Fountains, Statues, and Flowers

Fountains, Statues, and Flowers:

Studies in Italian Gardens of the Sixteenth and Seventeenth Centuries

Elisabeth Blair MacDougall

Dumbarton Oaks Research Library and Collection
Washington, D.C.

Chapters 2 through 7 were originally published as follows:

"*Il Giardino all'Antico:* Roman Statuary and Italian Renaissance Gardens," ed. R. Curtis, *Studia Pompeiana and Classica in Honor of Wilhelmina F. Jashemski,* II, New Rochelle, 1989, 139–54.

"The Sleeping Nymph: Origins of a Humanist Fountain Type," *Art Bulletin* 57 (1975), 357–65.

"*L'Ingegnoso Artifizio:* Sixteenth-Century Garden Fountains in Rome," *Fons Sapientiae: Renaissance Garden Fountains,* Dumbarton Oaks Colloquium on the History of Landscape Architecture 5, ed. E. B. MacDougall, Washington, D.C., 1978, 85–114.

"*Ars Hortulorum:* Sixteenth-Century Garden Iconography and Literary Theory in Italy," *The Italian Garden,* Dumbarton Oaks Colloquium on the History of Landscape Architecture 1, ed. D. Coffin, Washington, D.C., 1972, 37–59.

"Imitation and Invention: Language and Decoration in Roman Renaissance Gardens," *Journal of Garden History* 5 (1985), 119–34.

"A Circus, a Wild Man, and a Dragon: Family History and the Villa Mattei," *Journal of the Society of Architectural Historians* 42 (1983), 121–30.

Frontispiece: *Giardino segreto,* Ferrari, *Hesperides* (photo: Dumbarton Oaks)

Library of Congress Cataloging-in-Publication Data

MacDougall, Elisabeth B.
    Fountains, statues, and flowers : studies in Italian gardens of the sixteenth and seventeenth centuries / Elisabeth Blair MacDougall.
        p.   cm.
    ISBN 0-88402-216-1
    1. Gardens, Italian—History—16th century.   2. Gardens, Italian—History—17th century.   3. Gardens—Italy—History—16th century.   4. Gardens—Italy—History—17th century.   I. Title
SB457.85.M33   1993
712'.0945'09031—dc20
                                            93-9546
                                            CIP

Contents

Dedication

To the memory of my father who encouraged me to become
an art historian
and to
Richard Krautheimer
who taught me how to be one

Introduction

This volume of the collected essays of Elisabeth Blair MacDougall honors her director-ship of the program of Studies in Landscape Architecture at Dumbarton Oaks for sixteen years, from its establishment as a major center for the study of landscape in 1972, until her retirement in 1988. The initial conception for the program followed from the interests of Mrs. Robert Woods Bliss. While she was still active, occasional fellows, such as Georgina Masson and Peter Willis, came to use the library acquired by Mrs. Bliss. It contained both rare books and a general research library of several thousand volumes. Beatrix Farrand advised Mrs. Bliss on the design and maintenance of the gardens at Dumbarton Oaks and library acquisitions until her death in 1959. Mrs. Bliss also ap-pointed a committee of landscape consultants on the gardens in 1957, first chaired by Michael Rapuano. After the death of Mrs. Bliss in 1969, William R. Tyler, then director of Dumbarton Oaks, added the first scholar to the committee. The original committee evolved into an Advisory Committee, later renamed Senior Fellows Committee, first chaired by the historian of landscape David R. Coffin from Princeton University, then by Walter M. Whitehill, director of the Boston Athenaeum, Joseph Alsop, the columnist, myself, Alfred Frazer, and currently by Michel Conan. Eventually an advisory group was created solely for the gardens, and the program of Studies in Landscape Architecture continued to be supervised by the Senior Fellows Committee.

An initial symposium on the Italian garden was sponsored by the program in April 1971, and the papers, edited by David Coffin, were published in 1972, the first year of Elisabeth MacDougall's tenure.

While in charge of the program, she shaped the first, and still the only, center for the study of the history of gardens and landscape. She enlarged and regularized the fellowship program; developed a vigorous acquisition plan for the library that increased its holdings to more than 3,300 rare books and more than 13,000 books and periodicals in the research collection; instituted an annual symposium; and began a publication pro-gram that included six monographic studies in addition to nine volumes of symposia papers.

Professor MacDougall served on national and international committees related to the field. One example is her service, from 1973, on the Committee on Historic Gardens and Sites of the International Committee on Monuments and Sites. She also frequently taught History of Landscape at the Graduate School of Design at Harvard University and lectured widely on the history of landscape and gardens. MacDougall served on the landscape jury for the Rome Prize of the American Academy in Rome, and, to make the field of landscape history better known, she served in various elected and appointed positions in the Society of Architectural Historians, including membership on the Board of Directors, Secretary, First Vice-President, President, and Editor of the *Journal* of the Society from 1984 to 1987.

Prior to her appointment as director of the program, Elisabeth MacDougall had been an active scholar, preservationist, and academic. She attended Vassar College, the Institute of Fine Arts at New York University (where she studied with Richard Krautheimer), and Harvard University, where she received a Ph.D. with a dissertation on Roman sixteenth-century villa gardens. Her early publications and scholarly reviews include a detailed examination of Michelangelo's drawings for the Porta Pia in Rome. She was at Harvard when she decided to join the faculty at Boston University from which she was called to the landscape program at Dumbarton Oaks.

While in Cambridge and Boston, MacDougall showed a concern for conservation issues. She served first as Associate Survey Director and consultant to the Cambridge Historical Commission and co-author of Volume II of the Cambridge Architectural History Survey. She then was appointed a member and chair of the newly formed Boston Landmarks Commission.

During her sixteen-year tenure as director, Elisabeth MacDougall continued her scholarly activities by publishing a series of articles on Italian gardens, including papers on *The Sleeping Nymph*, sixteenth-century garden fountains in Rome, the gardens of the Villa Mattei, the decoration of Roman Renaissance gardens, and the use of ancient Roman statues in Renaissance gardens, each reprinted in this volume. She also prepared material that appears here for the first time on the style and development of Roman gardens in the sixteenth century, the garden of the seventeenth-century Piedmontese villa/castello at Venaria Reale near Turin, and on Cardinal Barberini's bulb garden in seventeenth-century Rome. These studies helped to reveal and define issues and directions in the field of landscape studies.

The masterful paper on garden iconography and literary theory in sixteenth-century Italian gardens, delivered at the first landscape symposium at Dumbarton Oaks in 1971, most likely weighed heavily in her appointment to head the program the next year.

In 1972, when Professor MacDougall was appointed, there was a single historical journal in the field, *Garden History*, several professional journals of landscape architecture, including *Garten + Landschaft*, *Landscape* (a pioneering periodical begun by J. B. Jackson), and *Landscape Architecture*, as well as a number of plant and horticultural journals. Sixteen years later, there were a number of new journals in the field, notable among them the *Journal of Garden History*, founded in 1981 by John Dixon Hunt, Elisabeth MacDougall's successor at Dumbarton Oaks. Articles on the history of gardens, both the vernacular and designed landscape, now appear frequently in journals of architecture, history, geography, and the history of art.

David Coffin, the first scholar to chair the Advisory Committee to the program of Studies in Landscape Architecture, in the preface to the volume of papers resulting from the initial symposium in the series dedicated to *The Italian Garden*, said

> this would seem to be the moment . . . [that] promises new ideas and new information. . . . The past decade . . . has seen a renewal of interest in the history of gardens, and recent efforts have been made to relate the Italian garden to other fields of scholarship. The literary historian of pastoral poetry, the scholar of land-

scape painting, and architectural historian concerned with the villa realize the garden is essential to their interests (pp. vii-viii).

Indeed the field has burgeoned. As the annual symposia at Dumbarton Oaks demonstrate, research in the history of landscape is flourishing. Scholars from other fields have found the issues raised in the history of landscape and garden both engaging and demanding. The establishment of the fellowship program that has attracted many of the leading scholars, the building of a major specialized library, and the series of symposia and other gatherings sponsored by the program have provided a significant stimulus to the study of landscape. Professor MacDougall's accomplishments at Dumbarton Oaks are unparalleled in the field.

The initiative, energy, and imagination that Elisabeth MacDougall brought to the program of Studies in Landscape Architecture at Dumbarton Oaks have not diminished. Her enthusiasm and leadership led to the presidency of the Society of Architectural Historians, and, in addition to maintaining her service on the Committee on Historic Gardens and Sites, she is also at work on a study begun a few years ago on the iconography of the throne room in later medieval and Renaissance palaces. For commitment and unrepressable optimism, for humor and vision, for scholarship and concern for fellows, Elisabeth Blair MacDougall has earned the affection and admiration of her colleagues and friends.

Henry A. Millon
27 April 1993

Preface

The essays in this volume are studies in the history of Italian gardens. The six in Part I are exact reprints of earlier publications; the introduction to Part I and the two articles in Part II have never appeared before. All of them are an outgrowth of my dissertation, "The Villa Mattei and the Development of the Roman Garden Style" (Harvard University, 1970). The first, "An Introduction to Roman Gardens of the Sixteenth Century," is a condensation and revision of the chapter in my dissertation in which I traced the history of gardens in Rome from the first decades of the sixteenth century to 1585 and the start of the Villa Mattei. I have abandoned the concept of linear development discussed in my dissertation and now propose a three-stage history, each stage marked by the introduction of important new formal or decorative features. I have described the unique social and political situation of Rome, which was the basis for the special character of Roman villa and garden building, and analyzed the design and spatial organization of the most important gardens of each stage. This is intended to serve as a background to the six following essays in which the sculptural and fountain decorations of the sixteenth-century gardens and their iconographic programs have been discussed.

The next six essays are arranged in a sequence that starts with a discussion of the use of ancient statues in Roman gardens (*"Il Giardino all'Antico"*) and continues on to the study of Sleeping Nymph fountains derived from an ancient statue type. *"L'Ingegnoso Artifizio,"* the next essay, examines the many different kinds of fountains used in Roman gardens and the importance of water in the gardens' design and use. *"Ars Hortulorum,"* the earliest chronologically but the next in this sequence, relates two garden features found in almost all the Roman gardens of the sixteenth century, the grotto-nymphaeum and the wilderness or grove, to their sources in ancient literature, while "Imitation and Invention," which is an expansion and in some senses a revision of the previous essay, places the use of allegorical programs in garden decorations in the context of literary and rhetorical theory of the period. The final essay of this group, "A Circus, a Wild Man, and a Dragon," applies the methods and theories developed in the previous essays to the interpretation and explanation of the iconography of the program of the Villa Mattei decorations.

Part II consists of two new essays. The first, "Venaria Reale," is about the seventeenth-century villa built by Carlo Emanuele II, ruler of Piedmont, starting in 1660. My interest in it developed when I investigated seventeenth-century stage sets as a possible source for the reconstruction of the appearance of gardens, or at least as a source of information for the way they were seen by their patrons. The link between theater and garden has long been recognized; however, Venaria Reale was unusual because the design of one of its most prominent features was engendered by a stage set.

PREFACE

"A Cardinal's Bulb Garden," a study of three Barberini manuscripts, represents an attempt to make up for a side of garden history that I have egregiously neglected in my other garden essays, the plants grown in them. I started with an inventory of a seventeenth-century *"Giardino Segreto"* at the Palazzo Barberini in Rome. Two other Barberini manuscripts, one a horticultural treatise and the other a presentation album of flower paintings, provided the opportunity, virtually unique for this period, to reconstruct the planting of a garden, to know the appearance of the plants and how they were grown.

Over the many years that the research and writing of these essays have occupied, I have received much generous support and inspiration from the institutions where I did research and from my colleagues and friends. I have acknowledged specific debts at the start of the individual articles; here, I would like to make more general acknowledgments.

I have expressed my thanks before to James S. Ackerman and John Coolidge for their advice and assistance on my dissertation, which they directed. It is a pleasure to state once more my gratitude for their help then and for the many times since when they have given me the benefit of their knowledge and experience.

I am particularly grateful, too, to Irving Lavin and the late Howard Hibbard who suggested the potential of a dissertation on gardens at a time when I was stymied by the topic I originally selected. The late Wolfgang Lotz introduced me to Roman studies in a seminar on Roman Baroque Architecture given in Rome the summer of 1957. For this and the generous advice and support he gave as Director of the Bibliotheca Hertziana when I was preparing my dissertation and later research I am extremely grateful. From those Roman years, I would like to thank Irving and Marilyn Aronberg Lavin, Henry Millon, and the late Howard Hibbard and Milton Lewine for introducing me to the intricacies of research in the archives and libraries there and in Florence and in Turin. They were generous in sharing their knowledge and the results of their own research, and countless discussions with them, usually over the dinner table in a Roman trattoria, illuminated and expanded my work. A number of other friends participated in our talks, but I would particularly like to thank Kathleen Weil-Garris Brandt, Christoph Frommel, Konrad Oberhuber, and Alfred Frazer. Unfortunately, Georgina Masson will never read my words of gratitude for her generosity in sharing material and ideas on so many different aspects of the history of Italian gardens; her pioneering studies showed the way for most subsequent work, mine included. I am also indebted to Claudia Lazzaro and Mirka Beneš for our many stimulating conversations and their generous sharing of information. I offer my warmest thanks to Frederick Meyer for his meticulous reading of "A Cardinal's Bulb Garden" and his patience in correcting the botanical material.

Research for these essays was done at many different institutions. These include the Biblioteca Apostolica Vaticana, the Archivi di Stato in Rome, Florence, Modena, and Turin, and the Biblioteche Nazionali in Rome and in Turin. The Library of the German Archaeological Institute in Rome, the Biblioteca Reale in Turin, the Biblioteca Marcelliana in Florence, and the British Library in London were also important sources for my research. I am grateful to their respective librarians, archivists, and staffs. The American Academy Library and the Bibliotheca Hertziana in Rome have been the base upon which I depended and from which all "hunting expeditions" started. I am especially grateful to their staffs for their assistance and cooperation.

PREFACE

I am indebted to Harvard University, the Italian Ministry of Foreign Affairs, and the John Simon Guggenheim Memorial Foundation for the grants that provided support for my research and travel in Italy.

Finally, I want to thank Dumbarton Oaks for providing the opportunity that my appointment as Director of Studies in Landscape Architecture from 1972 to 1988 gave for research there and elsewhere. Thanks are also due to all the friends who held fellowships there during my years as Director of Studies for the stimulating discussions and sharing of knowledge which has added so much to my own work.

I am deeply grateful to the former director of Dumbarton Oaks, Robert Thomson, to the present director, Angeliki Laiou, and to the Senior Fellows Committee of Landscape Architecture Studies for undertaking the publication of these essays. Thanks are also due to Joachim Wolschke-Bulmahn, the Director of Studies in Landscape Architecture, John Dixon Hunt, the former Director of Studies, Glenn Ruby, Publishing Manager, Frances Kianka and Matthew Rieck in the Publications Office, and all the other members of the Dumbarton Oaks staff who took my photographs, found my books, and generally created order out of my otherwise chaotic ways.

Elisabeth Blair MacDougall
Cambridge, Massachusetts
31 December 1992

Part I
The Sixteenth Century

An Introduction to Roman Gardens
of the Sixteenth Century

As an introduction to the following essays, which are studies of sculptural decorations and iconographic programs in sixteenth-century Roman gardens, this chapter will trace the history of design and describe the social and political conditions in which they were created. One may speak of an Italian Renaissance garden style; villas throughout Italy in this period had gardens with formal, geometric plans, used similar types of plants in similar ways, and were decorated with fountains and statues with similar forms and subjects. But there were also distinct regional variations in style that were related to the differing social and political structures of the various regions and the role of agriculture in the local economy. The type of patronage and the location of villas in relation to the city were especially influenced by such factors.

In principalities with hereditary rulers such as Ferrara, Mantua, and, in the last two-thirds of the century, Florence, villas were predominantly built and owned by the ruling family (d'Este, Gonzaga, and Medici). Many were close to the city and were used for a day's recreation by the ruler and his court. Those built by aristocrats and other members of the court were fewer in number and smaller in scale and often part of an agricultural estate. In states governed by oligarchies, such as Genoa, Bologna, and Venice, even when one family was dominant, greater numbers of villas of roughly equal size and importance were built. Where the owners' income was primarily from agriculture, as in the Veneto or the Lombardy plain, villa buildings had agricultural as well as recreational functions, and gardens tended to be minimal in size.

Rome was unique in its social structure and in the existence of villa sites within the city walls, unlike other cities on the peninsula (Fig. 1). The true "urban" center in the sixteenth century was the low area bordering the Tiber; the hills in the northwest part of the city (that is, the Pincio, Quirinal, Esquiline, Aventine, and Celio) were almost uninhabited at the beginning of the century. In the next one hundred years these hills were built up with villas like those in suburban areas outside the walls in other cities. Elsewhere, gardens inside the walls were usually attached to the owner's primary residence. In Rome, primary residences were almost always in the urban center by the Tiber—the gardens above on the hills were used for short visits and as an escape from the heat and unhealthy conditions of the low lying land by the river.[1]

[1] This essay was written several years ago, before the appearance of D. Coffin, *Gardens and Gardening in Papal Rome,* Princeton, 1991. Our factual material is drawn from the same primary and secondary sources, and since we are in basic agreement about these, I do not feel it necessary to give references to the factual information in his book. My interpretation of the development of garden design in the 16th century differs

1

1. Dupérac map of Rome, 1577 (photo: Dumbarton Oaks)

Yet the names these villas within the walls were given, *giardino* or *horto* (Giardino del Bufalo, Horti Farnesiani) were a recognition of their essentially urban nature. Their layouts also reflected their urban situation, combining the extensive sites, elaborate decorations, and small casinos characteristic of the *villa suburbana* with the strict enclosures and limited views of palace gardens. These "intraurban" gardens in Rome were unique. A truly suburban group of villas was constructed just outside the walls of the city; their layout was similar to suburban villas elsewhere. Recognition of their location is apparent in the fact they were called villas (Villa Giulia, Villa Borghese) even though they were used, like the properties within the walls, for recreation and short sojourns.[2]

All patrons, in Rome as elsewhere, also had country estates. In other parts of Italy they were usually farmed, and often were a chief source of revenue for the patron. Romans' country estates were commonly located in the hill towns near Rome, such as Frascati and Tivoli, as were those of the ancient Romans, and they were used only as an escape from the heat of the city. None seem to have been attached to agricultural, income-producing property.[3] This was in part due to the structure of papal society, for many villa builders were members of papal, princely, or patrician families from other parts of Italy, and their agricultural income was derived from their home farms and hereditary estates.[4]

Another factor that influenced the creation of villas in Rome was the nature of its rulership. Although the governance of Rome and the papal states in the sixteenth century was similar to that of other states with hereditary rulers, the politics of papal elections prevented the establishment of dynastic succession. With the exception of the Medicis (Leo X and Clement VII), each sixteenth-century pope came from a different family, and from a different region of Italy.[5] Each, upon election, brought relatives to Rome and appointed new court officials, all of whom wanted villas and palaces of their own. Since most properties built by their predecessors remained in the possession of the original owners and their family, even though financed by the pope and hence by church money,

---

from Coffin's at many points, but it is beyond the scope of these essays to discuss specific differences. I leave it to the reader to compare the two texts.

[2] For a slightly different typology of villas, see C. Frommel, "La Villa Madama e la tipologia della Villa Romana nel rinascimento," *Bollettino del Centro Internazionale di studi di architettura Andrea Palladio* 11 (1969), 47–64.

[3] An exception might be the tannery built by Cardinal d'Este across the road from the lowest part of his villa in Tivoli; the run-off water from the fountains was used in the tanning process. It should be noted that citizens of Rome were required to own a *vigna* within three miles of the city walls to qualify as a legal citizen. This means that a small area of a villa outside the walls frequently was set aside for use as a vineyard. This little known Roman statute and its significance for patterns of land holding is discussed by M. Beneš, "Villa Pamphilij: Family, Gardens, and Land in Papal Rome," Ph.D. diss., Yale University, 1989, I, 36, n. 38. Her citation for this information is L. Nussdorfer, "City Politics in Baroque Rome (1623–1644)," Ph.D. diss., Princeton University, 1985, 26, n. 15.

[4] For discussions of social and economic history of 16th-century Rome, see J. Delumeau, *Vie économique et sociale de Rome dans la seconde moitié du XVIe siècle*, 2 vols., Paris, 1957–59; P. Partner, *Renaissance Rome, 1500–1559. A Portrait of a Society*, Berkeley, 1976; E. Sereni, *Storia del paesaggio agrario italiano*, Bari, 1961. See also D. Coffin, *The Villa in the Life of Renaissance Rome*, Princeton, 1979.

[5] 1503, Pius III, Piccolomini, Siena; 1503–13, Julius II, della Rovere, Savona; 1513–21, Leo X, de' Medici, Florence; 1522–23, Hadrian VI, Utrecht; 1523–34, Clement VII, de' Medici, Florence; 1534–46, Paul III, Farnese, Canino (Rome); 1550–55, Julius III, del Monte, Monte Sansavino; 1555, Marcellus II,

few could be acquired. Thus almost every pope built himself a villa, and the *Cardinali nipoti* and other papal relatives also built villas for themselves.[6] In addition, many cardinals who were not members of the pope's family were scions of the great noble families of other parts of Italy, and they too built impressive villas in the city and in the hills nearby.[7] Finally, one must add to this list of patrons members of the old nobility of Rome, the Colonna, Orsini, and Caetani, as well as members of the papal court, such as Baldassare Turini de Pescia, Julius II's datary, Agostino Chigi, his banker, Angelo Colocci and Hans Goritz, protonotaries for Julius II, or Leone Strozzi, an official at the court of Sixtus V. Thus the unique combination of the social and political character of Rome, the existence of a large, ever increasing circle of patrons coming from a nobility seated away from Rome, and the availability of open space within and just outside the city walls created a climate for the almost explosive cycle of villa and garden construction during the sixteenth century—more than eighty were either built *ex novo* or totally reconstructed in Rome in those one hundred years, many more than were built in other centers. Money was abundant, warfare did not draw on the resources of the patrons as in other cities, and the materials for building and decorating villas were easily available.

This great period of villa building began with the construction of the Cortile del Belvedere at the Vatican Palace in Rome (Fig. 2). There, for the first time, all the forms and themes that were to dominate garden design in Rome, and to a certain extent the rest of the peninsula, for the next one hundred years or more were brought together in a unified whole. Today it is hard to conceive of the Belvedere Court as a garden, for its original space has been cut in two by the Sixtus V library wing, and the upper terraces are no longer planted as they once were nor accessible to visitors.[8] As originally conceived by Bramante for Pope Julius II (1503–13), the area between the palace and the upper ridge of the Vatican Hill to the north was divided into three parts by a series of ascending terraces. Long corridor wings connecting the palace to the structures at the far end of the upper terrace enclosed the cortile—the upper end terminated in an exedra and

---

Cervini, Montepulciano; 1555–59, Paul IV, Carafa, Avellino; 1559–65, Pius IV, Medici, Milan; 1566–72, Pius V, Ghislieri, Alessandria; 1572–85, Gregory XIII, Boncompagni, Bologna; 1585–90, Sixtus V, Peretti, Grottammare; 1590, Urban VII, Castagno, Rome; 1590–91; Gregory XIV, Sfondrati, Cremona; 1591, Innocent IX, Facchinetti, Bologna; 1592–1604, Clement VIII, Aldobrandini, Fano. All but three of them built villas or helped finance villas for relatives.

[6] Examples of the former include the Belvedere Court and the Casino in the Vatican gardens built respectively by Julius II and Pius IV, the Villa Giulia on the Via Flaminia built by Julius III, and the Villa Montalto near San Giovanni in Laterano built by Sixtus V. *Cardinali nipoti* gardens include the Horti Farnesiani on the Palatine built for Cardinal Alessandro Farnese, the so-called nephew (actually grandson) of Paul IV and the gardens on Monte Magnanapoli on the slopes of the Esquiline, improved by Cardinal Aldobrandini, nephew of Clement VIII.

[7] Examples include the Villa Madama, started by Cardinal Giulio de' Medici, later Clement VII; the Villa Medici on the Pincio—a reconstruction by Cardinal Francesco de' Medici, son of the Grand Duke of Tuscany, of a villa started by the Riccis, nephews of Cardinal Giovanni Ricci, treasurer of Julius III; and the two villas, one on the Quirinal and one in Tivoli, built by Cardinal Ippolito d'Este, son and brother of successive dukes of Ferrara and Modena.

[8] For the history of the construction and of the later alterations to the Belvedere Court, see J. Ackerman, *The Cortile del Belvedere*, Studi e documenti per la storia del Palazzo Apostolico Vaticano 3, Vatican City, 1954.

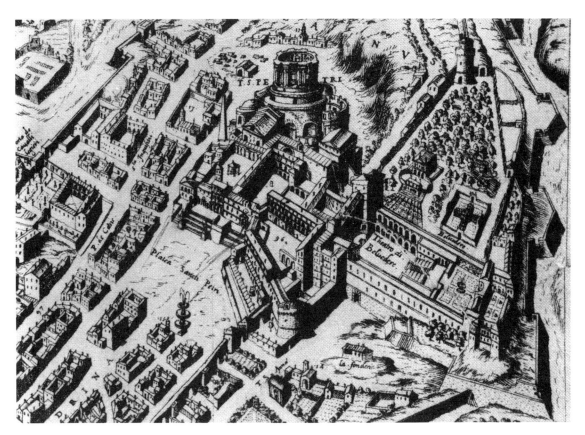

2. Bird's-eye view of Belvedere, Vatican Palace, from Dupérac map of Rome, 1577
(photo: Dumbarton Oaks)

screen wall that hid from view a villa built by Pope Innocent VIII (1484–92). A wall at the lower end of the cortile masked the irregular walls of the palace. A giant staircase flanked by two towers connected the lowest terrace to the intermediate one, and it was linked to the upper terrace by ramps framing a nymphaeum (Fig. 3).[9] Early views show that the two upper terraces were laid out in a regular geometric grid of planting beds; both had fountains placed on the central axis (Fig. 4). The design was strictly architectonic and axial. All the major elements of the design were masonry constructions; plant materials played a subordinate, purely decorative role. A strong central axis, which was established by the fountains, the nymphaeum and paths in the two upper terraces terminated at the centers of the palace facade and of the exedra. Irregular forms, such as the non-axial siting of the fifteenth-century villa were disguised or hidden, and the space between the older building and the new construction was itself organized by a

[9] Parts of the ramps are still to be seen in the courtyard behind the library wing. The nymphaeum was destroyed when the library was built.

5

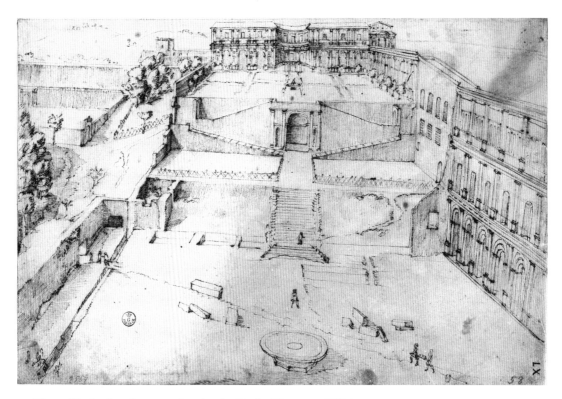

3. View of Belvedere in 1545, drawing by Dosio, Florence, Uffizi
   (photo: Gabinetto Fotografico Uffizi)

4. View of Belvedere by Hendrik van Cleve, 1550, Brussels, Royal Museum (photo: Royal Museum)

6

symmetrically arranged series of niches and wall spaces designed to exhibit the pope's collection of ancient Roman statues.[10] This latter space, however, was open on the western side to an area enclosed by the outer Vatican walls in which a grove of trees was planted (see Fig. 2).

The most important innovation of the design for the Belvedere Court was the boldness with which an enormous space (ca. 250 × 900 meters) was organized and manipulated as an active force. Gardens of the early Renaissance had small and essentially negative spaces defined by surrounding walls; large areas, such as the park rebuilt and decorated by Alfonso I and his successor, Ferrante, at the Castel Nuovo in Naples, were neither conceived as nor organized into coherent architectural designs.[11] The Belvedere Court, in contrast, like the great architectural complexes of antiquity, was the result of a concept of space as a positive force molded and organized by the architectural forms.

The inspiration for the design was indeed that of antiquity, for the court was part of Julian II's program to create at the Vatican monuments whose scale and scope rivaled the achievements of Imperial Rome. The new St. Peter's would surpass the Pantheon, the additions to and decorations of the Palace recalled the imperial palaces of the Palatine, while the Belvedere Court was to be comparable to ancient imperial villas, many of which were still visible, although in a ruinous state, at this period.[12] This program for the revival of antiquity was accompanied by a conscious adoption of ancient architectural forms, such as the arcades and screen walls of the court whose design emulated the articulation of walls at the Colosseum and the Pantheon, while the terraces and exedra were derived from the Temple of Fortuna Primigenia at Palestrina.

Another important innovation at the Belvedere was the display of ancient statutes in the courtyard behind the exedra. Collections of statues had been formed in the previous century but no attempt seems to have been made to create a formalized setting for them. At the Belvedere, niches for the statues were arranged symmetrically around the enclosing walls, and large Tragedy and Comedy masks, also of ancient origin, were placed in roundels above the niches (Figs. 5, 21). Two statues were made into fountains (see Figs. 19, 24), and another pair were set in the center of the court.[13] In addition to the statues, the court was decorated with an arrangement of orange trees in pots, and it opened on the west side with a loggia to a grove informally planted with grass, mulberrys, and cypresses.

There can be no doubt that the Belvedere Court was planned for a diversity of recreational uses by the pope and the court. As early as 1509 the lower court, usually referred to in later documents as the *cortile del teatro* was used for a bull fight, a *"festa taurorum,"* while the information that the baby elephant given to Pope Julius by King

[10] For a full discussion of the history of the statue court and the statues in it, see H. Brummer, *The Statue Court in the Vatican Belvedere*, Acta Universitatis Stockholmiensis. Stockholm Studies in the History of Art 20, Stockholm, 1970.

[11] G. Hersey, *Alfonso II and the Artistic Renewal of Naples, 1485–1495*, New Haven and London, 1968.

[12] I owe this interpretation to J. Ackerman, "The Belvedere as a Classical Villa," *Journal of the Warburg and Courtauld Institutes* 14 (1951), 70–91.

[13] Brummer, *Belvedere*, 186–204. For further discussion of statue display in Roman gardens, see below, *"Il Giardino all'Antico:* Roman Statuary and Italian Renaissance Gardens" (hereafter "Giardino all'Antico") and "The Sleeping Nymph: Origins of a Humanist Fountain Type" (hereafter "Sleeping Nymph").

Facciata del cortile ddle flatue, che resta addofo alla Cleopatra

5. Belvedere Statue Court,
eighteenth-century
drawing,
London, British Library
(photo: British Library)

Emmanuel of Portugal was stabled there, suggests that there was a collection of exotic animals kept there for the amusement of the courtiers.[14] The upper terraces lent themselves to the learned conversation and leisurely strolling so much a pattern of the life of the papal court at that time, while the statue court provided the stimulation of viewing great works of art and a visible reminder, even a reconstruction, of the ancient Roman past.

An equally influential but differing model for sixteenth-century gardens was provided by another villa, the Villa Madama, even though only a fraction of the grandiose design was actually completed. It was begun by Cardinal Giulio de' Medici in 1518, and continued after he was elected Pope Clement VII in 1523. The site on Monte Mario, outside the walls of Rome, was a steep hill which sloped down to the river Tiber. Unlike the design of the Belvedere which organized and manipulated an area strictly confined both visually and physically by the delimiting wings, the Villa Madama was to have swept down the hill in a series of terraces which provided, at every level, vistas of the river and the hills beyond (Figs. 6, 7).[15] The terraces were organized along a central axis which led

[14] See C. Frommel, "Raffaello e il teatro alla corte di Leone X," *Bollettino del Centro Internazionale di studi di architettura Andrea Palladio* 16 (1974), 173–88. There is also information about life at the court of Leo X in D. Gnoli, "Orti letterari nella Roma di Leo X," *Nuova Antologia*, ser. 7, 269 (1930), 3–19, 137–48.

[15] Although Mario Bafile's reconstruction (published in *Il giardino di Villa Madama*, Istituto d'archaeologia e storia dell'arte. Opere d'arte 12, Rome, 1942, pl. IX) is not entirely in accord with recent scholarship, it gives a better idea of the topography of the villa than the San Gallo drawings. For a discussion of the chronology of the drawings, with earlier bibliography, see C. Frommel, "Die architektonische Planung der Villa Madama," *Römisches Jahrbuch für Kunstgeschichte* 15 (1975), 59–87.

6. Reconstruction by Mario Bafile of the Villa Madama design from surviving ground plans,
   Il Giardino di Villa Madama, pl. IX (photo: Dumbarton Oaks)

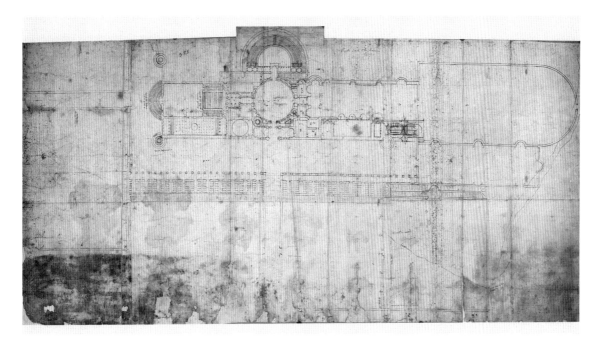

7. Plan of the Villa Madama by Antonio da San Gallo, the Younger, Florence, Uffizi,
   Gab. d. Disegni, UA 314 (photo: Gabinetto Fotografico Uffizi)

from the casino at the top of the site to the river, and the buildings were arranged along a second axis at right angles to the first. This latter extended from the entrance to the villa through a vestibule, circular atrium, and the casino to a succession of walled gardens with a grove beyond.[16] Like the Belvedere's, the design was predominantly architectural and classicizing.

There seems little doubt that it was influenced by Pliny the Younger's two letters describing his Laurentine and Tuscan villas, the sole surviving detailed accounts of ancient villas.[17] In a letter describing his plan, Raphael, the first architect of Villa Madama, described a sequence of spaces similar to those in Pliny's description of the Tuscan villa as well as a similar disposition of small pavilions and other amenities. He even repeatedly used words taken from Latin, such as *dieta* for pavilion and *cryptoporticum* for loggia, although the Italian names for these structures were in common usage.[18]

The design of the Villa Madama differed from that of the Belvedere Court in two important ways, both related to the difference in their location. The first was in the treatment of space. The Belvedere's design was based on the enclosure of a space which was then manipulated and organized internally. The Villa Madama project, on the contrary, used the sloping site to create a series of interactions with the surrounding area. Both its axes provided views beyond the garden precincts into the surrounding countryside. This can be explained by the fact that the two villas, according to Renaissance theory, were different types. The Villa Madama was a *villa suburbana,* a term applied to an estate near a city, that is, in a suburban location, used solely for recreation and not for agriculture. Where the topography of the site permitted, the gardens were usually placed on a slope, opening out to the view. Palace gardens, on the other hand, were customarily walled and enclosed, and the Belvedere Court, despite its great size, was originally a palace garden. Its name, *cortile,* reflected this concept; only after the area north and west of the ensemble were made into gardens does one find references to the *Giardini Vaticani.*

Their location also affected the functions they were expected to serve. The Villa Madama was outside the city walls of Rome and at a sufficient distance from the Vatican that accommodations were needed for the pope and for the retinue that ordinarily accompanied him outside the Vatican. Thus suites of rooms that could be used for overnight stays were planned in the casino, and one of the early designs shows a stable with stalls for more than a hundred animals. The casino also served as a place of reception for important visitors arriving from the north by the Via Cassia or Via Flaminia. It was the custom for such visitors to stop outside the city overnight or to pause to refresh themselves before making their ceremonial entrance into the Vatican or the city of Rome. There was no necessity for such accommodations at the Belvedere; the Vatican palace housed the pope, the Curia and the papal household, and visiting dignitaries.

[16] D. Coffin, "The Plans of the Villa Madama," *Art Bulletin* 49 (1967), 111–12. Frommel, "Architektonische Planung."

[17] Pliny, *Epistles,* 5.6; 2.17.

[18] P. Foster, "Raphael on the Villa Madama: The Text of a Lost Letter," *Römisches Jahrbuch für Kunstgeschichte* 11 (1967–68), 308–12.

Despite their differences, both the Belvedere Court and the Villa Madama created precedents that influenced garden design for the next two hundred years. Their essentially geometric and axial design was expressed and created entirely by man-made forms; plants were used only to cover surfaces and fill out the design. To this extent the influence of these two gardens spread throughout Italy; one can find similar formal characteristics in gardens in every part of the peninsula.

Equally influential was the important role their sculpture and fountains played both in the organization of space and in garden decoration, and the influence of antiquity on their design and their decorations. Ancient precedent was sought: ancient statues or their replicas were preferred, and ancient mythology was the source used for their decorative programs.

Two features of these villa gardens, however, were to become more prevalent in Rome than in other parts of Italy. One was the informal, non-architectonic area found in both that provided a visual contrast to the severe geometry of the principal garden.[19] At the Belvedere the grove visible from the statue court created the contrast; at the Villa Madama an area beyond the hippodrome-shaped terrace was arranged in ascending levels that culminated in a grotto decorated with ferns and stalactites to resemble a natural cave.

The second was the role played by ancient statues in the gardens.[20] Instead of their display as a collection of valuable objects, a practice already common in the previous century, the statues were used as ornaments or as part of a decorative scheme. In the statue court of the Belvedere the statues were arranged symmetrically and evenly around the walls, not in random piles as in some earlier collections. At the Villa Madama, ancient statues were placed in niches in the loggia, and in the walled garden at that level, in what appears to have been a carefully coordinated composition.[21] This was possible in Rome where ancient statues were easily acquired and large collections could be formed.

The influence of the Belvedere and Villa Madama can be traced throughout the sixteenth century in Rome. There were enclosed gardens with interior space divisions—the Medici villa on the Pincio or, an extreme example, the Villa Giulia (Figs. 8, 9). Others took advantage of a hilly site to provide views outside their boundaries—examples include the d'Este garden on the Quirinal, or the Villa Montalto (Figs. 10, 11). Gardens in this period were laid out with formal and axial plans, yet the plan almost always included a grove or an informally planted area, such as those in the Medici and d'Este gardens.

[19] See below, "Ars Hortulorum: Sixteenth-Century Garden Iconography and Literary Theory in Italy," (hereafter "Ars Hortulorum") for a discussion of this feature. It should be noted that gardens in other parts of Italy also had groves and other informal features, but they were used to trap birds, (the ragnaia) or confine animals as well as serving an ornamental function. The Roman groves apparently were purely decorative.

[20] This is the subject of several of the following articles: see "Giardino all'Antico," "Sleeping Nymph," and "A Circus, a Wild Man, and a Dragon: Family History and the Villa Mattei" (hereafter "Circus").

[21] Fig. 8 and the others showing the early 16th-century Roman sculpture gardens were made by the Dutch artist, Marten van Heemskerck, during his sojourn there in the early 1530s. They are published by C. Huelsen and H. Egger, Die römischen Skizzenbücher von Marten van Heemskerck, Berlin, 1913–16.

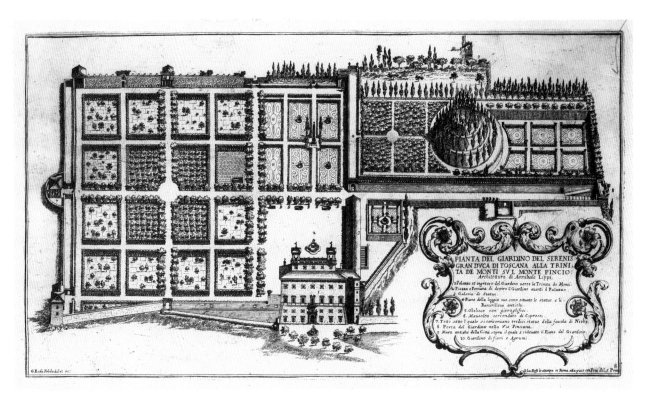

8. Bird's-eye view of the Villa Medici, ca. 1680, G. Falda, *Li giardini di Roma*, pl. 8 (photo: Dumbarton Oaks)

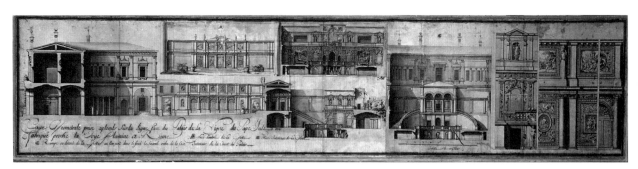

9. Villa Giulia, longitudinal section, seventeenth-century drawing attributed to Oppenordt, Rome, Museo di Villa Giulia (photo: Gabinetto Fotografico Nazionale)

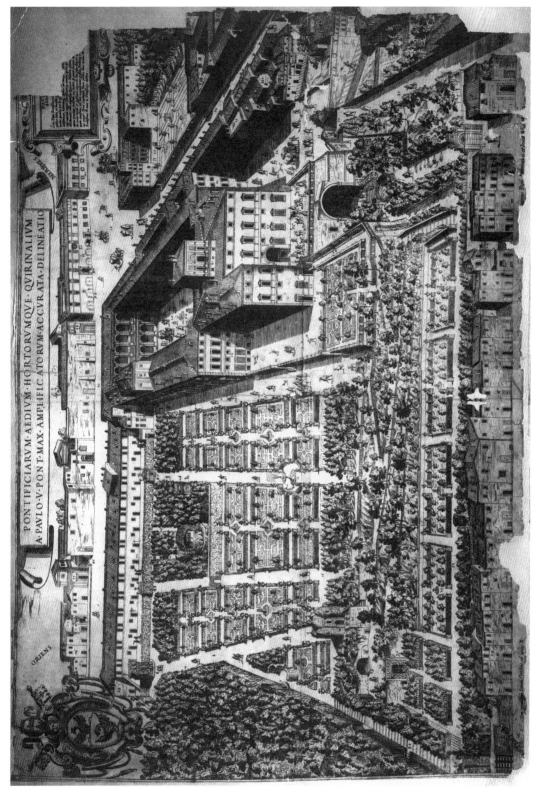

10. Perspective view of the d'Este villa on the Quirinal, Maggi, 1612, British Museum, Map Room, vol. 81, no. 72a (photo: British Museum)

13

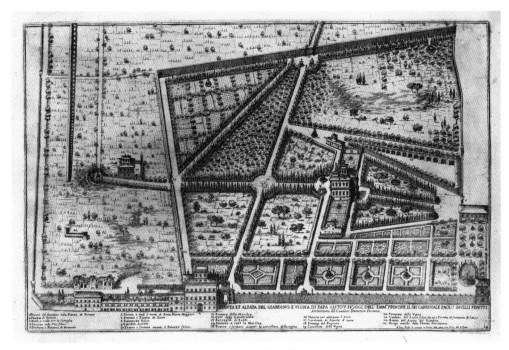

11. Bird's-eye view of the Villa Montalto, ca. 1680, Falda, *Li giardini,* pl. 14
(photo: Dumbarton Oaks)

Fountains and statues remained the principal form of ornamentation; until late in the century, the statues were predominantly ancient, and the iconographical programs were drawn from the mythology of antiquity.[22] Scarcely any, however, were of the grandiose scale and monumentality of the two early papal villas, and the only two that rivaled them, at least in extent, the Villa Montalto and the Villa Borghese, were built by a pope and a *Cardinal nipote* respectively.

Yet despite this continuity, several different stages in design and ornamentation can be traced in the gardens of Rome during the sixteenth century. In the first stage, in the decade before the Sack of Rome in 1527, the gardens show little reflection of the innovations initiated by the two great papal villas, and should be described as continuations of the late quattrocento style in Rome. Characteristic of this style is the garden built by Cardinal Emilio Cesi behind his palace on the Monte Sto. Spirito, now the site of the Pontifico Collegio Urbano di Propaganda Fide. The cardinal's extensive collection of ancient statues was set out in the garden in a rather haphazard arrangement along the garden walls; it is visible in the foreground of a painting by Hendrick van Cleef III (Fig. 12),[23] and in a drawing made by Heemskerck in the mid 1530s (see Fig. 18).[24] The

---

[22] See below, especially, "Giardino all'Antico" and *"L'Ingegnoso Artifizio:* Sixteenth-Century Garden Fountains in Rome" (hereafter "L'Ingegnoso Artifizio").

[23] See M. van der Meulen, "Cardinal Cesi's Antique Sculpture Garden: Notes on a Painting by Hendrick van Cleef III," *Burlington Magazine* 116 (1974), 14–22.

[24] An inventory of the collection was published by C. Huelsen, *Römische Antikengärten des XVI. Jahrhunderts,* Akademie der Wissenschaften zu Heidelberg, Philosophisch-historische Klasse, Abhandlungen 4 (1917), 11–35. See also D. Gnoli, "Il Giardino e l'antiquario del Cardinal Cesi," *Mitteilungen des Deutschen Archäologischen Instituts. Römische Abteilung* 20 (1905), 267–76.

12. Villa Cesi, above the Porta Cavallegieri, view by Hendrick van Cleef III, Prague, National Museum (photo: National Museum)

15

haphazard and informal placement of statues is also found in Heemskerck's other draw-ings of quattrocento gardens, as in, for example, the Giardino Galli (see Fig. 17), and so is the small walled area with its rectangular planting beds.

The layout of the garden of the Farnesina, built by Leo X's banker, Agostino Chigi, on the banks of the Tiber in 1508–11 was also a continuation of the quattrocento type even though Peruzzi's design for the Casino was innovative and established a new style for villa buildings.[25]

Only one of the gardens known from this period seems to have taken advantage of a sloping site. Built by Blosius Palladius, a humanist at the papal court, it descended a hill outside the city walls in several terraces; there were fountains at each level.[26]

One feature of the Villa Madama, however, was adopted in other gardens of this period, that is the grotto. Raphael's letter described a fountain in the area beyond the hippodrome garden as a cave cut in the hillside.[27] The pavilion at the top of the rise in the Villa Cesi was described as decorated with rocks that simulated the appearance of a cave, while the Farnesina had a nymphaeum under the riverside loggia—a small rocky room with benches. A cavelike nymphaeum also appeared at Blosius Palladius' garden.[28]

This first stage of garden building came to an end with the Sack of Rome in 1527, and little new appeared before 1540, but the following decades saw the creation of many new villas and gardens. Chief among these were three started around 1550, the Pio da Carpi villa (before 1550), the d'Este villa on the Quirinal, and the Villa Giulia on the Via Flaminia outside the walls of Rome. A fourth, the Ricci-Medici Villa on the Pincio, was built in the 1560s and 1570s.

All of them are characterized by increasingly complicated spatial arrangements and by elaborate fountain structures, sometimes with complex iconographical programs.[29] The hitherto undivided garden areas articulated by cross axes and rectangular planting beds began to be cut up into room-like spaces, often separated by walls or other visual barriers. The most extreme example is that found at the Villa Giulia (see Fig. 9), where the three successive spaces behind the casino were divided by walls, and made further complicated by the two lower levels introduced in the second courtyard (Fig. 48).[30] The

[25] See C. Frommel, *Die Farnesina und Peruzzis Architektonisches Frühwerk*, Berlin, 1961, for a reconstruc-tion of the garden plan.

[26] See below, "L'Ingegnoso Artifizio." For it and other humanist gardens of this period, see Gnoli, "Orti letterari."

[27] This portion of the letter is quoted in "L'Ingegnoso Artifizio," n. 19.

[28] See "L'Ingegnoso Artifizio" for a fuller description. For a description by Girolamo Rorario of the cavelike nymphaeum at the Palladius garden, see E. Battisti, *"Natura Artificiosa* to *Natura Artificialis," The Italian Garden*, Dumbarton Oaks Colloquium on the History of Landscape Architecture 1, ed. D. Coffin, Washington, D.C., 1972, 32–33, n. 72.

[29] The iconographical programs are the subject of discussion in "Ars Hortulorum," "L'Artifizio Inge-gnoso" and "Imitation and Invention: Language and Decoration in Roman Renaissance Gardens" (hereafter "Imitation and Invention").

[30] See T. Falk, "Studien zur Topographie und Geschichte der Villa Giulia in Rom," *Römisches Jahrbuch für Kunstgeschichte* 13 (1971), 101–78, for a history of the construction of the villa.

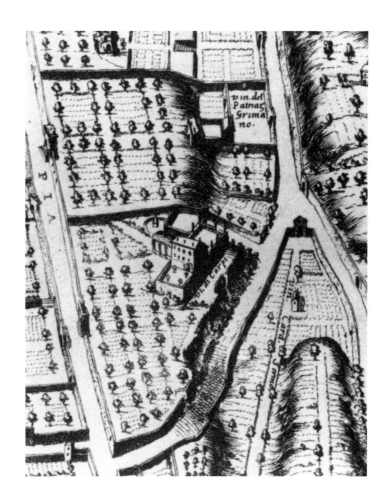

13. Pio da Carpi villa on the
Quirinal, bird's-eye view from
Dupérac map of Rome, 1577
(photo: Dumbarton Oaks)

Pio da Carpi villa also had several levels of terraces (Fig. 13) as well as a nymphaeum in a walled chamber on one of the terraces.[31] At the d'Este villa, also on the Quirinal, not only were there several walled-in areas next to the palace, but a green room was created in the flat open area of the garden by hedges in which niches were cut to accommodate statues (see Fig. 10 and the detail and plan, Figs. 25, 74).[32] Even the Villa Medici's garden, which in plan appears to be the traditional compartmented garden, was depicted in a painting in one of the small pavilions at the villa with pergolas covering all the paths, thereby creating a series of separate spaces (Fig. 14).

Frequently one of the enclosed spaces was a *giardino segreto*, that is a private walled area reserved for the use of the patron, family, and invited friends. The third enclosure at the Villa Giulia, visible at the far right of the Oppenordt view (Fig. 9) was evidently

[31] For the nymphaeum, see below, "Ars Hortulorum" and "L'Ingegnoso Artifizio."

[32] This area is described by the German architect Heinrich Schickhardt as "Es hat auch ein wilden gemachten Berg ungever uff 12 oder 14 sch[u] hoch, geht zu 3 zeiten herum . . ." See below, "Ars Hortulorum," n. 69, for full bibliographical citation. The statues described in the 1568 inventory published by Huelsen (*Antikengärten*, 113–17) as in "nicchi di cerchiate coperti d'hedera," were a Zeus and nude "King."

17

14. View of the Villa Medici, fresco in Garden Pavilion at the villa
(photo: Gabinetto Fotografico Nazionale)

one, while the gardens in front of the casino and on the hill above were more public.[33] A walled garden is visible in the Falda view of the Villa Medici (Fig. 8), and we know from the inventory of statues at the d'Este villa on the Quirinal that at least two areas were designated as *"giardini segreti."*[34]

Groves or informal areas became a more clearly defined and significant part of the design. At the Villa Giulia, the area between the palace and the upper garden was connected by a path with benches and inscriptions.[35] At the d'Este villa, the area called "il Boccaccio" in the inventory is shown in the Maggi view as densely planted with trees, as is the area between the rustic fountain and the Via Pia (see Fig. 10).

[33] These are described in the letter of Bartolommeo Ammannati to Marco Mantova Benavides, ms. Oliv. 374, Biblioteca Communale, Pesaro. See G. Balestra, *La fontana pubblica di Giulio III ed il palazzo di Pio IV sulla Via Flaminia*, Rome, 1911, 65ff. See also, D. Coffin, "The *'Lex Hortorum'* and Access to Gardens in Latium during the Renaissance," *Journal of Garden History* 2 (1982), 205–6. A revised version of this article appears in Coffin, *Gardens*, chap. 14, "The Public and the Roman Garden," 244–57. For the paths up the hill and the upper villa, see below, "Ars Hortulorum."

[34] For the inventory of 16 July 1568, in the Archivio di Stato in Modena, see Huelsen, *Antikengärten*, 113–17. Two heads are described as "Nei giardini segreti sopra le porte ch'entrano dalla banda del Cortile del Cipresso," and a fountain with several statues is described as in the "giardino segreto." See below, "L'Ingegnoso Artifizio," 72–73, and nn. 49–50.

[35] See below, "Ars Hortulorum," 91–92, and n. 16.

A third stage in the history of sixteenth-century gardens in Rome began in the last two decades of the century. Two features that mark this stage are the more abundant use of water in fountains, made possible by new water supplies, and the appearance of new types of fountain figures without classical prototypes. Both trends are exemplified in the cascades and new fountains added in the 1590s to the Vatican Gardens and to the d'Este villa on the Quirinal, by then a papal possession, for Pope Clement VIII (see Figs. 41, 59).[36] A third innovation, seen at the Villa Mattei, was the development of a sequential narrative that required the visitor to follow a fixed itinerary, a feature that first appeared at the Villa d'Este in Tivoli and the Villa Lante at Bagnaia.[37]

One final innovation occurred which materially altered the appearance of the gardens. Throughout the earlier years of the century planting beds had been bounded either by low, usually evergreen, hedges, or wicket fences, so that the view over the *compartimenti*, as they were called, was unimpeded, and from above they looked very much like a floral carpet. Sometime toward the end of the century, it became the custom to line the paths with high hedges, which obscured the view of the beds and strengthened the role of the *mostre*, or wall fountains placed as termini of the paths. Examples of this may be seen in the Greuter views of the Villa Montalto and Villa Borghese (Figs. 15, 16). By the date of the Falda views of these same gardens, the practice was well established (see Fig. 11). As the practice of delimiting the view of the surrounding garden developed, extensions beyond the walls created views outside the garden. At the Villa Montalto, for example, the major *viale* was extended sometime after 1590 beyond the walls of the garden to a hill in the *vigna*, from which there was a view over the surrounding area.[38] *Viali* until then had always been used as space dividers, their extension beyond the garden stopped by a wall or other closing device. At the Villa Montalto they are used to create a visual extension beyond the limits of the garden and as a dynamic rather than a static element in its organization.

Documentation of the built features of these villas, especially when there are contemporary views and plans, is very full, but there is very little information about their plants.[39] Payments for plant purchases rarely survive, and the depiction of plants in views

---

[36] See "L'Ingegnoso Artifizio," 86–87, App. II.

[37] See D. Coffin, *The Villa d'Este at Tivoli*, Princeton, 1960, chap. 5, and C. Lazzaro-Bruno, "The Villa Lante at Bagnaia: An Allegory of Art and Nature," *Art Bulletin* 59 (1977), 553–60, and C. Lazzaro, *The Italian Renaissance Garden*, New Haven and London, 1990, 243–69. Coffin suggests that the set itinerary was a way of controlling the movement of the public in gardens in "'Lex Hortorum'," 222–26. The Villa Mattei is discussed below in "Circus."

[38] This extension appears in the Falda engraving. The view from the hill would have included the ruins of the Baths of Diocletian, including the great exedra, at that time the villa of Cardinal du Bellay, and the basilicas of Santa Croce and San Giovanni Laterano. The Villa Montalto was the only estate within the walls of Rome with agricultural as well as garden areas. Maps and views of the villa are published in V. Massimo, *Notizie della Villa Massimo alle Terme Diocleziane*, Rome, 1936. I have not been able to consult M. Quast, "Die Villa Montalto in Rom. Entstehung und Gestalt im Cinquecento," Ph.D. diss., University of Bonn, 1988.

[39] Coffin, *Gardens*, App. I, publishes a list of plants dating from the 1570s to 1580s recommended for the Villa d'Este. See also Lazzaro, *Renaissance Garden*, 20–46, 323–25, for documentary evidence for plants in common use in the 16th century. Lazzaro's list, pp. 323–24, is especially helpful for it identifies with modern botanical names and English common names the plants known by their 16th-century Italian names.

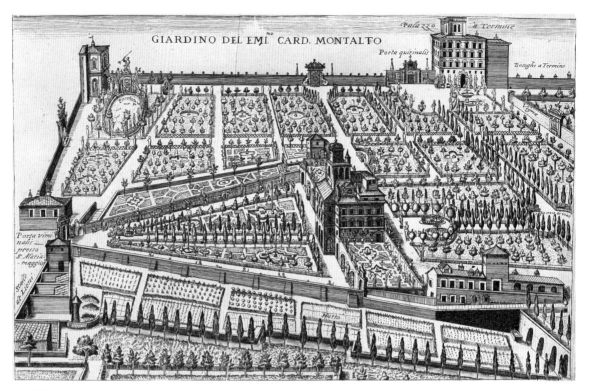

15. Villa Montalto, view by M. Greuter, ca. 1612 (photo: Dumbarton Oaks)

16. Villa Borghese, view by M. Greuter, ca. 1612 (photo: Dumbarton Oaks)

are usually too generalized to permit identification. Some clues can be gathered from names given sites on the views or in inventories such as the "Cortile dell'Olmo" at the Pio da Carpi villa on the Quirinal or the "Viale della Quercia" at the Villa Mattei.[40] Descriptions sometimes give information about plants, such as the reference in a 1523 description of the Belvedere Statue Court to laurels, mulberrys, cypresses, and orange trees or Boissard's description of several different kinds of citrus and jasmine at the d'Este villa on the Quirinal.[41] Plants were spalliered against walls and trained over frameworks to create pergolas, *cerchiate*, or the low fences around the planting beds, as a maintenance contract for the Villa Medici describes (see Fig. 14).[42] The topiary figures, so popular in the fifteenth century, do not appear in sixteenth century gardens in Rome.

That same Medici contract specifies that the superintendent is responsible for the care of the "Semplici, fiori, vasi et piante salvatiche e domestiche et arbori di frutta," and this provides almost the only proof that flowers were to be found in these gardens.[43] As Georgina Masson has shown, interest in flower collecting became very strong in the second half of the sixteenth century throughout Europe, and Italians were among the most fervent collectors.[44] In the seventeenth century, flowers were to be found in the *giardini segreti*.[45] These began to appear in Roman gardens in the same decades of the sixteenth century that the fervor for flower collecting developed, and in at least one case, the Villa Mattei, a *giardino segreto* is referred to as the "Giardino dei Simplici."[46] We must imagine then, gardens that were predominantly green, but with color accents provided by the fruits and flowers of the citrus and other flowering plants and shrubs. Foliage was usually evergreen and provided a strong contrast to the white marble statues and fountains with which the gardens were decorated. In this respect, their appearance was startlingly similar to ancient Roman gardens (see Fig. 23).[47] *Compartimenti* may have been planted in geometric patterns with the interstices filled with colored sands—this can be documented in other parts of Europe in the sixteenth century. Only the *giardini segreti* would have had the variety of textures and colors we associate with gardens today, and even they would not have had the quantities of flowering plants that are now common.

[40] The first appears in the inventory of statues there published by Huelsen, *Antikengärten*, 81–84. The latter in the 1614 inventory published by R. Lanciani, *Storia degli scavi di Roma*, III, Rome, 1907, 88–97, item 175, "Un Augusto a sedere nella nicchia sforata nel viale della . . . Quercia."

[41] The former is from a description by the Venetian ambassador, dated 11 May 1523, published in E. Alberi, *Relazioni degli ambasciatori veneti al Senato*, ser. 2, Venice, 1840, III, 114ff. The latter appears in J. J. Boissard, *Topographia Romae*, 2nd ed., Frankfurt, 1627, I, 94.

[42] The maintenance contract refers to "spalliere . . . tanto le basse quanto le alte," and to caring for the walls where there are esspalliered "Cedri" and "Melangoli" (both are ornamental citrus). ASF, Mediceo del Principato, filza 3882.

[43] See Lazzaro, *Renaissance Garden*, esp. 24–33.

[44] See G. Masson, "Italian Flower Collectors' Gardens in Seventeenth-Century Italy," *The Italian Garden*, Dumbarton Oaks Colloquium on the History of Landscape Architecture 1, ed. D. Coffin, Washington, D.C., 1972, 61–80.

[45] See below, "A Cardinal's Bulb Garden: A *Giardino Segreto* at the Palazzo Barberini in Rome."

[46] This appears in the rubric of the Lauro view.

[47] Reproduced in color in W. Jashemski, *The Gardens of Pompeii, Herculaneum and the Villas Destroyed by Vesuvius*, I, New Rochelle, 1979, fig. 204.

There are no records of designers of these gardens, and almost none for gardeners, although the names of the latter are sometimes found in salary rolls or papal accounts.[48] It is customary to assume that architects or even their patrons designed the actual layouts and planting plans[49] even though there was almost no theoretical literature on design or horticulture. Serlio included some parterre designs in his *Tutte le Opere d'Architectura;* the thirteenth-century treatise on agriculture, *Opus ruralium commodorum,* by Piero de' Crescenzi had several sixteenth-century editions.[50] Two treatises, one modeled on Crescenzi by Anton Doni, the other by Giovanvettorio Soderini, imitating ancient Roman agricultural writings, remained in manuscript until the twentieth century.[51] From Soderini we learn that there were simple arithmetical formulas for selecting the width of paths but nothing like the sophisticated calculation of proportions in building designs. The iconographical programs, on the other hand, are usually assumed to have been created by scholars attached to the papal court or patron's entourage.

A Roman patron's garden was an intimate part of his life. The unique conditions in the city of Rome made it possible for gardens to be situated closer to his main residence than was usual in other parts of the peninsula. It could be used for short respites from city life and as a display to his visitors. It was an index of his cultivation as well as his wealth, a demonstration of his link with antiquity as well as a statement about his position in his own world. As a consequence, the Roman garden of the sixteenth century was not just an assemblage of plants and statues in pleasing decorative patterns. Allegory as well as literary allusion provided moral lessons, personal aggrandizement, and intellectual puzzles. It is this aspect of these gardens that is examined in the succeeding articles.

[48] For a collection of evidence of gardeners in papal employ, see Coffin, *Gardens,* App. III.

[49] In contrast in France at this time, gardeners can be identified—especially those employed by the rulers—and in successive generations they became garden designers, such as André LeNôtre and the Mollets.

[50] S. Serlio, *Tutte le Opere d'Architectura,* IV, Venice, 1600, 197–98; P. de Crescenzi, *Opus ruralium commodorum,* Venice, 1554. Other editions are listed by R. G. Calkins, "Piero de' Crescenzi and the Medieval Garden," *Medieval Gardens,* ed. E. B. MacDougall, Dumbarton Oaks Colloquium on the History of Landscape Architecture 9, Washington, D.C., 1986, 159.

[51] A. F. Doni, *Le Ville,* in *Scritti d'arte del Cinquecento,* ed. P. Barocchi, III, Milan, Naples, 1977, 321–57; G. Soderini, *Il trattato della cultura degli orti e giardini,* in *Opere,* ed. Bacchi della Lega, II, Bologna, 1903. Three other texts by Soderini, *I due trattati dell'agricoltura e della coltivazione delle vite* and *Il trattato degli arbori,* were published as vols. I and III of the *Opere* (Bologna, 1902, 1904), respectively.

Il Giardino all'Antico: Roman Statuary
and Italian Renaissance Gardens

Starting late in the fourteenth century, Italians began to build small suburban villas just within or just outside the walls of the city. Unlike the true country estates, which provided food and goods for trading, these were intended primarily for relaxation and escape from the cares of urban life; their term for this was *ozio*, derived from the Latin *otium*. They were places where a group of scholars might meet to discuss philosophy, read poetry or ancient literature, or merchants might discuss political affairs, give banquets, or listen to concerts.[1] Their appearance coincided with the revival of interest in ancient civilization, that is, the beginning of the Renaissance.

One of the chief interests of these groups of scholars and patrons, intellectuals and collectors was the acquisition of antiquities. They searched out coins and gems, and especially statues. Fragments as well as entire statues, reliefs and sarcophagi, even architectural remains, such as columns and capitals, architraves, consoles, and bases were avidly collected. All types of antiquities were studied and copied in drawings, as the many surviving sketchbooks testify.[2]

By the end of the fifteenth century some very large collections had been amassed. Some were displayed in palaces, as for instance Isabella d'Este's collection in her apartments in the ducal palace in Mantua.[3] In Rome, a favored site for such collections was the garden; of the almost forty collections of antiquities listed by Fra Giocondo at the end of the century at least half contained statues and statue fragments, and many were exhibited in their owners' palace or villa gardens.[4] One such collection was drawn by the Dutch artist Marten van Heemskerck in the 1530s (Fig. 17). It belonged to the wealthy

[1] For a discussion of early Renaissance gardens and their use, see E. Battisti, "*Natura Artificiosa* to *Natura Artificialis*," *The Italian Garden*, Dumbarton Oaks Colloquium on the History of Landscape Architecture 1, ed. D. Coffin, Washington, D.C., 1972, 1–36; D. Coffin, *The Villa in the Life of Renaissance Rome*, Princeton, 1979, chaps. 1, 2.

[2] R. Weiss, *The Renaissance Discovery of Classical Antiquity*, Oxford, 1969, esp. chaps. 5, 12, 13.

[3] Ibid., 197–98.

[4] For a discussion of the Fra Giocondo manuscript, see R. Lanciani, *Storia degli scavi di Roma e notizie intorno le collezioni romane di Antichità*, 4 vols., Rome, 1902–12 (repr. 1975), I, 96–98, and 100–121 for the list of the collections.

17. Ancient sculpture collection at the Giardino Gallo, Rome, drawing by Marten van Heemskerck, Berlin Sketchbook (photo: Library of Congress)

18. Ancient sculpture collection at the Villa Cesi, Rome, drawing by Heemskerck, Berlin Sketchbook (photo: Library of Congress)

Roman, Jacopo Gallo, and contained as well two statues by Michelangelo, the Apollo and the Bacchus with Young Satyr.[5] Yet another collector, Giuliano Cardinal della Rovere, may have placed the statue now called the Apollo Belvedere on the dome of a garden pavilion; on his elevation to the papacy in 1502 the statue was taken to the Vatican as the nucleus of the statue collection of the Belvedere Court.[6]

At first, the possession of antiquities was sufficient, and neither their condition nor the manner of their display was important (Fig. 18).[7] In the sixteenth century, however, the attitude towards the objects gradually changed as did their role in the garden. At the beginning of the century the garden was the place where statues were displayed with little regard for any of the kinds of arrangements we are accustomed to today, that is, chronological, geographical, or topical. By the end of the century the garden and its design had become the focus of interest, and the antiquities had become decorations, placed to accent a view or embellish a fountain.

This change in attitude can be traced in the gardens of Rome where the most important and the largest collections of antiquities were in the sixteenth century. Ancient statues existed in great quantities in the Roman ruins and were continually being discovered; in addition, the sixteenth-century patron saw himself as the continuer of the ancient tradition of patronage and collecting.[8] Outside Rome, ancient statue collections were smaller and, perhaps because of their rarity, were more frequently displayed within the palace or villa buildings.

It is not surprising that Julius II, the former Cardinal della Rovere, whose projects for rebuilding St. Peter's and the Vatican Palace have been characterized as an expression of his desire to recreate the splendors of ancient Rome, was the first to create a *giardino all'antico*. He commissioned the enclosure of the area between the Vatican Palace and the little casino on the high ridge of the Vatican hill built by Innocent VIII in the preceding century. The space between the casino and the exedral terminus of the great new terraced court was made into a garden for the display of the papal collection of ancient statues. This consisted of some of the most famous ancient statues then known: the Apollo Belvedere; the Laocoon group; statues of river gods, the Nile, Tigris, and Tiber; a figure of a reclining woman, then called Cleopatra but now identified as representing Ariadne (Figs. 19, 20).[9] The statues were placed in niches in the walls of the courtyard; there were fountains in the center and high on the walls were large masks which were reproductions of the ancient Comedy and Tragedy masks (Fig. 21). Even though the decoration of some of the niches, as they were depicted in the 1530s, was created later than the original statue installations, the arrangement of the regularly and

[5] C. Lee, "The Garden of Jacopo Gallo in Rome," Ph.D. diss., Brown University, 1981.

[6] H. Brummer, *The Statue Court in the Vatican Belvedere*, Acta Universitatis Stockholmiensis. Stockholm Studies in the History of Art 20, Stockholm, 1970, 44–46.

[7] The drawings of this garden, the Villa Cesi, and the Gallo garden were made by the Dutch artist Marten van Heemskerck during his stay in Rome in the 1530s. The drawings, now in the Print Department of the Berlin State Museum, were published by C. Huelsen and H. Egger, *Die römischen Skizzenbücher von Marten van Heemskerck*, Berlin, 1916.

[8] Many even claimed that they could trace their lineage back to Roman patricians and emperors.

[9] Each statue is discussed in a separate chapter by Brummer, *Belvedere*.

19. Ancient statue of river god, the "Tigris,"
as originally installed in the Belvedere Statue
Court, Vatican Palace, drawing by Heemskerck, Berlin Sketchbook
(photo: Library of Congress)

20. Statue group of Laocoon and his sons,
engraving by F. Perrier, *Segmenta nobili-
uim signorum et statuarum . . .* , Rome,
1638
(photo: Dumbarton Oaks)

symmetrically placed figures was provided for from the beginning. One must suppose
that the Belvedere Court was intended to be a replica of an ancient statue display.[10]

The question, however, is how did the collectors of the Renaissance derive their
ideas? There was very little evidence for the appearance of ancient gardens. Pliny's well-
known letters describing his two villas at Tusculum and Laurentum, probably the single
most important source known to the Renaissance, do not mention statues. Cicero described the purchase of statues and relief fragments for his villa, to place, he said, on the
walls of his library, and Pliny the Elder's chapter on marble in his *Natural History* includes
a number of references to statues in gardens in Rome.[11] Evidence was also provided by
the discovery of statues in what were known to be the sites of ancient villas, although
probably not as early in the sixteenth century as the construction of the Belvedere
Court.[12]

[10] Ibid., 218–19.

[11] Pliny, *Epistles*, 2.7; 5.6; Pliny, *Natural History*, 36.20; Cicero, *Epistolae ad Atticum*, 1.10; Martial, *Epigrams*, 3.29, describes a grove in a public park in Rome, the Porticus Liviae, with statues of wild beasts.

[12] The Laocoon was discovered in 1506 at a site then believed to be part of Nero's Domus Aurea, an
urban villa. Later in the century the statues of the Muses, formerly in the grotto of the d'Este villa on the
Quirinal, were found at Hadrian's villa in Tivoli. The Niobid group installed at the Villa Medici was found
on the site of the Horti Lamiani. For lists of other discoveries, see P. G. Hübner, "Detailstudien zur Gesch-

21. Mask decorations formerly in the
    Belvedere Statue Court, drawing by
    Francisco de Hollanda, Escorial
    Sketchbook
    (photo: Dumbarton Oaks)

In addition, a number of sarcophagi and reliefs which seem to show statues arranged in colonnaded loggias or placed on fountains may have been the inspiration for statue displays in the Renaissance (Fig. 22). Despite the scarcity of information these early gar-dens were startlingly similar in appearance to suburban gardens of antiquity. Paintings, which were not discovered in Pompeii until the eighteenth century, look as if they were the models for the early sixteenth-century gardens (Fig. 23).

One feature of Julius II's collection in the Belvedere, and one which would be commonly found later, was the grouping of sculpture of different provenances and functions to make an ensemble. This is true of the Cleopatra/Ariadne fountain, in which the free-standing statue, probably originally a decoration in a Hellenistic palace or garden, was placed above a sarcophagus which served as the catchpool for the water that dripped from the rocky niche, and, if we are to believe a contemporary poem, from the statue's breasts (Fig. 24).[13] Another example of the many such combinations was in the villa of Emilio Cardinal Cesi located on the Gianicolo above the piazza of St. Peter's. The collection, which was formed in the 1520s and which consisted of more than one hundred and fifty statues, included a satyr with a wine sack placed over a large footed basin that served

---

ichte der antiken Roms in der Renaissance," *Mitteilungen des Deutschen Archäologischen Instituts. Römische Abtei-lung* 26 (1911), 288–328. The more famous statues are discussed in F. Haskell and N. Penny, *Taste and the Antique: The Lure of Classical Sculpture, 1500–1900,* New Haven and London, 1981.

    [13] Brummer, *Belvedere,* 154.

22. Roman sarcophagus representing the Labors of Hercules, Rome, Villa Borghese (photo: Anderson)

23. Ancient painting of a Mars statue in a garden, Pompeii, House of Venus (photo: Stanley Jashemski)

28

24. The Cleopatra/Ariadne fountain as
originally installed in the Belvedere
Statue Court, drawing by Hollanda,
Escorial Sketchbook
(photo: Dumbarton Oaks)

as a catchpool for the water flowing from the sack. Originally this group was placed
against the garden wall among a group of statues and fragments (see Fig. 18). In the
1540s, at a time when statue display was becoming more formal and decorative, the
group was placed in the center of one of the four planting beds, each of which had statues
placed at their four corners.[14]

The new attitude towards statues and their arrangement that began to appear in
the 1540s grew stronger in the succeeding decades. In the 1550s plans were made to
install statues in the first courtyard of the Villa Giulia in niches along the side walls. The
walls were articulated with a rich architectural framework, separating niches in which
statues were to be placed, and the placement of the statues was symmetrical in relationship to the central group on each wall and to the statues on the facing wall.[15]

In the 1560s Ippolito Cardinal II d'Este leased a palace on the Quirinal hill to use
as a refuge from the heat and unhealthy conditions of the lowlands by the Tiber where

[14] C. Huelsen, *Römische Antikengärten des XVI. Jahrhunderts*, Akademie der Wissenschaften zu Heidelberg,
Philosophisch-historische Klasse, Abhandlungen 4 (1917), 3–4.

[15] The arrangement was described by the architect Bartolommeo Ammannati in a letter dated 2 May
1555 to Marco Mantova Benavides. The letter, preserved in the Biblioteca Communale in Pesaro (ms. Oliv.
374), was published with emendations of spelling and punctuation by G. Balestra, *La fontana pubblica di Giulio
III ed il palazzo di Pio IV sulla Via Flaminia,* Rome, 1911, 65ff. For an interpretation of the decorative program,
see "Imitation and Invention," 122.

his chief residence was located. The palace is now the residence of the president of Italy, and the sixteenth-century garden was replaced by a landscape-style design in the eighteenth century. Its original appearance, however, can be reconstructed from a number of pre-eighteenth-century views, while engravings of the individual statues in the collection that the cardinal formed and had displayed in the garden give evidence of the extent of that collection. Additional information is supplied by an inventory of the statues in 1568.[16] Of interest are the number of statues that had been or were in the process of being restored. In earlier collections the statues or their fragments were left as they were found; now parts were added to make a statue complete, an indication that mere antiquity was no longer satisfactory. A complete work of art was required.[17] Further evidence of the difference in attitude is provided by the many statues that had been adapted for use in the garden fountains by the sculptor Cioli. A fountain in one of the garden loggias had a restored female figure whose left breast had been pierced so water would spout from the nipple. In niches on either side of her were two Bacchus statues, one with an animal whose mouth had been perforated to make a water spout, the other with a wine sack which had been similarly treated.[18]

There were two interesting sculptural ensembles at this villa. The first, in a grotto beneath one of the palace terraces, contained a statue of Apollo with a lyre. Eight figures of muses were placed in the grotto walls. The other, referred to as the "Fontana del Bosco," was at the rear of an open plaza in the center of a grove of trees. The small structure in which the fountain was placed seems to have been a sort of pergola or pavilion covered with greenery. Inside there was a rocky mount with a shepherd boy on top, in front of it was a figure of a Venus with two putti at her feet (Figs. 25, 26, 27). Small satyrs with vases on their head stood in side niches and a "Ganymede with a swan" was in the water pool in front (see Fig. 73).[19] The latter was probably a replica of the Hellenistic statue type of a boy with a goose, a popular decoration in fountains of this period. A payment to the restorer Cioli, which may refer to this statue, speaks of remaking his "pincerello" so that he could appear to piss.[20] The plaza in front of the little pavilion, according to a German traveler at the beginning of the seventeenth century, was lined with wall-like hedges with deep niches in which stood statues of a Jupiter, a "king," a Ceres, and a Hermes restored as a Roman emperor.[21] Unlike the earlier statue

---

[16] Huelsen, *Antikengärten*, 113–17.

[17] Typical of the kinds of restoration undertaken are those described in the payments to the sculptor Valerio Cioli for work done on statues in the d'Este collection; see A. Venturi, "Ricerche di antichità per Monte Giordano, Monte Cavallo e Tivoli nel secolo XVI," *Archivio storico dell'arte* 3 (1890), 196–206.

[18] ". . . per aver fatto la testa . . . et aver finite le gambe e bucatola quella zinna manca della Venere ch'è esposta nella fontana della loggia . . . per aver rappicciato quel Bacco ch'è nella fontana della loggia . . . e di più si cuciò quello animale perchè buttasi acqua . . . e quell'altro che tiene l'otra in ispala si busò l'otra per gitar l'acqua"; Venturi, "Ricerche," 198.

[19] Huelsen, *Antikengärten*, 99.

[20] "Per aver bucato quel putto dell'oca e refattogli el suo pincerello appropriato a questo effetto del pisciare"; Venturi, "Ricerche," 198.

[21] A description by the German architect Heinrich Schickhardt, who visited the garden ca. 1600, says "Vor diesem Felsem [sc. the fountain described above] hat es einen schenen Platz, so mit Gewechs wie

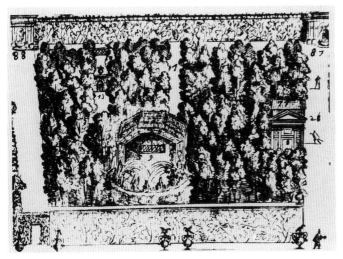

25. The *fontana rustica* in the d'Este villa on the Quirinal, Rome, detail of Maggi view, ca. 1600 (photo: British Library)

26. The rocky mount of the *fontana rustica* in the d'Este villa on the Quirinal, Rome, engraving in G. Maggi, *Fontane diverse . . . di Roma,* Rome, 1618 (photo: Dumbarton Oaks)

27. Venus, Eros, and Anteros statue group formerly in the *fontana rustica* in the d'Este villa on the Quirinal, engraving from G. de Cavalieri, *Antiquae statuae . . . ,* Rome, 1585 (photo: Dumbarton Oaks)

31

groupings I have been describing, these two ensembles are derived from descriptions of ancient sites. The Apollo grotto recalls that Apollo, the *Musagete,* was the leader of the nine Muses and that his chief cult was in connection with the Delphic oracle whose prophesies were made in the great cavern there. The second group, at least the part under the pergola, is like the small sanctuary described by Pausanias (1.19.2) of "Aphrodite in the Garden" on the slopes of the Acropolis in Athens. He says of the sanctuary that the cult statue was not placed in the temple but rather was outside in the surrounding garden. Although we now know a number of Greek vases that show the Athenian statue seated in front of a hilly background and with two erotes accompanying her, an arrangement very similar to the d'Este group, it is unlikely that any of them were known in the sixteenth century.[22]

One final *giardino all'antico* must be discussed; one which survives in something like its original form. I refer to the Villa Medici on the slopes of the Pincio above the Piazza di Spagna. The hill, which lay outside the walls of republican Rome, had a long history as the location of villas; the gardens of Lucullus and of other members of the Roman aristocracy were there.[23] In 1576, Ferdinando Cardinal de' Medici bought land and a casino from the Ricci family. He remodeled the casino, built a gallery for his sculpture collection, built a mount, which he named Parnassus, over the remains of an ancient temple, and replanted and reorganized the gardens.[24]

In 1583, he purchased the della Valle sculpture collection, one of the largest formed in the first decades of the century. Many of the reliefs and statues from that collection were placed on the garden façade of the casino remodeled by the cardinal (Fig. 28). An inventory made at the end of the century lists friezes and other reliefs, masks, heads, and thirty-six statues.[25] The inspiration for this innovation in the use of antiquities as façade decoration seems to have been ancient sarcophagi or possibly a reconstituted arrangement of fragments (Fig. 29).

In the same year, a major discovery was made in a vineyard near San Giovanni in Laterano. The approximately fourteen statues were a group representing the story of the slaying of Niobe and her children by Apollo and his sister Diana in revenge for a

Mauren unfangen; hat vertiefte Muschlen [niches] darin marbelsteine Bilder stehen." Schickhardt's manuscript (Stuttgart State Library, cod. hist. Q 148) was partially published by W. von Heyd, *Handschriften und Handzeichnungen Württembergischen Baumeisters Heinrich Schickhardt,* Stuttgart, 1902. His description of various features in the d'Este villa appears in Huelsen, *Antikengärten,* 121–22. The other statues in this group are listed on pp. 99–100.

[22] E. Langlotz, *Aphrodite in den Gärten,* Abhandlung, Sitzungsberichte der Heidelberger Akademie der Wissenschaften, Philosophisch-historische Klasse 2 (1954).

[23] P. Grimal, *Les jardins romains,* 2nd ed., Paris, 1969, 126–27.

[24] G. Andres, *The Villa Medici in Rome,* New York, 1976.

[25] "Inventario delle Masseritie et altre robbe che si trovano nel palazo et giardino del S.mo Gran Duca di Toscana alla Trinita de Monti"; dated 22 June 1598. See F. Boyer, "Un inventaire inédit des antiques de la villa Médicis," *Revue archéologique,* ser. 5, 30 (1929), 256–70. He identifies the manuscript as Archivio di Stato, Firenze, Fondo Medicea 587, but I have been unable to trace the document by this number or by concordances with the newer numbering system.

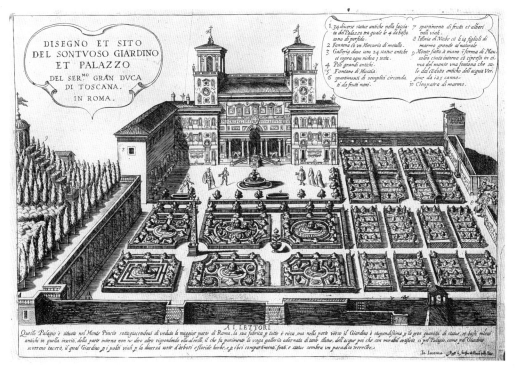

28. Bird's-eye view of the garden of the Villa Medici, Rome, with the Niobid group installed, engraving in M. Greuter, *Vedute e giardini di Roma*, Rome, 1623 (photo: Fogg Art Museum)

29. Renaissance reconstruction of an ancient relief and statues in an architectural setting, Vatican Museum (photo: Anderson)

Par hæsitatio est Nioben cum liberis morientem,   Scopas, an Praxiteles fecerit   Plin, l.36,e5,   in Ortis Mediceis.

30. Ancient statue group of the Niobids as displayed in the Villa Medici garden, Rome,
      engraving by Perrier, *Segmenta* . . . (photo: Dumbarton Oaks)

slighting remark Niobe had made about their mother, Latona. In all probability the statues that were found were the group donated to the temple of Apollo in the Campus
Martius at the beginning of the Christian era.[26] They were purchased by the cardinal for
the very large price of 1800 scudi and, after restoration, installed as a group in the
garden. A few nonrelated figures were added, such as the rearing horse (Fig. 30). The
statues, which have since been moved to Florence where they are now in the Uffizi, were
set against an architectural frame at the end of the major axis of the garden and were its
major decorative feature (see Fig. 28).

   At the Villa Medici the transformation started in the early sixteenth century was
complete. The Belvedere display of sculpture in a garden had been replaced by the
Medici garden decorated with sculpture. Ancient sculpture, at least in the garden, was
no longer valued for its antiquity alone, no longer acceptable in a fragmented state.
Restored statues were now arranged in ways that appear to emulate ancient groups and
used as important focal points in the design of the garden.

   This transformation sheds light on the nature of classicism in the Renaissance. Although the collectors wished to create gardens in the style of antiquity, they had little

[26] For the history of the discovery of the group, their purchase by Ferdinando de' Medici, installation
at the villa, and subsequent removal to Florence, where they are now on display in the Uffizi, see G. A.
Mansuelli, *Galleria degli Uffizi: Le sculture*, Rome, 1958, 101–9.

reliable information on which to base their recreations—much less, for instance, than architects and painters had. Nevertheless, they arrived at solutions very much like those we can now prove existed in Roman times. Their creations were not imitations but genuine inventions in the spirit of the classical past. They saw themselves as the revivers and continuers of a tradition: *renovatio* not *imitatio* was their ambition and their achievement.

The Sleeping Nymph:
Origins of a Humanist Fountain Type

In 1512 a newly excavated statue of a reclining female was installed as part of a fountain in the Belvedere Statue Court at the Vatican.[1] In a drawing dated 1538–39 (Fig. 24), the statue is shown set in a niche against a rocky grottolike background.[2] Water drips down the rocks and flows from two orifices into an ancient sarcophagus supported by two dolphins and a shell. The statue, now identified as an Ariadne, was then believed to represent Cleopatra. As such, it may have been a component of an overall allegorical program of decoration in the statue court,[3] but the figure and setting also corresponded closely to the image evoked by an epigram then believed to be ancient. "Huius nympha loci, sacri custodia fontis / Dormio dum blandae sentior murmur aquae. / Parce meum quisquis tangis cava marmora somnum / Rumpere: sive bibas, sive lavere taces."

The poem had appeared among the inscriptions compiled by Michael Fabricius Ferrarinus in a manuscript dated between 1477 and 1484. It was accompanied by a description. "On the banks of the Danube where there is a sculpture of a sleeping nymph in a beautiful fountain. Under the figure is this epigram."[4]

I am indebted to Marilyn Aronberg Lavin, whose question, "Why do nymphs sleep?," provided the stimulus for this essay.

[1] For details and documents concerning the installation of the Cleopatra statue in the Belvedere Court, see H. Brummer, *The Statue Court in the Vatican Belvedere*, Acta Universitatis Stockholmiensis. Stockholm Studies in the History of Art 20, Stockholm, 1970, 154. For the discovery of the statue, see W. Amelung, *Die Sculpturen des vaticanischen Museums*, I, Berlin, 1903, 636, n. 414.

[2] The dating of the Hollanda drawing is discussed by Brummer, *Belvedere*, 155. There is no documentation for the rocky setting prior to the drawing. However, I believe that the background was part of the original setting because the Fausto di Capodiferro poem quoted on p. 38 clearly reflects the *Huius nympha loci* which calls for a cave setting.

[3] See Brummer, *Belvedere*, 220–22, for a political interpretation of the Cleopatra fountain. He also suggests that the figure might have been construed as a nymph (p. 171). Another interpretation of the fountain is expressed by E. Gombrich, "Hypnerotomachiana," *Journal of the Warburg and Courtauld Institutes* 14 (1951), 122–24.

[4] "Super ripam Danuvii in quo est sculpta nympha ad amoenum fontem dormiens, sub figura est hoc epigramma," Paris, Bibl. nat. lat. 6128, fol. 114r and Reggio, Bibl. comm. cod. C. 398, fol. 28r. The Paris manuscript is after 1477, the Reggio is dated 1486. The epigram appears in *Corpus inscriptionum latinarum* (hereafter *CIL*), Berlin, 1863–1940, VI, 5, 3*e. Although Smetius stated doubts about the authenticity of the

The relationship of the Vatican fountain to the topos of the sleeping nymph was recognized at the time of its installation. For example, a poem about the fountain attributed to Evangelista Maddaleni Fausto di Capodiferro and written before the death of Pope Julius II in 1513 borrows from the epigram. "Fessa soporifero Fontis susurro / Perspicui, dulcis frigidulique fruor. / Accaedas tacitus, tacitusque lavere bibasque. . . ."[5]

In the decade following the construction of the Cleopatra fountain two more versions were built by two humanists at the court of Pope Leo X, Angelo Colocci and Hans Goritz.[6] Colocci's was inscribed with the whole epigram, whereas Goritz's had a shortened version, *Nymphae, Loci/Bibe. Lava/Tace*.[7] Later in the century many more replicas of the fountain appeared in Rome both with and without the inscription, and the type also spread to other parts of Italy; one in Venice and two in Sicily can be documented.[8] Throughout the century the topos remained a popular one; it was soon adopted in other media. For example, Cranach painted a female nude lying by a well inscribed with an abbreviated version of the epigram.[9] A drawing by Dürer also shows a figure reclining by a well inscribed with the full epigram, and a relief on a fountain in St. Wolfgang, Germany, has the same figure type personifying water.[10] The persistence of the literary theme is suggested by Michelangelo's quatrain on the Medici Chapel statue of Night, a figure posed very similarly to the Cleopatra-Ariadne type.

"I prize my sleep and more by being stone / As long as hurt and shamefulness endure / I call it lucky not to see or hear / So do not waken me, keep your voice down."[11]

The association of sleeping nymph, cave, and epigram remained constant in the early sixteenth century; the statue form did not. The earliest fountains for which there is visual evidence have two different types. The half-clothed, half-recumbent Cleopatra-Ariadne figure differs in many respects from the other documented early figure, the nude nymph of the Colocci fountain (Fig. 31). Neither is identical to the ancient Roman fountain nymph type, which was not used until later in the sixteenth century (Fig. 32).[12]

---

epigram in the mid-16th century, it was retained in compilations of ancient inscriptions until the 19th century when Mommsen included it in the *CIL* collection of forgeries.

[5] Quoted by Brummer, *Belvedere*, 221. The relationship between the two poems was pointed out by O. Kurz, "*Huius nympha loci*: A Pseudo-Classical Inscription and a Drawing by Dürer," *Journal of the Warburg and Courtauld Institutes* 16 (1953), 174–75.

[6] See pp. 48–51.

[7] *CIL*, VI, 5, 4*c.

[8] The Sicilian fountains were reported by Don Vincenzo di Giovanni at the end of the 16th century. See V. di Giovanni, *La topografia antica di Palermo dal secolo X al XV*, II, Palermo, 1890, 367–70. The Venetian example is mentioned by M. Meiss, "Sleep in Venice," *Proceedings of the American Philosophical Society* 110 (1960), 350, n. 13.

[9] M. Liebmann, "On the Iconography of the *Nymph of the Fountain* by Lucas Cranach the Elder," *Journal of the Warburg and Courtauld Institutes* 31 (1968), 434–37.

[10] The Dürer drawing is discussed by Kurz, "*Huius nympha*," 171–77. For the fountain relief, see F. Saxl, "A Heathenish Fountain in St. Wolfgang," *Journal of the Warburg and Courtauld Institutes* 1 (1937), 182–83.

[11] C. Gilbert, "Texts and Contexts of the Medici Chapel," *Art Quarterly* 34 (1971), 391–409. The poem (Girardi, 247), written in 1545–46, is given here in C. Gilbert's translation (*Complete Poems and Selected Letters of Michelangelo*, New York, 1965, no. 245).

[12] For a discussion of the ancient sleeping nymph figure type and a list of examples, see C. Praschniker and H. Kenner, *Der Bäderbezirk von Virunum*, Vienna, 1947, 79–81 and 80, n. 52.

31. Sleeping nymph fountain in garden of Angelo Colocci, engraving by
J. J. Boissard, *Romanae urbis topographia*, Rome, 1585, IV, pl. 25
(photo: Biblioteca Apostolica Vaticana)

Many aspects of the sleeping nymph fountain have been examined before, but several questions remain unanswered. No one has traced the origin of the epigram, although it was identified as a Renaissance forgery by Mommsen in the corpus of Latin inscriptions.[13] The origins of the figure types and their relationship to ancient sources have not been fully explored. Finally, no one has yet explained the widespread and enduring popularity of the topos.

THE HISTORY OF THE EPIGRAM

Previous discussions of the sleeping nymph theme have been based on the inclusion of the epigram as an ancient inscription in two compendia by Ferrarinus, and there has been no speculation as to its origin. Its appearance in an earlier manuscript, a collection of *excerpta*, epitaphs, and verses made by Bartolommeo della Fonte, has been ignored.[14] In della Fonte's manuscript the epigram is given the superscription, "Recently invented

[13] It is listed among the forgeries in the *CIL;* cf. n. 4 above.
[14] Kurz, "*Huius nympha*," 172, refers to the presence of the epigram in della Fonte's manuscript but does not speculate on the significance.

in Rome. It is by Campanus."[15] Other epigrams by Campanus included in della Fonte's manuscript permit his identification as Giovanni Antonio Campani, a Roman humanist at the Vatican and the biographer of Pope Pius II.[16] After the death of the pope in 1464 Campani taught at the Florence Academy when della Fonte was a student there.[17] The manuscript itself appears to have been compiled before 1470.[18]

Much that is puzzling about the epigram is made clear by the establishment of its date and author. Its poetic form is totally unlike other Renaissance inscription forgeries, which are usually simple dedications, or at most a distich.[19] In contrast, as a literary invention produced in the circle of humanists of Rome and Florence, its form and content are easily explained. The epigram recalls Ovid's description of Rhea Sylvia in the *Fasti*. The image of a girl resting by an urn of water lulled to sleep by the soft sound of the water (*murmur blandae aquae*) is similar in both.[20] The form of the poem and its feeling are nearer to Greek Hellenistic pastoral and lyrical poetry. Epigrams of this style became popular at this time, for the period of the composition of the *Huius nympha loci* coincides with the first diffusion in Italy of knowledge of the Planudean collection of Greek epigrams, now called the Greek Anthology.[21] It was also the period when the influence of Greek scholars from Byzantium was at its highest, and when the study of Greek literature became widespread in the universities and academies. Campani, a protégé of Cardinal

[15] Florence, Riccardiana, Cod. 907, fol. 172r. "Romae recens inventum. Campani est." I am indebted to Dr. Gino Corti for his investigation of the manuscript and transcription of portions of it. Phyllis Bober has recently pointed out to me that *inventum* was used more commonly in this period for "discovered," and that the superscription can also be translated as "Recently discovered in Rome. It belongs to Campani." In view of the other reference to Campani in the della Fonte ms. (fol. 187v), she agrees with me that the less common sense of *inventum* is intended here. I am indebted to her for pointing out the alternative meaning.

[16] An epigram by Campani to Pope Pius II in this ms., fol. 187v, is included in the published works of Campani, *Opera Campani omnia,* 2nd ed., Venice, 1495, fol. XV. A biography of Campani appears in this edition. For further information about Campani, who wrote a biography of Pius II, see M. E. Cosenza, *Biographical and Bibliographical Dictionary of the Italian Humanists and of the World of Classical Scholarship,* 2nd ed., rev. and enl., Boston, 1962–67, s.v.

[17] For the facts concerning della Fonte's student years, see C. Marchesi, *Bartolommeo della Fonte (Bartholomeus Fontius), contributo alla storia degli studi classici in Firenze nella seconda metà del quattrocento,* Catania, 1900, 11. In della Fonte's *Annales* (Riccard. Cod. 1172A) for the year 1465, he writes, "His temporibus doctrina et ingenio clari erant Campanus Romae, Pontanus Napoli, Baptista Albertus et Landinus et Schola Florentiae" (Marchesi, 11, n. 3).

[18] Inclusion of epitaphs to Pope Pius II (d. 1464) and a letter dated 9 August 1464 give a terminus post quem. Other epitaphs give a terminus ante quem of 1470.

[19] Characteristic examples are to be found in *CIL,* VI, 5.

[20]

> Silvia Vestalis—quid enim vetat inde moveri?—
>   Sacra lavaturas mane petebat aquas.
> Ventum erat ad molli declivem tramite ripam:
>   Ponitur e summa fictilis urna coma.
>   . . . . .
> Dum sedet, umbrosae salices volucresque canorae
>   Fecerunt somnos et leve murmur aquae,
> Blanda quies furtim victis obrepsit ocellis,
>   Et cadit a mento languida facta manus.
>   —*Fasti,* 3.11–20

[21] J. Hutton, *The Greek Anthology in Italy to the Year 1800,* New York, 1935, 3.

Bessarion, was undoubtedly familiar with the Greek Anthology, for Bessarion owned a complete copy of the Planudean collection of epigrams.[22] In addition, both Bessarion's Academy in Rome and Pomponio Leto's, of which Campani was also a member, were noted for their promotion of studies in Greek literature and its translation.[23] Campani's poems testify to the strong influence on him of Greek poetry.[24]

Thus the form chosen by Campani was one particularly in vogue at that time, and the subject matter of his epigram, a nymph, was equally popular. Starting with Boccaccio's *Ninfale fiesolana,* nymphs were the subject of a number of novels, of which the *Hypnerotomachia polifili* is the best-known example of the quattrocento. Nymphs also played an important role in the poetry of the period.[25] Campani's epigram, then, can be seen as a typical product of the poetic tastes of the humanists of his time.

The process by which the poem became known as an ancient inscription is not so clear, for the gap in time and place between its appearance in Bartolommeo della Fonte's manuscript and its inclusion in the Ferrarinus compendium needs explanation. Possibly the history of the inscription collections of Cyriacus of Ancona provides the needed link. Cyriacus, the famous traveler of the first half of the fifteenth century, made numerous compendia of inscriptions, and all the later fifteenth-century compilations are at least partially dependent on his.[26] The two compendia by Ferrarinus in which the Campani epigram appears have recently been shown to descend from a lost Cyriacus manuscript.[27] Cyriacus' work was known to Bartolommeo della Fonte; he served as a transmitter of some of the material, and copies of Cyriacus' writings appear in his own manuscript.[28] Greek epigrams appear in surviving inscription collections by Cyriacus. Is it not possible that della Fonte, who forged other inscriptions, inserted the Campani epigram in one of his copies of the Cyriacus material, and that this was Ferrarinus' source?[29]

In the next known citation of the epigram after its appearance in the two compendia

---

[22] D. J. Geanakoplos, *Greek Scholars in Venice, Studies in the Dissemination of Greek Learning from Byzantium to Western Europe,* Cambridge, Mass., 1962, 72.

[23] "Il Bessarione ed il Campani," *Bessarione* 1 (1879), 610–17.

[24] Campani's poems are published in *Epistolae et poemata,* ed. Mencken, Leipzig, 1707. See especially *Carmina* on p. 55 and *Ad Phoebum* on p. 83.

[25] G. Boccaccio, *Ninfale fiesolana,* written 1340s, ed. prin., Venice, 1477. For the importance of the *Hypnerotomachia,* see p. 48. Nymphs as subject matter for poetry are discussed by E. Callara, *La poesia pastorale,* Milan, n.d., 170–80 and passim.

[26] The vexed problem of the interrelationship of the 15th-century inscription compendia was discussed by Mommsen, *CIL,* VI, 1, cols. xl-xlv. This was modified by E. Ziebarth, "De antiquissimis inscriptionum syllogis," *Ephemeris epigraphica* 9 (1905), 187–352. See especially pp. 188–213 for the Cyriacus mss.

[27] C. Mitchell, "Felice Feliciano *Antiquarius,*" *Proceedings of the British Academy* 47 (1961), 197–221. He traces the Feliciano and Ferrarinus mss. to lost archetypes of Cyriacus of Ancona.

[28] See F. Saxl, "Classical Inscriptions in Renaissance Art and Politics," *Journal of the Warburg and Courtauld Institutes* 4 (1944), 19–46; B. Ashmole, "Cyriac of Ancona," *Proceedings of the British Academy* 45 (1959), 25–41.

[29] Epitaphs and epigrams from ms. Riccardiana 907 containing the *Huius nympha loci* also appear in a della Fonte manuscript that contains Cyriacus of Ancona material. A list of the contents of the manuscript, formerly in the Ashmole Collection, is to be found in Saxl, "Classical Inscriptions," 44–46. The manuscript is now in Oxford, Bodl. Lat. misc. d.85. See C. Trinkaus, "The Poetics of Bartolommeo della Fonte," *Renaissance Studies* 7 (1960), 151, n. 5.

32. Roman statue of water nymph, Rome, Vatican Museum (photo: Alinari)

33. Ariadne, formerly in the Cleopatra Fountain, Rome, Vatican Museum (photo: Alinari)

by Ferrarinus, it is described as "in horto cardinalis S. Clementis." This occurs in a manuscript written in Rome ca. 1495 and is repeated in a second one of ca. 1500. The writing of the latter has been identified as that of a Vatican scribe active between 1490 and 1510.[30] The Cardinal of San Clemente in these years was the nephew of Pope Sixtus IV, Domenico della Rovere, a man noted for his interest in architecture and antiquity. Thus the epigram was known at least by 1495 to the humanist court circle for which the later fountains were built, and Campani, who died in 1477, could not claim authorship of his now fully established "ancient" inscription.

THE FIGURE TYPE AND ITS SETTING

The early sleeping nymph figures had a number of characteristics in common, although there were variations in pose and clothing. All were semi-recumbent, with their heads propped on one arm and their legs crossed at the ankle or lower leg. This pose is close to the ancient convention for the representation of sleep. Two figures, those in the Vatican and Colocci fountains (Figs. 31, 33), have an arm bent over their head, and this pose is the one most often encountered in later versions of the fountain. Yet this was not the position of the ancient water nymph figure (Fig. 32) nor that of the figure illustrated in the *Hypnerotomachia polifili* (Fig. 34). The latter, which contributed to the popularity of the fountain, derives from a well-known Dionysiac sarcophagus type, Ariadne's discovery by Bacchus on the island of Naxos.[31] It is important to note, however, that the Ariadne figure on these sarcophagi was most often represented with one arm bent over her head (Fig. 35)[32] and that a number of sarcophagi with this figure type were prominently displayed and frequently drawn during the fifteenth and sixteenth centuries.[33] Thus all the early fountain figures can be shown to derive from one ancient figure type, the Ariadne. This figure has some similarities to the ancient water nymph figure (Fig. 32) as well as to the river god figure type (Fig. 19), yet enough differences to suggest that the choice was based on reasons other than similarity.

First, it seems unlikely that the ancient figure type was known in the late fifteenth and early sixteenth centuries. The first representation of one is in a Heemskerck drawing of the mid-1530s.[34] There is no visual evidence that the figure type was used in any

[30] For the date of the first manuscript, Berlin, Hamilton 26, see Ziebarth, "De antiquissimis syllogis," 317. The second manuscript, formerly in the Wardrop Collection, present whereabouts unknown, is discussed by J. Wardrop, "Notes: Six Italian Manuscripts in the Department of Graphic Arts," *Harvard Library Bulletin* 7 (1953), 222; the epigram is illustrated, pl. 11b.

[31] See n. 48.

[32] Fig. 35 is published by F. Matz, *Die dionysischen Sarkophage, Die antiken Sarkophagreliefs*, IV, repr. Berlin, 1961, no. 214, pp. 383–85, pl. 223. Others are on pls. 224–37.

[33] One sarcophagus of this type was attached to the wall of San Giovanni in Laterano in Rome. It was drawn by Gentile da Fabriano and Pisanello. I am indebted to Hellmut Wohl for calling these drawings to my attention. For further discussion of these drawings, both in Milan, Ambrosiana Cod. F 214 inf., fols. 13r, 14v, see B. Degenhart and A. Schmitt, "Gentile da Fabriano in Rom und die Anfänge des Antikenstudiums," *Münchner Jahrbuch der Bildenden Kunst* 11 (1960), 119, 128.

[34] C. Huelsen and H. Egger, *Die römischen Skizzenbücher von Marten van Heemskerck*, I, Berlin, 1916, 28.

35. Ariadne unveiled by satyr, detail of sarcophagus, Kent, Hever Castle (photo: Deutsches Archäologisches Institut)

34. Fountain of Venus, from *Hypnerotomachia polifili*, Venice, 1499, fol. d8 (photo: Dumbarton Oaks)

fountain in the sixteenth century, nor do there appear to be sixteenth-century replicas, as is the case for other popular fountain figure types.[35] Since there were inadequate visual prototypes for a sleeping nymph, the creators of the fountain turned to literary sources.

Two myths are the most probable source for the idea of a nymph sleeping by a spring. The first tells of Amymone, a young girl who was sent for water but fell asleep while hunting for it. A satyr discovered her but was prevented from seducing her by the intervention of Neptune who drove away the satyr and created a spring by thrusting his trident into a rock. The tale ends with the seduction of Amymone by Neptune.[36] Another less well-known myth tells of Byblis, a girl who was turned into a nymph or a spring as punishment for her illicit love for her brother.[37] Both myths evoke images of sleep and seduction.

[35] For a list of known ancient sleeping nymph figures, see Praschniker, *Bäderbezirk*, 79–81 and 80, n. 52. Additions to this list were made by B. Kapossy, *Brunnenfiguren der hellenistischen und römischen Zeit*, Zurich, 1969, 18.

[36] Hyginus, *Fabulae*, 169, but see also Ovid, *Metamorphoses*, 2.240, where the name is given to a fountain.

[37] Ovid, *Metamorphoses*, 9.452, cf. Theocritus, *Idylls*, 7.114. For a list of other myths about nymphs and satyrs, see G. Pozzi and A. Ciapponi, "La cultura figurativa di Francesco Colonna e l'arte veneta," *Lettere italiane* 14 (1962), 160.

A specific pose for such a figure was suggested by a passage in Propertius describing his mistress, "like Ariadne lying on the shore from which the ship of Theseus sailed away, or like Andromeda freed from the rock, who at long last in softer slumber lay, or like a maenad dizzy with the dance, flinging herself beside the river bed."[38] Figures with this pose were given a specific descriptive name in antiquity, *anapauomenai;* the name appears in a description of a painting in Pliny's *Natural History.*[39]

Thus ancient literary tradition called for the representation of a fountain nymph as a reclining sleeping figure, and Pliny and Propertius seemed to indicate that there was a specific pose associated with the tradition. Of the numerous ancient reclining and recumbent statues known in the Renaissance only one had the requisite connotation of sensuousness and abandon suggested by the passage from Propertius and the two nymph myths—the Ariadne type.[40] Even in antiquity, the Ariadne pose, which seems to have been a Hellenistic invention,[41] was adapted for other scenes with similar connotations. Thus Bacchus is represented in this pose in the celebration of his union with Ariadne, and Rhea Sylvia is represented similarly in the sarcophagus showing her discovery by Mars (Figs. 36, 37). Drunken Silenus and the sleeping Endymion are two other examples.[42]

The rocky or grotto setting for the nymph fountains was simpler in derivation. Literary sources were quite clear. In addition to the cave of the nymphs described in the *Odyssey,*[43] Virgil's description in the *Aeneid* of the *domus nympharum* was the *locus classicus.*[44] It was well known in the Renaissance that nymphs were worshiped in caves, and indeed that the origin of the nymphaeum, that is, the architectural fountain, was to be found in natural grottoes with springs. Many of these were described by Pausanias and Pliny.[45]

---

[38] Propertius, 1.3, trans. H. E. Butler, Loeb Classical Library, London, 1924, 9.

[39] Pliny, *Natural History,* 35.99. For a discussion of the word *anapauomenai* and the relevant literary sources, see K. Dilthey, "Archeologisches Streifzüge. I. Uber zwei Gemälde des Aristides," *Rheinisches Museum für Philologie* 25 (1879), 151–58. See also T. Birt, "Die Vaticanische Ariadne und die dritte Elegie des Properz," *Rheinisches Museum für Philologie* 50 (1895), 31–65, 161–90.

[40] Sleeping hermaphrodites and Cupids slept on their back with one arm crossed over their chest, or prone. For examples, see S. Reinach, *Répertoire de la statuaire grecque et romaine,* I, Paris, 1920, 352–54, 371. Dead figures, such as Meleager, were represented on their sides with a pendant arm. See Robert, *Antike Sarkophage-Reliefs, Einzelmythen,* III, Berlin, 1904, no. 230a, pp. 297–98, pl. 78, and Matz, *Dionysischen Sarkophage,* fig. 88, 2.

[41] Birt, "Vaticanische Ariadne," 166–74.

[42] In addition to Fig. 36, see Matz, *Dionysischen Sarkophage,* no. 77, p. 187, pl. 92 (Arbury Hall), and no. 82, p. 197f, pl. 94 (Oxford). The Rhea Sylvia sarcophagus appears in Robert, *Einzelmythen,* III, no. 188, pp. 228–32, pls. 60–61. For a drunken Silenus, see Matz, idem, no. 108, p. 251, pl. 134 (Rome, Terme). For an Endymion, Robert, idem, no. 55, p. 72, pl. 15. For further lists of figures with this pose, see Birt, "Vaticanische Ariadne," 63–65. Meiss also points out that the pose was not confined to Ariadne figures ("Sleep in Venice," 351, n. 25).

[43] Homer, *Odyssey,* 13.102–12.

[44] "Fronte sub adversa scopulis pendentibus antrum, / intus aquae dulces vivoque sedilia saxo, / Nympharum domus. . . ."; Virgil, *Aeneid,* 1.166–68.

[45] For citations of texts by ancient authors referring to caves and grottoes, see G. W. Elderkin, "The Natural and the Artificial Grotto," *Hesperia* 10 (1941), 125–37; G. Roux, "Le val des muses et les musées chez les auteurs anciens," *Bulletin de correspondence héllénique* 78 (1954), 22–48.

36. Bacchus and Ariadne, detail of unidentified sarcophagus
(photo: Deutsches Archäologisches Institut)

37. Mars and Rhea Sylvia, sarcophagus, Rome, Palazzo Mattei
(photo: Deutsches Archäologisches Institut)

38. Ariadne deserted by Theseus, detail of relief, Rome, Vatican Museum
(photo: Deutsches Archäologisches Institut)

Visual precedents were also numerous. Many Bacchus and Ariadne sarcophagi showed Ariadne leaning against a pile of rocks, as did a number of coins (Fig. 38).[46] In addition, some of the ancient reliefs known in the Renaissance represented nymphs, often with satyrs and Pan, and these also had a grotto setting.[47]

To sum up, the epigram began as a poetic invention by Campani in the style of the lyric poetry of the Greek Anthology. It soon migrated, possibly by its introduction into compendia by Bartolommeo della Fonte, into the early sylloges where its authenticity was bolstered by the added description of the sculpture of the sleeping nymph and the fountain on the banks of the Danube. The pose of the figure was derived from a well-known type, the reclining Ariadne, which was given justification by the ancient texts, the myths, and the tradition of the *anapauomenai* type. The rocky background or grotto was also derived from a combination of literary and visual traditions.

[46] For examples of the scene on coins, see F. Imhof-Blumer, "Nymphen und Chariten auf griechischen Münzen," *Journal international d'archéologie numismatique* 2 (1908), pl. IX, figs. 18–19. Fig. 38 is a detail of a relief (Vatican Museum, Gallerie delle Statue, no. 416) that was discovered in the 16th century and assembled with other fragments in its present columniated frame at that time. See Amelung, *Sculpturen*, I, n. 416.

[47] Examples of reliefs depicting nymphs in caves are represented in S. Reinach, *Répertoire des reliefs grecques et romaines*, II, Paris, 1912, 27, 4; 80, 1; 142, 2.

THE SPREAD OF THE FOUNTAIN TYPE AND THE REASONS FOR ITS POPULARITY

In addition to the sources already discussed, the creator of the Belvedere Statue Court may have been influenced by the fountain described and illustrated in the *Hypnero-tomachia polifili*. The text describes a relief set between the columns of an octagonal edifice, the fountain of Venus. It depicts a partially clad sleeping nymph reclining on the ground; hot and cold water issue from her breasts to fall in a porphyry vase below. A satyr is unveiling her, while nearby are two infant satyrs holding urns and serpents.[48] The illustration (Fig. 34), which does not agree in all its particulars with the description, is derived from a Dionysiac sarcophagus (Fig. 35).[49] The *Hypnerotomachia*, with its extended description of the Garden of Venus and numerous illustrations of topiary work and garden structures, exerted a strong influence on Renaissance garden decoration. At least one visitor to the statue court saw a relationship between the Cleopatra fountain and the text of the *Hypnerotomachia*: in a letter to Lelio Gregorio Giraldi, Pico della Mirandola compared the statue court to a Garden of Venus and spoke of water appearing to trickle from the breasts of the figure of Cleopatra.[50]

For the visitors to the other two sleeping nymph fountains of the period there were different associations, and these were the decisive factor in the popularity of the fountain type. One of the fountains was in the garden of Angelo Colocci, *abbreviatore* in the court of Pope Julius II and *cameriere* and *segretario* to Popes Leo X and Clement VII. Colocci's property, purchased in 1513, was on the Pincio near the Fontana di Trevi.[51] Colocci's collection of ancient statues and inscriptions was displayed in the garden which was entered by a portal with an inscription exhorting the visitor to leave anger and fatigue behind. A part of the ruined aqueduct of the Aqua Claudia ran through the garden, and a relief with a reclining sleeping nymph was placed in one of the arches of the aqueduct (Fig. 31). The epigram appeared in Roman lettering below the relief. Numerous poems dedicated to this arrangement confirm that it was a fountain.[52]

[48] F. Colonna, *Hypnerotomachia polifili*, Venice, 1499, fol. d8. See now the annotated edition of G. Pozzi and L. Ciapponi, *Francesco Colonna, Hypnerotomachia polifili*, Padua, 1964.

[49] This was first discussed by F. Saxl, *Lectures*, I, London, 1957, 162f, and more extensively by Meiss, "Sleep in Venice," 350–51, in his discussion of the influence of the illustrations on Giorgione's Dresden *Venus*.

[50] ". . . Cleopatrae, cuius quasi de mammis destillat fons vetustorum instar aqueductuum. . . ." The letter is discussed by Gombrich, "Hypnerotomachiana."

[51] Biographical material about Angelo Colocci is to be found in F. Ubaldini, *Vita di Mons. Angelo Colocci, studi e testi*, ed. V. Fanelli, Vatican City, 1969, 256. The garden is discussed on pp. 38–60. For the date of purchase of the property, see ibid., 28. Discussion of the garden and its collection also appears in D. Gnoli, "Orti letterari nella Roma di Leo X," *Nuova Antologia*, ser. 7, 269 (1930), with a revised version in D. Gnoli, *Roma al tempo di Leo X*, ed. U. Gnoli, Rome, 1938, 136–63. For further information on the Colocci garden, see C. P. Gioia, *Gli orti colocciani in Roma*, Foligno, 1893.

[52] The inscription is cited in J. Mazzocchi, *Epigrammata antiquae urbis*, Rome, 1521, and L. Mauro, *Antichità di Roma*, Rome, 1556, 97, as being in the Colocci garden. The engraving appears first in J. J. Boissard, *Romanae urbis topographia*, IV, Rome, 1598, pl. 25. Boissard was in Rome in the 1550s. See J. Janker, "Die Porträtstiche des Robert Boissard . . . an dem J. J. Boissard'schen Sammelwerke," *Repertorium für Kunstwissenschaft* 7 (1883–84), 418. The engraving of the relief appears also in B. Montfaucon, *L'Antiquité expliquée*, I,

The second fountain of this period was in the garden of Hans Goritz, a Swiss human-ist, who was a *protonotario apostolico* in 1512 and later *maestro delle suppliche*. Corycius, as Goritz called himself after the old man from Corycius in Virgil's *Georgics*,[53] owned prop-erty near the Basilica of Maxentius and Constantine, in an area now occupied by the Via dei Fori Imperiali. There was a small building with a large salon on the ground floor, a loggia, and a grotto with a sleeping nymph fountain inscribed with the shorter version of the epigram.[54]

Both Colocci and Goritz frequently assembled groups of friends in their gardens for the study of ancient literature, for philosophical discussion, and for poetry-reading contests. The groups were called "Academies," following the tradition revived in the fif-teenth century in Florence, Naples, and Rome. Unlike the Florentine Academy, these groups did not engage in formal instruction but rather remained associations of pro-fessional humanists and scholars.[55] The tradition for the use of gardens for this kind of meeting goes back to the time of Plato. Socrates met his friends in a grove with a stream outside the city of Athens. Plato's Academy also met in a grove with a shrine dedicated to the Muses.[56] Aristotle tutored Alexander in a glade with a grotto dedicated to nymphs.[57] These traditions were also emulated in ancient Rome and were revived again in the fifteenth century in Florence, Rome, and Naples. Poggio Bracciolini wrote that he had named his villa near Careggi "Accademia" as Cicero had his in Tusculum, both recall-ing the Academy of Plato.[58]

Ancient traditions linked nymphs with Muses, and they too were associated with springs and grottoes. Thus the Muses were proprietary deities of the Hippocrene spring on Mt. Helicon and the Castalian spring at the shrine of Apollo in Delphi. Since nymphs

pt. 2, 1719, pl. 220. Boissard, *Topographia*, V, pl. 78, also illustrates a base with the shortened inscription (see p. 38) and the legend "in domo Salviatorum." The poems are published in Gioia, *Orti colocciani*, passim. A number also appear in Ubaldini's life of Colocci. See nn. 64–65 for specific references.

[53] It should be pointed out that *Corycius* can also refer to the Corycian cave on Mt. Parnassus, and hence the name can be interpreted as the Parnassian old man, a sense that goes well with Goritz's position as a patron of poetry.

[54] For Hans Goritz, see D. Gnoli, "Orti letterari," 151–53. I have been unable to find a copy of the frequently cited A. Colocci, *Angelo Colocci ed Hans Goritz*, Fabriano, 1922, which may have additional material. For the site of the Goritz garden, see U. Gnoli, "Ceramiche romane del cinquecento," *Dedalo* II (1921), 199–202. Gnoli found an inscription, "I. Coritius. Trevir MDXVII," which suggests the date of the garden and fountain. *Coryciana*, a group of poems assembled by Blosius Palladius and published in 1524, contains a number of poems dedicated to the fountain. See p. 50.

[55] For the Florentine Academy, see A. della Torre, *Storia dell'Accademia platonica di Firenze*, Florence, 1902. For the Roman "Academies," in addition to Gnoli, "Orti letterari," and Gioia, "Orti colocciani," see M. Maylender, *Storia delle accademie d'Italia*, IV, Bologna, 1930, 320–27.

[56] H. I. Marrou, *Histoire de l'éducation dans l'antiquité*, 3rd ed., Paris, 1955, 261–63. For Socrates, see Plato, *Phaedrus*, 230B. Plato's Academy is described by Pausanias 1.30.2. P. Boyancé, *Le culte des Muses chez les philosophes grecs: Études d'histoire et de psychologie religieuses* (*Bibliothèque des écoles françaises d'Athènes et de Rome*, 141), Paris, 1937, 260–67.

[57] Plutarch, *Lives*, Alexander, 7.3.

[58] Della Torre, *Accademia platonica*, 538–40. For the name of Cicero's villa at Tusculum, see Cicero, *Tusculanae disputationes*, 2.3; 3.3. Idem, *Epistolae ad Atticum*, 1.4. Pomponio Leto called his garden on the Quirinal "Accademia"; see Ubaldini, *Angelo Colocci*, 66.

were deities of springs, Muses were also considered nymphs.[59] Lelio Giraldi, a member of the Colocci circle, summed up current ideas concerning Muses in his *De musis syntagma*, written in 1509. They were first called nymphs, he says, only later Muses. They were particularly associated with poetry but also represented all the disciplines of thought. They were virtuous maidens who not only presided over the separate arts but also inculcated in writers the desire to do well, to please, and to instruct.[60] Cicero summed this up with the statement that to live with Muses was to live with education and refinement.[61]

The connection between the Muses and the fountains in the gardens of Colocci and Goritz can be seen in the poems written to these men about their fountains. Blosius Palladius edited a collection of poems, entitled *Coryciana*, in which his introduction dedicated to Goritz says in part, "Nam eo bonorum atque eruditorum virorum ea cohors coit, ac diem celebrat, ut in tuas hortis medias Athenas, emporiumque doctrinarum possis videri illo die includere et musas de Helicone et Parnasso deductas, in Tarpcium et Quirinalem tuis hortis imminentis trasferre. . . ."[62] The poet Aléandre wrote that one lived in Goritz's garden, "sepositis curis cum Musis."[63] Another series of poems preserved in a manuscript formerly in Colocci's collection celebrated his fountain and garden.[64] Many are dedicated to the virgin of the Aqua Virgine (as the Aqua Claudia was then known) but relate her to the virginal Muses in such poems as "Quam bene confugit virgo in tua tecta COLOTI / Non alio poterat tutior in esse loco. / Iam sua nomen habet Nympha: et te praeside, Virgo / Incipit Aonis vatibus esse liquor."[65] Even more specific is Battista Casali's epigram: "Redde Helicona mihi, redde, inquit Apollo sorores / Dic ubi sunt, inquam: dicam, ait, ex tripode / Musae habitant spretis Bassi pentralia Delphis / Hic aeternis fons scatet uber aquis. / Redde libens, inquam te, Phoebe tuisque tibique / Non alio poteris gratior esse loco. / Musarum sed me sacris admitte volentem / Casalioque meam prolve fonte sitim."[66] Yet another ended, ". . . Jure Hospiti Coloti / Musarum Domus hospita et bonorum."[67]

Thus to the contemporaries of Colocci and Goritz the sleeping nymph fountain was a symbol of the presence of the Muses who presided over the newly reborn academies of

---

[59] See Daremberg and Saglio, *Dictionnaire des antiquités grecques et romaines*, IV, pt. 1, 124–28, s.v. "Nymphae"; Pauly-Wissowa, *Real-Enzyclopedie*, s.v. "Musai," and W. F. Otto, *Die Musen und der göttliche Ursprung des Singen und Sagens*, 2nd ed., Düsseldorf-Cologne, 1956, 20.

[60] L. G. Giraldi, *De musis syntagma*, published in *Opera omnia*, G. Gaes and P. Colomesi, eds., Basel, 1696, 556–68.

[61] Cicero, *Tusc. disp.*, 5.23, 66.

[62] B. Palladius, ed., *Coryciana*, Rome, 1524, intro.

[63] Ibid., 34. He also referred to Colocci as "le grand nourisson des muses et d'Apollon." See J. Pacquier, *L'Humanisme et la réforme: Jerome Aléandre*, Paris, 1900, 113.

[64] Ubaldini, *Angelo Colocci*, 48–59.

[65] Vat. lat. 3388, fol. 199v, as quoted in Gioia, *Orti colocciani*, 13. A somewhat different transcription appears in Ubaldini, *Angelo Colocci*, 52.

[66] Vat. lat. 3388, fol. 199r, as quoted in Gioia, *Orti colocciani*, 12.

[67] Quoted without name of author, in A. Colocci, *Poesie italiane latine*, ed. G. Lancellotti, Jesi, 1772, 17.

learning and the reborn art of poetry.[68] As Gallo said of the grotto on the Tiber at the Farnesina, "antrum aptum poetis."[69]

This imagery pervaded the literature of the period.[70] Giulio Simone in his *Oratio de poetice et musarum triumpho* of 1517 hailed Pope Leo X as Apollo Musagetes, calling the Vatican hill a new Mt. Parnassus with a new Hippocrene spring.[71] The frescoes of the Muses added at this time to the decoration of the papal hunting villa, La Magliana, are probably a visual expression of this concept of Leo X and his role as patron of literature.[72] Sleeping nymph fountains were not the only form of the topos. Blosius Palladius' garden near the Vatican had two naturalistic rocky fountains referred to as Parnassus,[73] and the Giardino del Bufalo adjoining Colocci's garden had a Parnassus fountain and frescoes of the Muses.[74]

The identification of the nymph as a Muse does not explain why the nymph figures are always represented as asleep. Meiss suggests a relationship to the metaphor frequently encountered in Renaissance literature of the Muses, asleep since antiquity, reawakened by the new writers.[75] I am inclined to believe that the combination of traditions already discussed is sufficient explanation. First, the best-known myth, that of Amymone, involves sleep as does Ovid's description of Rhea Sylvia. In addition, Propertius' ode,

[68] Meiss, "Sleep in Venice," 358, refers to the concept of poetry reawakened after centuries of sleep. For further discussion of this metaphor, see B. L. Ullman, *Studies in the Renaissance* (*Storia e letteratura: raccolta di studi e testi,* 51), Rome, 1955, 12–23.

[69] E. Gallo, *De viridario Augustini Chigii Patrittii . . . ,* Rome, 1511, 25v. Printed in the margin beside Gallo's description of the grotto at water level of the Tiber at the Farnesina. The description concludes with, "Perpetuo hic intus resonant suavissimi Phoebi / Musarumque novem inter se discrimina vocis. / Concilium hic intus vatum: quo sancta poete / Conveniunt vario tractate Poemata versu. / Constiti: et comitem largo sermone moratur."

[70] See examples quoted by Ullman, *Studies in the Renaissance,* 18, 23.

[71] G. Simone Siculo, *Oratio de poeticae et musarum triumpho,* Rome, 1518, fol. Eii ". . . ad Leonum decimum verum μουσαγετην & verum apollinem. . . ." In the margin of the following page, "Roma Virtutum domicilium mons vaticano Parnassus tiberina fluenta Fons caballinus Athene poetica musae Apollo decimus.i.Leo decimus. . . ."

[72] The frescoes, representing Apollo and the Muses, each Muse identified by an inscription, are now in the Museo di Roma. For their date, see L. Bianchi, *La villa papale della Magliana,* Rome, 1942, 64.

[73] G. Rorario, *Quod animalia bruta ratione utantur melius homine. Libri duo,* II, Paris, 1648, 117. The letter of dedication is dated 1547. Translated in Gnoli, "Orti letterari," 160–61, ". . . il vitreo fonte dell'acqua stillante con leve susurro dalla rupe simulata per le stallattiti di Tivoli: mostravo loro l'altra fontana di fronte, levemente cadente da una simile rupe. . . ." Flaminio writes in a poem quoted by Gioia, "Orti colocciani," 10, ". . . relicta Apollo / Cirrha Pieridesque vos frequentant, / Ex quo deliciae suae suique / Amores Blosius vireta vestra / Cirrae praetulit Aonique monti." Thus by implication the villa is a new Parnassus.

[74] R. Kultzen, "Die Malereien Polidoros da Caravaggio im Giardino del Bufalo in Rom," *Mitteilungen des Kunsthistorisches Instituts in Florenz* 9 (1959–60), 99–120. He does not seem to have known the Boissard description, *Topographia,* I, 117. "Huic hortulo fons est additus, ex trophis marinis efformatus affabre in speciem rupes naturalis. . . . Disposita sunt diversis in locis conchylia preciosa . . . ," nor Aldrovandi's, "Qui è una fonte bizarra e rustica vaghissimamente composte così nel monticello scabro, onde esce l'acqua, come nel suolo istesso, che si calpesta et in ogni altra sua parte" (*Statue,* 288).

[75] Meiss, "Sleep in Venice," 358. For another interpretation of sleep as a metaphor, see H. Muruter, "Personifications of Laughter and Drunken Sleep in Titian's *Andrians,*" *Burlington Magazine* 115 (1973), 521–23.

which suggests the existence of an established pose, is a description of his sleeping mistress. Finally, the sculptured prototypes also represent a sleeping figure.

The Sack of Rome in 1527 caused the dispersal of the circle of humanists and poets responsible for the flourishing of this cult of the Muses and poetry. Also lost was the optimism and conviction in the revival of antiquity that gave the circle its vitality and self-confidence. Popes of the next generation were more interested in temporal power than in poetry and classicism. After the Sack, sleeping nymph fountains and statues became common outside the original humanist circle, but the unity of the original topos was destroyed. Thus the Cesi garden had a sleeping nymph statue with the inscription, but there was no fountain.[76] Aldrovandi's description of ancient statue collections in Rome, written in 1550, shows that the use of the statue type was widespread, although the statue was rarely a part of a fountain.[77] In addition, the use of a sleeping figure as a fountain decoration was extended to other figure types. At the d'Este villa on the Quirinal, for instance, the rustic fountain had a sleeping shepherd figure, and the Villa Giulia had two sleeping Venuses.[78] The fountain in the grotto room of the Farnese Palace at Caprarola had a sleeping Cupid.[79]

New allegories were created around the sleeping nymph theme. Cardinal Pio da Carpi's villa on the Quirinal had a grotto fountain or nymphaeum with a reclining sleeping nymph. The other statues in the grotto, however, were of satyrs, erotes with birds, and a Hercules, and an inscription at the entrance gives the key that the nymphaeum was a Garden of the Hesperides where man loses worldly cares; it was not the Castalian spring that inspires man to poetry.[80]

With the period of the Counter Reformation a more somber and conventionally religious note was introduced. The Belvedere fountain was dismantled, and the Cleopatra-Ariadne figure installed at the end of one of the Bramante corridors connecting the Vatican Palace to the villa of Innocent VIII. The room's ceiling decorations represented scenes from the Old and New Testaments, and the intention evidently was to relate the water of the fountain to the sacrament of baptism.[81] The Papacqua fountain at

[76] For a discussion of the Cesi garden, see "Giardino all'Antico" and "Ars Hortulorum." See now M. van der Meulen, "Cardinal Cesi's Antique Sculpture Garden: Notes on a Painting by Hendrick van Cleef III," *Burlington Magazine* 116 (1974), 14–24. C. Huelsen, *Römische Antikengärten des XVI. Jahrhunderts,* Akademie der Wissenschaften zu Heidelberg, Philosophisch-historische Klasse, Abhandlungen 4 (1917), 36, for the source of this information.

[77] U. Aldrovandi, *Delle statue di Roma,* published with L. Mauro, *Antichità di Roma,* Rome, 1556. See, for example, his description, "In casa di M. Domenico de Negris presso a S. Marco . . . si vede una Ninfa ignuda dalla metà in su, e giacendo dorme e tiene nella mano sinistra una urna" (pp. 259–60).

[78] The d'Este fountain is discussed in "Ars Hortulorum," 107. For the statues at the Villa Giulia, see T. Falk, "Studien zur Topographie und Geschichte der Villa Giulia in Rom," *Römisches Jahrbuch für Kunstgeschichte* 13 (1971), 173.

[79] L. Partridge, "The Sala d'Ercole in the Villa Farnese at Caprarola," *Art Bulletin* 53 (1971), 480–86, figs. 32–33.

[80] See "Ars Hortulorum," 105–8.

[81] Brummer, *Belvedere,* 254–64.

the Chigi Palace in Soriano nel Cimino adapts the reclining nymph figure to a female satyr nursing an infant, possibly a representation of the birth of Bacchus taken from Philostratos' *Imagines* (Fig. 39). The other relief there represents Moses striking the rock, suggesting another allegory on salvation through baptism.[82] The Villa Lante at Bagnaia has a grotto on one of the intermediate levels in which the reclining figure type is used with figures of wild men and snakes, an apparent image of primitive life.[83] Finally, two public fountains at the Quattro Fontane in Rome have sleeping nymph figures, but they symbolize Faith and Courage (Fig. 40). Thus the original association with the Muses and the creation of poetry disappeared by the middle of the sixteenth century, and in the second half of the century new literary themes developed around the figure type. At the same time, however, decorations related to the Muses and Parnassus continued, divorced from the association with the sleeping nymph. At the Villa Lante, the top two pavilions were called *Mansiones musarum*. A statue of Pegasus creating the Hippocrene spring is to be found on one of the upper levels of the d'Este villa in Tivoli, and a grotto with a fountain, an Apollo Musagetes, and statues of the Muses was built in the d'Este villa on the Quirinal in Rome.[84]

A hiatus occurs in the history of the sleeping nymph fountain during the seventeenth century. Neither the form nor the content seems to have appealed as a fountain type.[85] A curious revival, however, of both the fountain and the ideas originally associated with it took place in England in the eighteenth century. In 1725 Alexander Pope described the grotto in his garden at Twickenham, saying, "It wants nothing to compleat it but a good statue with an inscription, like that beautiful antique one which you know I am so fond of, 'huius nympha loci. . . .'" He goes on to give a translation, "Nymph of the Grot, these sacred springs I keep / And to the Murmur of these Waters sleep; / Ah, spare my slumbers, gently tread the cave! / And drink in Silence or in silence lave!"[86]

In the 1740s at Stourhead, possibly as a result of Pope's influence, Henry Hoare also built a grotto in which he placed a copy of the Belvedere Cleopatra-Ariadne figure and a statue of a river god. Under the Ariadne figure, which served as the source of a

[82] The fountain was built between 1561 and 1579. One of the most bizarre creations of the period, the fountain is little known. For another interpretation of the meaning of the fountain, see S. Lang, "Bomarzo and Soriano, A Study in Iconography," *Architectural Review* 121 (1953), 427–30. For the date, see P. Egidi, "Soriano del Cimino e l'archivio suo," *Archivio della Società romana di storia patria* 26 (1903), 393.

[83] The Villa Lante was started in the 1560s. The grotto, "di Diana o Venere," is on the park side of the garden. It is neither described nor illustrated in A. Cantoni, F. Ariello, et al., *La Villa Lante di Bagnaia*, Milan, 1960. The grotto, its decoration, and significance are discussed in C. Bruno, "The Villa Lante at Bagnaia," Ph.D. diss., Princeton University, 1975.

[84] For the Villa d'Este in Tivoli, see D. Coffin, *The Villa d'Este at Tivoli*, Princeton, 1960, 33, fig. 34. For the Quirinal grotto, see "Ars Hortulorum," 108, 110–11. Both statue and grotto were erected in the 1560s.

[85] The figure type continued to be found in paintings but more likely as a result of Giorgione's and Titian's influence. See Meiss, "Sleep in Venice."

[86] Letter to Edward Blount, June 1725. Quoted by E. Malins, *English Landscaping and Literature, 1660–1840*, London, 1966, 35.

39. Papacqua fountain, view of whole, Villa Chigi, Soriano nel Cimino
    (photo: Bibliotheca Hertziana)

40. Figure of Faith in fountain at the Quattro
    Fontane, Rome
    (photo: Gabinetto Fotografico Nazionale)

stream running through the grotto and out into a lake beyond, was placed Pope's translation of the epigram. Another inscription at the entrance to the grotto labeled it a *Domus nympharum*.[87] Thus the image, the epigram, and the idea were once more reunited.

Thirty years later Thomas Jefferson proposed a grotto be built lined with pebbles and with a figure placed on a couch of moss. Pope's translation of the epigram was to be the inscription.[88] Although the grotto was never constructed, Jefferson's project is a testimony to the enduring fascination of the sleeping nymph.

[87] K. Woodbridge, *Landscape and Antiquity: Aspects of English Culture at Stourhead 1718 to 1838*, Oxford, 1970, 2, 35, n. 56.

[88] "The ground above the spring being very steep, dig into the hill and form a cave or grotto. Build up the sides and arch with stiff clay. Cover this with moss. Spangle it with translucent pebbles from Hanover-town, and beautiful shells from the shore at Burwell's ferry. Pave the floor with pebbles. Let the spring enter at a corner of the grotto, pretty high up the side, and trickle down, or fall by a spout into a basin, from which it may pass off through the grotto. The figure will be better placed in this. Form a couch of moss. The English inscription will then be proper." [Here he quotes the Pope translation, see p. 53; T. Jefferson, *Pocket Account Book*, 1771.] I am indebted to George Hersey for bringing this quotation to my attention.

L'Ingegnoso Artifizio:
Sixteenth-Century Garden Fountains in Rome

Claudio Tolomei's letter of 26 July 1543 refers to his pleasure in the recently rediscovered "ingegnoso artifizio" of the making of fountains. His development of this idea provides the key for understanding much of the nature of fountains in Rome in the sixteenth century and their significance to their owners and visitors.

> The ingenious skill, newly rediscovered to make fountains, such as used to be found in Rome, where art was so blended with nature that one could not discern whether the fountains were the product of the former or the latter. Thus some appeared to be a naturalistic artifice while others seemed an artifice of nature. In these times they endeavor to make a fountain appear made by nature itself, not by accident, but with a masterful artistry.[1]

This paradox, the artificial creation of a setting that appears a product of nature, as in the Scoglio fountain at the Vatican (Fig. 41), or the use of materials of nature to create the illusion of man-made form, as in a water spout at the Villa d'Este (Fig. 42), lies behind the design of most of the dominant fountain types of the period. A similar contradiction existed in fountain iconography. Nature and its forces or the evocation of creations of the intellect, such as the topoi of pastoral poetry, constituted the most prevalent subject matter. Paradoxically, however, a natural element, such as a river, was personified and usually incorporated into fountains that were architectonic or at least restrained in their naturalism.[2] In contrast, the Papacqua fountain, which almost certainly illustrates a written, that is, man-made subject, was given the appearance of a creation of nature (Fig. 43).[3]

[1] C. Tolomei, *Delle lettere di M. Claudio Tolomei*, Venice, 1550, 41–43. See "Ars Hortulorum," 104.

[2] River gods appeared in fountains in the Belvedere Statue Court (see p. 61), in nymphaeum decorations at the Villa Giulia, in fountains at the Villa Lante della Rovere at Bagnaia, in the Casino in the upper garden at Caprarola, to name only a few examples.

[3] For the history of the Casino and its fountain, see M. Festa Milone, "Il Casino del Cardinale Madruzzo a Soriano nel Cimino," *Quaderni dell'Istituto di Storia dell'Architettura* 17–19 (1970–72), 71–94. There is some similarity between the fountain and a passage in Philostratus the Elder's *Imagines*, 1.14. "Semele," a description of the birth of Dionysus. ". . . for sprays of ivy grow luxuriantly about it and clusters of ivy berries and now grape-vines and stalks of thyrsus . . . for the Earth will take part with the Fire in the Bacchic revel and

41. *Scoglio* fountain, Vatican Gardens, engraving by G. Falda, *Le fontane di Roma*, III, 3 (photo: Dumbarton Oaks)

42. Water fan, Villa d'Este, Tivoli (photo: Naomi Miller)

43. Papacqua fountain, view of wall with reclining nymph, Villa Chigi, Soriano nel Cimino (photo: Bibliotheca Hertziana)

There is more to the history of fountains in Rome than this sophisticated, intellectual current. The various sensual pleasures of water were an important aspect, and the very availability of water was often a determining factor in the design. Water was still a luxury in the first half of the sixteenth century. Of the many aqueducts that had brought water into ancient Rome, only the Acqua Vergine was in operation at that time, while the rest of the city depended on the Tiber or on wells for its water.[4] Until its refurbishment in the sixteenth century, the water pressure of the Acqua Vergine was low;[5] neither it nor the Tiber could provide the volume or pressure of water required for the hills of Rome, but it was on the hills that the villas and gardens were constructed as an escape from the

make it possible for the revellers to take wine from springs and to draw milk from clods of earth or from a rock as from living breasts. Listen to Pan, how he seems to be hymning Dionysus on the crests of Cithaeron, as he dances an Evian fling. And Citharaeron in the form of a man laments the woes soon to occur on his slopes . . . and Magaera causes a fir to shoot up besides him and brings to light a spring of water, in token, I fancy, of the blood of Actaeon and of Pentheus," trans. A. Fairbanks, Loeb Classical Library, London, 1931, 59, 61. See also, S. Lang, "Bomarzo and Soriano, A Study in Iconography," *Architectural Review* 121 (1953), 427–30.

[4] The evidence for the history of the ancient aqueducts appears in R. Lanciani, *Le acque e gli acquedotti di Roma antica*, Rome, 1881 (repr. Rome, 1975). The ancient and modern history of the Acqua Vergine is on pp. 333–42. Other books which deal with the ancient and modern water supply of Rome include W. V. Morton, *The Fountains of Rome*, New York, 1966, and C. d'Onofrio, *Le Fontane di Roma*, 2nd ed., Rome, 1962, especially 9–136, for the Cinquecento public fountains.

[5] Lanciani, *Acquedotti di Roma*, 340.

heat and crowded conditions of the lower regions.[6] Thus there were few garden fountains early in the century, and use of water in them was very restricted. It was not until the introduction of new water sources late in the century that fountains become more numerous (both private and public), and only then does one find water used lavishly and as a major component of the design.

Availability of water influenced design. This was one of the chief differences between the fountains of Rome and those in the nearby hills. The Villa d'Este in Tivoli and the Villa Lante in Bagnaia were noted for the abundance of their water.[7] Even today water from each of these villas constitutes the major source of supply for their respective villages. Thus the cascades and water stairs found in the gardens in the hill country did not appear in Rome, although many gardens had ample room for fountains of this type.

Yet another feature is peculiar to Rome. The earliest sixteenth-century fountains used ancient statues, and for most of the century only these or modern copies were used for fountain figures.[8] Elsewhere in Italy, even in the nearby Campagna and Lazio, fountain statues were modern and usually free variations on ancient types.[9] One rarely finds an important sculptor employed to make fountain figures in Rome; indeed the few that have survived from the sixteenth century are of an extremely poor quality and made of peperino, a soft volcanic stone.[10] In Florence, in contrast, sculptors of great renown were commissioned to do garden fountains; the figures were of marble and metal.[11]

The story of the development of Roman fountains begins at the Vatican with the Belvedere. Although there were both gardens and fountains in Rome in the fifteenth century, nothing remains of them, and the little evidence that has survived suggests that the fountains were simple, non-figural, and unimportant in the overall design of the garden.[12] The tradition of large-scale figural fountains as a dominant feature of the design started at the Belvedere.

[6] For the distribution and location of villas and gardens in Rome in the 16th century, see above, "Introduction," 1–22.

[7] D. Coffin, *The Villa d'Este at Tivoli,* Princeton, 1960, 9; A. Cantoni, F. Ariello, et al., *La Villa Lante di Bagnaia,* Milan, 1960, 43.

[8] See pp. 64–65.

[9] An interesting contrast is provided by the fountains at the d'Este villa on the Quirinal in Rome (now the presidential palace, the Palazzo del Quirinale) and the Villa d'Este in Tivoli. In the former, ancient statues were used in all the fountains (see pp. 72–73), while in the latter most of the fountain figures were modern and the ancient statues there were used in the terraces and entrances to grottoes. See T. Ashley, "The Villa d'Este and the Collection of Ancient Statues which it Contained," *Archaeologia* 61 (1908), 242–50 and plan opposite 223.

[10] Examples include the river god statues at the Villa Giulia, which were originally covered with stucco (see p. 68), the fountain figures of the adjoining Villa Poniatowski, and a reclining river god on the *mostra* of a fountain at the Villa Mattei on the Celio. Other examples are at Bagnaia and Caprarola.

[11] For examples of the Florentine villa fountains, see B. Wiles, *The Fountains of Florentine Sculptors and their Followers,* Cambridge, Mass., 1933. Examples of fountains by Tribolo, Ammannati, Bandinelli, etc. are discussed and illustrated. See also, D. Heikamp, "Ammannati's Fountain for the *Sala Grande* of the Palazzo Vecchio in Florence," *Fons Sapientiae: Renaissance Garden Fountains,* Dumbarton Oaks Colloquium on the History of Landscape Architecture 5, ed. E. B. MacDougall, Washington, D.C., 1978, 115–74.

[12] A fountain was planned for the Vatican gardens during the reign of Nicholas V. See T. Magnuson, *Studies in Roman Quattrocento Architecture,* Uppsala, 1958, 136, for the text of the description. A pyramidal shaped fountain is shown in the Vatican gardens in the Gozzoli view of Rome in Sant'Agostino, San Gemignano (illustrated in Magnuson, *Quattrocento Architecture*). Fountains which presumably existed in the gardens

Ackerman believes that a major reason for the development of the plan to connect the Vatican palace with Innocent VIII's villa on the ridge to the north was to provide space for the exhibition of Julius II's collection of antiquities.[13] The Laocoon, discovered in 1506 in the ruins of the Baths of Titus, was the first to be installed there;[14] other statues included the Apollo Belvedere, the Venus Felix, and by 1512 the monumental statue of the sleeping Ariadne, believed in the sixteenth century to represent the dying Cleopatra (Fig. 24). The statue was placed in the corner niche, most likely with the rocky setting that appears in Hollanda's drawing of 1538/9. Later on a river god figure, the so-called Tigris, was set in another corner niche lined with *cipollacio*, a striated green stone (Fig. 19). Many of the features that dominated the fountains of the first half of the sixteenth century are to be found here. First, the statues are ancient, as were the sarcophagi placed below the niches as catch pools. Other parts, however, were new—the marine animals supporting the sarcophagi and the architectural settings. The minor role of water in the design is also characteristic of the period. Contemporary descriptions speak of water dripping down the rocks, and Heemskerck's drawing shows only two small streams of water in the Tigris fountain. The reference in a contemporary poem to water trickling from the Cleopatra figure's breast is probably poetic license—an echo of the nymph fountain described in the *Hypnerotomachia polifili*.[15]

Single-figure wall fountains such as these are the most prevalent type in the first quarter of the century. Few freestanding figural fountains can be documented in this period. This may be accidental. Many of the ancient statues then recognized as fountain types were best suited for installation in a niche because of their frontal and horizontal poses.[16] Water supply must also have been a determinant. A reservoir could be built

---

of palaces like the Palazzo Venezia, the Giuliano della Rovere (now Colonna) Palace at the Santi Apostoli, and the Domenico della Rovere Palace in the Borgo have not survived.

[13] J. Ackerman, *The Cortile del Belvedere,* Studi e documenti per la storia del Palazzo Apostolico Vaticano 3, Vatican City, 1954, 18.

[14] H. Brummer's *The Statue Court in the Vatican Belvedere* (Acta Universitatis Stockholmiensis. Stockholm Studies in the History of Art 20, Stockholm, 1970) has a full bibliography of the earlier literature. See his Plate I for a plan of the statue court and the location of statues in it. The dates for the discovery of the various statues and their placement in the court are to be found on pp. 44–47, 75–78, 123, 135, 139, 154–58, 186–88, 191–95, 207, 212.

[15] "... Cleopatrae, cuius quasi de mammis destillat fons. ..." Letter of G. F. Pico della Mirandola quoted by Brummer, *Belvedere*, 154. The description of the nymph fountain appears in F. Colonna, *Hypneroto-machia polifili*, Venice, 1499, fol. d8. For further discussion of the topos of the sleeping nymph fountain, see "Sleeping Nymph," 37–55. P. Bober's "The *Coryciana* and the Nymph Corycia" (*Journal of the Warburg and Courtauld Institutes* 40 [1977], 223–39) places the topos in the context of neo-Platonic thought of the late 15th and early 16th century and interprets it as an expression of "*voluptas* imbued with Christian morality, ... [and] the perfect fusion of nymph-cult and reverence for the Virgin. ..." In regard to my discussion of the origins of the fountain type, I would like to thank Ernst Kitzinger for pointing out to me the existence of a Roman statue in the Ariadne pose reclining on a base with a river landscape of water and marine animals. The statue, now in the Denman collection in San Antonio, was formerly in the Wilton House collection, a large part of which was purchased in Italy. It is therefore possible that the figure and its association with water was known in the Renaissance. See H. Hoffman, *Ten Centuries that Shaped the West*, Greek and Roman Art in Texas Collections, Houston, 1970, 36–41, illus. Frontispiece, figs. 12a–c.

[16] Documentation of ancient statues known in Rome before 1527 is limited, but the early sketchbooks give some idea of the range of variety. In chronological order these sketchbooks are:

behind a wall or niche to store the water used when the fountain was turned on. While elaborate effects could not be obtained with this system, reservoirs were especially suited to the trickling and gentle flow of water so often described in the early fountains.

In addition to the Sleeping Nymph/Cleopatra and the River God figures, a number of other ancient statues can be documented in fountains of this period. One of the most popular was the Eros with Urn (Fig. 44), but one can also find satyrs with wine sacks, Venuses with bowls (Fig. 45), and even animals such as the elephant head fountain at the Villa Madama.[17] Most of these figures were placed in simple wall niches with little or no architectural decorations, but more elaborate designs did exist. The nymphaeum attributed to Bramante at Genazzano represents the most architectonic type. This pavilion was set on a hill above a dammed stream, probably with a surrounding garden. The central rear exedra shows remains of a rectangular basin with a hole in the center rear wall for the water outlet; it may have been used for dining. The octagonal room, though, with its two meter deep pool and waterspouts on the walls at shoulder height must have been a bath.[18]

In contrast to this sophisticated architecture in a natural setting was the grotto at the Villa Madama with its cavelike fountain. Vasari describes the fountain as built in a crevice in the hill, decorated with *tartari* and colored stones from which water fell in

---

ca. 1491. Codex Escurialensis. Escorial, Cod. 28. II. 12.

ca. 1500–1503. Amico Aspertini, Wolfegg, Fürstliche Sammlungen, Wolfegg Codex.

1532–35. Amico Aspertini. London, British Museum, 1898–11–23–3.

Before 1552. Amico Aspertini. London, British Museum, 1862–7–12–394 to 435.

1532–36. Heemskerck. Berlin, Kupferstich Kabinett, Heemskerck Ms.

1538–39. Francisco d'Ollanda. Escorial, Cod. 28. II. 20.

1535–50. Basel, Cod. U4.

1550–55. Pighius. Coburg, Veste, Hz. II.

1550–53. Cambridge, Trinity College, Cod. R. 17.3.

A number of other sketchbooks are known in addition to this list. See A. Schmitt, "Römische Antikensammlungen im Spiegel eines Musterbuchs der Renaissance," *Münchner Jahrbuch der Bildenden Kunst* 21 (1970), 99–128. See also, P. Bober, *Drawings after the Antique by Amico Aspertini*, Studies of the Warburg Institute 21, London, 1957, 96–101. A discussion of statues known in Renaissance Rome is in P. G. Hübner, *Le statue di Roma*, Forschungen herausgegeben von der Bibliotheca Hertziana 2, Leipzig, 1912, but see the review of C. Huelsen in *Göttingische gelehrte Anzeigen* 176 (1914), 257–311. For more information on the sketchbooks, see A. Michaelis, "Römische Skizzenbücher nordischer Künstler," *Jahrbuch des kaiserlich Deutschen Archäologischen Instituts* 6 (1891), 123–72, 218–38; 7 (1892), 83–99.

[17] The Eros with the urn and a satyr with a wine sack are visible in Heemskerck's (Berlin, Kupferstichkabinett, vol. I, 25) drawing of the walled garden of the Cesi villa located on the southern arm of the Vatican hill above the Porta de' Cavallagieri. See C. Huelsen, *Römische Antikengärten des XVI. Jahrhunderts*, Akademie der Wissenschaften zu Heidelberg, Philosophisch-historische Klasse, Abhandlungen 4 (1917), 2, 21, 23. A Venus with a bowl and a standing Eros were present at the Chigi villa, now the Farnesina, by 1550. For the elephant head fountain at the Villa Madama, see R. Lefèvre, "La fontana dell'elefante a Villa Madama," *Capitolium* 26 (1951), 81–90. A description is in Vasari-Milanesi, VI, 556. U. Aldrovandi, *Di tutte le statue antiche, che per tutta Roma . . . si veggono. . . .*, Venice, 1558, lists six male river gods, two female river gods, two sleeping nymphs, five boys with urns, three Silenus and Bacchus figures, five marine figures or human figures with marine animals. They were not all used in fountains but their role as fountain figures was recognized.

[18] C. Frommel, "Bramantes 'Ninfeo' in Genazzano," *Römisches Jahrbuch für Kunstgeschichte* 12 (1969), 137–60.

44. Eros with urn, Villa Cesi, drawing by
    M. van Heemskerck, Berlin Sketchbook, II,
    fol. 62v
    (photo: Deutsches Archäologisches Institut)

45. Roman statue of nymph with bowl,
    Rome, Museo Vaticano
    (photo: Alinari)

46. Roman statue of Eros with goose,
    Rome, Museo Capitolino
    (photo: Alinari)

drops and jets. The top held a large lion's head that was planted round with ferns and other greens.[19] Another nymphaeum, or more properly, grotto, was built under the loggia on the banks of the Tiber at the Chigi villa, that is, the Farnesina. A description of 1511 tells us that it consisted of a small rocky room with benches. Water from the Tiber flowed into a pool and flowed out again to the river.[20]

Thus it can be shown that in this period, roughly the first quarter of the sixteenth century, a number of different types of fountains had developed, the most elaborate of which were without real prototypes from the fifteenth century. Models must have been sought, and for this period the sources were most likely to have been classical. What was known then about the ancient fountains? Three problems are involved: first, what statues were recognized as fountain figures; second, what was the physical evidence of the arrangement of ancient fountains; and third, what evidence came from literary sources?

It is apparent that a great many ancient fountain figures were known and recognized as such, even as early as the fifteenth century. Fountain figures such as the Boy with Fish by Verrocchio, now in the Palazzo Vecchio in Florence, are certainly based on late Hellenistic types such as the Eros with the Goose in the Museo Capitolino in Rome (Fig. 46).[21] A drawing attributed to the School of Mantegna suggests that another common type, the Eros with Urn, was also known in the fifteenth century.[22] Although the River God and the Ariadne/Cleopatra types appear to have been the most frequently used figures in the early sixteenth century, drawings and prints show many others had also been rediscovered.[23] These include various Bacchic fountain types, satyrs, standing

[19] "E dopo questo [the elephant fountain] fece un'altra fonte, ma selvatica, nella concavità d'un fossato circondato da un bosco, facendo cascare con bello artifizio da tartari e pietre di colature d'acqua gocciole e zampilli, che paravano veramente cosa naturale; e nel più alto di quelle caverne e di que' sassi spugnosi avendo composta una gran testa di leone, a cui facevano ghirlanda intorno fila di capelvenere ed altre erbe artificiosamente accomadate . . .", Vasari-Milanesi, VI, 556. This must be the same fountain referred to in the letter attributed to Raphael, ". . . una bella fonte & fa uno mezo circulo cavato nello monte adorno di varij nichi marini et tartari dacqua ch[e]varij partimentij secondo ch[e] piacuto allo Artifice co[n] lij sedilj atornno. . . ." Published by P. Foster, "Raphael on the Villa Madama: The Text of a Lost Letter," *Römisches Jahrbuch für Kunstgeschichte* 11 (1967–68), 311.

[20] E. Gallo, *De viridario Augustini Chigii Patrittii* . . . , Rome, 1511, fols. 25v–26r, quoted in C. Frommel, *Die Farnesina und Peruzzis Architektonisches Frühwerk*, Berlin, 1961, 42.

[21] See Wiles, *Fountains of Florentine Sculptors*, 8–9, fig. 14.

[22] Ibid., 6–7, fig. 8.

[23] In addition to statues which appear in the sketchbooks listed above (n. 16), books illustrating ancient statues show the range of ancient statues known in the 16th century. The most important of these are G. B. de Cavalieri, *Antiquarum statuarum urbis Romae* . . . , Rome, 1561, with new and enlarged editions in 1570, 1574, 1585, 1594, and J. J. Boissard, *Romanae urbis topographia*, Frankfurt, 1598, but based on his stay in Rome in the 1550s. Other books with engravings of statues include: L. Vaccarius, *Antiquarum statuarum urbis Romae icones*, Rome, 1584; J. Franzini, *Icones statuarum antiquarum urbis Romae*, Rome, 1589; F. Perrier, *Icones et segmenta nobilium signorum et statuarum quae Romae extant. . . .* , Paris, 1638; and G. Giacomo de Rossi (de Rubeis), *Insigniores statuarum. . . .* , Rome, n.d. Many of these books are simply reissues of the de Cavalieri with added plates and a new publisher. See B. Lowry, "Notes on the *Speculum Romanae Magnificentiae* and Related Publications," *Art Bulletin* 34 (1952), 46–50, and T. Ashby, "Antiquae Statuae Urbis Romae," *Papers of the British School at Rome* 9 (1920), 107–58. Another important source for the knowledge of ancient statues in Rome is Aldrovandi, *Le statue antiche*.

nymphs, and Venus figures. Genre figures such as the *putto mingens* were known very early, as were the Boy with a Goose and the Boy with a Dolphin.[24] There is evidence that restorations were made to figures or groups in order to accommodate them to new fountain use. A sack was added to the satyr figure in the Vatican, for instance, while a number of figures were bored with holes for water.[25] Usually, the latter were statues recognizable as fountain types.

There was, however, almost no direct evidence of the architectural settings of fountains in antiquity. Only two great fountain installations survived in Rome, the Trophei Marii and the Septizodium. The former was not recognized as a fountain structure until the 1550s; the latter has only recently been identified as such.[26] A third ancient fountain, the Meta Sudans (Fig. 47), visible near the Colosseum until its destruction in the 1930s, certainly accounts in part for the popularity of the rocky naturalistic fountain.[27] Other physical evidence was available in the form of reliefs, some of which were fountains.[28] It is uncertain whether any representations of actual ancient fountains were known in the

[24] Renaissance examples of the *putto mingens* are illustrated in Wiles, *Fountains of Florentine Sculptors*, figs. 11, 12. See also, G. de Terverant, "L'Origine des fontaines anthropomorphes," *Académie royale des sciences, des lettres et des beaux arts de Belgique, Classes des lettres. . . . Bulletin* 38 (1936), 122–29. Ancient examples of the boy strangling the goose type are in the Museo Capitolino, Rome (illustrated in M. Bieber, *The Sculpture of the Hellenistic Age*, rev. ed., New York, 1961, fig. 285), and the Vatican Museum (Galleria dei Candelabri IV, 60). An example of the boy with the dolphin is in the Museo Nazionale, Naples.

[25] For the addition to the satyr figure (Vatican, Galleria dei Candelabri II, 40), see G. Lippold, *Die Sculpturen des Vaticanischen Museums*, III, Berlin, 1936, pl. 2, 185. A list of ancient fountain figures arranged by type (ca. 115) is to be found in B. Kapossy, *Brunnenfiguren der hellenistischen und römischen Zeit*, Zurich, 1969, 12–53. A more thorough discussion of some of the statue types listed by Kapossy is in E. Curtius, "Die Plastik der Hellenen an Quellen und Brunnen," *Abhandlungen der Akademie der Wissenschaften zu Berlin*, Philosophisch-historische Klasse (1876), 139–72. I have not seen a copy of E. Lange, "Die Entwicklung der antiken Brunnen Plastik," Ph.D. diss., Göttingen, 1920, which appears to have a more complete discussion of ancient fountain types and their chronology. See also, N. Neuerburg, *L'architettura delle fontane e dei ninfei nell'Italia antica*, Memorie dell'Accademia di archeologia lettere e belle arti di Napoli 5, Naples, 1965, which includes a discussion of some Renaissance fountains. For examples of ancient statues adapted for fountain use, see A. Venturi, "Ricerche di antichità per Monte Giordano, Monte Cavallo e Tivoli nel secolo XVI," *Archivio storico dell'arte* 3 (1890), 198–99. Payments to the sculptor Valerio Cioli for statues at the d'Este villa on the Quirinal, published by Venturi, include "per aver rappicciato quel Bacco ch'è nella fontana della loggia . . . e di più si cucciò quello animale perchè buttasi acqua . . . e quell'altro che tiene l'otra in ispala si busò l'otra per gitar l'acqua . . ." and "per aver fatto la testa . . . et aver finite le gambe e bucatola quella zinna manca della Venere ch'è esposta nella fontana della loggia. . . ."

[26] The first description of the Trophei Marii as a fountain *mostra* is that of Boissard, *Topographia*, I, 87. The Septizodium was believed to be part of the facade of the imperial palaces on the Palatine. See E. Nash, *Bildlexikon zur Topographie des antiken Rom*, II, Tübingen, 1961, 302.

[27] Ibid., II, 61–63.

[28] Examples include the so-called Amalthea relief in the Lateran Museum, originally in the Giustiniani collection formed in the 16th century (W. Helbig, *Führer durch die öffentlichen Sammlungen Klassischer Altertumer in Rom*, 4th ed., Tübingen, 1963, no. 1012, inv. 9510), illustrated in T. Schreiber, *Die hellenistische Reliefbilder*, Leipzig, 1894, pl. 21. For other examples of reliefs used in fountains, see T. Schreiber, *Die Wiener Brunnenreliefs aus Palazzo Grimani . . .*, Leipzig, 1888, and H. von Rohden and H. Winnefeld, *Architektonisches Römische Tonreliefs der Kaiserzeit*, Berlin, 1911. It is difficult to determine how many of these reliefs were known in the Renaissance. The only Roman 16th-century garden fountain known to me with relief sculpture was in a garden near the Basilica of Maxentius, first owned by Eurialo Silvestri, later by Don Alessandro Medici,

47. Meta Sudans, Rome, engraving from G. Lauro, *Antiquae urbis splendor . . .*, Rome, 1612–28, pl. 138 (photo: Dumbarton Oaks)

Renaissance, but some forms of arrangements and installations seem to be related to antiquities known by then.[29]

There is no evidence that any ancient paintings were known in the Renaissance that depicted fountains or grottoes. Some of the Pompeian frescoes, however, show arrangements that were remarkably close to compositions made in the Renaissance—an example is the House of Romulus and Remus, where the combination of nymphs, satyrs, fountains, and trelliswork seems to anticipate the rustic fountains of the mid-sixteenth century. It is also interesting to see what fountain figure types were not used. Some of the obvious marine deities, Neptune, or figures, such as tritons, or dolphins do not appear in fountains until later in the century.

---

which finally became the Pio Istituto Rivaldi. The polychrome majolica decorations by Luca della Robbia are now in the Museo di Roma. For the garden, see G. Incisa della Rochetta, "Il palazzo ed il giardino del Pio Istituto Rivaldi," *Capitolium* 9 (1933), 213–34, and R. Lanciani, *Storia degli scavi di Roma e notizie intorno le collezioni romane di Antichità*, II, Rome, 1902, 213–18.

[29] Some reliefs, such as the Trajanic fragment in the Vatican (Gallerie delle Statue 401a; Helbig, *Führer*, 140), appear to represent nymphaea or fountains, but seem to have had no influence on Renaissance fountains. On the other hand, the arrangement of statues in architectural settings, as they appeared in sarcophagi and other reliefs, must have influenced the design of the larger mid-century architectural fountains. See pp. 73–75 and Figs. 29, 55.

The only other source of knowledge was literary, but textual sources were not as helpful for fountains as for other forms of art. Descriptions of villas such as those by Pliny the Younger, mentioned fountains, but with considerably less detail than is found in his garden descriptions.[30] Vitruvius was silent about fountains, and the agricultural treatises, which occasionally mentioned pleasure gardens, also ignored them.

What remains were descriptions by Pausanias, Pliny the Elder, and other geographers and natural historians. In these, specific references to fountains and springs in various sanctuaries—the fountain at the sanctuary of Delphi, or the sanctuary of the Muses on Mt. Helicon, for instance—provided generalized ideas but little specific detail.[31] Technical books, such as Philo's *Pneumatica* and Heron's *Automata*, undoubtedly provided a source for the fascinating and elaborate mechanical devices that appear in the late sixteenth century—the water organs, singing birds, and other fantasies.[32] Certain other sources, such as Martial's epigrams, made known the location and some general details of the appearance of fountains, such as the Egeria, Appiades, or the Camena in Rome.[33]

A third literary source was poetic. The odes, eclogues, and epigrams of Greek and Roman writers contain many references to water, natural springs, and grottoes. The pastoral and bucolic mood created by the poets formed an important background for Roman Renaissance fountain design. Specific knowledge of ancient fountains was less important than the subject matter and mood created in the works of Ovid, Horace, and the Greek pastoral poets. The dominant image projected was naturalistic with rocky caves, tumbling streams, woodland lakes; the mood was elegiac or nostalgic.[34]

[30] The following fountains at Tusci, the Tuscan villa, are described by Pliny. "In the centre [of the courtyard] a fountain plays in a marble basin, watering the plane trees round it. . . ."; ". . . a small fountain with a bowl surrounded by tiny jets which together make a murmuring sound."; ". . . just below the windows in front is an ornamental pool . . . with its water falling from a height and foaming white when it strikes the marble."; "Water gushes out through pipes from under the seat [in the hippodrome] . . . is caught in a stone cistern and then held in a finely worked marble basin which is regulated by a hidden device so as to remain full without overflowing. A fountain opposite plays and catches its water, throwing it high in the air so that it falls back into the basin. . . ." *Letters*, vol. 6, trans. B. Radice, Loeb Classical Library, Cambridge, Mass., 1969, 334, 345, 351.

[31] J. R. Smith, *Springs and Wells in Greek and Roman Literature*, New York, 1922, gives citations for descriptions in ancient literature under the name of the individual springs.

[32] Water organs were built at the Villa d'Este at Tivoli, where there also was a fountain with singing birds, at the Quirinal for Clement VIII in the 1580s, and at Pratolino near Florence where there were a number of other automata. For the *Pneumatica* and Heron's *Automata*, see G. Brett, "The Automata in the Byzantine Throne of Solomon," *Speculum* 29 (1954), 477–87, with earlier bibliography.

[33] Fountains and grottoes of ancient Rome, known to have existed in the Renaissance, include the Egeria, Juturna, Camena, and Lupercal. Except for Martial's vague reference to statues of nymphs in the Ganymede fountain (*Epigrams*, 7.50) and the visible remains of the Egeria fountain (see N. Miller, "Domain of Illusion," 183, n. 22), little was known of the physical appearance of the fountains. See Lanciani, *Topografia*, 220–36, and F. Castagnoli, *Topografia e urbanistica di Roma antica*, Bologna, 1969, 103–5.

[34] For a chronological survey of gardens in ancient Roman literature, see P. Grimal, *Les jardins romains*, 2nd ed., Paris, 1969, 353–424. H.-D. Reeker, *Die Landschaft in der Aeneis*, Spadanata: Studien zur klassischen Philologie und ihren Grenzgebieten 27, Hildesheim and New York, 1971, discusses the more rustic topoi in Latin poetry. See also, K. D. White, *Country Life in Classical Times*, London, 1977, esp. chaps. 3, 9.

A group of fountains belonging to humanists of the court of Pope Leo X are reflections of this poetic mode. Angelo Colocci and Hans Goritz had small gardens in the city, one near the present Via del Tritone, the other near the Forum of Trajan. A third garden, that of Blosius Palladius, was outside the city near St. Peter's. Colocci's and Goritz's gardens had sleeping nymph fountains, a type derived from the Ariadne/Cleopatra fountain in the Belvedere.[35] Palladius appears to have had a more elaborate garden than the others. It was built on a terraced hillside with fountains and pools on each level. At the entrance, a fountain was surrounded by marble benches shaded by laurel trees; beyond, a slope was planted with lemon trees, and at the top of the slope was a terrace where Palladius gave dinners. It had an artificial cliff on each side with stalactites—water ran down them into two pools and overflowed onto the slope. A third fountain or pool in the center of the terrace was shaded by a pergola with grapevines.[36] All three of the gardens were used for discussions, poetry reading, Greek lessons, and other humanist activities.[37] Each evoked a presiding Muse the sleeping nymph—or created a Mt. Helicon, the deity and site linked to poetry in ancient literature.

The types of fountains developed in the first quarter of the sixteenth century continued to be repeated, with ever-increasing elaboration, for most of the rest of the century. In the 1520s the Cesi garden on the hill above the Porta Cavaleggeri had two fountains—a Boy with Urn and a Satyr with a Wine Sack (Fig. 18).[38] In the 1550s the Villa Giulia not only had four boys with urns, but the nymphaeum also included river gods, a reclining nymph and herms (Figs. 48–50).[39] The Vatican Ariadne and the Colocci and Goritz sleeping nymph fountains were individual fountains in simple settings. In the 1540s the Pio da Carpi villa had a nymphaeum which, in addition to a sleeping nymph

---

[35] See "Sleeping Nymph," 48–49.

[36] A description of the garden appears in G. Rorario, *Quod animalia bruta ratione utantur melius homine. Libri duo*, II, Paris, 1648 (letter of dedication dated 1544), 117–19. It is translated by D. Gnoli, "Orti letterari nella Roma di Leo X," *Nuova Antologia*, ser. 7, 269 (1930), 160–61. A similar fountain decorated with shells and with a rocky base for a waterfall was in the Giardino del Bufalo. It is described by Boissard: "Huic hortulo fons est additus, ex trophis marinis efformatus affabre in speciem rupes naturalis, ... Disposita sunt diversis in locis conchylia preciosa, quae margaritarum referunt splendorum, et ingentes cochleae. Indicae ludicissimae, colore Iridis et unionum. Totaque hec rupes artificiosa venustissime tegitur lauris, cedris, tarariscis, & aliis arboribus, quae praebent umbram fonti subiecto; sub quibus simulachra sunt tria Musarum elegantissima: . . . ex rupe fontis eiaculatur aquae limpidissimae, per tubos et canales creneos mirando artificio. Litostratum ex marmoribus compactum est exquisitissimos, opere tessellato, ex chalcedonico, Porphyro, Alabastro, Thasio, Pario, Ophite, Marmoridum, & Aethiopum lapidus: Opus summa admiratione dignum." Boissard, *Topographia*, I, 117. For a history of the Bufalo garden, see R. Kultzen, "Die Malereien Polidoros da Caravaggio im Giardino del Bufalo in Rom," *Mitteilungen des Kunsthistorisches Instituts in Florenz* 9 (1959–60), 99–120.

[37] Gnoli, "Orti letterari," passim.

[38] Aldrovandi's description of the boy with urn fountain (*Le statue antiche*, 124) corresponds to its appearance in the Heemskerck drawing dated 1532/34. By 1550 when Aldrovandi's description was written, the satyr had been moved from its position by the wall of the garden and stood in one of the planting beds in the center of the garden.

[39] The boys with urns appear in an elevation of the lower level of the nymphaeum (London, Royal Institute of British Architects, Chatsworth Devonshire Collection, 8/6v) and are also visible in the Hieronymus Cock engraving of the nymphaeum illustrated in T. Falk, "Studien zur Topographie und Geschichte der Villa Giulia in Rom," *Römisches Jahrbuch für Kunstgeschichte* 13 (1971), fig. 19.

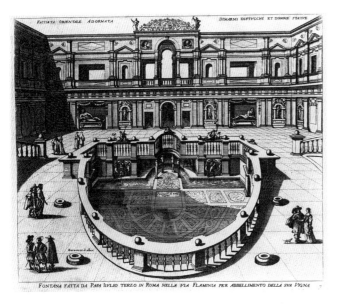

48. Nymphaeum of the Villa Giulia, Rome, engraving
after Hieronymus Cock, in Falda, *Le fontane*, III, 6
(photo: Dumbarton Oaks)

50. Lower level of nymphaeum, Villa Giulia, Rome, detail
of drawing, ca. 1555, London, Royal Institute of British
Architects, Burlington-Devonshire Collection, 8/6v
(photo: Royal Institute of British Architects)

49. Upper level of nymphaeum, Villa Giulia, Rome, drawing, ca. 1555, London,
Royal Institute of British Architects, Burlington-Devonshire Collection, 8/6r
(photo: Royal Institute of British Architects)

in a rocky setting, had a pool with figures of Erotes with birds, standing statues along the sides of the structure, including a Hercules, a nymph, a satyr, and a relief on the entrance facade with an inscription which set the mood for the interior.[40] A drawing by Giacomo della Porta has been identified as the design for the fountain group at the end wall of the nymphaeum. While the group in della Porta's drawing does not correspond exactly to the description and the engraving of the nymph statue printed in de' Rossi, the design nevertheless is characteristic of the elaborate fountains of the period.[41]

[40] See "Ars Hortulorum," 105–6, Figs. 71–73. Sometime during this period, probably during the reign of Pius IV, a fountain was built and decorated with statues at the Belvedere. The record of the statues, which were sold or given away by Pius V a few years later, was published by Michaelis, "Statuenhof," 60–62. He believed that the niche referred to was the Nicchione. The location of the statues within the list, however, makes it more likely that it was the one at the north end of the intermediate terrace which is now the small cortile behind the Vatican Library. Drawings by Ammannati, 1532–33 (Cambridge, Mass., Fogg Art Museum, 1934, 214r) and Dosio, 1558–61 (Florence, Uffizi, Dis. arch. 2559) show a high niche framed by paired pilasters, with smaller niches in the wall of the niche proper. See Ackerman, *Belvedere*, figs. 25–26. He publishes no documents of work there in this period but points out the importance of statues to the decorative program of Pirro Ligorio, then architect of the Belvedere (ibid., 95–96). This niche was later decorated with *imprese* and characteristic late 16th century decorations. See D. Parasacchi, *Raccolta delle principale Fontane dell'inclitta citta di Roma*, Rome, 1647, fig. 35. The inventory of the statues in and near the fountain is as follows:

> Nel nicchio grande a piè di detta piazza, che fa fonte
> Puttini quattro con Urne in spalle: Ultimo febraro Facchini 8
> Appolo, alto p. 6
> Tre Ninfe
> Mirtoessa
>
> Giunone
> Angerono
> Un Fauno, alto p. 6
> Mercurio colla borsa in mano
>
> In faccia del detto Nicchio
> Nettuno, alto p. 8
> Un Fiume a giacere, e sopra un[a] Testolina
> Apollo Tenedo: Ultimo Febraro Facchini 8
> Un altro Fiume a giacere, e sopra una Testolina: Ultimo Febraro Facchini 4.

Michaelis, "Statuenhof," 61–62. Another fountain group of the period, also published by Michaelis (ibid., 63), included:

> dos Iunones chiquittas con sus pavones al lado que echan aqua.
> Dos Satiros que ni mas ni menos achan aqua chiquittos el uno es antiqua y son entrambos gratiosos et hara en bueno vista en la fontana donde havieren de servir.
> Una Venus echada midiana que tan bien echa aqua.
> Dos ninos con un cornucopia cadauno en la mano por los quales echan aqua.
> Dos serenas [Sirens] con dos cabezas de leones por los lados, las quales echan tan bien agua.
> Quatro mascarsa chiquittas razonables con algunos pedacos de piedra para adornar la fontana.

An unusual decorative device in a fountain in the Palazzo Bocabelli was described by Boissard, *Topographia*, I, 45: "Domus Bocabellorum. In ascensu Capitolij habitant Bocabelli: in quorum aedibus . . . fons ostenditur venustissime constructus artificio, ex tophis & conchylis marinis: unde limpidissimae caturiunt aquae; in iis supernatant pisces artificiales subnixi filis aeneis subtitissimis, quae ad aquarum motum crispantur, & videntur leniter pisces moveri." Ibid., 45.
[41] See W. Gramberg, *Die Düsseldorfer Skizzenbucher des Guglielmo della Porta*, Berlin, 1964, 39–40.

Two changes occurred—fountains became multifigured compositions in elaborate architectural or imitation naturalistic settings, that is, nymphaea and grottoes. Single-figure fountains became rare, but small basins and pools were regularly used to adorn the garden beds. The change in content is similar. The earlier fountains had served as backdrops for the activity taking place in the garden—and the activity seems to have been primarily sedentary and reflective. The fountains set the mood and pleased the senses. They provided an excuse for the writing of poetry and were in fact often the subject of the poem.[42] In the period after 1530 the fountain becomes a narrative—it has a story to tell, often one with a complicated allegorical program. One must move into it or even move from one fountain to another in order to unravel the significance of the tale—Vasari refers to *poesie* in his description of a series of garden decorations.[43]

An early example of this new kind of fountain design was described by the humanist Annibale Caro in 1538.[44] It was a grotto with several rooms. The entrance wall was made of *asprone,* a kind of black spongy tufa, laid in irregular courses with holes left for plants. Caro says it was made to represent a "pezzo d'anticaglia rósa e scantonata." Inside the grotto, the walls and ceilings were made to appear like natural rock. In the room entered first, two fountains were built in corner niches of rough stones. A statue of a river god and a *pelaghetto* (it appears to be a basin with irregular, eroded edges) were placed above ancient sarcophagi in the niches like, Caro says, the river god at the Belvedere. Water for these fountains was stored in a reservoir behind the wall. The tops of the niches were pierced with small holes, surrounded by *tartari,* and water fell like rain through the holes into the sarcophagi; water also ran down the back of the niche and along the base of the statue, dropping through small holes to the sarcophagus and a lower pool. In the other niche water was forced into the bottom of the basin so that jets rose on the surface of the water, and the water overflowed into the sarcophagus. Caro emphasizes the sounds of the water and describes the pair of vessels suspended above the ceiling that reverberated when water ran through them.

The growing elaborateness of the fountains coincided with a period when many villas were built. To name the most outstanding, the Pio da Carpi (now the Barberini Palace) was started in the 1540s, the Villa Giulia in the 1550s, the d'Este on the Quirinal, the Ricci (later Medici) on the Pincio, and the Casino Pio IV at the Vatican in the 1560s.[45]

---

[42] Examples are to be found in the collection of poems dedicated to Hans Goritz, B. Palladius, ed., *Coryciana,* Rome, 1524.

[43] ". . . l'arcivescovo di Cipri . . . avendo egli una casa . . . nella quale aveva acconcio un giardinetto con alcune statue ed altre anticaglie . . . fece chiamare Perino . . . ed insieme consultarono che e' dovesse fare intorno alle mura di que; giardino molte storie di baccanti, di satiri, e di fauni, e di cose selvagge, alludendo ad una statua d'un Bacco che egli ci aveva, antico, che sedeva vicino a una tigre: e così adornò quel luogo di diverse poesie." G. Vasari, *Le vite de' più eccelenti pittori. . . .*, ed. Milanesi, V, Florence, 1878, 597–98.

[44] Letter by A. Caro to G. Guidiccione dated 13 July 1538, in *Lettere familiari,* ed. A. Greco, I, Florence, 1956, 105–9. See App. I.

[45] For the dates of the Pio da Carpi villa and the Villa d'Este, see Huelsen, *Antikengärten,* 43–44. The dates of the Ricci villa (now Medici) are discussed by G. Andres, *The Villa Medici in Rome,* I, New York, 1976, 118, 140. See Falk, "Villa Giulia," for the dates of its construction. G. Smith, *The Casino of Pio IV,* Princeton, 1977, 8–15, gives dates of the Casino.

51. Casino of Pio IV, Vatican Gardens, engraving from G. Vasi, *Delle Magnificenze di Roma*, Rome, 1747–61, X, 182 (photo: Library of Congress)

A similar burst of villa building occurred in the country—with the Villa d'Este at Tivoli, the Gambara (now Lante) at Bagnaia, and the Farnese at Caprarola.[46] Few of the fountain complexes have survived; none are in their original state. Perhaps the most complete is the fountain at the Casino Pio IV. It was conceived as a nymphaeum, with casino and court. Elaborate stuccoes cover the facades of the casino and the loggia (Fig. 51), and statues, now removed, decorated the court and the fountain side of the loggia.[47] Although this is the most elaborate of all the designs of the period, the cast of characters is familiar—satyrs and Pan, Apollo and Muses, Muses on Mt. Helicon, and the Hippocrene spring. Similarly, statues of Apollo and the Muses were features of the decoration of the nymphaeum at the d'Este villa on the Quirinal.[48] The rustic fountain there was embel-

[46] For the dates of the three villas listed, see Coffin, *Villa d'Este*, 14, n. 2, and idem, "Some Aspects of the Villa Lante at Bagnaia," *Arte in Europa: Scritti di storia dell'arte in onore di Edoardo Arslan*, I, n.p., 1966, 569–75.

[47] Smith, *Casino*, 15–17.

[48] The inventory of 16 July 1568 (published by Huelsen, *Antikengärten*, 113–17, and in Fiorelli, *Documenti*, II, 157–62) lists the following: "Nella fontana da basso: Nel mezzo di essa fonte è un Apollo qual'è come il naturale con l'arpa sotto il braccio destro; nella sinistra mano tiene l'accetta con queste lettere sopra *Secur. Tenedia*. Nelli nicchi che sono attorno essa fontana vi sono: Otto statue di Muse della medesima gran-

lished with a Venus and Eros, a sleeping shepherd or Silenus, two small satyrs with vases on their heads in the side niches, and a putto with a goose in the lower basin (Figs. 26, 27).[49] The loggia fountain had statues of Aesculapius and Diana in the side niches with two Bacchus figures above. These had been adapted for fountain use; one had the sack on his shoulder pierced, the other's animal was given a hole from which water poured. In the center niche a Venus figure was flanked by nymphs; a reclining river god was below her.[50]

Unlike the earlier fountains, the inspiration for which appears to have been almost entirely literary, the compositions of this period seem to derive from antiquity or from what was conceived to have been ancient designs. It is difficult to reconstruct the appearance of most of these fountains. None in Rome have survived in their original form, and even the best preserved, the fountain at the Casino of Pio IV, has had significant alterations.[51] Basically, however, there were three main types: the simple *tazza* (Fig. 52) usually without sculptural decoration, such as were used in the planting beds at the d'Este villa on the Quirinal; wall fountains, the next most common; and nymphaea or grottoes, the most elaborate type. Wall fountains, which could be as ornate as the multifigured ones at the Villa d'Este, or the later example at Caprarola (Fig. 53), appear to have followed the tradition established at the Belvedere.[52] Figures were set in niches with either a rustic

---

dezza dell'Apollo, . . ." This nymphaeum was rebuilt and a water organ placed in its rear exedra at the end of the century. See L. Salerno, "La fontana dell'organo nei giardini del Quirinale," *Capitolium* 36 (1961), fasc. 4, 3–9.

[49] The inventory lists, "Una Carita nuda che sta a sedere, ha un panno sopra le cosse, et nella sinistra mano un grappo d'uva, et li sono dalle bande dui puttini che li fanno vezzi. Sopra di questa statua nel monte si vede un pastore che sta a giacere con un otre sotto 'l braccio manco per gettar aqua. Dalle bande sono due caverne dove sono due satiretti piccoli in piedi con un vaso per ciascuno in capo. Nel laghetto che fa essa fontana è un Ganimede piccolino in piedi che scherza con cigno et lo lega con una benda." The Maggi view of the Quirinal of the first decade of the 17th century (see L. Dami, "Il giardino Quirinale ai primi del' 1600," *Bolletino d'arte* 13 [1919], 113–16 and plate) shows a trellised structure with indications of greens trained over the trellis. Some of the figures, especially the seated "Carità"—a Venus figure—can be identified in Cavalieri, while the rocky structure on which the shepherd reclined is represented in G. Maggi, *Fontane diverse che si vedano nel alma città di Roma*, Rome, 1618 (Figs. 26–27).

[50] The inventory lists: "nel nicchio del mezzo Tre statue, nel mezzo una Venere Tutta nuda, et dalle bande Due Ninfe con li panni nel mezzo in giù quanto il naturale. Sotto la Venere è Una statua vestita che sta giacere fatta per un Fiume o vogliam dire fonte, ha la testa di stucco. Fuori del nicchio di mezzo sono quattro altri nicchi piccoli; nelli dui primi a man diritta è un Esculapio col bastone et serpe, nell'altro una Diana con l'arco in mano mezzo del naturale; nelli dui più alti sono Due Bacchetti nudi con uve in mano et attorno il capo, assai più alti sono Due Bacchetti nudi con uve in mano et attorno il copo, assai più piccole delle altre." For the figures adapted for fountain use, see n. 25.

[51] Smith, *Casino*, 17–18. The articulation and the surface decoration of the fountain on the downhill side of the loggia at the Casino have been drastically altered, and statues there and in other parts of the Casino have been removed. Several series of fountain views were issued in the 17th century that include important 16th-century fountains. The earliest of these series is Maggi, *Fontane*. It was reissued with added plates in 1645 and 1651. Parasacchi, *Raccolta*, also uses some of the Maggi plates. G. Giacomo de Rossi, *Le fontane di Roma nelle piazze e luoghi publici. III. Le fonte ne' palazzi e ne' giardini di Roma . . . disegnate et intagliate da Gio. Francesco Venturini*, Rome, 1691, has the most accurate views of the highest artistic quality.

[52] See p. 61 for the Belvedere fountains.

52. *Tazza* fountain, detail of bird's-eye view of the
d'Este villa on the Quirinal, Rome, from Falda,
Li giardini, pl. 5 (photo: Dumbarton Oaks)

53. Fountain in the Castello Farnese,
Caprarola
(photo: Anderson)

54. Fountain formerly in the Villa Montalto, now in
Via Luciano Manara, Rome (photo: Alinari)

rocky setting (a *Scoglio*), with architectural articulation, or with a combination of both. A frame with heavy architectural membering was placed outside the niche. The fountain now at the foot of the Gianicolo (Fig. 54), but formerly in the Villa Montalto, is an example of the type. It held, according to the inventory of 1655, a statue of a *"priggione,"* and an elevation of it from the late nineteenth century shows a rocky pile with water flowing from its top to the basin below.[53] Many-figured wall fountains appear to have simply multiplied and repeated the essential unit. Both single- and multi-figured fountain designs derived from Roman sarcophagi and reliefs. One such, a relief in the Vatican Museum (Fig. 29), reassembled in the sixteenth century, certainly reflects the type of composition then favored in fountain design.[54] Other ancient reliefs show the probable source of the architectural and stucco decorations commonly found in the wall fountains (Fig. 55).[55]

The grottoes and nymphaea, that is, cavelike or freestanding architectural enclosures, are even less well known. It seems safe to say that the rustic, artificial caves were not common; the grotto described by Caro and the rustic fountain at the d'Este villa on the Quirinal are the only two documented.[56] For the others, such as the d'Este Apollo and Muses grotto, or the Pio da Carpi Sleeping Nymph nymphaeum, one must assume that the walls were articulated by the same flat architectural forms and decorated with the same overall stucco, mosaic, or shell incrustations that survive at the Casino of Pio IV at the Vatican and can be seen in the sixteenth-century drawings of the Villa Giulia.[57]

The sarcophagi also appear to have suggested a sculptural style for those figures made for the fountains. Many of the Dionysiac sarcophagi known in this period were second century or later.[58] The crude carving, deeply incised surfaces, and nonhuman

[53] The inventory date of 3 May 1655 is in ASR, Fondo Giustiniani. Armadio Unico Peretti, vol. 20. For the history of the Villa Montalto, see V. Massimo, *Notizie istoriche della Villa Massimo,* Rome, 1836. The Fonte del Prigione appears on pl. v.

[54] Vatican, Gallerie delle Statue, 416; Helbig, *Führer,* 147.

[55] The relief illustrated, from the Tomb of the Haterii, was not discovered until the 19th century.

[56] See pp. 72–73.

[57] London, Royal Institute of British Architects, Burlington-Chatsworth Collection, 8/6r. The incrustation is still visible in the large drawings of the villa, now in the Director's office there. See fig. 15 of F. Land Moore, "A Contribution to the Study of the Villa Giulia," *Römisches Jahrbuch für Kunstgeschichte* 12 (1969), 171–94. There are three large sheets in all, a ground plan, an elevation of the casino facade, and a sheet with one longitudinal section, three transverse sections and various details. First published by A. Della Seta, *Il museo di Villa Giulia,* Rome, 1918, they are also reproduced by M. Bafile, *Villa Giulia, l'architettura e il giardino,* Istituto d'archaeologia et storia dell'arte. Opere d'arte 14, Rome, 1948, pls. I, VI–VII. I believe they can be identified with the drawings prepared by Oppenordt, a French pensioner of the Academy in Rome in the 1690s, and described in a memoire by La Teulière, director of the Academy, in 1697. "Le Ser Oppenordt a fait plusieur dessins des plux batiments qui soient à Rome et au tour de Rome meme: Il a achevé le dessein . . . du petit palais de la Vigna de Jules 3. De tous ces Batiments il a tiré le plan, l'élévation et la coupe et presque tous d'une grandeur qui n'est pas ordinaire. . . ." The whole memoire is quoted in H. La Pauze, *Histoire de l'Académie de France à Rome,* I, Paris, 1924, 115. For a new analysis of the nymphaeum, see C. Davis, "Villa Giulia e la 'Fontana della Vergine,'" *Psicon* 3 (1977), 133–41.

[58] F. Matz, *Die dionysischen Sarkophage,* I, Berlin, 1968, figs. 9, 39, 45, 51.

55. Detail of relief from Tomb of Haterii,
Vatican, Lateran Museum (photo: Deutsches
Archäologisches Institut)

56. Satyr Head, detail of Papacqua fountain,
Villa Chigi, Soriano nel Cimino
(photo: Bibliotheca Hertziana)

57. Faun Head, detail of late third-century
sarcophagus, Rome, Museo Nazionale
delle Terme, inv. no. 124711
(photo: Deutsches Archäologisches
Institut)

appearance of figures on these sarcophagi were perhaps interpreted as evidence of a satyrical style, a *stile rustica* appropriate for the representation of the woodland and pastoral figures in the fountains. This must be true of the head from the Papacqua fountain (Figs. 56, 57; see also Fig. 39). Possibly also this type of carving was adapted to give the impression of antiquity when an ancient statue was not available.

Most of these fountains had complicated allegorical programs, some of which defy interpretation. However, in general, the themes are built around two ideas. One is the stimulation of intellectual activity through the influence of Apollo and the Muses with the accompanying suggestion of the return to an Arcadian or Golden Age. The other develops around the concept of water as benefactor, fructifier, life-giver—this accounts for the Aesculapius statues, the Venus, and the Bacchic figures. Usually these are thinly disguised metaphors for the generosity and virtues of the patron. Graham Smith has recently described the program of decorations of the Casino Pio IV as one that reflects the humanistic and intellectual aspirations of the pope.[59] The d'Este grotto with its statues of the Muses and Apollo—a true cave of the nymphs[60]—must refer to the cardinal's patronage of the arts, just as the decorations of the Tivoli villa have been shown to celebrate his virtues and his family lineage.[61]

Indeed, the themes of fountains in Tivoli, Caprarola, and Bagnaia are much the same, but the forms they take are very different. The country villas had the space and the volume of water to exploit for the manipulation of space and of vision and metaphor as well. The Villa Lante fountains are an extended demonstration of the contrast between art and nature.[62] The fountains in the park are of animals—they are small and almost disappear in the setting, while in the garden fountains dominate the scene.[63] Emphasis is on architecture and man's control of nature. One enters the park by the Pegasus fountain and ascends through the natural surroundings. At the top one emerges by the *Mansiones musarum,* and descends through an increasingly manipulated and constructed landscape. Every experience in the garden is related to the theme. At the Villa d'Este, just one of the transverse axes starts with the Pegasus fountain, continues with the Oval Fountain with its personifications of the Tibertine Sibyl and the two local rivers, Erculaneo

[59] G. Smith, "The Stucco Decorations of the Casino of Pio IV," *Zeitschrift für Kunstgeschichte* 36 (1974), 116–56.

[60] For the topos, see N. Miller, "Domain of Illusion," *Fons Sapientiae: Renaissance Garden Fountains,* Dumbarton Oaks Colloquium on the History of Landscape Architecture 5, ed. E. B. MacDougall, Washington, D.C., 1978, 117, and "Sleeping Nymph," 45.

[61] Coffin, *Villa d'Este,* chap. 5.

[62] This interpretation is derived from C. Lazzaro, "The Villa Lante at Bagnaia," Ph.D. diss., Princeton University, 1975. See also, C. Lazzaro-Bruno, "The Villa Lante at Bagnaia: An Allegory of Art and Nature," *Art Bulletin* 59 (1977), 553–60.

[63] Some of the surviving animal fountains of the park are illustrated in A. Cantoni, F. Ariello, et al., *La Villa Lante di Bagnaia,* Milan, 1960, figs. 64–67. Others are known from the drawings of Giovanni Guerra, in the Albertina, Vienna, published by J. Hess, "Entwürfe von Giovanni Guerra für Villa Lante in Bagnaia (1598)," *Römisches Jahrbuch für Kunstgeschichte* 12 (1969), 194–202, and W. Vitzthun, "Ammannatis Boboli-Brunnen in einer Kopie G. Guerras," *Albertina-Studien* 1 (1963), 75–79.

and Anio, and passes by way of the avenue of the one hundred fountains with their scenes from Ovid to culminate in the Rometta (Fig. 58).[64]

Despite the role of water in the rituals or beliefs of the Church, Christian imagery almost never appears. Only a few examples are known to me, and almost all use the story of Moses striking the rock in the desert to obtain water for the Jews.[65] This was interpreted as a precursor of the rite of baptism, with its implications of salvation.[66] In the 1550s the Belvedere Ariadne was moved to a room at the end of one of the wings connecting the palace to the villa.[67] It was installed above a rocky niche as a fountain, the ceiling of the room was painted with the scenes from the Old and New Testament (*Finding of Moses, Israelites Crossing the Red Sea, Baptism of Christ,* and *Christ and the Woman of Samaria*). The intention seems to be to contrast the eternal life conferred on the righteous through baptism, to the death suffered by sinners—remember that the Ariadne figure was believed to be a Cleopatra at this period.

Even more surprising is another example. The Papacqua fountain was set in a courtyard at right angles to a relief depicting Moses striking the rock. A third wall held figures representing virtues. This group was commissioned by Cardinal Madrucci, one of the leaders of the Council of Trent. After the finish of the Council, the cardinal retired to his villa in Soriano and, in what seems a rejection of the conciliar principles concerning art, had this complex built.[68]

Yet the Council of Trent may have had an influence on the history of fountains in Rome in the later part of the sixteenth century. Genre figures became popular, while the number of mythological figures waned.[69] Fountains added to the Quirinal gardens in the 1590s include a fountain of dwarves, a dog, a dragon (from the papal coat of arms), one called, mysteriously, "del mal tempo" and the waterfalls called "della Pioggia" (Fig. 59)

---

[64] See the Dupérac view reproduced in Coffin, *Villa d'Este*, fig. 1. The itinerary described extends the entire width of the garden and involves two of the upper levels.

[65] Exod. 17.6.

[66] L. Réau, *Iconographie de l'art Chrétien*, II, Paris, 1956, pt. 1, 176, 201.

[67] Brummer, *Belvedere*, 254–64.

[68] For information about the Papacqua, see n. 3. A slightly later example of the use of Christian themes is to be found in the modifications made by Clement VIII to the former Apollo and the Muses nymphaeum at the Quirinal. The new decorations include a scene of Moses striking the rock. Salerno, "Fontana del' Organo," 5. The theme also appears in the *mostra* of the Moses Fountain of the Acqua Felice, 1587. See d'Onofrio, *Fontane*, figs. 66–69.

[69] Genre figures also appeared in public fountains in this period. A manuscript guide to Rome, written during the reign of Sixtus V, "Cose antiche e moderne publiche e private in Rome e fuori anc.a forse lontano," published by R. Lanciani, "Il codice barberiniano XXX, 89," *Archivio della Società romana di storia patria* 6 (1883), 223–40, 445–95, gives a description of a fountain with a wolf on the corner of a house near the Palazzo Medici, ". . . la fontana grottesca con mezzo statua de lupo, la cui bocca de l'acqua in piccolo vasetto o conca. . . ." (446). Another fountain, near Castel Sant'Angelo, had a small lion (*leoncino*) set among stones (479). Two that survived from the period are the "Facchino" on the Via Lata and the "Pig" on the Via della Scrofa. D'Onofrio, *Fontane*, figs. 13, 48, respectively.

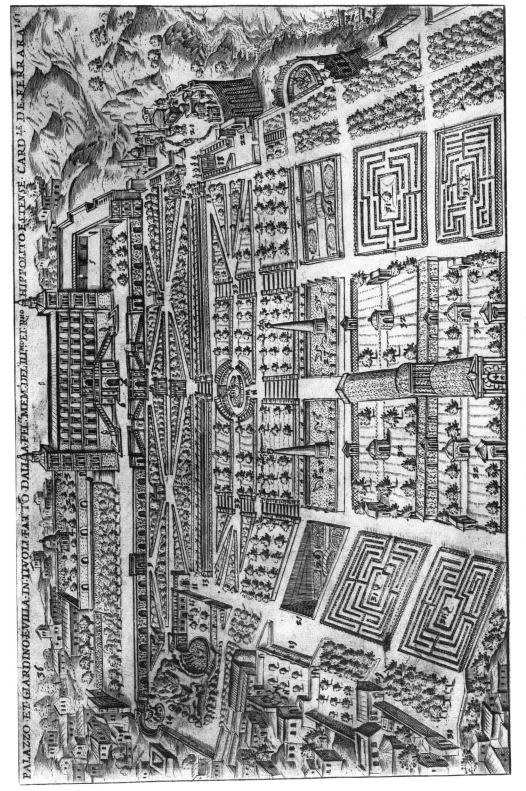

58. Villa d'Este, Tivoli, engraving after Dupérac view of 1563 (photo: Dumbarton Oaks)

79

59. *Fontana della Pioggia,* d'Este villa on the Quirinal, Rome, engraving from
G. Falda, *Le fontane,* I, 6 (photo: Dumbarton Oaks)

and "le Cascate."[70] Payments for the fountain of the dwarves in 1597 give an idea of the
kind of decorations used. The fountain was divided into three niches by columns with
grapevines colored green and blue; the bases and capitals were yellow, and the pedestals
below the columns had the pope's *impresa* in yellow and green. All this was set on a base
of *tartari*. The vaults of the niches were divided into compartments decorated with stars
and roses of shells against a pebble background and their walls articulated by yellow
and green pilasters. In the center niche there was a grotto of *tartari* with two life-sized
dwarves, made of stucco and painted in oil, in niches covered with red and green stones.
Above them in the main part of the niche were two bright blue stucco phoenixes and
above the arch of the niche was a "cherubino." The entablature over the whole fountain
was inlaid with pebbles of yellow, red, and white marble. The pope's coat of arms flanked

[70] The fountains appear in the view of the Quirinal by Maggi and are named on the rubric (Dami,
"Giardino Quirinale," 115 and pl. 1). Payments for work at the Fountain of the Dog, the "fontana del mal
tempo," and the cascades are in an account book of M. O. Pompeo Maderno et Compagni, ASR, Camerale
I, Giustificazione di Tesoro 23.17, 1595–96. Could the "fontana del mal tempo" be another name for the
Fontana del Pioggia?

by the coats of arms of the two cardinal *nipoti* surmounted the entablature, and the whole was finished off by a balustrade of alternating vases and plaques, the latter decorated with pebbles, shells, and masks.[71] A surviving fountain with similar polychrome incrustation is the Fonte degli Specchi at the Vatican.[72]

A great change occurred in fountain design at the end of the century as a result of the construction of the Acqua Felice by Pope Sixtus V.[73] This brought for the first time since antiquity a plenteous water supply with adequate pressure. The list of purchase and gifts of the water includes most of the major villas on the Quirinal and the Esquiline, and the effects were soon seen.[74] The two waterfalls at the Quirinal, constructed in the 1590s, had a volume of water unthinkable earlier (Fig. 59).[75] This kind of fountain immediately became popular in Rome, and the names given to them show how important the volume of water now available was. The two at the Quirinal were called the "Cascate"—the lower one also the "Fontana del Pioggia." A fountain with considerably less water in the Orti Farnesiani was named the "Fontana del Diluvio," and a fountain constructed at the Vatican during the pontificate of Paul V, while usually called the "Fontana dello Scoglio," was also occasionally referred to as the "Fontana del Diluvio."[76]

Another characteristic of fountains of the end of the century is the widespread use of *imprese* and heraldic animals. The first documentation of such decorations appear in the building accounts of the Villa Montalto, built by Sixtus V from 1580 to 1589.[77] All the fountains there were embellished with lions, stars, and *monti*, Peretti's *imprese*.[78] Later,

[71] The decorations are listed in a *Stima* in the account book referred to in n. 70, fols. 22–23. See App. II for a transcription. The fountain was changed under Paul V by additions of his *impresa* and the eagles and dragons of the Borghese coat of arms, see n. 75.

[72] Illustrated in I. Belli Barsali, *Le ville di Roma*, Milan, n.d., 219. See also details of the mosaic incrustation of the facade of the Casino Pio IV on pp. 218–19. Belli Barsali's dating of the fountain to the pontificate of Pius IV (ibid., 207) cannot be sustained, as the fountain house does not appear in the Cartaro map of Rome of 1576, nor in the less accurate Hendrik van Cleve view of 1589. The orientation of the Dupérac-Lafréry map of 1576 and the Tempesta of 1593 makes this area invisible. The first time the house is unmistakeably depicted is in the Greuter map of 1618. See Frutaz, *Le piante di Roma*, II, Rome, 1962, pls. 243, 260, 291, for the Cartaro, van Cleve, Greuter, respectively.

[73] L. Pastor, *History of the Popes*, XXII, St. Louis, 1932, 208–16. Morton, *Waters*, 117–22.

[74] The list of purchases and donations of water from the Acqua Felice is preserved in an 18th-century copy of the notarial acts (ASR, Presidenza delli Acquedotti Urbani, b. 24). It starts with the gift on 17 May 1588 of 6 *oncie* of water to Cardinal Farnese from the run-off of the Michelangelo fountain on the Campidoglio for his garden "a Campo Vaccino," that is the Orti Farnesiani. The grotto with the cascade fountain there dates from this period. Other recipients are Paolo Sforza for his garden "alle Terme," Cardinal Ascanio Sforza for the gardens of the Palazzo Colonna, Marc'Antonio Fiorenzi, Pietro Bandini, and Marzio Frangipani for their gardens, etc.

[75] Payments for changes in the water system and in the decorations of the "Cascate," in 1596 (ASR, Cam. I, Gius. di Tes. 23.17 [1595–96], fols. 11r, 15r) give a terminus ante quem for the construction of these fountains. Alterations and additions were made during the pontificate of Paul V (ASR, Cam. I, Gius di Tes. b. 40, 5, 3, int. 8 June 1614).

[76] For the dates of the Fontana dello Scoglio, see H. Hibbard, *Carl Maderno and Roman Architecture, 1580–1630*, London, 1971, 199–200. An early use of the name "del diluvio" is found at the Villa Lante in Bagnaia, where the volume of water permitted construction of a waterfall.

[77] See "Circus," 136–37. The accounts are in ASR, Cam. I, Fabriche, 1527, and include 22 *conti* and a *ristretto* of all accounts.

[78] See n. 75.

60. River god fountain, Rome, Quattro Fontane
(photo: Gabinetto Fotografico Nazionale)

Paul V substituted decorations of eagles and dragons, the animals of the Borghese coat of arms, for Clement VIII's *impresa* on the Fontana dei Nani at the Quirinal and built twin fountains with the same animals there.[79] Dragons and eagles are also important features of the Fontana dello Scoglio at the Vatican (Fig. 41).

The types of fountains developed during the sixteenth century continued in use in the seventeenth. Rustic fountains were built at the Villa Borghese, the Villa Aldobrandini in Frascati, and other sites. The simple *tazza* continued to be used as decoration of the *compartimenti* or planting beds. Architectural wall fountains also remained popular—examples to be noted are at the Palazzo Borghese, the Palazzo Rospigliosi-Pallavicini, and the Palazzo del Grillo, while standing figure fountains continued to be as rare as they had been in the sixteenth century. Instead of innovations in design, the seventeenth century is notable for its innovations in the use of fountains. Popes turned their thoughts and devoted their resources to the adornment and enrichment of public spaces, creating the great Baroque showpieces that dominate our image of Rome today.

Thus it is symptomatic that the sixteenth century ends with the construction of two fountains, a river god and a sleeping nymph (Figs. 60, 61), the same types that domi-

[79] Payments for the alterations and the new fountains in ASR, Cam. I, Gius. di Tes. b. 40, 4 (int. 5); 40, 15 (int. 12, 14).

61. Reclining nymph fountain, Rome, Quattro
Fontane (photo: Quattro Fontane)

nated at the start of the century. But now these fountains were public, built by Muzio
Mattei in payment for water from the Acqua Felice.[80] While the type is traditional,
the purpose of the fountain is new. The century started with evocations of Parnassus and
Mt. Helicon, the creation of an environment for pleasure. It went on to the elaborate
literary fantasies which could be understood only by the limited group of cultured aristocrats and literati. When, late in the century, symbols of personal and family identification,
the *impresa* and the heraldic animals, were added to the fountain decorations, the way
was opened for the politicization of fountains. Bernini's Barcaccia and Quattro Fiume
fountains are statements about the power of the papacy and the role of Christianity in
the world[81]—messages to impress and educate the populace at the same time that the
waters of the fountains literally showered them with the benefits of papal largesse.

[80] This obviously was a papal policy for financing public amenities. Muzio Mattei was given the run-off
water from two fountains at the Quattro Fontane, "per aver egli fabbricato le dette due fontane," and 8 *oncie*
from the Moses Fountain, the *castello* of the Acqua Felice, with the obligation, "debba fare la Piazza dell 4
Fontane a compenso." Giacomo Gridenzoni was given one and a half *oncie* of water, "per aver fatto a sue
spese una dell 4 Fontane" (ASR, Pres. delle Acqued., b. 24, 25 June 1588; 28 May 1593, respectively). Fabio
Mattei and Zeffiri Farratino were given water or allowed to purchase it cheaply in return for constructing
public fountains at other locations in Rome (ibid., 11 June 1591; 6 July 1602).

[81] For the iconography of the Barcaccia, see H. Hibbard and I. Jaffe, "Bernini's Barcaccia," *Burlington
Magazine* 106 (1964), 159–70. For the Quattro Fiume Fountain, see R. Preimesberger, "Obeliscus Pamphil-
ius: Beiträge zu Vorgeschichte und Ikonographie des Vierströmebrunnens auf Piazza Navona," *Münchner
Jahrbuch der Bildenden Kunst* 25 (1974), 77–162.

APPENDIX I

A Monsignor GUIDICCIONE, a Lucca

Tengo una di V. S. Reverendissima da Lucca per la quale mi domanda o descrizione o disegno de la fontana di Monsignor mio. E perché mi truovo ancora in Napoli, farò l'una cosa come meglio potrò, l'altra ordinerò a Roma che sia fatta quanto prima, benché mio fratello mi scrive che di già avea richiesto un pittor mio amico che la facesse. Io non iscriverò a V. S. l'artificio di far salire l'acqua, ancora che ciò mi paia la più notabil cosa che vi sia, poich'ella (secondo che scrive) ha l'acqua con la caduta e col suo corso naturale, e dirolle minutamente la disposizione del resto, secondo che mi ricerca. Monsignore ha fatto in testa d'una sua gran pergola un muro rozzo di certa pietra che a Roma si dice asprone, specie di tufo nero e spugnoso, e sono certi massi posti l'uno sopra l'altro a caso, o per dir meglio con certo ordine disordinato, che fanno dove bitorzoli e dove buchi da piantarvi de l'erbe, e tutto 'l muro insieme rappresenta come un pezzo d'anticaglia rósa e scantonata. In mezzo di questo muro è lasciata una porta per entrare in un andito d'alcune stanze, fatta pure a bozzi da gli lati, e di sopra a' sassi pendenti, a guisa più tosto d'intrata d'un antro, che d'altro, e di qua e di là da la porta in ciascun angolo è una fontana, e la figura di quella a man destra è tale: è gettata una volta de le medesime pietre, tra le due mura che fanno l'angolo, con petroni che sporgono fuor de l'angolo intorno a due braccia, e sotto vi si fa un nicchio pur bitorzoluto, come se fusse un pezzo di monte cavato. Dentro da questo nicchio è posto un pilo antico, sopra due zoccoli, con teste di lioni, il quale serve per vaso de la fontana. Sopra al pilo, tra l'orlo suo di dentro e il muro del nicchio, è disteso un fiume di marmo con un'urna sotto al braccio, e sotto al pilo un altro ricetto d'acqua, come quelli di Belvedere, ma tondo a uso di zana. L'altra fontana da man manca ha la volta, il nicchio, il pilo, il ricetto sotto al pilo, e tutto quasi nel medesimo modo che l'altra, salvo che dove quella ha il fiume sopra al pilo, questa v'ha un pelaghetto di quasi un braccio e mezzo di diametro, col fondo d'una ghiara nettissima, e d'intorno le sponde con certi piccioli ridotti come se fossero róse da l'acqua: e in questa guisa stanno ambedue le fontane. Ora dirò come l'acqua viene in ciascuna, e gli effetti che fa. Dentro dal muro descritto, più d'una canna alto, è un bottino o conserva grande d'acqua, commune a l'una fonte ed a l'altra, e di qui, per canne di piombo che si possono aprire e serrare, si dà e toglie l'acqua a ciascuna, ed a quella a man destra si dà a questo modo. La sua canna è divisa in due, e l'una, ch'è la maggiore, conduce una gran polla d'acqua per di dentro, in fino in su l'orlo del fiume descritto, e quindi, uscendo fuori, trova intoppo di certi scoglietti, che rompendola, le fanno far maggior rumore e la spargono in più parti, e l'una cade giù a piombo, l'altra corre lungo il letto del fiume, e nel correre trabocca per molti lochi, e per tutti romoreggiando versa nel pilo, e dal pilo (pieno che egli è) da tutto 'l giro de l'orlo cade nel ricetto da basso. L'altra parte di questa canna, la quale è una cannella piccola, porta l'acqua sopra la volta del nicchio, dove è un catino quanto tiene tutta la volta, forato in più lochi, per gli quali fori, per certe picciole cannellate, si mandano solamente gocciole d'acqua sotto la volta, e di là quindi come per diversi gemitii, a guisa di pioggia, caggiono nel pilo, e caggendo passano per alcuni tartari bianchi di acqua congelata, che si trovano ne la caduta di Tivoli, i quali vi sono adattati in modo, che par che l'acqua gemendo vi sia naturalmente ingrommata. E così tra 'l grondar di sopra e 'l correr da ogni parte si fa una bella vista e un gran mormorio. La fontana a man sinistra ha la canna pur divisa in due, e l'una ch'è la picciola, nel medesimo modo che s'è detto ne l'altra, conduce l'acqua di sopra a la volta a far la medesima pioggia per gli medesimi tartari, ed a cader medesimamente nel pilo. Ma l'altra parte più grande di essa canna la mette nel pelaghetto descritto, e quivi si sparte in più zampilli; donde schizzando con impeto, truova il bagno del pelaghetto che le fa resistenza, e rompendola viene a fare un bollore e un gorgoglio bellissimo e simile in tutto al sorger de l'acqua naturale. Quando il pelaghetto è pieno, cade per mille parti nel pilo e dal pilo per mille altre ne l'ultimo ridotto. E così tra il piovere, il gorgogliare e 'l versare e di questa fonte e de l'altra, oltre al vedere, si fa un sentir molto piacevole e quasi armonioso, essendo con il mormorar d'ambedue congiunto un altro maggior suono, il quale si sente e non si scorge donde si venga; perché di dentro fra 'l bottino e i nicchi di sopra di ciascuna d'esse sono artificiosamente posti alcuni vasi di creta grandi e sottili con il ventre largo e con la bocca stretta a guisa di pentole, o di vettine più tosto. Ne' quali vasi sboccando l'acqua del bottino, prima che giunga ne' catini già detti, viene a caderci d'alto, ristretta e con tal impeto che fa rumor grande per sé, e per riverbero moltiplica e s'ingrossa molto più. Per questo che, essendo i vasi bucati nel mezzo, in fino al mezzo s'empiono solamente, e posti col fondo come in bilico non toccano quasi in niun loco. Onde che fra la suspensione e la concavità loro, vengono a fare il tuono che v'ho detto; il quale continuato e grave, e più lontano che quei di fuori, a guisa di contrabasso s'unisce con essi e risponde loro con la medesima proporzione che lo sveglione a la cornamusa. Questo è quanto a l'udito. Ma non riesce men bella cosa ancora quanto a la vista, perché oltre che 'l loco tutto è spazioso e proporzionato, ha da gli lati spalliere d'ellere e di gelsomini, e sopra alcuni pilastri vestiti da altre verdure, un pergolato di viti sfogato e denso tanto, che per l'altezza ha de l'aria assai, e per la spessezza ha d'un opaco e d'un orrore, che tiene insieme del ritirato e del venerando. Si veggono poi d'intorno a le fontane per l'acque, pescetti, coralletti, scoglietti; per le buche granchiolini, madreperle, chiocciolette, per le sponde, capilvenere, scolopendie, musco ed altre sorti d'erbe acquaiole. Mi sono dimenticato di dire de gli ultimi ridotti abbasso de l'una fonte e de l'altra, che quando son pieni, perché non trabocchino, giunta l'acqua a un dito vicini a l'orlo, truova un doccione aperto, donde se n'esce, ed entra in una chiavichetta che la porta al fiume. E in questa guisa sono fatte le fontane di Monsignor mio. Quella poi del Sanese ne la strada del Popolo, se io non la riveggio, non m'affido di scrivere, tanto più che non l'ho mai veduta gittare, e non so le vie de l'acqua. Quando sarò a Roma, che non sia prima che a settembre, le scriverò più puntualmente che potrò. Intanto ho scritto a Monsignore che le mandi ritratto di tutte, e son certo che lo farà, sapendo quanto desidera di farle cosa grata. Io non ho saputo scriver queste più demostrativamente che m'abbia fatto; se la descrizione le servirà, mi sarà caro; quando no, aiutisi col disegno, e degnisi di dirmi un motto di quanto vi desidera, ché si farà tanto che V.S. ne resterà satisfatta. E quando bisogni, si manderà di Roma chi l'indirizzi l'opera tutta. La solitudine di V.S. mi torna in parte a dispiacere, per tenermi discosto da lei, ma considerando poi la quiete de l'animo suo e i frutti che da gli suoi studi si possono aspettare, la tollero facilmente. Né per questo giudico che s'interrompa il corso de gli onori suoi, perché a questa meta arriva talvolta più tosto chi se ne ritira, che chi vi corre senza ritegno. E con questo me le raccomando e le bacio le mani.

Di Napoli, a li 13 di luglio MDXXXVIII.

Stima della fontana dove sono li nani a tutta robba delli mastri eccetto li lomachi corredi et matroperle.

Per haver messo li tartari nel mezzo delli cartelloni et vasi	∇22
Per haver fatto li 4 vasi sop.a alli Cartelli coperti di spolvere e smalti et li frutti dentro a detti vasi	∇10
Per haver fatto 4 cartelloni sotto alli d.i vasi coperti di sassetti e cochiglie con maschere	∇12
Per haver fatto l'armi del Papa coperta di smalti et marmi, colli e spolveri	∇13
Per haver fatto doi Armi delli Cardinali coperti di spolveri di diverse colori	∇12
Per haver fatto 6 festoni dalli bandi di d.o Armi	∇13
Per haver abbozzato et coperto la Cornice sotto alle Cartellini et Armi coperta parte di spolveri et parte di sassate ed la [?] intagliato et goccio la torio et dintello et una foglia sotto	∇30
Per haver fatto il fregio sotto alla d.a cornice fatto di sassetti di serpentino et marmo bianco et rossi	∇15.30
Per haver fatto l'architrave ed una foglia intagliata	∇15.30
Per haver fatto 4 Capitelli Ionichi coperti di spolveri di marmo giallo	∇15
Per haver fatto 4 Colonne fatte a fogliami di vita coperte di spolveri di smalti verdi et turchino et pavonazzo il campo di granito	∇36
Per haver fatto 4 basi di d.e collonne coperte di spolveri di marmo giallo	∇6
Per haver fatto 4 piedestalli sotto alle d.e Colonne dove sono l'imprese del papa fatti di sassetti gialli et verde il zoccolo fatto di tartari tutti	∇26
Per haver fatto l'Arme del S.r Gio: francesco sotto a quella del Papa	∇6
Per haver fatto la mostra del Arco della Nicchia di mezzo coperta di marmo giallo di sassetti cochiglie et tellini	∇6
Per haver fatto doi triangoli del d.o arco fatti di sassetti gialli et serpentine	∇3
Per haver fatto la mostra delli altri doi archi simili a quello di mezzo	∇3
Per haver fatto 4 triangoli delli doi archi sop.a d.i ed l'imprese del Papa fatti di sassetti verdi e gialli	∇6
Per haver fatto doi sottarchi piccoli fatti a partimenti ed sassetti et cochiglie	∇10
Per haver fatto il sottarco grande di mezzo fatto a partimenti con sassetti di serpentino et rossi et conchiglie	∇8
Per haver fatto la volticella della Nicchia grande scompartita a quadri con stelli et rose di cochiglie ed li Campi di sassetti	∇12
Per haver fatto un Cherubino sopra l'arco della Nicchia grande	∇60
Per haver fatto doi fenice di stucco ed il Campo di spolvere di smalti turchini nelle nichie sopra li nani	∇6
Per haver fatto la mostra del arco sop.a la grotta di tartari ed un listello di smalti doro ed doi piani di spolveri ed una lumaca che fa guscio	∇2
Per haver fatto la Cimasa al imposta della volta et archi intagliata et coperta di spolvere di smalto cochighlie	∇20
Per haver fatto 6 pilastri sotto alle d.e cimase dove sono l'imprese del Papa ed 3 partimenti per pilastro coperti di spolveri di smalti et marmi et parte di sassetti	∇28

Per haver fatto 6 membretti ed li pilastri fatti di sassetti gialli .... $\nabla 14$

Per haver fatto doi nani di stucco fatti del naturale coloriti a olio .... $\nabla 25$

Per haver fatti doi nichie dove sono li nani fatti di sassetti rossi et verde et parte di tartari ed li piedestalli sotto alli nani .... $\nabla 24$

Per haver fatto la nichia grande fatta de tartari ed le doi passatore et membretti fatti di marmo bianchi ed un profilo di smalti doro ed una lumaca attorno che fa guscio .... $\nabla 15$

Per haver fatto il piedestallo sotto al apollino fatto di sassetti .... $\nabla 3$

Per haver adornato lo scoglio della nichia grande sotto all apollino sino al [?] della peschiera coperto di tartari et breccia .... $\nabla 10$

Per haver adornato doi altri scogli dalle bande sotto alle nani simili al d.e. .... $\nabla 10$

Per haver adornato la fontana del specchio de tartari et breccie et doi cartelli overo mēsoli sotto il vaso coperti di spolvere .... $\nabla 10$

    ASR. Cam. I. Gius. di Tes. 23. 17, 1595–96, fols. 22r–v.

Ars Hortulorum: Sixteenth-Century Garden Iconography and Literary Theory in Italy

To Richard Krautheimer

Interpretation of Renaissance garden forms and themes has been hampered by the lack of direct evidence as to their meaning. No written iconographical programs have survived, and indeed there is not much evidence for their existence in the sixteenth century. Only Vasari explains the entire theme of a garden in his description of the decorations of the Medici villa at Castello.[1] Later writers, such as Tesauro, the seventeenth-century Turinese scholar, give evidence that unified decorative themes existed and explain their aim. His arrangement of statues at Racconigi, with their accompanying inscriptions, were intended, he says, to promote contemplation of celestial astronomy as well as of human philosophy.[2]

Although the programs of some individual gardens have been elucidated,[3] not enough evidence has been accumulated to show a common background or source for Renaissance garden iconography nor to permit the interpretation of commonly found garden decorations. Aesthetic theory of the period, however, provides the information necessary to understand this background and the process of development of garden

[1] G. Vasari, *Le vite de' più eccelenti pittori.* . . . , ed. Milanesi, Florence, 1878, VI, 78–84. See also, L. Chatelet-Lange, "The Grotto of the Unicorn in the Garden of the Villa di Castello," *Art Bulletin* 50 (1968), 51–58.

[2] "Peroche volendo il Principe Tomasso termina tutti gli angoli de' Quadri del Perterro [sc. Racconigi] con qualche Statua misteriosa sopra suoi Piedistalli, che compievano il numero di 61, sicome quel Giardino nella Primavera pare un cielo stellato di fiori; Così vennemi nel pensiero di rappresentare in ogni Statua una delle *Imagini celesti*, che uguagliano apunto quel numero . . . nella forma che da' Poeti, secondo le lor favole misteriose, ci vengono effigiati. Et di ciascuna statua formai un' Emblema col suo Epigramma nel Piedestallo, per dichiarar la Favola & applicarla à qualche moral documento. Si che . . . chiunque passeggiasse per il Giardino, potesse vedere il Cielo in terra, & conoscere quasi tutte le favole de' Poeti & impara Documenti utili alla vita humana. . . ." E. Tesauro, *Il Cannocchiale aristotelico*, Turin, 1670, 710–11.

[3] For interpretations of iconographical programs of gardens, see, in addition to Chatelet-Lange, "Grotto of the Unicorn," the following: D. Coffin, *The Villa d'Este at Tivoli*, Princeton, 1960, 78–97; K. Schwager, "Kardinal Pietro Aldobrandinis Villa di Belvedere in Frascati," *Römisches Jahrbuch für Kunstgeschichte* 9–10 (1961–62), 370–79; D. Heikamp, "La grotta grande del Giardino di Boboli," *Antichità viva* 4 (1965), fasc. 4, 30–33. I am indebted to Dr. Wolfgang Lotz for calling my attention to the Heikamp article.

themes and decoration. The dominant doctrine of the period is summed up by "ut pictura poesis," Horace's dictum that poetry is analogous to painting in its aims and effects, or, to paraphrase a saying attributed to another ancient writer, that painting is mute poetry and poetry a speaking picture. Renaissance critics interpreted the doctrine as meaning that art should emulate poetry, and they applied to the creation of works of art, principles that, in late antiquity, had been formulated for poetry and other genres of *belles lettres*.[4] These tenets included a requirement to imitate models from antiquity and to choose subject matter from established themes, or *topoi*. Art was required to edify and uplift as well as to give pleasure.[5]

For the Renaissance patron or humanist faced with the development and design of a garden, these requirements created a dilemma. Required to emulate antiquity, he had little concrete evidence to draw upon. Actual remains of ancient gardens were scarce and frequently misinterpreted.[6] No treatises on landscape architecture had survived. Indications in Vitruvius and the horticultural treatises were scanty.[7] What remained were the fragments of information to be found in other ancient texts. Pliny the Younger's description of his two villas, the most complete factual information available, was studied minutely.[8] Other texts, where references were more oblique, seem to have been culled systematically.[9]

A study of two features frequently found in Renaissance gardens, the grove or *boschetto*, and the fountain grotto or nymphaeum, shows the use of another precept of the aesthetic doctrine of the period, the choice of subject matter from established literary themes. Indeed, it is only through knowledge of the literary background that the purpose and meaning of the grove and nymphaeum can be understood.

The existence of groves and irregular or naturalistic areas in Renaissance gardens is often ignored.[10] The Renaissance garden is usually thought to be entirely architectural

[4] For a discussion of the doctrine, "ut pictura poesis," and its reinterpretation in the Renaissance, see R. Lee, "Ut Pictura Poesis: The Humanist Theory of Painting," *Art Bulletin* 22 (1940), 197–269; republished in paperback, New York, 1968.

[5] Lee, "Ut Pictura Poesis," 226–28.

[6] The hippodrome garden on the Palatine was believed to be an atrium at this period and is so labeled on the 1576 Dupérac map of ancient Rome, reproduced in A. Frutaz, ed., *Le piante di Roma*, Rome, 1962, pl. 39. The nymphaeum at the Horti Liciniani was believed to be a temple. I am grateful to John Pinto for his information about villa remains visible in the Renaissance. These included Hadrian's villa in Tivoli, the Horti Liciniani near the Porta Maggiore in Rome, the Villa of Maxentius on the Via Appia, the villa at Settebasso, and the Domitian villa at Castel Gondolfo.

[7] Vitruvius, *De Architectura*, VI, vi. The four agricultural treatises known in the Renaissance were: Cato, *De agri cultura;* Varro, *Rerum rusticarum;* Palladio, *De re rustica;* Columella, *Res rustica;* published together in the Renaissance as *Rei rusticae scriptores*, ed. prin., Venice, 1472.

[8] Pliny's description of his villas at Laurentium and Tusci are to be found in *Epistles*, 2.7; 5.6. For discussion and interpretation of the letters, see H. Tanzer, *The Villas of Pliny the Younger*, New York, 1924, with earlier bibliography, and K. Lehmann, *Plinius Caecilius Secundus: Lettere scelte con commento archeologico*, Testi della scuola normale di Pisa 3 (1936), 42–59.

[9] For references to gardens or villas in Latin writings, see especially, G. Lafaye, "Jardins," *Dictionnaire des antiquités grecques et romaines*, ed. Daremberg and Saglio, III, pt. 1, 276–93.

[10] See, however, G. Argan, "Landscape Architecture," *Encyclopedia of World Art*, VIII, col. 1068.

and formal, an attitude that goes back to the eighteenth century and which is typified by this poem by Pope:

> On ev'ry side you look, behold the Wall:
> No pleasing intricacies intervene,
> No artful wildness to perplex the scene:
> Grove nods at grove, each Alley has a brother,
> And half the platform just reflects the other.
> The suff'ring eye inverted Nature sees,
> Trees cut to Statues, Statues thick as trees.[11]

Yet it is possible to show that there were indeed informal or naturalistic areas of importance to the garden design. They were not, as Pope said, planted symmetrically with regard to each other, nor were they part of the farm, as distinct from the garden of the villa.

The Villa Lante at Bagnaia, dating in the late 1560s, is usually discussed entirely in terms of the formal terraced gardens in front and behind the two casinos, while the informal park to the side is ignored (Fig. 62).[12] The park, however, contained fountains of a type ordinarily found only in the formal parts of gardens, that is, the fountains of Bacchus, of the Dragon, the Unicorn, and the Duck. Still another, the fountain of Pegasus, was clearly a key point in the overall program, linked in idea to the upper pavilions, the *Mansiones musae*.[13] Even the terraced garden did not consist entirely of low, geometrical plantings; the terrace in front of the upper pavilions had a beech grove.[14]

Again, at the Villa Giulia in Rome, built in the 1550s, discussion is always restricted to the enclosed courtyards and the nymphaeum.[15] The surrounding hills, which were planted with *selvatiche* at the time of the construction of the villa, have been thought to be part of the farm. Ammannati's description of 1555, however, makes it clear that the casino and its courtyards were sited in relationship to the hills (". . . col palazzo si è voluto obbedire ad una bella ed amena valle"), and that the wooded slopes of the hills were also part of the garden. There were paths leading to a casino and loggia on the upper level

[11] "Epistle to Lord Burlington," lines 114–20, quoted by E. Malins, *English Landscaping and Literature, 1660–1840*, London, 1966, 38–39.

[12] For the history of the villa, see A. Cantoni, F. Ariello, et al., *La Villa Lante di Bagnaia*, Milan, 1960. The date is discussed by D. Coffin, "Some Aspects of the Villa Lante at Bagnaia," *Arte in Europa: Scritti di storia dell'arte in onore di Edoardo Arslan*, I, n.p., 1966, 569–75.

[13] See Giovanni Guerra's drawings of the Villa Lante in the Albertina, Vienna, published by J. Hess, "Entwürfe von Giovanni Guerra für Villa Lante in Bagnaia (1598)," *Römisches Jahrbuch für Kunstgeschichte* 12 (1969), 194–202. The Bacchus fountain is illustrated in fig. 12 of that article.

[14] So named in the Lauro print (Fig. 62) and the Guerra drawing.

[15] J. Coolidge, "The Villa Giulia: A Study of Central Italian Architecture in the Mid-Sixteenth Century," *Art Bulletin* 25 (1943), 177–225, and F. Land Moore, "A Contribution to the Study of the Villa Giulia," *Römisches Jahrbuch für Kunstgeschichte* 12 (1969), 171–94. See T. Falk, "Studien zur Topographie und Geschichte der Villa Giulia in Rom," *Römisches Jahrbuch für Kunstgeschichte* 13 (1971). For information on herms, C. Huelsen, "Die Hermeninschriften berühmter Griechen und die ikonographischen Sammlungen des XVI. Jahrhunderts," *Mitteilungen des Deutschen Archäologischen Instituts. Römische Abteilung* 16 (1901), 128–29, 144.

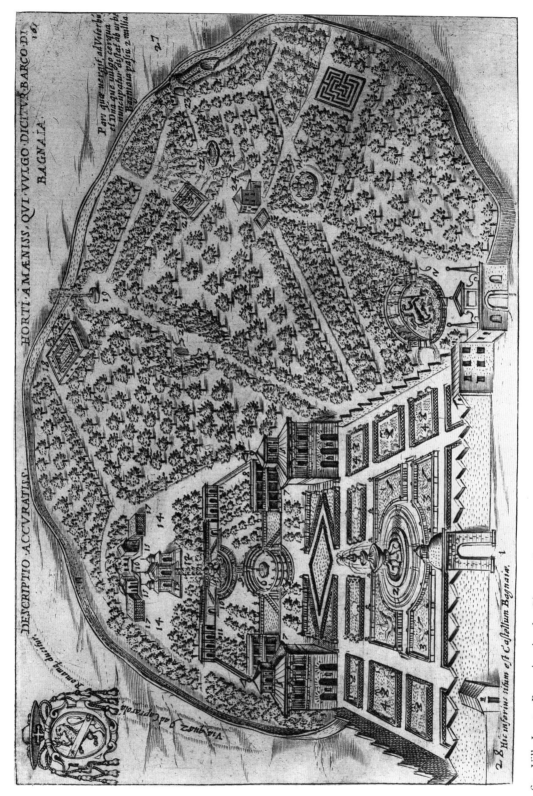

62. Villa Lante, Bagnaia, view by Giacomo Lauro, early seventeenth century (photo: Dumbarton Oaks)

92

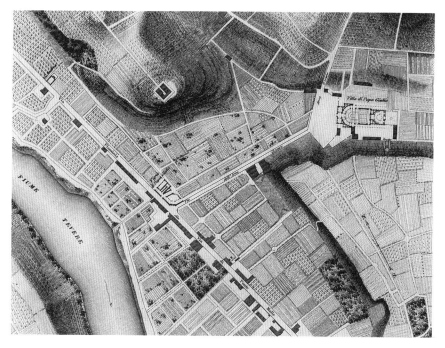

63. Villa Giulia, Rome, topographical plan by Letarouilly (photo: Dumbarton Oaks)

of the property. Along the paths, which were decorated with ancient herms, were resting places with arbors, benches, and tables. A smaller grove with a loggia was situated behind the church of Sant'Andrea, and still another grove was planted in the area between the public fountain and the casino (Fig. 63).[16]

An examination of other villas show that *boschetti* and informal planting occurred everywhere. Cardinal Pio da Carpi's villa, on the site of the present Palazzo Barberini, had a large park, called a *vigna* in a 1550 description, but nevertheless decorated with statues, arbors, and fountains.[17] The d'Este villa also on the Quirinal, now the site of the Palazzo Quirinale, was famous for its *boschetti*. One on the brow of the Quirinal hill surrounded a trelliswork temple, another near the Via Pia, now Via XX Settembre, contained a rustic fountain, while a third was planted in front of the Grotto of Apollo and

[16] Ammannati's description is in a letter to Marco Mantova Benavides dated 2 May 1555. The letter, preserved in a copy in Pesaro, Bibl. Oliveriana, cod. 374/II, fols. 91–96, was published with emendations of spelling and punctuation by G. Balestra, *La fontana pubblica di Giulio III ed il palazzo di Pio IV sulla Via Flaminia*, Rome, 1911, 65ff.

[17] The history of the Carpi villa is given by C. Huelsen, *Römische Antikengärten des XVI. Jahrhunderts*, Akademie der Wissenschaften zu Heidelberg, Philosophisch-historische Klasse, Abhandlungen 4 (1917), 43–54. A description of the villa in 1550 appears in U. Aldrovandi, *Delle statue di Roma*, published with L. Mauro, *Antichità di Roma*, Rome, 1556, 122–38.

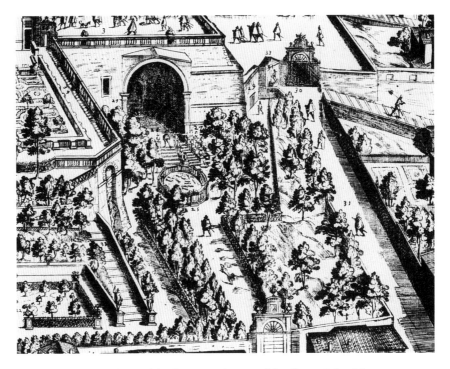

64. D'Este villa on the Quirinal, Rome, Grotto of Apollo and the Muses,
detail of Maggi view of 1612 (photo: British Museum)

the Muses on the lower slopes of the hill (Figs. 25, 64).[18] Boissard's description of the late
1550s says that nowhere in Rome are to be seen trees more diverse or more splendid in
their cultivation.[19] He closes his description by saying that the villa is inferior to the Carpi
villa in the diversity and number of ancient statues but far superior in the number of
its trees.

By the 1580s the naturalistic plantings often were equal in area and importance to
the formal. At the Villa Mattei only the flat area near the casino was organized into
regular geometric planting beds (Fig. 65).[20] The rest of the villa consisted of *boschetti*, one
near the entrance gate containing statues of a shepherd with a mastiff at his feet, of kids

[18] The cardinal first leased the land in 1550 and the major planting was completed ca. 1555 (see n. 19).
Payments for the fountains date in 1560–61. For this and other facts, see Huelsen, *Antikengärten*, 85–122,
and J. Wasserman, "The Quirinal Palace in Rome," *Art Bulletin* 54 (1963), 204–44.

[19] "(Horti Ferrariensis cardinalis) quibus nulli Romae videntur arborum diversarum cultu splendidi-
ores, et aedificio mirabilis artificii, quod ex arboribus consertis simul et implicatis Labyrinthum efficiunt."
From J. J. Boissard, *Topographia Romae*, I, Frankfurt, 1597, 94. Boissard's description dates from his six year
stay in Italy, starting in 1555, see J. Janker, "Die Porträtstiche des Robert Boissard . . . an dem J. J. Boissard'schen Sammelwerke," *Repertorium für Kunstwissenschaft* 7 (1883–84), 418.

[20] The Villa Mattei, or Giardino Celimontana as it was known in the 16th century, was built by Ciriaco
Mattei in the 1580s. For a history of the garden and its decorations, see "Circus," 127–40.

94

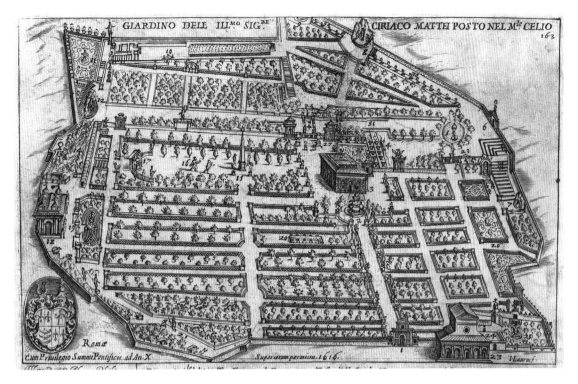

65. Villa Mattei, Rome, view by G. Lauro, 1616 (photo: Biblioteca Vaticana Apostolica)

and goats playing and eating, of a wolf, a wild boar, and deer. The lower garden was entirely taken up by *boschetti* and *ragnaie,* an especially thickly planted grove, while the connecting slopes were treated *"a laberinto."*

The examples in Rome were not unique. Castello, the Medici villa near Florence, had a large *boschetto* on the uppermost terrace (Fig. 66), the Boboli Garden in 1584 appears to have been planted in dense groves (Fig. 67), and Pratolino was almost entirely devoted to *boschetti* and an informal design (Fig. 68).[21]

Not all gardens evoked the pastoral or benign side of nature. The Sacro Bosco at Bomarzo was certainly intended to provoke feelings of fear and confusion. Visitors who penetrated the labyrinth at the Villa Mattei may have felt more than surprise to discover a dragon at its center.[22]

[21] Figs. 66 and 68 are reproductions of the lunettes painted by Utens in 1599 showing the Medici villas. For a list of the series, dates of Castello and the Boboli garden, see W. Smith, "Studies on Buontalenti's Villas," Ph.D. diss., New York University, 1958, 78–79, 183–84. For Pratolino, see idem, "Pratolino," *Journal of the Society of Architectural Historians* 20 (1961), 155–68.

[22] An interpretation of the program of the Sacro Bosco is proposed by M. Calvesi, "Il sacro bosco di Bomarzo," *Scritti di storia dell'arte in onore di Lionello Venturi,* I, Rome, 1956, 369–402. The dragon in the labyrinth at the Villa Mattei is listed in the inventory of 1614 published by R. Lanciani, *Storia degli scavi di Roma e notizie intorno le collezioni romane di Antichità,* III, Rome, 1907, 96.

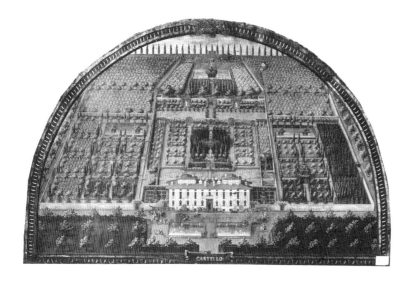

66. Villa Medici, Castello, view in 1599 by Utens, Florence, Museo Storico di Firenze (photo: Gabinetto Fotografico Uffizi)

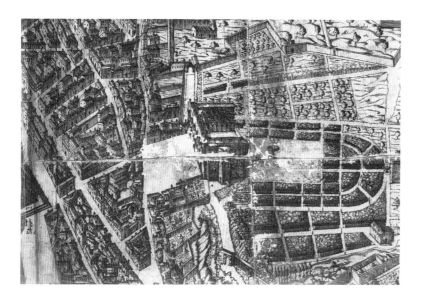

67. Boboli Gardens, Florence, detail of Bonsignori map of 1584 (photo: Gabinetto Fotografico Uffizi)

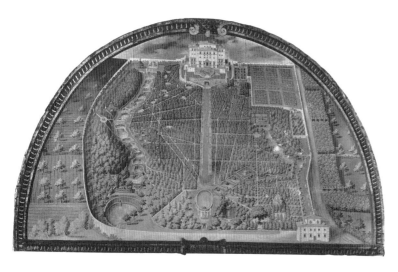

68. Villa Medici, Pratolino, view in 1599 by Utens, Florence, Museo Storico di Firenze (photo: Gabinetto Fotografico Uffizi)

It is difficult to trace the evolution of the *boschetto* and the informal plantings in gardens. Battisti has pointed out the existence of a trend toward naturalism in Florence in the late fifteenth century.[23] Rucellai's description of his villa Quaracchi shows it included both a formal garden and a *boschetto* with winding paths, a labyrinth, small trellis pavilions, and a small hill planted with evergreens. His language is of interest here. In the *boschetto* he speaks of a *viottola* or path, while in the formal garden he uses the word *viale;* the pavilions are called *capanne* or huts, while the formal garden had a pergola and a loggia; even the hill is given a rustic name, *pogiuolo*.[24] Thus the contrast between the formal and the informal was deliberate in both the description and the actual garden. At the Belvedere in Rome, a description of 1524 mentions the area west of the courtyard, saying that the loggias on that side open on some meadows, a small hill, and a grove.[25]

Despite scattered early examples, the focus of the development seems to have been in Ferrara, in the series of d'Este gardens built near the city walls. As early as the 1470s Borso d'Este built the garden of San Giorgio. He used the earth left over from the construction of a new rampart in the city walls to make the garden's most prominent feature, a tall artificial mount.[26] A description written shortly after the garden's destruction in the early seventeenth century reads: "Entering by the great gate near the church of St. George there was a large plaza with the palace on the right built by Duke Alfonso I. . . . In perspective from the gate and at the exit of the piazza was a thick wood with many types of trees. In its center was a fountain surrounded by a labyrinth. To the right of the wood . . . there was a small garden. On the left . . . there was a large mountain artificially constructed . . . with a beautiful grotto; within, the first room was round with niches decorated with *grottesche* and beyond one entered a small square room covered with mosaics. . . . The mountain had paths leading up and down covered by pergolas with vines and other greens. At the summit a small open space was enclosed by a pergola of larch. . . . This mountain was planted informally ("era senz' ordine piantata ed imboschita di varie piante").[27] A representation of this *Montagnola,* as it was called, has been iden-

---

[23] See E. Battisti, "*Natura Artificiosa* to *Natura Artificialis*," *The Italian Garden,* Dumbarton Oaks Colloquium on the History of Landscape Architecture 1, ed. D. Coffin, Washington, D.C., 1972, 24–36.

[24] "Vedesi una siepe grossa intorno al detto orto [the *boschetto*], che gira braccia 400, d'allori, fichi, susini, vite e ruvistichi, sanguini, ginepri, pruni di more; più quantità di segiole nella detta siepe fasciate e coperte d'allori e ruvistichi . . . E più, nel detto orto v'è uno oratorio d'allori tondo con panche da torno . . . con uno andirivieni a botte . . . E più, una chapanna quadra d'albeti e allori chon panche da torno, . . . E più, una chapanetta di ginepro . . . E più, v'è uno pogiuolo, verde d'ogni tempo, d'abeti e albori . . . alto braccia octo, e gira d'intorno braccia ciento di sotto e di sopra braccia cinquanta, con cierte vie nel mezzo del monte da poterlo girare intorno intorno," A. Perosa, ed., *Giovanni Rucellai ed il suo Zibaldone: I. Il Zibaldone Quaresimale,* Studies of the Warburg Institute 24, London, 1960, 22.

[25] An anonymous description dated 11 May 1523, quoted in J. Ackerman, *The Cortile del Belvedere,* Studi e documenti per la storia del Palazzo Apostolico Vaticano 3, Vatican City, 1954, 145.

[26] I am grateful to Mrs. Margaret Licht for the information that Borso d'Este was responsible for the construction of the *Montagnola.*

[27] M. Guarini, *Compendio historico delle chiese di Ferrara,* Ferrara, 1621, 295–96.

69. Montagnola, Ferrara,
view in Libania-Melius
tapestry,
Paris, Musée des Arts
Décoratifs
(photo: Fiorentini)

tified recently, showing a pyramidal shaped hill thickly planted with various trees (Fig. 69).[28]

By 1516 one of the most famous of the d'Este *Delizie* was under construction. This was the Belvedere located on a small island in the river Po near the walls of the city of Ferrara.[29] Destroyed in 1598 by papal troops to make way for a new fortress, only descriptions have survived. The island, apparently lozenge shaped, had its main buildings at the end nearest the city. A staircase led up from the river to a forecourt with a bronze fountain in the form of a tree trunk, its branches formed by streams of water. Behind, the palace enclosed a small courtyard planted with many flowers. The rest of the island was given over to a large park planted with a great diversity of trees. It served as a preserve for a collection of domestic and exotic wild animals, but there were also pools and grottoes in the park. One writer said that one might expect to find Diana relaxing from the hunt in one of the pools or Pan seeking respite from the savage mountain tops in the grottoes.[30]

Thus a well-documented tradition for naturalistic and informal planting can be traced back to the fifteenth and early sixteenth centuries in Ferrara. Later gardens of

[28] The *Montagnola* appears in the background of a tapestry in the Louvre representing the Libanus-Melia myth. Identified by F. Gibbons and published in his, "Ferrarese Tapestries of Metamorphosis," *Art Bulletin* 48 (1966), 409–11, and fig. 1.

[29] For the date of the villa, see A. Trotti, "Le delizie di Belvedere illustrate," *Atti e memorie della deputazione di storia patria ferrarese* 2 (1889), 10.

[30] Scipione Balbo Finalese, *Pulcher Visus Calliopsis Divi Alphonsi Ferrariensium Ducis*, ed. G. B. Phaellus, Bologna, 1531. I have seen only the translation published by G. Pazzi in *Le "Delizie Estensi" e l'Ariosto*, Pescara Riviera, 1933, 45–50. A number of descriptions are published by Pazzi, pp. 35–70. She points out passages in the *Orlando Furioso* that refer directly to the Belvedere and which were inserted in the text after 1530. It seems possible to me that the design of the Belvedere was influenced by Ariosto's description of the island of Alcina (Canto VI, stanzas 20–22).

the d'Este in Ferrara had an equal dominance of groves and parks. It is clear that Cardinal Ippolito was continuing the Ferrarese tradition in his villa on the Quirinal. Boissard's description shows that the number of *boschetti* was considered unusual in Rome at that time, so the influence of this garden may account for their new importance there later in the century.[31]

At the same time that the *boschetto* was growing in importance a change took place in the relationship between the spectator and the garden. The early Renaissance garden was primarily static and could be viewed in its entirety from a fixed point of view. To borrow from literary terminology, it had a unity of space and time. The gardens after the 1520s consisted of a series of successive spaces, isolated from each other physically and visually. They could only be experienced through movement, and the relationship between spectator and garden became active rather than passive. The arrangement of terraces at Castello (Fig. 66), the planting, and the position of the connections between the terraces called for movement from one space to another and from one level to another, as did the succession of courtyards at the Villa Giulia (Fig. 70). Pratolino, with its series of fountains, statue groups, grottoes, and pools suggests an itinerary was planned by which a theme could be revealed in a succession of episodes (Fig. 68). It might be termed a form of narrative with continuity provided by the spectator confronting different experiences in succession.

Precedents for the existence of groves and other naturalistic elements, for gardens arranged in series of spaces, and even for smaller details such as animal groups in groves existed in antiquity. Pliny the Younger described at his villa in Tusci a meadow near a circular walled garden which "owes as many beauties to nature, as all I have been describing within (i.e., the walled garden) does to art."[32] In the hippodrome garden, also at Tusci, some parts were planted formally, but "on a sudden in the midst of the elegant regularity you are surprised with an imitation of the negligent beauties of rural nature."[33] Martial described a villa with "laurel groves, plane groves and airy pine groves, . . . on every side babbles the water of a stream."[34] In another epigram he speaks of the Agrippa park in the Campo Marzio: "Where figures of wild beasts adorn the plane grove is to be seen a she bear."[35]

This scanty factual evidence, however, was supplemented by one of the most popular and enduring literary themes, that of garden and landscape description. In antiquity such descriptions were found not only in epic poetry but also in a separate genre, the rhetorical set piece developed from the *argumentum a loco* and the eulogistic descriptions

[31] See n. 19.

[32] Pliny, *Epistles*, 5.6, trans. M. Melworth and W. Hutchinson, Loeb Classical Library, New York, 1915, 383.

[33] Ibid., 339.

[34] Martial, *Epigrams*, 12.50, trans. W. Ker, Loeb Classical Library, New York, 1929, 353–54.

[35] Ibid., 3.19, trans. 175. The epigram describes a child playing in the grove who puts his hand in the bear's mouth, "but an accursed viper lay hid in the dark cavern of the bronze, alive with a life more deadly than that of the beast itself. The boy perceived not the guile but when he felt the fang and died. Oh, what a crime was this that unreal was the bear."

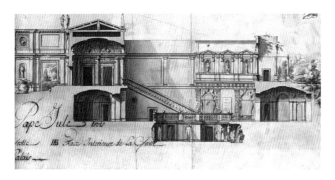

70. Villa Giulia, longitudinal section of courtyards, detail of Fig. 9, Rome, Museo di Villa Giulia (photo: Gabinetto Fotografico Nazionale)

71. Villa Pio da Carpi, Rome, relief of shepherd from nymphaeum, engraving by J. J. Boissard (photo: Biblioteca Apostolica Vaticana)

72. Villa Pio da Carpi, Rome, grotto and sleeping nymph of nymphaeum, engraving by G. Giacomo de Rossi (photo: Archivio Capitolino di San Pietro)

73. Villa Pio da Carpi, Rome, Amor with bird from nymphaeum, drawing by P. Jacques (photo: Deutsches Archäologisches Institut)

of rhetorical exposition. In addition, pastoral poetry provided further literary models of descriptive imagery.[36]

For the Renaissance these various literary genres provided specific themes associated with both gardens and natural landscape. In one group can be placed subjects with associations of pleasure, perfection, and nostalgia. Gardens or meadows were often used to symbolize an idyllic place, remote in time or place, such as the Blessed Isles (sometimes identified with the Garden of the Hesperides), the Elysian Fields, and the conflation of both with the concept of the Golden Age.[37] Homer's description of the Elysian Fields sets the tone for the other worldly perfection of this garden-like place.

> Snowfall is never known there nor long frost of winter, nor torrential rain, but only mild and lulling airs from the ocean bearing refreshment for the souls of man.[38]

Virgil's description of Elysium reaffirms the idyllic note.

> To joyous sites they came and lovely lawns, blest seats in woods which no misfortune scathes; fields clothed in ampler air, bathed in new light, purple—their own sun shades it, their own stars.[39]

More specific details are given for another type of garden, the Garden of Love described by Claudian.

> The mountain's height slopes down into a plain that golden hedge encircles guarding its meadows with a yellow metal. Fair is the enclosed country, ever bright with flowers. . . . Afar shines and glitters the goddess' many coloured palace, green gleaming by reason of the encircling globe. . . . In the midst is a courtyard rich with fragrant flowers that yields a harvest of perfume.[40]

Here the luxury of Venus' dwelling is enhanced by the luxuriance of the natural surroundings.

[36] E. R. Curtius, *European Literature and the Latin Middle Ages,* trans. W. Trask, New York, 1963, 193–94.

[37] Much of the discussion that follows is based on A. Giamatti, *The Earthly Paradise and the Renaissance Epic,* Princeton, 1966. For concepts of paradise, Elysian fields, and the Golden Age, see pp. 11–47. H. Levin, *The Myth of the Golden Age in the Renaissance,* Bloomington, 1969, deals primarily with English literature, but see pp. 3–24 for a discussion of the literary background.

[38] Homer, *Odyssey,* 4.564–68, trans. R. Fitzgerald, Garden City, N.Y., 1961, 81.

[39] Virgil, *Aeneid,* 6.637–41, trans. J. W. McKail, Modern Library, New York, 1950, 120. All further quotations are from this translation.

[40] *Epithalamium de Nuptiis Honori Augusti,* 56, trans. M. Platnauer, Loeb Classical Library, New York, 1922, 247–48.

In contrast, pastoral life was celebrated in Virgil's eclogues, and a nostalgia expressed for the simpler pleasures of rural existence.

> Tityrus, thou where thou liest under the covert of spreading beech, broodest on thy slim pipe over the Muse of the woodland: we leave our native borders and pleasant fields; we fly our native land, while thou, Tityrus, at ease in the shade teachest the woods to echo fair Amaryllus.

This eclogue closes,

> Never hereafter shall I, stretched in a green cave see you afar hanging from the tufted rock: no song shall I sing.[41]

In a less nostalgic mood Horace wrote of the pleasures of country life.

> Tis pleasant, now to lie beneath some ancient ilex tree, now on the matted turf. Meanwhile the rills glide between their high banks; birds warble in the woods; the fountains plash with their flowing waters.[42]

Another tradition emphasized the dangers and temptations of nature symbolized by the deceits and temptations of the enchanted garden of Circe, the frightful wood in which she transformed Picus into a bird, or the marshes of the Stymphalian birds.[43]

Thus, established literary forms brought to the Renaissance a climate of allusion and of associations with the yearning for the perfections of the Golden Age, the brilliant luxury of the gardens of the gods, or the nostalgic simplicity of pastoral life. Alternatively, nature could threaten through its innate savagery or through the temptations of earthly passions. This imagery and allegory cast a poetic veil over the Renaissance perception of nature, especially as it pertained to gardens and the natural landscape.

Landscape description inherited from antiquity reappeared in Renaissance litera-

[41] Virgil, *Eclogues*, 1.1–5, 1.75–76, trans. 265–67.

[42] Horace, *Epodes*, 2.23–28, trans. C. E. Bennett, Loeb Classical Library, New York, 1914, 367.

[43] For instance, the description of Circe's enchantment of a wood. "The woods, wonderful to say, leaped from their place, the ground rumbled, the neighboring trees turned white, and the herbage where her poisons fell was stained with clots of blood. The stones also seemed to voice hoarse bellowings, the bayings of a dog was heard, the ground was foul with dark, crawling things, and the thin shades of the silent dead seemed to be flitting about. . . . She touched the frightened wondering faces with her magic wand, and at the touch, horrid beastlike forms of many shapes came upon the youths. . . ." Ovid, *Metamorphoses*, 14.406–15, trans. F. Miller, Loeb Classical Library, New York, 1951, 325.

ture, especially in the epic poetry of the late fifteenth and of the sixteenth centuries.[44] The ancient theme of the vicissitudes of the wandering hero was transformed by the inheritance from medieval secular poetry into the tribulations of the knight on a quest.[45] With the transformed protagonist, gardens and landscapes came to assume a new role. In antiquity the various types of landscapes or gardens had served as a backdrop or setting, isolated as a description, in which the action took place. Interaction between setting and deed did not occur. Also in the Middle Ages the garden is most often the spot where people assembled to hear tales of action. For instance, in the Decameron a group of young people "went out to a lawn of thick green grass entirely shaded from the sun. A soft breeze came to them there." The queen made them sit down in a circle on the grass, commanding them to tell their tales since "to walk around at this hour would be foolish."[46]

Starting in the fifteenth century with Boiardo's *Orlando Innamorato* and Colonna's *Hypnerotomachia polifili,* landscape and garden began to play an active role in the furthering of the action and the exposition of the narrative.[47] By the second decade of the sixteenth century elements of nature had even been given a speaking role. In the *Orlando Furioso,* Ruggiero, arriving at Alcina's island, ties his steed to a myrtle. Suddenly the bush begins to speak; it is Astolfo, a knight transformed by Alcina into a plant.[48] A more important example of interaction between narrative and landscape occurs in the description of Ruggiero's life with Alcina. Their time was spent

> often in banquets—they were always festive—in tournaments, plays, in bathing, in dancing. Now close to the fountains, in the shade of the arbors, this amorous couple read from the classics. Now they go hunting the trembling hares through shadowy valleys and brightly lit hills. Now the trained dogs make the foolish pheasants spring screaming from pastures and thickets. Now they trap thrushes by the fragrant junipers.[49]

In each case the action of the protagonists is linked with the landscape.

The center of the revival of epic poetry with its extended landscape descriptions and its new emphasis on the relationship between action and setting was the court of Ferrara. Boiardo, Bernardo Tasso, and Ariosto were officials, Torquato Tasso was supported as

[44] Giamatti, *Earthly Paradise,* chaps. 3, 4.

[45] See P. Rajna, *Le fonti dell'Orlando Furioso,* 2nd ed., Florence, 1900, 141–63, and V. Vivaldi, *Sulle fonti della Gerusalemme Liberata,* 2nd ed., Turin, 1901.

[46] *The Decameron of Giovanni Boccaccio,* trans. J. Payn, New York, 1930, 29.

[47] Boiardo, *Orlando Innamorata,* ed. prin., Venice, 1505, but completed by 1500, and F. Colonna, *Hypnerotomachia polifili,* Venice, 1499. See, for example, in the second book the scene of the two maidens murdered in a wood, where the wood itself ("uno agreste Nemore, arbusto, & umbrifico bosco, di proceri & vasti arbori consito, & silvestrato, di horridi spini luco . . .") frightens the hero even before he hears the maidens' cries.

[48] Ariosto, *Orlando Furioso,* VI, 26–28.

[49] Ibid., 31–32, translation of the author.

court poet.[50] It is probably no coincidence that two of the scholars responsible for the development of the Renaissance theory of poetics, Giraldi and Scaliger, were also at the Ferrarese court.[51]

Thus the practice of using groves and other natural landscape forms developed in the center where a revival of ancient epic and pastoral poetry and drama was taking place. Themes or *topoi* from literary sources provided the general mood evoking either the pastoral, such as the Villa Mattei's grove with its shepherd and sheep, or thoughts of the Golden Age or Garden of the Hesperides in the wandering paths of the Villa Giulia, or the park of the Ferrarese Belvedere.

The literate visitor to these gardens had these references in mind. A description of the Cesi villa, formerly on the ramparts above the Porta Cavalleggieri, called it a *locus amoenus*. Aldrovandi termed the Carpi villa a *paradiso terrestre*. Vasari called the murals of bacchantes, satyrs, and fauns in the garden of the Archbishop of Cyprus "diverse poesie."[52]

But one must go deeper than this to understand the significance of the *boschetto* and the irregular paths and plantings. Pliny gives the key in his description of the juxtaposition of the formal and informal areas in his garden. A meadow owes as many beauties to nature as the formal gardens to art. In the midst of the formal planting in the hippodrome garden one is surprised with an "imitation of the negligent beauties of rural nature."[53] The same contrast occurs frequently in descriptions of Renaissance gardens. Taegio, for instance, in describing Scipione Simonetta's garden in Milan, in 1559, says: "Here art and nature, at times in rivalry show their utmost in contests; at times joined, united and reconciled together, they create stupendous things."[54] The humanist and scholar Claudio Tolomei, in a letter of 1543, described his pleasure in a fountain in the garden of a Signor Agapito. The fountain demonstrates, he says,

> The ingenious skill, newly rediscovered to make fountains, such as used to be found in Rome, where art was so blended with nature that one could not discern whether the fountains were the product of the former or the latter. Thus some appeared to be a naturalistic artifice while others seemed an artifice of nature. In these times they endeavor to make a fountain appear made by nature itself, not by accident, but with a masterful artistry.[55]

[50] For the positions of Boiardo, Ariosto, and the Tassos, see E. G. Gardner, *Dukes and Poets in Ferrara*, London, 1904.

[51] For their role, see J. E. Spingarn, *A History of Literary Criticism in the Renaissance*, New York, 1899, 3–59, and V. Hale, Jr., "Renaissance Poetics," *Encyclopedia of Poetry and Poetics*, ed. Preminger, 690–95. A stimulating resumé of court life at Ferrara and the interconnections between courtiers, artists, and poets is to be found in F. Gibbons, *Dosso and Battista Dossi*, Princeton, 1968, 3–23.

[52] Description of the Villa Cesi, written before 1550 by Martin Waescapple, published in Huelsen, *Antikengärten*, 36–37, and see Aldrovandi, *Statue di Roma*, 289. Vasari's description of the Archbishop of Cyprus' garden in *Vite*, V, 597.

[53] See p. 99, and nn. 32–33.

[54] B. Taegio, *La villa: Un dialogo*, Milan, 1559, 102.

[55] Letter to G. B. Grimaldi, dated 26 July 1543, published in *Delle lettere di M. Claudio Tolomei*, Venice, 1550, 41–43: ". . . l'ingegnosa artifizio nuovamente ritrovato di far le fonti, il qual già si vede usato in più

The paradox of art created from nature itself, as a garden was, was expressed in Tasso's description of Armida's garden:

> So with the rude the polished mingled was
> That natural seemed all and ev'ry part;
> Nature would Craft in counterfeiting pass,
> And imitate her imitator, Art.[56]

The paradox was heightened by the contrast; formal gardens created from the materials of nature and natural settings created by the skill of the designer. Order was created out of disorder, which was to be feared. Taegio said that the country villa was cultivated to contrast with the dangers of untamed nature, "le quali quantunque senza horrore rare volte reguardar si possano."[57]

The *boschetti* and the rustic elements present in gardens should be seen then not only as a generalized imitation of literary *topoi,* the grove, the wild wood, etc., and as an evocation of mood, nostalgia, luxury, or fear, but also as a constant reminder of an intellectual and philosophical concern: the role of man in the world of nature, and the creation of order from chaos.[58]

The process of the conversion of the literary *topos* into a garden form may be followed in even greater detail in a type of nymphaeum, a grotto with statues and a fountain, that became prevalent in Rome in the sixteenth century. Early sixteenth-century nymphaea, such as Bramante's at Genazzano or in the Belvedere, were architectural and formal.[59] There was no evocation of a natural grotto, nor is it clear that they were decorated with statues. In contrast, a number of nymphaea of the 1540s, 1550s, and 1560s seem to evoke a natural grotto as well as the *topos* of the cave of the nymphs.[60] In the Carpi villa on the Quirinal there was a nymphaeum in a courtyard, now destroyed but described in detail by Aldrovandi in 1550.[61] It was a small rectangular chamber with a

---

luoghi in Roma, ove mescolando l'arte cò la natura, non si sa discernare s'ella è opera di questa or di quella; anzi hor altrui pare un naturale artifizio, e hora una artifiziosa natura: in tal modo s'ingegnano in questi tempi rassembrare una fonte, che da l'istessa natura, non a caso, ma cò maestrevol arte sia fatta." I am grateful to Dr. Wolfgang Lotz for calling this letter to my attention. See W. Lotz, *Architecture in Italy, 1400 to 1600,* trans. M. Hottinger, Harmondsworth, 1974. This quotation is also discussed in "L'Ingegnoso Artifizio," 57.

[56] The translation by E. Fairfax, *Jerusalem Delivered,* London, 1749, from *Gerusalemme Liberata,* Canto XVI, 10: "Stimi (si misto il culto è co'l negletto) / sol naturali e gli ornamenti e i siti / Di natura arte che per diletto / l'imitatrice sua scherzando imiti."

[57] Taegio, *La Villa,* 115.

[58] For a fuller discussion, see E. W. Taylor, *Nature and Art in Renaissance Literature,* New York, 1964.

[59] The nymphaeum at Genazzano has been attributed to Bramante by C. Frommel, "Bramantes 'Ninfeo' in Genazzano," *Römisches Jahrbuch für Kunstgeschichte* 12 (1969), 137–60. For the nymphaeum at the Belvedere, see Ackerman, *Belvedere,* 24–25.

[60] Homer's description of a cave of the nymphs on Ithaca (*Odyssey,* 13.104–12) is the start of the *topos.* See B. Tamm, "Auditorium and Palace," *Stockholm Studies in Classical Archaeology* 2 (1965), 168–79, and J. des Gagniers, P. Devamberg, et al., *Laodicée du Lycos: Le Nymphée: Campagnes 1961–63,* Quebec, 1969, 137–67, for the grotto in antiquity and other examples of the literary *topos.*

[61] See n. 17.

loggia in front. Over the door was a relief of a seated shepherd with the inscription, "At secura quies et nescia fallere vitae" (Fig. 71). At the far end of the nymphaeum the figure of a sleeping nymph in a rocky grotto was placed over the fountain basin (Fig. 72), and on the sides of the basin were two reclining putti holding aquatic birds whose beaks spouted water (Fig. 73). On either side of the fountain were statues of a faun and a water nymph, the former with a goatskin flask, the latter with a vase. At the entrance to the chamber was a statue of Hercules, holding the apples of the Garden of the Hesperides.[62]

The inscription over the entrance to the nymphaeum is a quotation from Virgil's *Georgics* in a passage praising country life. Although the country man is deprived of the luxuries of the city,

> yet theirs is a repose without care and a life that knows no fraud, but is rich in treasures manifold. Yea, the ease of broad domain, caverns and living lakes and cool vales; the lowing of the kine and soft slumbers beneath the trees—all are theirs.[63]

The nymphaeum, then, is an evocation of the pastoral life with the key to its meaning given by the inscription over the entrance. Presided over by rustic figures, the theme of repose without care was echoed by the sleeping nymph fountain. It, in fact, was a version of one of the most common fountain types of the first half of the sixteenth century, a type which had its origins in a supposedly ancient fountain described by Michael Fabricius Ferrarius in the late fifteenth century.[64] He wrote of a grotto with a statue of a sleeping nymph found in Hungary and with an accompanying inscription that has been translated: "Nymph of the Grot, these sacred springs I keep and to the murmur of these waters sleep. Ah, spare my slumbers, gently tread the cave; and drink in silence or in silence lave."[65]

Aldrovandi breaks off in the middle of his description of the Carpi nymphaeum to exclaim that Carpi's villa is an earthly paradise—nothing is lacking that would make it more perfect.[66] He continues that the most perfect part of the villa is the fountain in the

---

[62] Aldrovandi, *Statue di Roma*, 288–89.

[63] Identified by Huelsen, *Antikengärten*, 57; the line is from the *Georgics*, 2.467–70, trans. 320–21.

[64] For sleeping nymph fountains and the history of the inscription, see O. Kurz, "*Huius nympha loci:* A Pseudo-Classical Inscription and a Drawing by Dürer," *Journal of the Warburg and Courtauld Institutes* 16 (1953), 171–77. See now H. Brummer, *The Statue Court in the Vatican Belvedere*, Acta Universitatis Stockholmiensis. Stockholm Studies in the History of Art 20, Stockholm, 1970, 168–84.

[65]   "Huius Nympha loci, sacri, custodia fontis
Dormio, dum blandae sentio murmur aquae,
Parce meum, quisquis tangis cava marmora somnum
Rumpere, seu bibas, sive lavere, tace."

CIL, VI, 5, 3*e. Pope's translation is found in a letter to Edward Blount of June 1725, quoted in Malins, *English Landscaping*, 35. See "Sleeping Nymph," 37–43.

[66] "Ma quella che avanza ogni meraviglia, è questa artificiosa e piacevolissima fontana, fatta in questa sua grotta con tant'arte e modo, che non si può maggiore amenità ne diporto per un spirto gentile e sciolto dalle passioni volgari, desiderare," Aldrovandi, *Statue di Roma*, 300.

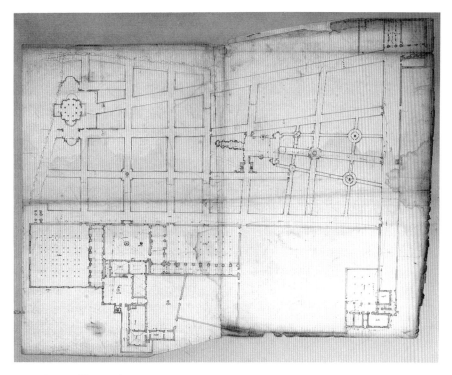

74. D'Este villa on the Quirinal, Rome, plan after 1561, New York, Metropolitan
Museum of Art, no. 49.92.8 (gift of Janos Scholz and Mrs. Anne Bigelow
Scholz in memory of Walter Bigelow Rosen)

nymphaeum. Perfectly suited for a gentle soul freed from vulgar passions ("sciolto dalle
passione volgare"), it reveals to the world a shadow of heaven's repose.[67]

The nymphaeum was more than an evocation of the simple pleasures of rural life.
It was intended to remind the viewer of the more perfect world of the Golden Age,
symbolized by the statue of Hercules with the apples of the Garden of the Hesperides.

Another nymphaeum, more fully incorporated into a garden setting, was a less literal representation of an ancient text. At the d'Este villa on the Quirinal, one of the
nymphaea was in the middle of a large *boschetto* (Figs. 10, 74).[68] A U-shaped grotto terminated in a rocky mount about twelve feet high on which lay the figure of a shepherd
pouring water from his flask. Below him sat a Venus with two Erotes, while the pool of
the fountain held another Eros with a swan. The rocky sides of the grotto had niches
with child satyrs holding vases on their heads. A forecourt with ivy covered trelliswork
niches held more statues, and the entire complex was entered by a gate flanked by two
statues of Muses.[69]

---

[67] ". . . poi che mostra al mondo un' ombra de' riposi del cielo"; ibid.

[68] See n. 18.

[69] A description by German architect Heinrich Schickhardt (Stuttgart, Landesbibl. cod. hist. Q 148,
24v–26r), published by Huelsen, *Antikengärten*, 121–22, says in part, "Es hat auch ein wilden gemachten
Berg ungever uff 12 oder 14 sch[u] hoch, geht zu 3 zeiten herum, hin den sitzt ein Weibsbild. . . . Es felt das
Wasser an allen Orten mit grosem Rauschen über die Felsen ab."

A grove or grotto of Venus was represented, corresponding in many details to a passage in Claudian's *Epithalamium . . . Palladio . . .* :

> It chanced that Venus had one day retired into a cave overgrown with vines to woo sleep amid its alluring cool, and had laid her goddess limbs on the thick grass, her head upon a heap of flowers. The vine branches stir gently in the breeze. . . . Round her lie too the nymphs of Ida and hard by beneath a lofty oak tree the three Graces sleep with interlaced arms, while the other trees swarm with amorini at play.[70]

A second nymphaeum at the d'Este villa was built into the substructure of the palace. A vaulted room with a semicircular apse contained a fountain with a statue of Apollo; on the sides were the statues of eight Muses.[71] In front of the grotto was a grove of trees visible in the Maggi view of 1612 (Fig. 64).[72] The whole was intended as a replica of an ancient sanctuary dedicated to the Muses. It also recalls Virgil's fourth eclogue invoking the Muses of Sicily and a time when "thine own Apollo reigns."[73] Again, as in the Carpi nymphaeum, a second level of meaning was involved. Sanctuaries of the Muses evoked contemplation of philosophy, for Pausanias had described Plato's Academy meeting in a grove with an altar dedicated to the Muses, and Aristotle taught Alexander in another such sanctuary.[74] The totality of knowledge was recalled here too, for in antiquity the Muses were the origins of all knowledge. Virgil, in a passage in the *Georgics*, invoked the Muses to,

> . . . show me the pathways of the sky, the stars, and the diverse eclipses of the sun and the moon's travails; whence is the earthquake; by what force the seas swell high . . . why winter suns so hasten to dip in Ocean, or what hindrance keeps back the lingering nights.[75]

Cicero said to live with the Muses is to live with education and refinement.[76]

Most of the nymphaea with figures of sleeping nymphs were associated with poetic creation. The Muses were thought to be water nymphs because of their association with the spring of Hippocrene, literally the source of poetry, on Mt. Helicon.[77] Nowhere is this association more beautifully expressed than in a Greek epigram from the Palatine Anthology:

---

[70] Claudian, *Epithalamium dictum Palladio . . .* , lines 1–25, trans. M. Platnauer, Loeb Classical Library, New York, 1922, II, 205, as *Carminum Minorum Corpusculorum*, XXV (XXX, XXXI).

[71] Huelsen, *Antikengärten*, 103–4.

[72] Published by L. Dami, "Il giardino Quirinale ai primi del' 1600," *Bollettino d'arte* 13 (1919), 113–16.

[73] *Eclogues*, 4.1–10.

[74] Plato's Academy is described by Pausanias 1.30.2. Aristotle's grotto in Plutarch, *Lives*, Alexander, 7.3.

[75] *Georgics*, 2.475–83, trans. 321.

[76] "Quis est omnium, qui modo cum Musis, id est cum humanitate et doctrina, habeat aliquod commercium, qui se non hunc mathematicum malit quam illum tyrannum," Cicero, *Tusculanae disputationes*, 5.23, 66, quoted in Curtius, *European Literature*, 228.

[77] For literary references to the Muses, see Curtius, *European Literature*, 228–46, and G. Roux, "Le val des muses et les musées chez les auteurs anciens," *Bulletin de correspondance hellénique* 78 (1954), 22–48. For Muses as nymphs, see Pauly-Wissowa, XVI, 1, 692–93.

Pour for me, Muses, a draught of clear delightful song, the rain of Heliconian melody sweetened by your lips. For all, for whom is shed the drink of the fountain that gives birth to poets, delight in the clear song of your verse.[78]

An example of the association of sleeping nymph fountains and poetry occurred in the German humanist Goritz's garden at the foot of the Capitoline. A small grotto there contained a sleeping nymph fountain with an inscription derived from the poem already quoted: "Nymphae Loci, Bibe, Lava, Tace."[79] Poetry contests were held there, and the competing verses were attached to an altar set up near the nymph. These competitions recall the contests held at the nearby Temple of Hercules Musarum in antiquity, where enthusiasm was frequently so great that the sound of poetry being declaimed could be heard beyond the sanctuary walls.[80]

These various nymphaea provide perfect examples of the interwoven themes and sources characteristic of the creation of gardens and their decorations in the sixteenth century. Each conformed to a specific literary theme, and the basic composition came close to being a replica of a specific text. This might be called the *Inventio*, that is, the choice of subject matter.[81] Specific factual information from antiquity, however, provided both the justification for and the prototypes of the physical appearance. In the case of the Apollo and the Muses grotto at the d'Este villa, the architecture was close to the Canopus at the Villa of Hadrian in Tivoli.[82] The Venus grotto was similar to descriptions of grottoes by Pliny the Elder,[83] and also conformed to the description of a surviving nymphaeum at Lago Albano, which the anonymous artist of the Codex Destailleur said was "ornamented with shells, pumice, and pebbles set in mosaic. The sides of the small niche had a perpetual spallier of ferns, the fronds of which dripped with purest water" (Fig. 75).[84]

Arrangements of groups of statues as garden decoration were known to have existed in antiquity. Many sculpture groups discovered in the early sixteenth century were found on the site of ancient gardens, among them several groups of Muses.[85] Thus the architectural and decorative forms were copied after antiquity—*Emulatio*.[86]

---

[78] Declamatory epigram 364 by Nestor of Laranda, trans. W. R. Paton, Loeb Classical Library, New York, 1917, 199.

[79] Goritz's garden is described by D. Gnoli, "Orti letterari nella Roma di Leo X," *Nuova Antologia*, ser. 7, 269 (1930), 137–40.

[80] B. Tamm, "Le Temple des Muses à Rome," *Opuscula Romana* 3 (1961), 157–67.

[81] Lee, "Ut Pictura Poesis," 210–11.

[82] N. Neuerburg, *L'architettura delle fontane e dei ninfei nell'Italia antica*, Memorie dell'Accademia di archaeologia lettere e belle arti di Napoli 5, Naples, 1965, 53–59, and figs. 81, 82.

[83] Pliny, *Natural History*, 31.20.

[84] St. Petersburg, Hermitage, Codex Destailleur A, fol. 22. Half of this nymphaeum with the description also appears in Destailleur B, fol. 20.

[85] The most famous of the ancient groups, the Laocoon was found in the Domus Aurea but was thought to have been moved there from one of the imperial gardens. The Niobid group was excavated in 1583 on the site of the Horti Lamiani, and at least one of the several groups of Muses discovered in the Renaissance came from Hadrian's villa in Tivoli, see H. von Huebner, *Römische Funde*, Berlin, 1960, 17–27.

[86] Lee, "Ut Pictura Poesis," 205–7.

75. Nymphaeum at Albano, drawing from Codex
Destailleur B, fol. 20, St. Petersburg,
Hermitage
(photo: Deutsches Archäologisches Institut)

Yet the artist by his combination of themes went beyond the literal representation of a literary *topos* to create a more complicated image, evoking wider associations and deeper implications—the Garden of the Hesperides as the shadow of the repose of Heaven, the sanctuary of the Muses as the source of poetry and of humanist education. In this lies the exercise in part of *Dispositio,* that is, the arrangement or composition, and in part of *Expressio,* the devices by which the spectator was brought to respond to the work of art. Ultimately the spectator was carried beyond the initial sensual pleasure to an edifying and uplifting contemplation of philosophy and life.[87]

Thus the precepts of the *ars poetica* were adapted to an *ars hortulorum,* and Horace's "ut pictura poesis" became *ut poesia hortis.*

Yet a word of caution is necessary. The principles discussed and the literary imagery interpreted provide the general framework by which garden forms and decorations can be interpreted. Beyond this primary level, however, one can be sure there were specific programs with allegorical references to ideas and events connected with the patron. To return once more to d'Este's nymphaeum of Apollo and the Muses, the inventory of 1568 describes the Apollo as a seated figure with a harp, the conventional image of an Apollo Musagetes.[88] But he also held an axe, and the pedestal was inscribed "Secur. Tenedia." Huelsen has identified this as a passage from Cicero referring to an obscure

[87] Ibid., 218–20.
[88] Huelsen, *Antikengärten,* 103. For Apollo Musagetes, see Pauly-Wissowa, I, 1, 453ff.

Greek hero, Tenes.[89] It refers specifically to the Tenedian axe, a term used in antiquity for a hasty and ill-considered action. Tenes used an axe to cut a rope mooring his father's ship to a dock, thus condemning his father to a death at sea.[90]

Without venturing into a morass of Oedipal fantasy, one cannot avoid the supposition that some personal allegory is represented here, one that I am unable to interpret. So I will echo the description of the pastoral intermezzi at a performance of Plautus' *Captives*: "Such was the performance, novel in its contrivance; I have described the outer shell; the kernel of the nut and the allegorical meaning I will leave to you to interpret."[91]

[89] Cicero, *Ad. Frat. Q.*, II, 11, 2.
[90] W. R. Halliday, "Tenes," *Classical Quarterly* 21 (1927), 37–44.
[91] Letter of Floriano Dulfo to the Duke of Mantua, dated 8 July 1496, published by A. d'Ancona, *Origini del teatro italiano,* 2nd ed., Turin, 1891, II, 372.

Imitation and Invention:
Language and Decoration in
Roman Renaissance Gardens

In an earlier essay on this subject, I explained that my conclusions were only a preface to an introduction to a prolegomenon to sixteenth-century garden iconography and literary theory.[1] This paper represents the results of more than a decade of further study and thought and both expands on and, in some ways, alters the earlier study. Specifically, I was and am concerned with examining the influence of literature on garden decorations in sixteenth-century Rome and in tracing the way literary and art theory governed the selection of subject matter and the iconographical programs of these decorations. The previous discussion centered on the presence of groves or *boschetti* and the significance of some grottoes in gardens in sixteenth-century Rome. Here I shall discuss the use of statuary and relief sculpture and their role in several Roman gardens.

The patrons of these gardens had factual information about the design of ancient gardens derived from literary sources, such as Pliny the Younger's descriptions of his villas at Tusci and Laurentum,[2] as well as from the remains of the imperial villas in and near Rome. The ways in which they used their villas, and their ideas of what villa life should be, derived from the ancient concept of *otium* and *villeggiatura*.[3] Descriptions of their villas or laudatory poems about them derived from Latin and Greek prototypes,[4]

[1] See "Ars Hortulorum," 89–111.

[2] Pliny, *Epistles,* 2.7; 5.6. Earlier discussions of these letters include H. Tanzer, *The Villas of Pliny the Younger,* New York, 1924; D. Coffin, *The Villa in the Life of Renaissance Rome,* Princeton, 1979, passim.

[3] Ibid., Part 1.

[4] Raphael's letter describing the Villa Madama not only follows the format of ancient descriptive texts but uses Latin words for the directions of the winds and for parts of the villa for which an adequate Italian vocabulary existed, e.g., "dietae," "cryptoporticus," etc. Published by P. Foster, "Raphael on the Villa Madama: The Text of a Lost Letter," *Römisches Jahrbuch für Kunstgeschichte* 11 (1967–68), 308–12. For further reference to parallels between Raphael's letter and Pliny's description of his villas, see now J. Shearman, "A Functional Interpretation of Villa Madama," *Römisches Jahrbuch für Kunstgeschichte* 20 (1983), 313–28. Egidio Gallo's poetic description of Agostino Chigi's villa, the present Farnesina, in which an elaborate *concetto* of a visit by Venus to the garden is the vehicle for its description, is clearly modeled on such ancient prototypes

while their imaginations peopled their groves and gardens with the deities of ancient mythology and the rustics of pastoral poetry.[5]

Despite the rich variety of information surviving from antiquity, little was known about the decorations of ancient gardens. Statues were known to have been used, from sources such as Pliny the Elder's chapters on stone in his *Natural History*,[6] and his evidence was corroborated by the many discoveries of statues at ancient villa sites.[7] Less was known about fountains or painted decorations.[8] Thus the nature and form of decorations in sixteenth-century gardens are more of an invention, less reliant on ancient prototypes than were their design or their owner's attitude toward them.

The decorations consisted almost entirely of statues and fountains. Structures, such as the pavilions and follies found in eighteenth-century landscape parks, were rare, and it was even rarer for them to have content. An exception would be the two pavilions at Villa Lante called the *Mansiones musarum*, which clearly are significant in the iconographical program.[9] Plants which we consider the chief ornament of gardens today played a minor role as a physical ornament, and there is little evidence that they were allegorized.[10]

Paintings, for obvious reasons, were also rare; there is evidence, however, for a cycle of painted decorations in a pavilion in the del Bufalo garden and in the garden of the Archbishop of Cyprus, both in Rome. The former consisted of three scenes from the Perseus legend and a Parnassus with Pegasus and the Muses.[11] The latter Vasari described as "storie di baccanti, di satiri, e di fauni, e di cose selvagge," chosen to go with an ancient statue of Bacchus seated on a tiger.[12]

---

as Claudian's *Epithalamium dictum Palladio* . . . Gallo's poem (Rome, 1511) is reprinted inpart by C. Frommel, *Die Farnesina und Peruzzis Architektonisches Frühwerk*, Berlin, 1961, 42.

[5] For instance, a description of a pond at a d'Este villa, the Belvedere, in Ferrara, reads "Here Diana rests from the fatigue of war . . . , the Dryads come to recover from their labors and bathe their virgin limbs. Even Pan, tired of the thick forests, comes and stretches out . . . ." Scipione Balbo Finalese, *Pulcher Visus Calliopsis Divi Alphonsi Ferrariensium Ducis*, ed. G. B. Phaellus, Bologna, 1531. I have translated from the Italian translation published by G. Pazzi, *Le "Delizie Estensi" e l'Ariosto*, Pescara Riviera, 1933, 45–46. For additional discussion of the infuence of Latin pastoral poetry on the Renaissance perception of gardens, see "Ars Hortulorum," 101–2.

[6] Pliny, *Natural History*, 36.20.

[7] The chief source of information on the discovery of ancient statues in Rome is P. G. Hübner, *Le statue di Roma*, Forschungen herausgegeben von der Bibliotheca Hertziana 2, Leipzig, 1912, but see the review of C. Huelsen, *Göttingische gelehrte Anzeigen* 176 (1914), 257–311.

[8] For a summary of Renaissance knowledge of ancient fountains and fountain figures, see "L'Ingegnoso Artifizio," 64–67. I cannot find evidence that paintings depicting gardens, such as have been found in Pompeii and Herculaneum, were known in the Renaissance.

[9] C. Lazzaro-Bruno, "The Villa Lante at Bagnaia: An Allegory of Art and Nature," *Art Bulletin* 59 (1977), 553–60.

[10] Candace Adelson has discovered (verbal communication) a Medici document in which plants in a garden are given allegorical significance. We do not know enough about plants actually used in the gardens of the period, but many associations were known from antiquity, such as the metamorphoses of Narcissus, Iris, and Hyacinth, the connection of the poppy with sleep, oaks with Jupiter, or grapevines with Bacchus. The argument against their use in iconographical programs has been "ex silentio."

[11] R. Kultzen, "Die Malereien Polidoros da Caravaggio im Giardino del Bufalo in Rom," *Mitteilungen des Kunsthistorisches Instituts in Florenz* 19 (1959–60), 99–120.

[12] G. Vasari, *Le vite de' più eccelenti pittori. . . .*, ed. Milanesi, V, Florence, 1878, 597.

Statues, which were the primary decoration, were used in varying ways during the century. In the first half of the century and especially in Rome, the garden was an outdoor museum for the display of a collection of antiquities; notable examples include the Cesi garden near the Vatican, the della Valle terrace garden in their town palace, and the d'Este, Medici, Mattei, and Giustiniani collections in their various villas in and outside Rome.[13] The statues were selected and displayed for their value as antiquities, a value not based on completeness or decorative arrangements (Figs. 17, 18).[14] Even in gardens primarily devoted to display, statues and reliefs were also used as decorations. Herms were placed at the four corners of each planting bed in the Cesi villa;[15] they lined the path from the lower to the upper garden at the Villa Giulia.[16] Starting in the 1530s statues were placed in niches as the terminus of a view, on pedestals in prominent locations, or assembled in groupings in fountains. However, with rare exceptions, elaborate decorative schemes did not appear until the 1540s and 1550s.[17]

These are the decades when reliefs also began to play a prominent role in the decorations of some gardens. The Villa Giulia, started in 1550, once had relief panels over the wall separating the first from the second courtyards (Fig. 76).[18] The lower register had *imprese* of Pope Julius II, and the upper had four reliefs of the four elements.[19] Venus and marine deities represented Water, Air was Juno with the winds, and Fire was represented as a scene of men sacrificing to the first fire, a tree struck by lightning. In an unusual use of biblical sources, Earth was personified as Eve with Cain and Abel. The center panel over the door to the next courtyard showed Hercules as a river god and a fleeing nymph, the virgin of the Aqua Vergine. Ammannati attributed the name of the latter to the fact that it flowed alongside the river Ercole without mixing with it. The

[13] Lists and inventories of the statue collections of the Cesi villa, Pio da Carpi villa and the d'Este villa on the Quirinal were published by C. Huelsen, *Römische Antikengärten des XVI. Jahrhunderts*, Akademie der Wissenschaften zu Heidelberg, Philosophisch-historische Klasse, Abhandlungen 4 (1917). Information about the Medici collection is in G. Andres, *The Villa Medici in Rome*, New York, 1976, with earlier bibliography. The inventory of the collection of Villa Mattei is published in R. Lanciani, *Storia degli scavi di Roma e notizie intorno le collezioni romane di Antichità*, III, Rome, 1902–12, 83–86. The only source of information on the collection at the Giustiniani villas is the set of illustrations of the statues in *Galleria Giustiniani del Marchese Vincenzo Giustiniani*, Rome, 1631.

[14] For a history of statuary display in Roman 16th-century gardens, see "Giardino all'Antico."

[15] Huelsen, *Antikengärten*, 19. They are visible in the detail of Dupérac's map of Rome of 1577 he publishes (Fig. 2).

[16] C. Huelsen, "Die Hermeninschriften berühmter Griechen und die ikonographischen Sammlungen des XVI. Jahrhunderts," *Mitteilungen des Deutschen Archäologischen Instituts. Römische Abteilung* 16 (1901), 11–75.

[17] The Belvedere Statue Court at the Vatican and the former della Valle terrace garden are notable exceptions of elaborate decorative schemes involving statues built before 1530.

[18] For a discussion of the drawings and their attribution, see "L'Ingegnoso Artifizio," 75, n. 57.

[19] The decorations are described by Ammannati in a letter to Marco Mantova Benavides dated 2 May 1555. A copy of the letter is preserved in Pesaro, Bibl. Oliveriana, cod. 374/II, fols. 91–96. It is published with emendations of spelling and punctuation by G. Balestra, *La fontana pubblica di Giulio III ed il palazzo di Pio IV sulla Via Flaminia*, Rome, 1911, 65ff. The description of the end wall of the first courtyard is as follows:

> Nella faccia in fronte . . . si vedano quattro colonne di misti, doi nere e doi di verde mischiate d'altri colori, . . . ; et quattro colonne di marmi venati . . . Et vi sono scolpiti le due imprese ch'erano di Papa Giulio la Giustizia et la Pace et la Fortuna, presa dall virtù per i cappelli, negli altri doi la Charità et la Religione. [In the] ordine di sopra . . . vi sono cinque quadri con fregetti et altri ornamenti . . . In quel di mezzo vi è un Hercole assiso in atto difiume, ed una feminina apresso in habito

76. Villa Giulia, rear wall of the
first courtyard, detail of Fig. 9,
Rome, Museo di Villa Giulia
(photo: Gabinetto Fotografico
Nazionale)

interior court also contained a relief representing the discovery of the source of the Aqua
Vergine by Roman soldiers, a story related by the ancient writer Frontinus in his history
of the aqueducts of Rome.[20]

A decade later elaborate reliefs were used to decorate the walls of the casino and
loggia of the *Giardino Secreto* of Pope Pius IV at the Vatican (started 1558). The casino
has the coat of arms of the pope and of eight of his cardinals. The loggia has reliefs of
Apollo with a lyre; he and the muses are seated on Mt. Helicon. The sides and rear of
the structure are decorated with scenes from ancient myths about water.[21]

An important difference existed between the painting cycles, the relief panels, and
the sculptural decorations. Painting cycles and reliefs, especially in the first third of the
century, tended to be literal depictions of the scene or event described in their literary
sources. Thus the Villa Giulia relief of the discovery of the Aqua Vergine is exactly as
Frontinus described it; the Perseus cycle at the Giardino del Bufalo is an accurate render-
ing of Ovid's recounting of the story.

In contrast, statue groups were not literal, although some groups from antiquity,

di vergine che fugge. Che dinota l'acqua della fontana secreta, . . . et chiamasi quest' acqua vergine,
perchè correndo col fiume Hercole, non si meschola co' lei. Gli altri quatro sono i quatro elementi;
per la terra é posto Eva et suoi figliuoli; per l'acqua Venere et Dei marini; per l'aria Giunone et altri
venti e cose d'aria per far ricca l'historia. Per il fuoco è posto il modo che dicano fu trovato il primo
fuoco; et è questo; un bosco d'alberi sbattuto dal vento, intorno al quale si vedono gente far sacrifici
ed altre cose ch' s'opera il fuoco.

[20] Frontinus, *De aquis urbis, Romae*, I, 10, Eng. trans. C. Bennett, London, 1925, 350.
[21] G. Smith, *The Casino of Pio IV*, Princeton, 1977, 31–53.

such as the Laocoon installed in the Belvedere Statue Court early in the century, or the Niobid group unearthed in the 1580s and displayed in the garden of the Villa Medici (Figs. 20, 30), were faithful representations of their written sources.[22]

In contrast, sixteenth-century groupings, whether of ancient or modern statues, were customarily assembled to create new scenes or narratives. For instance, at the Medici villa at Castello, near Florence, mountain personifications, river gods, the Four Seasons, Hercules and Antaeus, Venus, and busts of Medici ancestors were combined to create a statement about the power and virtues of Cosimo de Medici.[23] Near Turin, the Regio Parco, built for Carlo Emanuele I at the end of the century, was a *summa* of human knowledge and experience. Two of its paths represented the senses—with labyrinths, ditches, and precipitous inclines symbolizing their dangers—and the liberal arts. The second path was lined with statues of men in noble professions and of outstanding virtue and fame. A third path represented the "major studies" and was adorned with statues of lawmakers and poets whose work could guide one to Truth. The fourth was dedicated to the mathematical sciences and among other ornaments had globes, spheres, and figures holding mathematical instruments. The central, and longest, path was dedicated to theology. Along it were statues of priests and Greek and Latin inscriptions designed to induce the mind to contemplation of the Divine.[24]

Another difference existed between decorations of interiors of buildings and those of gardens. Scenes derived from biblical sources were common in the former, even in nonreligious settings such as audience halls, *saloni*, even bedchambers. Despite the abundance of literal and figurative garden and pastoral imagery in the Bible and in patristic writings, overt or allegorical Christian themes rarely appeared in secular gardens.[25]

The explanation is to be found in the Renaissance theory of decorum or appropriateness. *Decoro* prescribed subject matter and style according to the location and function of the work of art. Thus city styles and rustic could be differentiated, and places for state occasions were distinct from those for recreation.[26] *Istorie*, that is, some mythological and most historical (including biblical) scenes, were appropriate for city and state occasions; pastoral and rustic scenes were appropriate for the country, the garden, and for recreation.[27]

[22] H. Brummer, *The Statue Court in the Vatican Belvedere*, Acta Universitatis Stockholmiensis. Stockholm Studies in the History of Art 20, Stockholm, 1970, 73–119. For the Niobid group, see now G. A. Mansuelli, *Galleria degli Uffizi: Le sculture*, Rome, 1958, 101–9.

[23] D. Wright, "The Villa Medici at Olmo a Castello: Its History and Iconography," Ph.D. diss., Princeton University, 1976, 286–342.

[24] A. Scotti, "Giardini fiorentini e torinesi fra '500 e '600. Loro struttura e significato," *L'Arte*, n.s. 6 (1969), 47.

[25] An exception is the Papacqua fountain in the Madruzzo palace in Soriano nel Cimino. One wall has a reclining female satyr and other mythological figures, but the second wall is a representation of the biblical scene of Moses striking the Rock. See M. Festa Milone, "Il Casino del Cardinale Madruzzo a Soriano nel Cimino," *Quaderni dell'Istituto di Storia dell'Architettura* 17–19 (1970–72), 71–94.

[26] A useful discussion of the concept of *decoro* appears in P. Barocchi's critical note and comment on G. Andrea Gilio, *Dialogo nel quale s' ragiona degli errori e degli abusi de' Pittori circa l'istorie*, Camerino, 1564, in *Trattati d'arte del cinquecento fra manierismo e controriforma*, ed. P. Barocchi, III, Bari, 1962, 521–43.

[27] L. B. Alberti's concept and definition of *istoria* dominated Renaissance aesthetics. See H. Mühlmann, *Aesthetische Theorie der Renaissance: L. B. Alberti*, Bonn, 1981, 162–63.

The process of selection of decorations appropriate for site and function can be observed in a letter of Annibale Caro outlining a set of decorations for the Villa Giulia. For the grotto he recommended *grottesche* in the rustic style, with plants, snakes, bats, owls, and similar animals. He suggested three possibilities for the figural decorations. One he termed *"fantasie salvatiche"* with singing shepherds, dancing nymphs, satyrs, fauns, and Silenuses. A second *concetto* was based on the fact that the grotto was located under a hill; Caro recommended the depiction of human underground activities such as mining. A third series was derived from mythological scenes which took place underground or in a cave; Vulcan at the Forge, the rape of Proserpina, Odysseus blinding Polyphemus were among the suggestions. Caro's preference for a depiction of Circe in her grotto surrounded by the men she had turned into animals is not explained in the letter.[28]

The concept of appropriateness required gardens to be decorated with the deities and spirits found in pastoral poetry or with mythological scenes in natural settings. This explains the abundance of statues of nymphs, satyrs, Silenus, Bacchus, and Pan in Roman gardens of the sixteenth century. There were also the goddesses of nature: Diana, Flora, Ceres, and Pomona. Fountains and pools were peopled with figures associated with water, Neptunes, river gods, water nymphs (Figs. 19, 45), or marine monsters and their attributes.[29] Aldrovandi describes a fountain with putti riding two marine monsters with elephant heads from which water issued, and another with a reclining female holding a cornucopia full of flowers and fruits, because, he explains, "the cornucopia symbolizes the fertility born of rivers."[30] Wine was also associated with abundance and fertility, so many fountains were decorated with statues of satyrs with wine sacks, such as the one erected in the Cesi garden in the 1540s (Fig. 77).[31]

A few themes, in addition to the pastoral ones, were used constantly in sixteenth-century gardens in Rome. One of the most popular in the first half of the century was the nymph in the grotto *topos*. In addition to the Cleopatra/Ariadne/Sleeping Nymph group,[32] caves and grottoes provided settings for some of the ancient goddesses. There were Venus grottoes in both the d'Este villas, and two grottoes with unidentifiable female figures at the Villa Lante in Bagnaia.[33] Despite the fact that there were two well-known

[28] Letter to I. Soperchio, 15 May 1551, published in A. Caro, *Lettere familiari*, ed. A. Greco, II, Florence, 1959, 99–100.

[29] The lists and inventories published by Huelsen, *Antikengärten*, are the basis of this information. See also the descriptions of statues at various garden sites by U. Aldrovandi, *Di tutte le statue antiche, che per tutta Roma . . . si veggono. . . .* , Venice, 1558.

[30] "Finsero anco i fiumi col Corno della copia, per dinotare una somma abodontia di tutte le cose ala vita necessaria . . ."; Aldrovandi, *Le statue antiche*, 116.

[31] The statue is shown in a Heemskerck drawing of the 1530s standing against a garden wall. Aldrovandi's description of 1555 (*Le statue antiche*, 123) places it in one of the four planting beds in the middle of the garden.

[32] See "Sleeping Nymph," 37–55.

[33] C. Lazzaro, "The Villa Lante at Bagnaia," Ph.D. diss., Princeton University, 1975, 73. D. Coffin, *The Villa d'Este at Tivoli*, Princeton, 1960, 82.

77. Statue of Satyr with wine sack
in the Villa Cesi, Rome, engraving by F. Perrier, *Segmenta* . . .
(photo: Dumbarton Oaks)

ancient fountain/grotto/nymph *topoi*—the Homeric Cave of the Nymphs and Ovid's description of Diana and her nymphs bathing in a natural pool by a cave[34]—no exact replica
of either is to be found in a garden in Italy until the monumental group of Diana at the
Hunt was made for the waterfall at Caserta in the eighteenth century.[35]

In the representation of heroes and episodes in their lives, Hercules appears most
frequently, but was used to signify many different things. The stories of his labors had
been allegorizcd since the late Middle Ages and had come to signify in most cases the
triumph of virtue over vice, but other meanings were also expressed by his presence. At
the Villa Giulia, according to Ammannati's description, statues were placed (or were to
be placed) in the niches of the long walls of the first courtyard (Fig. 78). In the center on
one side were Mars and Venus; Bacchus and a faun were in the corresponding niche on
the other side. In addition, there were several statues related to a sylvan or pastoral
setting: two "forest deities," a Vertumnus, a Pomona, and a Pan.[36] Next to the Mars and

---

[34] Homer, *Odyssey*, 13.102–12; Virgil, *Aeneid*, 1.166–68.

[35] G. Hersey, *Architecture, Poetry and Number in the Royal Palace at Caserta*, Cambridge, Mass., 1983, 113–
22, and figs. 5–18.

[36] "Et fra i colonnati [articulating the side walls of the courtyard] vi sono accomodati quattrodeci nicchie,
sette nella faccia a man destra e sette alla sinistra; et in ciaschuna vi è una statua antica. Nella faccia a man
dritta nel mezzo vi son doi figure in un pezzo di marmo. Marte et Venere in atto di far carezze a Marte, che
con estrema dolcezza et pietà cerchi di tenerlo seco; . . . L'altra nicchia che segue a questa dalla destra mano
vi è un Hercole tutto ignudo appoggiato sulla clava, qual tiene sotto il braccio sinistro; ed ha nella destra
mano tre pomi. Seguita l'altra nicchia, nella quale è dentro il dio Pan con le sue zampogne e una pelle in
mano; del resto è tutto ignudo. Nel'altra nicchia vi è la statua di Lavinia figlia del Re Latino. L'altre tre da
sinistra, a quella di mezzo; in una Venere e Cupido che scherza con l'arme di Marte; nell' altra un deo
selvano; et nel' altra una femina vestita d'habito longo. Al' incontro vi sono l'altre sette statue della medisima

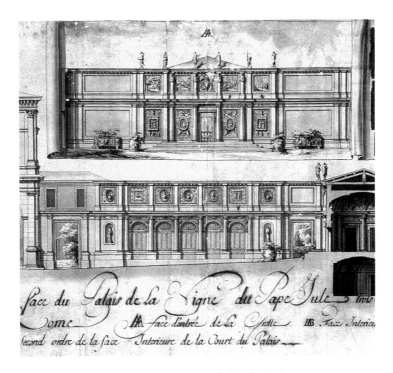

78. Villa Giulia, side walls of courtyard, detail of Fig. 9, Rome,
Museo di Villa Giulia (photo: Gabinetto Fotografico Nazionale)

Venus were a Venus and Cupid with Mars' armor. There were also two Hercules—one facing Lavinia, the daughter of the king of Rome, the other facing Vertumnus—and finally Ammannati described a Dejanera and a Commodus dressed as Hercules. In the ovals above were busts of Roman emperors. Since Mars and Venus were patron deities of Rome and Vertumnus and Pomona figure in a myth about early Rome, we have here an invocation of Rome and its history. Hercules has a double role; his pairing with Lavinia refers to the founding of Rome, while connecting him to Vertumnus specifies his role as a patron god of gardens.[37] The presence of Bacchus and the faun and of Cupid playing with the arms of Mars suggested that the cares of state are to be laid down and the pleasures of the country enjoyed under the protection of the sylvan deities and Hercules.[38]

Hercules' journey to the Garden of the Hesperides accounts for his presence in many gardens, for it invokes the idyllic carefree garden of the myth. This association is

---

grandezza delle dette. In quella di mezzo vi e un Bacco che s'appoggia ad un Fauno, e nel' altre una sol figura per nicchia, e son queste Vertunno, Pomona et Hercole; Dejanera, ed un Comodo in habito d'Hercole et un deo selvano." Ammannati Letter, Balestra, p. 65. Ammannati mentions busts of Trajan, Vespasian, and Titus on one wall, and on the other Augustus, Tiberius, and Claudius.

[37] M. Grant and J. Hazel, *Gods and Mortals in Classical Mythology*, Springfield, 1973, ss.vv. Pomona and Vertumnus, Heracles, Lavinia.

[38] J. Hall, *Dictionary of Subjects and Symbols of Art*, London, 1974, s.v. Mars.

certainly present at the Villa d'Este at Tivoli.[39] Yet, as David Coffin has shown, the program, and to some extent the layout, developed around the theme of Hercules at the Crossroads, or his choice between virtue and evil.[40] In addition to his role invoking the *concetto* of the d'Este garden as a modern Garden of the Hesperides and a representation of moral choice, Hercules was also used as a personification of the patron and as a reminder that the d'Este family claimed descent from him.[41]

In yet another role, Hercules appeared as a symbol of the virtues of a just ruler at the Medici villa at Castello, where a statue group of Hercules and Antaeus dominated the middle terrace of the gardens. The subjugation of Antaeus, in the moralizing versions of the Hercules cycle, had come to symbolize the overcoming of earthly temptations, while the other labors were also interpreted as examples of virtue overcoming vice.[42] This was the purpose of the numerous Hercules statues and fountains related to his labors at the Villa Mattei. Here the Hercules references served to narrate the passage of the patron's father, Alessandro Mattei, from childhood to the development of spiritual virtues and to the afterworld.[43]

Surpassing the frequency of Herculean imagery in sixteenth-century gardens are the *topoi* of Apollo, the Muses, Pegasus, and Mt. Parnassus or Mt. Helicon. There was scarcely a garden from the Villa Madama in the second decade of the sixteenth century to the Villa Aldobrandini in the early seventeenth century without their presence. The list includes the Giardino del Bufalo, the Casino of Pio IV, the two d'Este villas, the Villa Lante at Bagnaia, Pratolino—the Medici villa near Florence—and the Villa Mattei in Rome; undoubtedly there were more.[44]

In general we can account for their presence with a quotation from Pirro Ligorio, the antiquarian and probable designer of the Villa d'Este at Tivoli:

> The good Muses . . . , their Mnemosyne, Apollo, Minerva and Hercules [yet another allegorical significance] . . . signify the labours and happy days of those who are dedicated to higher things, and who lead man to the everlasting pleasures of the greatest knowledge, to high and profound meditation on seeing with the eyes of the mind how wonderful is the Prime Mover who made the heavens and the earth, so varied in its inspirations. Thus the force and the essence of the Divine Light can be recognized in *plants and animals* [my italics].[45]

In addition to the broad significance given them by Ligorio, various combinations of themes (Apollo and the Muses, the Muses and Mt. Parnassus, Pegasus and Mt. Helicon, etc.) were manipulated to create a number of different allegories. At the Villa d'Este in Tivoli, the Pegasus on the hill above the river gods and the Oval Fountain has been

[39] Coffin, *Villa d'Este*, 78–79.

[40] Ibid., 80–83.

[41] Ibid., 85.

[42] Wright, "Medici Villa," 286–302.

[43] See "Circus," 127–40.

[44] The group of Apollo and the Muses is described in B. Sgrilli, *Descrizione della regia villa, fontane e fabbriche di Pratolino*, Florence, 1742.

[45] Quoted from an unidentified manuscript by Pirro Ligorio in the Biblioteca Nazionale, Turin, by Smith, *Casino*, 56, n. 5.

interpreted as an allusion to Cardinal d'Este and his patronage of the arts.[46] The Muse and Mt. Parnassus fresco placed above a fountain at the Giardino del Bufalo is a reference to poetry and the Heliconian spring. At the d'Este villa on the Quirinal, Apollo and the Muses were placed in a grotto with fountains; the addition to the conventional representation of Apollo with a lyre (the Apollo *Musagetes* type) of the axe and an inscription *"Secur. Tenedia"* suggests that a new meaning has been given to the grouping—one that I am unable to interpret.[47]

However, the interpretation of two other appearances of the *topos,* at the Villa Lante in Bagnaia and the Villa Mattei, is more straightforward. At the former, the Fountain of Pegasus and the Muses is an introduction to the narrative, which has been interpreted as a parable of the Golden Age, its destruction, and the postdiluvian development of civilization.[48] Similarly, the presence of the sarcophagus of the Muses at the entrance to the garden path announces the start of the narrative of the life of the hero, Alessandro Mattci.[49]

A pattern may be discerned in the use of decorations during the century. In the first third there were few groupings of statues and few fountains to which an allegorical meaning was attached. Assemblies of statues were haphazard; quantity appears to have been more important than quality or completeness. In the last decades of the century a trend toward a close adherence to the written source appeared. The Parnassus at the Villa Aldobrandini in Frascati (Fig. 79) is as literal in its composition as was Raphael's painted version in the Stanza della Segnatura at the beginning of the century.

It was during the middle decades of the century that the most elaborate decorations with the most complicated allegories were popular. The range of subject matter used was limited, especially if compared to the variety found in painted cycles in palaces or villa buildings. Yet many different meanings and allegories were created by changing combinations of statues and their attributes. The process was analogous to that of writing. In each garden a *concetto* was developed and a text was created from a vocabulary of Greek and Roman mythology. The nouns, that is, the individual statues, could be modified by a change in attributes, such as the Apollo with the axe at the Quirinal garden, or by association with other statues, such as the juxtaposition of the Hercules statues with different figures at the Villa Giulia. The combinations, either groupings or sequential arrangements, created the sentences, the text. One may, for instance, compare the arrangement of statues and reliefs in the first courtyard of the Villa Giulia to inscriptions frequently found at the entrances to gardens, the Lex Hortorum. Many of the themes found in these appear at the Villa Giulia: the establishment of the identity of the patron (Giulius III's coat of arms and *imprese*); the history of the site or locale (Mars and Venus, Vertumnus and Pomona, Hercules and Lavinia); the exhortation to lay aside cares and the reference to a pastoral setting (Cupid with the armor of Mars, Bacchus, and faun).[50]

---

[46] Coffin, *Villa d'Este,* 87.

[47] See "Ars Hortulorum," 108.

[48] For a different interpretation, see Lazzaro-Bruno, "Art and Nature," 555.

[49] See "Circus," 127–40.

[50] D. Coffin, "The '*Lex Hortorum*' and Access to Gardens in Latium during the Renaissance," *Journal of Garden History* 2 (1982), 202–8.

79. Parnassus fountain at the Villa Aldobrandini, Frascati, engraving by D. Barrière,
Villa Aldobrandina Tusculana, Rome, 1631 (photo: Dumbarton Oaks)

This mode of composition relied on the use of readily identifiable statue types and conventional associations of meanings, but not on the use of a myth or poem in a literal way. Indeed, it is the expectation that a single literary source is the basis of garden iconographical programs that accounts for difficulties in deciphering them and for the variety of interpretations of individual decorative ensembles. The Papacqua fountain in Soriano nel Cimino, for example, has been interpreted on the one hand as a reconstruction of a temple dedicated to the Bono Dea and accompanied by the sylvan figures described by Ovid, "demigods, rustic divinities, nymphs, fauns, and satyrs and sylvan deities upon the mountain slopes," but elsewhere as a representation of Semele described in Philostratus' *Imagines*.[51] Bomarzo, where the program is not based on the familiar ancient literary sources, has engendered interpretations of the significance of its allegory almost as numerous as the enigmatic figures displayed there.[52]

Clare Robertson has proposed that a similar process of invention was used by Annibale Caro in developing the program for the ceiling of the Camera dell'Aurora at Caprarola and for an unexecuted loggia decoration for Vicino Orsini in the castle at Bomarzo.[53] She also demonstrated that most of the scenes and individual figures in the decorations were derived from sixteenth-century mythographic compilations rather than directly from literary sources. Robertson proposed that the appearance in the 1540s of texts like L. G. Giraldi's *De deis gentium syntagma*, which was one of Caro's sources, or Cartari's *Le imagini . . . degli dei* coincided with the development of the extremely complicated iconographical programs characteristic of that decade and later,[54] or possibly were the result of a demand for this type of handbook, a sort of iconographer's ready reference book.

This way of developing an iconographic program, whether in painting cycles or in garden decorations, and creating a text or narrative from isolated images or statues, has a striking resemblance to theories current at this time for creating a memory system. As Frances Yates has observed, the belief was that memory could be developed by establishing a mental image of a place inhabited by or decorated with images. The images served to recall the successive key ideas or topics needed to organize a speech or oration. The first century B.C. treatise on rhetoric, *Ad Herrenium,* uses an analogy similar to the one proposed above of the similarity between the construction of this method of recall to writing: "For the places are very much like wax tablets or papyrus, the images like the letters, the arrangement and disposition of the images like the script, and the delivery [the reference is to an oration] is like the reading."[55]

[51] The first is S. Lang's "Bomarzo and Soriano, A Study in Iconography," *Architectural Review* 121 (1953), 427–30. The second is my proposal in "L'Ingegnoso Artifizio," 57, n. 3.

[52] M. Darnall and M. Weil, "*Il Sacro Bosco di Bomarzo*: Its 16th-Century Literary and Antiquarian Context," *Journal of Garden History* 4 (1984), 1–94. See the Critical Bibliography, pp. 82–88, for a review of earlier and differing interpretations.

[53] C. Robertson, "Annibal Caro as Iconographer: Sources and Methods," *Journal of the Warburg and Courtauld Institutes* 45 (1982), 179.

[54] L. G. Giraldi, *De deis gentium syntagma*, Basle, 1539. V. Cartari, *Le imagini . . . degli dei*, Venice, 1556.

[55] F. Yates, *The Art of Memory*, London, 1966, 6–7, quoting in translation from *Ad Herenium*.

Since rhetoric, the art of persuasion, was considered the proper goal of all forms of art, it is not surprising to discover that common methods underlay the construction of "text" in garden decorations as well as painting cycles, and indeed the invention of *imprese* as well. Literary theory also provides an explanation for the differing subject matter. In sixteenth-century theory a distinction was made between *istorie* and *poesie;* the one, Varchi says, merely describes the visual world, while the other imitates what lies within—the concepts and passions of the soul. In his *Paragone* of painting and sculpture, he says that narrative poetry, or *istorie*, resembles painting which, he says elsewhere, imitates externals, "corporate bodies and their lineaments," while the poetry whose subject is *poesie* is like sculpture.[56] Both Vasari and Armenini refer to the subject matter considered appropriate for garden decorations as *poesie*. In describing the paintings on the garden wall of the palace of the Archbishop of Cyprus, Vasari concludes, "e così adornò quel luogo di diverse poesie." Armenini, writing at the end of the century in his *Dei veri precetti della pittura,* sums up the subjects appropriate for outdoor decoration as, "giuocchi di pastori, di ninfe . . . fauni, satiri, silvani, centauri, mostri marini con altre cose acquatiche e selvagge." He ends by saying that they should be "nel modo che si trovano essere finti nei libri de'Buoni poeti."[57]

While these remarks should still be considered preliminary, a few conclusions may be drawn about garden decorations in the sixteenth century. A rough chronology can be traced with a progression from the display of statues as antiquities at the beginning of the century, to decoration with statues chosen as appropriate for garden settings, to the elaborate *concetti* that began to appear in the 1540s. Literary theory and the several *Paragone* of the period held that *poesie* were *invenzioni*, not bound by the same rules of realism and literalness that governed *istorie*. At least one influential critic, Varchi, found statues most suitable for the expression of concepts and inner things, in other words, *poesie*, not *istorie*, and statues, of course, were more suitable for the decoration of gardens than paintings. Thus the precepts of *decoro,* on what was suitable subject matter for garden decorations, were reinforced by the theory that statues were appropriate for *invenzioni* rather than *imitationi,* or the literal representation of literary texts.

This leaves unexplored the question of the *concetti* themselves. We have seen that a limited range of *topoi* were manipulated to create a large number of differing programs. Were there deeper meanings, as many believe there were in the literature and painting decorations of the period?[58] The possibility cannot be excluded, but it seems unlikely. The attitude of the sixteenth century is clear; a garden was a place for relaxation and pleasure, to be decorated with "*cose allegre,*" as Armenini prescribes. It was not the place to contemplate the deep philosophical or religious questions that painting cycles evoked. Pico della Mirandola's proud statement about his exegesis of a Latin text: "If I am not

[56] L. Mendelsohn, *Benedetto Varchi's 'Due Lezzioni': Paragoni and Cinquecento Art Theory,* Ann Arbor, 1981, chaps. 2, 3.

[57] G. B. Armenini, *De' veri precetti della pittura,* Ravenna, 1587, bk. 3, chap. 13.

[58] E. Wind, *Pagan Mysteries in the Renaissance,* London, 1967; A. Patterson, *Hermogenes and the Renaissance: Seven Ideas of Style,* Princeton, 1970; D. C. Allen, *Mysteriously Meant: The Rediscovery of Pagan Symbolism and Allegorical Interpretation in the Renaissance,* Baltimore, 1970.

mistaken, it will be intelligible to only a few," no doubt applies to the *concetti* of garden decoration. To that special educated few, however, it would have been evident that meaning was concerned with the contrasts of art and nature, or with pride of family and place, or with the evocation of the pastoral heritage of classical antiquity. In *Mysteriously Meant,* Don Cameron Allen refers to "anagogic holes and grottos that are found throughout the landscape of Renaissance poetry."[59] Neither *decoro* nor literary theory of the period would have permitted anagogic holes or tropological grottoes in the poetry of the Renaissance landscape.

[59] Allen, *Mysteriously Meant,* 91.

A Circus, a Wild Man, and a Dragon:
Family History and the Villa Mattei

In 1610 Ciriaco Mattei, Roman nobleman and official, drew up his will. Much of its contents were related to the disposition of his villa on the Celio and to the large and renowned collection of ancient sculptures and inscriptions that he had assembled there and in his city palace. He reviewed the history of the villa and its gardens, which were probably constructed between 1581 and 1586:

> Qual giardino per prima et da quaranta anni sonno era vigna, et io con molto spesa sollecitudine et tempo l'ho redutto in forma di giardino con haverci fatte molte et diverse statue pili tavole intarziate, Vasi, Quadri di pitture et diversi marmi . . . et fattovi varie et diverse fontane et reduttolo in quel buon stato nel quale al presente si trova nel che dico, et confesso realmente, haver speso più di sessanta mila scudi. . . . [1]

After the deaths of his two sons who were to own the property jointly, he placed an entail on it with the title to descend to the oldest male descendant. The collection of antiquities and contemporary sculpture and painting was included in the entail, and he specified in the will that nothing movable, nothing attached or built into a structure was to be removed from the villa.[2] Even the attempt to dispose of any of the objects would

---

This article is an expanded and revised version of one chapter of my dissertation, "The Villa Mattei and the Development of the Roman Garden Style," Harvard University, 1970.

[1] The will, dated 26 July 1610, is in the Archivio di Stato, Rome, Atti Notaio Ottavio Capogalli, Anno 1610, vol. 486, fols. 334–69. It was published in its entirety by R. Lanciani, *Storia degli scavi di Roma e notizie intorno le collezioni romane di Antichità,* III, Rome, 1907, 83–86. The dates of construction are derived from two inscriptions, formerly inside the entrance gate of the villa, now lost but recorded in G. C. Amaduzzi and R. Venuti, *Vetera monumenta quae in Hortis Caelimontanis et in Aedibus Matthaeiorum adservantur . . .,* I, Rome, 1779, xxii (hereafter *Monumenta Mattheiana*). They are printed in S. Benedetti, *Giacomo del Duca e l'architettura del cinquecento,* Rome, 1972, 333–34, n. 6. The attribution of the design to Giacomo del Duca is undocumented. It first appears in P. Trotti, *Ritratto di Roma moderna,* Rome, 1638, 35. Benedetti's discussion emphasizes the formal aspects of the design.

[2] The passage reads, ". . . il detto Giardino con tutti suoi membri et pertinenze, et con tutte et singole statue, vasi, pili, Teste, Busti, tavole intarziate, quadri di pitture adobamenti, et supellettili con tutti ornamenti di qualsivoglia sorte tanto fatti come da farsi, et tanto fissi et murati come non fissi et amovibili di tutte qualità et quantità et tanto antichi quanto moderni nessuna cosa eccettuata. . . ." Lanciani, *Scavi,* 85.

have caused the title of the property to pass to the next succeeding heir.[3] To assure that his wishes would be carried out he directed that an inventory of his possessions be made within a month of his death, so that ". . . si possa conservare et fare conservare da posteri il detto giardino nel stato che si retrova."[4]

Unfortunately, at the end of the eighteenth century the Mattei descendants, a collateral branch of the family, were able to persuade Pope Benedict XIV to break the entail, and the collection in the garden was dispersed. Many pieces bought by the pope remain in the Museo Pio-Clementino at the Vatican. More than one hundred bought by the antiquarian Jenkins were sold in England.[5] In the early eighteenth century the family sold the property; after passing through several hands it was acquired by the city of Rome in the 1920s for use as a municipal park.[6] Almost nothing remains today of the original garden layout or of the statues and fountains which once decorated the grounds.

Ciriaco Mattei died on 10 October 1614, and the inventory he had called for was made, or at least notarized, on 15 November of the same year, slightly later than the month stipulated in his will.[7] Because the inventory was made sequentially according to the location of the objects in the gardens and buildings, as was customary in the sixteenth century, it may be used as a basis for the reconstruction of the appearance of the gardens and their decorations. Further, the list of statues was divided in two parts. The first was of marble statues, the majority of which were ancient or believed to be ancient.[8] Included in the second section were statues made of peperino, a soft volcanic stone. In all probability they were modern and made especially for the villa.[9] The location of a number of

[3] Ibid., ". . . se detti miei figli . . . o loro descendenti tentassero o ardissero di vendere o alienare qualsivoglia statue, busti o teste, tavole o altri marmi, o pitture, o qualsivoglia altro ornamento di qualsiasi qualità o valore (etiam che fusse di poco valore), ipso iure, et ipso facto caschi et s'intendi cascato et privato della proprietà et usufrutto, et di ogni commodo di detto Giardino . . . et in esso succeda, et debba succedere quello che succede et vien chiamato alla detta primogenitura come se il detto alienante, et contrafaciente fusse realmente morto. . . ."

[4] Ibid.

[5] The entail was broken by Clement XIV in 1770. For a history of the agreement and a record of the sculpture traced to other collections, see L. Hautecoeur, "La vente de la collection Mattei et les origines de la Musée Pio-Clementin," *Mélanges d'Archéologie et d'Histoire* 30 (1910), 57–75. The inventory of 1614 listed 76 statues, 19 herms, 10 reliefs, 17 altars and sarcophagi, 13 heads and busts, 10 animals, and 3 vases, all of marble and presumably ancient. In addition, 25 statues, 15 herms, 6 chests, 28 animals, and 17 vases of peperino were listed. The collection of ancient statuary was remarkable for its quality as well as its size. Although almost 100 paintings are inventoried, they are described so vaguely that they cannot be identified. The painting collection, however, was not renowned as was the sculpture collection.

[6] The later history of the Villa is discussed by M. Pasolini, "Villa Mattei e i giardini a Roma," *Roma* 3 (1925), 173–76, and I. Belli Barsali, *Ville di Roma: Lazio I,* Milan, n.d., 384–85.

[7] The full inventory was published by Lanciani, *Scavi,* III, 88–97. A slightly amended version appears in Benedetti, *Giacomo del Duca,* 493–505. I have quoted the relevant items in the footnotes.

[8] Since some of the statues are called modern in the first list, as for example, "un Settimio moderno con il petto di Alabastro . . . ," or "Un Antino moderno dell'istessa grandezza ivi vicino," and many of the statues can be identified as ancient, I have assumed that those not called modern were ancient or believed to be.

[9] The second part of the inventory begins, "Seguitano le statue, Animali, vasi et altri ornamenti di Peperino." The fountain figures and most of the statues associated with the iconographic program were made of peperino. See pp. 129–30, 133.

the statues as given in the inventory is corroborated by the earliest known view of the villa, a large print signed by Mattheo Pampano and Giacomo Lauro with a dedication to Ciriaco by Andrea Panarazzi. It is dated 1614, the year of Ciriaco's death (Fig. 80).[10]

The Pampano-Lauro print is a bird's-eye view which emphasizes the most prominent features of the garden, the two casinos, the flat area with obelisk called the *Prato*, and the labyrinth, but provides a very confusing picture of the topography of the site. This, however, is clarified by the two views that appeared in Falda's *Li giardini di Roma* later in the century (Figs. 81, 82).[11] The bird's-eye view shows that the garden was built on several levels. There was a large, flat area stretching from the entrance gate to the main casino. Behind the casino the Celian hill sloped precipitously, and this area was organized in a series of ramps and terraces. The lowest part of the hill was planted as a grove or *boschetto* and a small walled terrace with elaborately designed flower beds was a *giardino secreto*. The southwest side of the garden was supported by retaining walls, and a sloping path led down from the loggia (called the Casino di S. Sisto on the Lauro view) overlooking the valley to the lowest level. The Lauro view shows a second *giardino secreto* beyond the main casino; this evidently was removed to allow for the enlargement of the casino sometime later.[12]

In the upper garden, the most prominent feature was the *Prato*, a large open area terminated by a stepped exedra with an edicule containing a colossal bust of Alexander the Great in its center (Figs. 83, 84).[13] The middle of the *Prato* was occupied by the Capitoline obelisk, which had been donated to Ciriaco by the Roman *Conservatori* in 1582.[14] Two large lions guarded the entrance to the *Prato*, two ten-foot peperino statues

[10] A reduced version of this print with a dedication to M. P. Fugger, Baron of Kyrchberg and Waissenhoren, appears in G. Lauro, *Antiquae Urbis Vestigia quae nunc extant . . .*, Rome, 1628, pl. 36. The existence of a few large versions of the plates of other villas published in the 1628 volume suggests that all the gardens included also had larger earlier views.

[11] G. Falda, *Li giardini di Roma con le loro piante, alzate e vedute in prospettive . . .*, Rome, n.d. [1680?], pls. 17, 18.

[12] The evidence of the several views is somewhat conflicting, but the casino in the Lauro view does not reach the retaining wall that separates the upper from the lower garden, while in the Falda view it is shown as extending to the line. The change may have coincided with the enlargement of the gardens in the 1650s by Duke Girolamo Mattei, attested to by an inscription recorded in *Monumenta Mattheiana*, I, xxxiii, and F. Martinelli, *Roma ricercata nel suo sito*, Rome, 1650, "Questo giardino Mattei è stato del Signor Duca Girolamo Mattei accresciuto di fabrica e di sito, et arrichito di maggior copia d'acqua, e d'ogni varietà d'agrumi. . . ." The gardens were enlarged on a line running from the *Fontana del Tritone* to the *Fontana d'Atlante* and beyond (nos. 18 and 13, fig. 81), down the hill along the lane leading from the piazza in front of the church of the Navicella to SS. Giovanni e Paolo. The new fountains are attributed to Bernini and illustrated in G. Falda, *Le fontane di Roma nelle piazza e luoghi publici della città*, III, Rome, n.d. [ca. 1690], pls. 18, 19.

[13] "Una Testa grande di Alessandro Magno con il petto di trevertino a capo al prato con una iscrittione sotto." Lanciani, *Scavi*, III, 84. This and subsequent quotations describing sculpture are from the inventory. See n. 7.

[14] Decree of 11 September 1582, quoted by C. d'Onofrio, *Gli obelischi di Roma*, Rome, 1965, 204, n. 1. An inscription formerly on the base of the obelisk is quoted in *Monumenta Mattheiana*, I, xxv. "Ciriacus Matthaeum Obeliscum hunc a populo Romano tibi datum a capitolo con Hortos suos Coelimontanos trastulit . . . ut hortorum eius pulchritudo publico etiam ornamento augeretur. Anno 1582." An engraving of the obelisk by N. van Aelst (d'Onofrio, *Obelischi*, fig. 92) shows the four bronze-colored peperino statues of satyrs listed in the inventory arranged around its base.

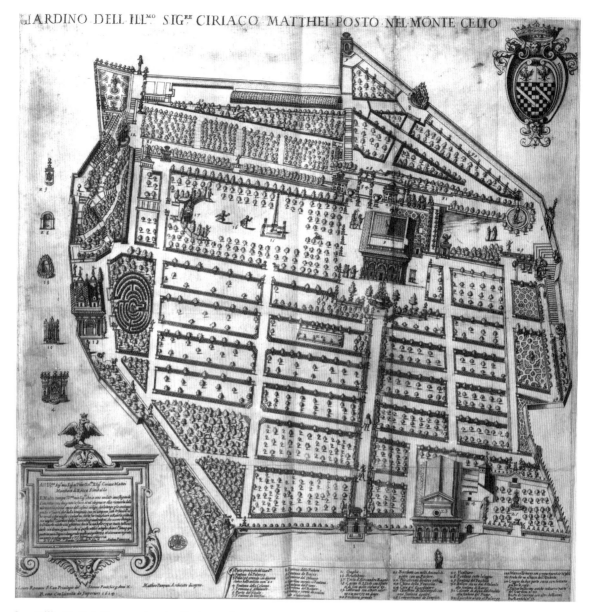

80. Villa Mattei, Rome, view by G. Lauro in 1614 (photo: British Library, Top K 81.70a)

were placed at the ends of the exedra, and in the open area there was a peperino group
called "Brutto Buono e Ragazzo che fanno a sassi" (Fig. 80, no. 16).[15] Other decorations
of the *Prato* included the four bronze-colored peperino satyrs and a number of hunting
dogs.[16]

The shape of the *Prato* is that of a Roman circus or hippodrome, a layout popular
in the Renaissance. Other examples of this period, however, such as the one in the Villa
Madama, were treated like gardens, undoubtedly in emulation of Pliny's description of

[15] "Doi leoni grandi di peperino nell'entrata del prato; Doi statue grandi di palmi 14 l'una di peperino
a capo al prato finte di bronzo; Un Bruttobuono di peperino in mezzo al detto prato, et un ragazzo pur di
peperino all'incontro che fanno a sassi."

[16] "Un cane inglese grande di peperino nell'entrata del prato; Quattro satiri di peperino intorno alla
loggia di color di bronzo; Quattro Cani grossi doi Barboni, et doi Corsi di peperino depinti al naturale in
mezzo al viale del prato; Doi livrieri di peperino dietro alla testa di Alessandro magno incontro all'Ercole."

130

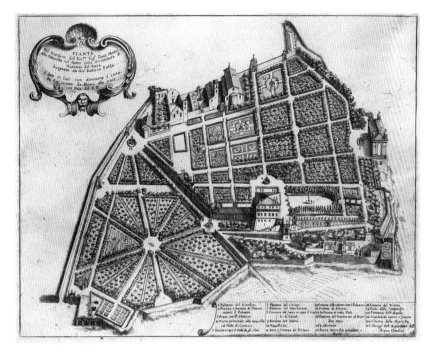

81. Villa Mattei, bird's-eye view by Falda, *Li giardini*, pl. 17
(photo: Dumbarton Oaks)

82. Villa Mattei, perspective view by Falda, *Li giardini*, pl. 18 (photo: Dumbarton Oaks)

131

83. Villa Mattei, view of *Prato* and casino, eighteenth century,
ex-collection Maraini (photo: Gabinetto Fotografico Nazionale)

84. Villa Mattei, colossal bust of Alexander the
Great and its edicule, *Monumenta Matteiana*,
Rome, 1774, I, 7 (photo: Library of
Congress)

a hippodrome-shaped garden at his villa at Tusci.[17] The *Prato* is unique because it was made to appear like a true circus, with an obelisk placed in the center, as though on a *spina,* with the vases and lions at the casino end arranged like the *carceres,* and with its curved stepped exedra. The obelisk, believed to have come from the Circus Flaminius, appears in sixteenth-century reconstructions of the Circus, such as Ligorio's or Panvinio's (Fig. 85).[18] A stepped exedra similar to the one in the garden is represented in the Roman relief said to have been discovered during the construction of the Mattei-Paganica palace (Fig. 86).[19] The "Brutto Buono e Ragazzo" may have been, in fact, a representation of a gladiatorial combat,[20] and even the lions and dogs should be considered an evocation of the animal contests held in circuses.[21]

A possible explanation for the specific references to ancient circuses in the *Prato* is to be found in the connection between the Mattei family and the Circus Flaminius. At that time it was believed that the site of the circus lay near the foot of the Capitoline and near the group of palaces belonging to the Mattei family.[22] Pirro Ligorio, in an unpublished manuscript quoted by Lanciani, described the site as situated between the Piazza Margana and the Calcarara fountain. He added that the visible remains had been destroyed for the construction of a palace by Ludovico Mattei, the present Palazzo Mattei-Paganica.[23] Onofrio Panvinio in his treatise about ancient circuses added that one of the long walls of the circus was on the Via delle Botteghe Oscure, where Alessandro Mattei, Ciriaco's father, had built a palace in 1564.[24] Thus the several family palaces in the area

[17] Pliny, *Epistles,* 5.6, 32–35. *Circus* is the Latin name for the elongated rectangles with curved ends used primarily for chariot races and horse races. *Hippodromos* is the Greek name, but Pliny referred to his garden as a *hippodromus.*

[18] Pirro Ligorio's engravings of the Circus Maximus and the Circus Flaminius were issued by Antonio Lafréri and are usually included in the so-called *Speculum Romanae Magnificentiae* collections. They date in the 1550s. The plates in Onofrio Panvinio's *De Ludis circensibus libri II,* Verona, 1600, are slightly altered versions of the Ligorio plates and were made earlier than the publication of Panvinio's book.

[19] The relief is still to be seen attached to a wall in the Palazzo Mattei-Paganica courtyard. Ligorio is the source of the information about the discovery of the relief. See n. 23.

[20] The figures of these statues are shown, in the Lauro view (Fig. 80), in contemporary dress, but they appear to hold round disclike stones in their hands. See, for example, the illustration in G. Mercuriale's *De arte gymnastica libri sex,* Venice, 1573, which shows figures in tunics throwing round disks in the air, with the *metae* of a circus in the background (illustrated in D. Coffin, "Pirro Ligorio and Decoration of the late Sixteenth Century at Ferrara," *Art Bulletin* 38 [1955], 177–78, fig. 10).

[21] For the variety of contests and games that took place in the ancient circuses, see Daremberg and Saglio, *Dictionnaire des antiquités grecques et romaines,* s.v. "Circus."

[22] For a discussion of the original location of the Circus Flaminius, see E. Nash, *Pictorial Dictionary of Ancient Rome,* I, London, 1961, 472.

[23] Pirro Ligorio wrote: "Il sito del circo Flaminio cominciava dalla piazza de'Margani et finiva appunto al fonte di Calcarara, abbracciando tutte le case de' Mattei. . . . Da questo lato de' Mattei il circo pochi anni fa era in gran parte in piedi. . . . La parte più intera era appunto dove è fondata la casa di Messer Lodovico Mattei il quale ha cavato un gran parte dei fondamenti del circo in quel luogo et trovatovi fra le altre cose una tavola di marmo in forma di fregio intagliato con puttini che sopra carri fanni il giuoco circense. . . ." (Quoted in Lanciani, *Scavi,* II, 65, as Ligorio, Circhi, ms. unidentified.)

[24] O. Panvinio, *De Ludis Circensibus,* 51: "Cuius longitudo [sc. Circus Flaminius] protendebatur ab area domus Marganiae, ubi in hemicycli formam desinebat, usque ad nova viam Capitolinam, ubi Carceres et XIII ostia erant: latitudo vero fuit ab aedibus Ludovici Matthaei usque: ad calcariae fontem ubi est officini tinctoris ambiens eo circuitu apothecas obscuras Matthaeiorum."

Alessandro Mattei's palace on the Via delle Botteghe Oscure, attributed to Ammannati, is the present

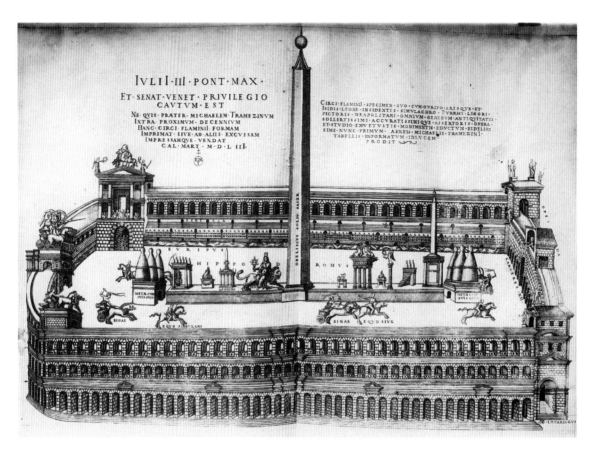

85. Circus Flaminius, reconstruction by Pirro Ligorio, 1550s (photo: Deutsches Archäologisches Institut)

86. Ancient relief of circus and chariot race, in situ, Palazzo Mattei-Paganica, Rome, engraving from Daremberg and Saglio, *Dictionnaire des antiquités*, I, 2, fig. 1521 (photo: Dumbarton Oaks)

had been built on the site believed to be that of the Circus Flaminius, and their construction had been the chief cause of the destruction of the ancient remains still visible in the first half of the century. Ciriaco's hippodrome-shaped *Prato* can be seen, then, as a symbolic replica of the ancient structure, and as an evocation of that part of Rome with which his family had been associated for one hundred years or more.[25]

Another theme can be discerned in the arrangement of some of the statues and fountains in other parts of the garden. There was an unusual predominance of Hercules statues—several freestanding and two herms by the aviaries[26]—and two of the major fountains had themes from the Hercules legend. The *Fontana del Diluvio,* in the lower garden had a peperino statue of Hercules and the Hydra, and the fountain in the lower garden had a figure of Atlas with a globe.[27] A third fountain, the *Fontana delle Colonne* had spiral columns of a type associated with the Pillars of Hercules (Fig. 87), and the labyrinth, with its peperino dragon in the center and its two "sirens" at the entrance evokes the Garden of the Hesperides.[28]

There seems, indeed, to have been an itinerary planned for visiting the garden, which finished at the lower end with the *Fontana del Diluvio.* The start was at the entrance to the *Boschetto degli Animali* (Fig. 80, no. 21) where the great sarcophagus of the Muses, now in the Museo Nazionale delle Terme, was placed (Fig. 80, no. 22; Fig. 88).[29] A path wound through the grove, or *Boschetto,* which contained a number of peperino statues of animals both wild and domesticated (goats, sheep, a wild boar, a wolf, deer) and a life-size statue of a shepherd with a mastiff at his feet.[30] The path ended in the open area

---

Palazzo Caetani. It was believed that the name of the street, *delle Botteghe Oscure,* derived from the shops built in outer arcades of the long side walls of the Circus. The earliest of the Mattei palaces surviving in that area, the Palazzo Giacomo Mattei, is behind the Caetani palace and faces on the Piazza Mattei. Lodovico's palace, the Palazzo Mattei-Paganica, is between them, and a fourth Mattei palace built by Asdrubale, Ciriaco's brother, in the late 16th century, faces on the Via Caetani. Together they occupy an entire block. See C. Pietrangeli, ed., *Guide Rionali di Roma, Rione XI. S. Angelo,* 2nd ed. rev., Rome, 1971, 55–68, for discussion and bibliography.

[25] The history of the Mattei family was traced in a series of articles by G. Antici-Mattei, "Cenni storici sulla nobile e antiche famiglia Antici, Mattei, e Antici-Mattei," *Rivista Araldica* 39–42 (1941–44). The installments relating to Ciriaco Mattei's branch of the family are to be found in 41 (1943), 231–38, 265–74, 299–309. Unfortunately, the series stopped before the history of Ciriaco's generation was published.

[26] A life-sized figure behind the edicule with the head of Alexander, two herms at the entrance to the aviary, two marble figures at the entrance to the labyrinth, and another marble figure on the balustrade of the *peschiera.*

[27] "In primis nella fontana del Diluvio una statua d'Ercole con l'idra; Un Atlante con una palla sopra di peperino che butta l'Acqua nella peschiera."

[28] "Un Drago di Peperino in mezzo al detto laberinto; Doi lettucci di peperino con li suoi cuscini, et sirene da capo nell'entrare del detto laberinto."

For an interpretation of the significance of the Pillars of Hercules in the Renaissance, see E. Rosenthal, *"Plus Ultra, non plus ultra,* and the Columnar Device of Emperor Charles V," *Journal of the Warburg and Courtauld Institutes* 34 (1971), 204–28. The association of the Garden of the Hesperides with the other world is discussed by G. de Terverant, *Attributs et symbols dans l'art profan, 1450–1600,* Geneva, 1955, 311–12. See also B. Giamatti, *The Earthly Paradise and the Renaissance Epic,* Princeton, 1966.

[29] "Un Pilo grande di marmo antico alto palmi 5. longo palmi xj. con le nove muse et altre figure quasi di tutto rellievo che posa sopra doi mezzi leoni, et sopra vi sono doi teste di mezzo rellievo."

[30] "Doi capre che cozzano assiemi di peperino nel boschetto dell'Animali; Un Cervo di peperino colco nel detto boschetto et un Caprio che pasce pur di peperino; Un Caprone detto colco in detto boschetto, et

87. Villa Mattei, *Fontana delle Colonne*, sketch by Hubert Robert, eighteenth century, location unknown (photo: Gabinetto Fotografico Nazionale)

between the Casino di S. Sisto (Fig. 80, no. 18) and the entrance to the labyrinth. Continuing in that direction one came to steps that led to the lower garden through another grove. In this was to be found the *Fontana del Bollore* (Fig. 80, no. 13) and a rough-cut granite "idol."[31] At the foot of this path stood the *Fontana del Fiume* (Fig. 80, no. 12), fragments of which still survive.[32] The inventory lists a peperino statue of a river god and two marble Minervas in the arch openings of the fountain *mostra*.[33] The path led downhill from this fountain along the *Viale delle Iscrizioni*,[34] the sloping path along the niched re-

<hr>

una Volpe pur di peperino colca; Una Capra di peperino in piedi con la testa alta in detto boschetto; Un porco cignale di peperino a sedere in detto luoco; Un Montone di peperino che pasce in detto loco; Un pastore di peperino alto palmi 9 in detto boschetto; Un cane mastino a giacere ai piedi di detto pastore."

[31] "Un Idolo di granito roscio dentro al boschetto del bollore."

[32] Illustrated in Benedetti, *Giacomo del Duca*, figs. 285–87, but captioned erroneously as *Fontana del Nettuno*.

[33] "Un fiume di peperino che butta acqua dentro un vaso di sperone in faccia del viale delle iscrittioni antiche; Doi Minerve armate nella fontana del fiume alte palmi 6 l'una i doi nicchie sfondate."

[34] The inscriptions were not inventoried but three statues were listed as being in niches along this wall. At the end of the list of peperino statues the inventory states, "Oltre le cose suddette si fa mentione che vi sonno molte iscrittioni antiche in marmo affisse nel già detto viale chiamato delle iscrittioni."

88. Sarcophagus with the Muses, formerly Mattei collection, now Rome,
   Museo Nazionale Romano (photo: E. Richter)

taining wall of the upper garden (Fig. 80, no. 6), past the *Fontana delle Colonne* (Fig. 80, no. 4; Fig. 88) to the *Fontana d'Attalante* (Fig. 80, no. 5). From there a number of paths could be chosen, but most would have led to the *Fontana del Diluvio* (Fig. 81, no. 9) with its statues of Hercules and the Hydra (Item 200). Steps nearby led to the *giardino secreto*.

The Hercules theme may also be explained by topographical and personal associations. By tradition, the Celio was believed to be the site of the battle of Hercules and Cacus.[35] Hercules was identified in antiquity as the patron deity of athletes and gladiators, and thus Hercules statues were an appropriate decoration to accompany the *Prato*'s circus theme. More significantly, the temple of the Hercules Musarum, one of the three cults of Hercules in Rome, was believed to have been located in the Piazza Mattei.[36] Finally, Ciriaco's birthday, 12 August, was the day believed to be dedicated to the cult of Hercules Magnus Costodes, the temple of which was also located near the Mattei possessions.[37]

A cycle of Hercules' deeds was not intended, however, for not all the canonic twelve labors were included. In addition, three, that is, the labyrinth as Garden of the Hesperi-

[35] The Hercules legends are summarized in M. Grant and J. Hazel, *Gods and Mortals in Classical Mythology*, Springfield, 1973, s.v.

[36] Röscher, *Lexikon der griecheschen und römischen Mythologie*, I, pt. 2, col. 2997.

[37] Ciriaco's epitaph, published by Antici-Mattei, "Cenni storici," 270, gives the date of his death as 10 October 1614 and his age at death as 69 years, 1 month, 28 days. August 12th was actually sacred to the cult of Hercules Victor, but during the Renaissance a misreading of some inscriptions caused a confusion in the dates of the respective cults. See Röscher, *Lexikon*, I, pt. 2, col. 2927. The major 16th-century commentary on the legends of Hercules, L. G. Giraldi, *Huic libello insunt L. G. Giraldi Hercules Vita . . .*, Basle, 1539, gave the erroneous date.

des, the *Fontana delle Colonne* as the Pillars of Hercules, and the *Fontana d'Attalante* have connotations of the other world and of Stoic virtues.[38] Hercules, himself, as a mid-sixteenth-century commentary on the legends explains, was seen as a personification of the triumph of intelligence over vice, his club as signifying philosophy and his lion skin, prudence. The story of the destruction of the Hydra was also commonly interpreted in the sixteenth century as an allegory of the triumph of virtue over vice.[39]

With this symbolism in mind, the itinerary described in the garden can be interpreted as an extended allegory of the life of a virtuous man. It starts with the introduction to the narrative presided over by the Muses and philosophers.[40] The *Boschetto degli Animali* represents youth, a kind of Golden Age, symbolized by the intermixture of wild and domestic animals.[41] In the labyrinth, the protagonist receives the three golden apples which, according to Giraldi, signified three virtues, rather awkwardly called those of absence of wrath, greed, and lust. The path then leads down a steep, rocky path, past the "idol" (temptation?) to the *Fontana del Fiume*, with statues that promise abundance and intelligence.[42] From there, the passage leads by the collection of inscriptions imparting the wisdom of the ancients, and passes the *Fontana delle Colonne* or the limits of the world. The "Attalante" Fountain symbolizes the virtues of steadfastness and courage, while the Hercules and Hydra fountain represents the hero's conquest of vice.[43]

Although allegorical cycles in which the patron was personified by a hero from mythology and his deeds and virtues celebrated in the guise of history and legend were frequent in the sixteenth century,[44] another possibility seems more probable at the Villa Mattei. The *Prato*, as the most prominent part in the garden, is the key. The bust of

[38] See n. 28.

[39] The following passages from Giraldi, *Hercules Vita,* are typical of 16th-century moralizations of Hercules and his deeds.

Hercules as a symbol of the conquest of vice: "Quidam Herculem nullum unquam fuisse opinati sunt, sed per eum humanae vim sapientiae significare, qua monstra quae in hominos animos grassantus, superbiam, libidinem, spurcitiam, desidiam, avariam, invidiam, caeterasque animi lobes sueramus" (col. 571).

Significance of the club and lion skin: "Alii philosophum Herculem putaverunt, atque idcirco illi ῥόπαλον, hoc est, *clavam* attributum volunt, qua ipsa phosophia significatur: & pellem leonis, qua prudentia."

For a discussion of the allegories on the myths of Hercules in the Renaissance, see M. René Jung, *Hercule dans la littérature française du XVI siècle,* Geneva, 1966.

[40] The philosophers are in niches on the sides of the sarcophagus. The use of Muses to introduce a narrative is also found at the Villa Lante in Bagnaia. See C. Lazzaro-Bruno, "The Villa Lante at Bagnaia: An Allegory of Art and Nature," *Art Bulletin* 59 (1977), 555.

[41] H. Levin, *The Myth of the Golden Age in the Renaissance,* Bloomington, 1969. Chapter 1 gives the ancient sources of this legend.

[42] Terverant, *Attributs,* 271.

[43] For Atlas, see Giraldi, *Hercules Vita,* col. 574.

Hercules and the Hydra: "Alii secretiore arcano fabulae locum datum volunt, quod scilicet Hercules animi sui ac continentiae ignita tamquam fece identidem reascentia libidinum caeterorumque vitiorum Lenaea capita represserit, atque penitus, extinxerit" (Giraldi, *Hercules Vita,* cols. 575–76).

[44] Such was the case at the Villa d'Este at Tivoli and the Villa Medici in Castello near Florence. See D. Coffin, *The Villa d'Este at Tivoli,* Princeton, 1960, 78–97, and D. Wright, "The Villa Medici at Olmo a Castello: Its History and Iconography," Ph.D. diss., Princeton University, 1976, Part II and especially 303–14. Note that both Cardinal d'Este and Cosimo de' Medici were rulers while Alessandro Mattei was not. This makes the choice of theme especially remarkable.

Alexander the Great in the place of honor in the exedra should be interpreted as a representation of Alessandro Mattei, Ciriaco's father. He had died in 1580 shortly before the beginning of the transformation of the former *vigna* into a villa.[45] There is a possibility that the obelisk was given to Ciriaco in honor of his father's service with the *Conservatori* of Rome, rather than his own, for Ciriaco's first known position with the municipal government was as *Conservatore* in 1584, two years after the donation of the obelisk.[46]

If we interpret the Hercules decorations as extolling the life and moral virtues of Alessandro Mattei, an explanation for the circus theme can also be proposed. Alessandro had been a prominent patrician and member of the government in Rome. For such distinguished citizens, ancient Romans had sometimes provided a memorial in the form of circus games. Most of the features of honorific funerals and funeral games described in ancient literature and discussed in the sixteenth and seventeenth century are present in the villa. The *Prato* in the shape of the hippodrome would be appropriate for *"Ludi Equestres,"* both the "Brutto Buono e Ragazzo" and the animals represent the *"Ludi Agonales seu Gymnici"*—that is, the gladiatorial and animal contests, while the narrative of the hero's life is a form of the *"Ludi Scenici sive Poetici et Musici."*[47] In addition, one should cite the head of Alexander, which corresponds to the life-size image, usually a bust, of the dead person carried in the funeral procession and placed at the grave, and the obelisk, for which there is ancient precedent as a monument to a famous person.[48] Even the satyrs by the obelisk can be explained by a passage from Dionysius Halicarnassus describing clowns (*"Satyricos"* in the seventeenth-century translation) and dancers in the funeral processions of illustrious men.[49]

[45] Antici-Mattei, "Cenni storici," 304.

[46] Ibid.

[47] F. Menestrier, *Traité des Tournois, Ioustes, Carrousels et autres spectacles publics,* Lyons, 1669, 12–13, names these three types of funeral games, quoting from ancient sources known in the 16th century. All three types seem to be represented at the Villa Mattei. It is tempting to apply his allegorical interpretation of chariot races in which "Les barrieres d'ou sortoient les chariots reprcsentoient le Naissance, les sept bornes, les sept AAges [sic] de la vie. . . . Les obelisques estoient les images de l'Ame qu'ils consideroient comme un feu qui s'elève vers le ciel. . . ." Ibid., 12. Unfortunately, I have found no 16th-century example of this interpretation which would add greater depth to the program I am discussing. The existence of "Ludi Scenici" as a type of funeral game may explain the figures associated with the theater which were placed in the *giardino secreto* next to the casino. These included a peperino statue "colorato al naturale che rappresenta un tal Emanuele portughese quasi moro che buffoneggia" and two masked figurines that represented Comedy and Tragedy.

[48] The publication closest in time to the Villa Mattei's construction is T. Porcacchi, *Funerali antichi di diversi popoli et nationi . . . ,* Venice, 1574. He says public funerals with games ". . . costumavano veramente . . . personaggi più illustri, che per qualche degna impresa havessero meritato honore et gloria sopra gli altri huomini" and that a statue and column erected in Scipio's honor "c'havesse parlato del imprese da lui fatte, cioè fosse stata contrasegno della gran virtù di lui" (p. 30). He mentions funeral feasts and annual celebrations on either the birth or funeral date, "Fu anchora usato dagli antichi, che qualunque in vita fosse stato sopra gli altri utile al publico, s'havesse con la virtù procacciato honori supremi; in morte, sepolto, o del publico, o del privato con magnificentia, fosse anchora con giuochi e spettacoli funebri, magnificamente honorato" (p. 56). Panvinio, *De Ludis Circensibus,* 85, also speaks of funeral games that took place in the circus.

[49] J. Kirchman, *De Funeribus Romanorum Libri Quatuor,* Hamburg, 1605, 160. "Quin etiam in illustrium virorum funeribus praeter alias pompas vidi & Satyricos choros qui lectulum praecedebant, et sicinnem saltationem saltabant: praecipue vero in fortunatorum virorum funeribus."

There is, of course, no proof of any sort for my interpretation of the decorative program at the Villa Mattei, nor is there any ready explanation why there is no record of any inscription or dedication to Alessandro. Yet the probability of a program of decoration devoted to the memory of Ciriaco's father is increased by the evident pride of family revealed in the introductory statement of his will:

> . . . qual giardino è stato anco di molta mia recreatione, et trattenimento, et di visto, et di esercito di virtuosi et *di reputatione non poca della casa* [emphasis mine] essendo visto, et visitandosi giornalmente non solo da personaggi et gente di Roma ma da forastieri con buona lode, et fama il che sia detto senza ostentatione et vangloria ma solo per verita et per essortatione delli miei posteri a conservarlo.[50]

Perhaps Ciriaco's desire to celebrate his father's virtue was due to a change in family status. Hitherto, the Mattei had been merchants and city officials. They held, for instance, the hereditary post of Captain of the Port.[51] Although they claimed descent from the family of Pope Innocent II (1130–43), they had never achieved the rank and preeminence of families such as the Orsini or Colonnas. Although they had married into distinguished families, they seem not to have been part of the papal court either as attendant nobles or members of the Curia.[52] After the Sack of Rome, however, the family fortunes improved. Two imposing family palaces were constructed, and a chapel built in Santa Maria d'Aracoeli. Girolamo, Ciriaco's brother, was made cardinal in 1586. Finally, in 1592 Pope Clement VIII granted the fief of Rocca Sinibaldi jointly to Ciriaco and his brother Asdrubale, and gave the former the title of marchese. Asdrubale was made Marchese di Giove in 1598.[53] Thus the period of Ciriaco's construction and embellishment of his villa coincided with the family's emergence into the upper aristocracy of Rome.

Ciriaco's pride in his garden and his desire to keep the decorations intact now become clear. The splendid collection of antiquities and the elaborate allegorical program were an index to his cultivation as well as his wealth, a demonstration of his links with antiquity as well as a statement about his position in his own world. The villa had indeed enhanced the renown of his family at the same time that it permanently enshrined the memory of his father.

---

[50] Lanciani, *Scavi,* 84.

[51] L. Huetter, "I Mattei custodi dei Ponti," *Capitolium* 7 (1929), fasc. 7, 347.

[52] For descent from the family of Pope Innocent II, see Antici-Mattei, "Cenni storici," 40 (1942), 77. He mentions Mattei marriages to the daughter of the Cardinal d'Estouteville, to a relative of Pope Alexander VII, to a Capodiferro, and to an Anguillara. The latter were distinguished Roman patrician families.

[53] Antici-Mattei, "Cenni storici," 41 (1943), 233–34, 305.

Part II
The Seventeenth Century

Venaria Reale: Ambition and Imitation in a Seventeenth-Century Villa

INTRODUCTION

Although the architecture of the late seventeenth and early eighteenth centuries in the Piedmont has been extensively studied and analyzed, earlier periods have been virtually ignored. This is particularly unfortunate for the years 1630 to 1680, an era of relative prosperity and peace. Starting with the reign of Vittorio Amedeo I (1630–37), continuing with the regency of his widow, Maria Cristina of France (1637–63), and the reign of his son, Carlo Emanuele II (1663–75), intense building activity changed the appearance of the city, expanded it, enlarged and transformed the royal residence in the capital, Turin, and added a ring of royal villas on the city's periphery.[1] Traditions of design and decoration developed which were to underlie and influence the more spectacular and better-known achievements of Guarini, Vittone, and Juvarra in the late seventeenth and early eighteenth centuries.[2]

The cultural traditions of Piedmont always reflected its geographic location, its political affiliations, and the French origins of its ruling family, the Savoy. Despite Piedmont's location in what is now the northwestern part of Italy it was governed for centuries from the French seat of the Savoys, Chambéry. Even when Turin became the capital and chief residence of the duke in 1563, ties remained strong with France, and these ties were constantly reinforced by intermarriages with the French royal family throughout the sixteenth and seventeenth centuries. Yet cultural ties (and political relationships) with north and central Italy were strong, and the presence of noted Italian artists, such as Palladio, who dedicated the third book of his *I Quattro libri dell'architettura* to Duke Emanuele Filiberto in 1575, or Federigo Zuccaro, whose *L'Idea de' scultori, pittori e architetti* was written in Turin, attests to Savoy interest in Italian art.

All illustrations are from Castellamonte, *Venaria Reale,* or in the Dumbarton Oaks Garden Library and photographed at Dumbarton Oaks unless otherwise noted.

[1] For studies of Turinese architecture of this period, see G. Brino, A. de Bernardi, et al., *L'opera di Carlo e Amadeo di Castellamonte nel XVII secolo,* Quaderni di Studio 5, Turin, 1966; C. Boggio, "Gli architetti Carlo ed Amedeo di Castellamonte e lo svilupp edilizio di Torino nel secolo XVII," *Atti del Società degli Ingegneri e degli Architetti di Torino* 29 (1895), 192–245; N. Carboneri, *Ascanio Vitozzi, un architetto tra manierismo e barocco,* Rome, 1966; *Mostra del barocco piemontese,* Turin, 1963, with additional bibliography. See now, M. Pollak, *Turin, 1564–1680; Urban Design, Military Culture and the Creation of the Absolutist Capital,* Chicago, 1991, 134–43, for a discussion of Carlo di Castellamonte's and his contemporaries urban planning. I have not been able to consult the exhibition catalogue, M. di Marco, G. Romano, eds., *Diana trionfatrice: arte di corte nel Piemonte del seicento,* Turin, 1989.

[2] I would like to thank Henry Millon for his help in this study. He introduced me to the subject of Piedmontese architecture, showed me how to locate the archival material, gave me copies of documents he had transcribed, and has even read this article for errors a non-specialist might make. Thanks are due also to the late Richard Pommer for his generosity in giving me material on the late years of Venaria Reale and guiding me to more. I should also like to thank the archivists of the Archivio di Stato in Turin for their generous advice and assistance.

During the half century with which we are concerned, ties with France were especially strong, for the mother and wife of Vittorio Amedeo I were princesses of the royal family, daughters or granddaughters of the French king, as was the first wife of his son, Carlo Emanuele II. The latter's second wife was from a cadet Savoy line. These links are reflected in the architecture of the period, especially during the regency of Vittorio Amedeo's widow, Maria Cristina, whose taste in art had been formed during her childhood at the court of Louis XIII.[3]

Maria Cristina's son, Carlo Emanuele II, continued the tradition of commissions in which an amalgam of Italian and French styles were combined to form a uniquely Piedmontese style. This may be clearly observed in the villa, Venaria Reale, which he constructed northwest of Turin starting in the late 1650s.[4] He began by improving an older "castle" to use as a hunting lodge, but shortly devised more elaborate plans "per sua habitatione e deporto con altre commodità convenienti alla sua reggia persona come gran Principe."[5] These included construction (or reconstruction) of a village on the main road leading to Turin, extensive gardens, elaborate garden structures, and two major enlargements of the original building.

An unusually complete record of the villa's appearance has survived in the views and descriptions published by its architect, Count Amedeo di Castellamonte, *VENARIA REALE, Palazzo di Piacere, e di Caccia, Ideato dall'Altezza Reale di CARLO EMANUEL II Duca di Savoia, Re di Cipro, &c Disegnato, e descritto dal Conte Amedeo di Castellamonte. L'Anno 1672.*[6] The text is a fictive dialogue between Castellamonte and Gian Lorenzo Bernini, the Roman architect and sculptor—a traditional form of architectural exegesis in which the visitor's questions give rise to very full descriptions and explanations. The accuracy of Castellamonte's text and the illustrations of the book are verified by the very full documentation preserved in the archives. Castellamonte's overall views (Figs. 1, 2) reveal the magnitude of the project. The estate was approached through a small town which was rebuilt along a central axis leading from the gate at the entrance to the town to the piazza

[3] A number of 19th-century histories are the best source for the lives of these 17th-century Savoys. See A. Manno and V. Promis, *Bibliografica Storica degli Stati della Monarchia di Savoia. I. Storia della R. Casa e della Monarchi*, Turin, 1884–1934. For Carlo Emanuele II and his widow, I have used G. Claretta, *Storia del Regno e dei Tempi di Carlo Emanuele II, Duca di Savoia, scritta su documenti inediti*, 3 vols., Genoa, 1877–78, and idem, *Storia della reggenza di Cristina di Francia Duchessa di Savoia con annotazioni e documenti inediti*, 3 vols., Turin, 1868–69. See also M. Viale Ferrero, *Le Madame reali di Savoia*, Turin, 1963.

[4] Material about Venaria Reale appears in the literature about Carlo Emanuele II and Amedeo Castellamonte, but only one study of it has been published. See V. E. Gianazzo di Pamparato, *Il Castello della Venaria Reale: Cenni storico-artistici con note, documenti e tavole illustrative*, Turin, 1888. Some of the documents published by Pamparato have not been traceable in the archives and are included here as he published them.

[5] Archivio di Stato, Turin, ASG 18, fol. 15r, 29 November 1660. See App. I for an explanation of my references to archival material.

[6] Although the title page gives a publication date, in Turin, 1672, it was not actually completed until 1679. *Termini post quem* for the text are the dates on p. 96 where Castellamonte speaks of occurrences ". . . nel corrente 1679. . . ." and on p. 98 where he quotes the text of an inscription on an institution supported by Maria Giovanna dated April 1679. Brambilla was paid for the drawings for the illustrations of the *gran salone* and Tasnière for the prints in 1675. See G. Claretta, *I Reali di Savoia, munifici fautori delle arti, contributo alla storia artistica del Piemonte del secolo XVII*, Turin, 1893, 13.

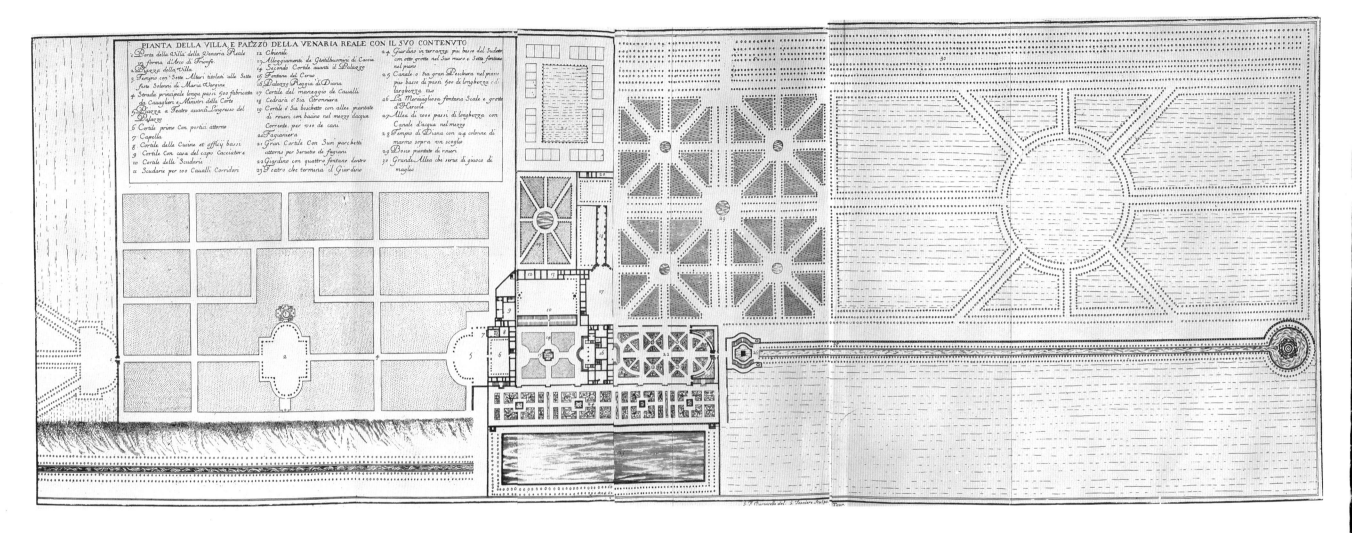

DISEGNO IN PROSPETTIVA
DELLA VILLA E PALAZZO DELLA

VENARIA REALE

CON IL SUO CONTENUTO
VEDUTO
DALLA PARTE DEL
SETTENTRIONE.

1 Villa Lunga in mezzo per laquale si va da Torino
alla Venaria Reale.
2 Piazza avanti la porta principale della Villa.
3 Borgo della Villa.
4 Atrio della Villa.
5 Piazza di Pietro avanti l'Ingresso del Palazzo.
6 Cortile dell'Hortaria.
7 Cortile della Cucina.
8 Cortile del Senato.
9 Piazza avanti il Palazzo.
10 Fontana del Cervo.
11 Scuderia.
12 Cortile piantato di rouere per uso di Caro.
13 Cortile de Guariani.

14 Citroniera.
15 Piazza ouero la Cittonera per Monaggio de Canali.
16 Palazzo Regio di Diana.
17 Giardino.
18 Oschetto di rouer.
19 Loania o Teatro.
20 Giardino basso.
21 Gran Canale.
22 Le scale e gran fontana dell'Hercole.
23 Due padiglione, a fianchi di detta fontana.
24 Allea grande.
25 Tempio di Diana.
26 Il Barco di Cervi.

G. Tasnieri Scill. i. Taur.

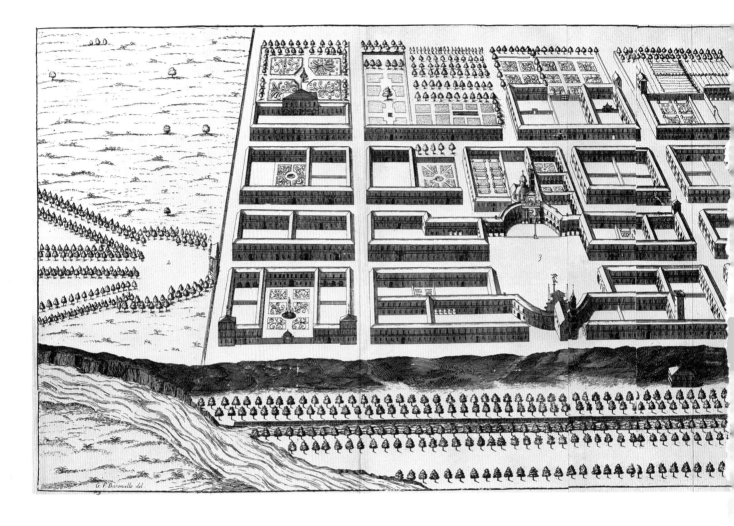

1. Bird's-eye view of Venaria Reale (unnumbered foldout)

in front of the villa. Individual plates show a palace, stables, orangery, an elaborate two-level garden with fountains and pavilions, and a large hunting park.

From these we can see that almost every feature combines both Italian and French traditions. The palace, for instance, with its pitched roof and forecourt arrangement, has a traditional French plan and elevation, yet the internal arrangement of central *gran salone* with attached wings divided into individual suites is unmistakably Italian. The decorations in the *salone* have many different origins. The stucco herms (Fig. 3) are derived from the book of herms by Sambin, published in 1572,[7] the hunting scenes on the upper walls were by a Flemish painter, Jan Miel,[8] but the moralizing mottoes appended to the mythological scenes here and in the lateral apartments derive from an old Italian tradition (Fig. 4).[9] The subjects and arrangement of the ceiling paintings in the apartments is specifically a Turinese tradition.[10]

Another characteristic of Venaria Reale, also true of other Piedmont designs of the period, is a curious mixture of *retardataire* and contemporary elements. The style of ornament at the villa, although usually French in derivation, can be traced to printed sources

---

[7] H. Sambin, *Oeuvre de la diversité des termes. . . .*, Lyon, 1572.

[8] Visible in Fig. 3. Four of these survive in the Palazzo Civico in Turin. They are nos. 63–67 in the exhibition catalogue, *Mostra del barocco piemontese*, Turin, 1963. One of these, no. 65, is illustrated as fig. 25. Also surviving from the *salone* decorations are four of the paintings showing "Huntresses of the Royal Family," by Carlo Claudio Dauphin. They are nos. 71–73 and figs. 28–29 in the *Mostra* catalogue.

[9] The tradition of moralizing epigrams will be discussed in another article. Examples of these are in the sequence of paintings with scenes of myths of Diana; the one showing Callista sent from the group of Diana's nymphs has the motto, "O non promette o non mancar in fede." In the Prince's apartment, in a Hercules cycle, the scene of Hercules capturing the stag with a golden horn is labeled, "Fa l'ossequio più illustre un fier commando." Compare these with mottoes at the Villa della Madama Reale, decorated in the 1640s, where, for instance, mottoes included "O' incauto error mostra la pianta il pianto" for the myth of Apollo's transformation of "Ciparesso" into a cypress tree to alleviate his grief, or "Chi trionfa d'amore merta l'allora" for Daphne. A few of the Venaria Reale decorations are illustrated in Castellamonte, and all the themes and mottoes are described in his text. Castellamonte says the "inventioni poetiche e morali, le imprese e li motti che V. S. [Bernini] andara osservando frà li ornamenti di questo Palazzo sono composte dal Gran Conte D. Emanuel Tesauro . . ." (p. 8). Tesauro, who left the Jesuit order in 1634 and became the tutor of Prince Emanuele Filiberto, second prince of Carignano, was a renowned Turinese scholar. See E. Derviaux, "Emanuele Tesauro, 1592–1675. Cenni biografici e bibliografici," *Miscellanea di Storia Italiana* 53 (1932), 653–73. Tesauro's book, *Il Cannocchiale aristotelico* (Turin, 1654), a compendium of mottoes, imprese, and instructions for devising them, was an important source for iconographical programs for festivities, painting cycles, and sculptural ornaments. He devised programs for several of the Savoy villas, including Racconigi. A reprint of the Turin, 1670 edition (Berlin, 1968) has a bibliography of recent studies of Tesauro and the role of emblems, imprese, etc. in Baroque art and literature.

[10] Not only was each room decorated with a single subject, but cycles on the same theme were spread over a whole apartment or in corresponding rooms of different apartments. One cycle in the four corner chambers (numbered 8 on the plan) represented the different kinds of hunts (earth, water, air, and underground-nocturnal), another, in the four main salons (numbered 6 on the plan) is devoted to the myths of Diana, the overall theme of the original iconographical program. This compares with other decoration cycles of the time. For instance, at the Villa di Madama Reale, her apartment was dedicated to the "Delitie delle Fronde, de' Fiori, e della Frutta." The subject of the cycle of another apartment there was "Le Delitie de' Conviti." The four chambers had scenes of the "Delitie delle Fonti, dei Fiumi, del Mare, della Caccia," respectively, while the cabinets had scenes of the "Delitie della Primavera, Estate, Autunno, Inverno." These are described in Filindo Il Costante [Filippo di San Martino, Count d'Agliè], *Le delizie della Vigna di Madama Reale*, Turin, 1667.

Parte interiore Sella Sala con suoi ornamenti Si pitture, e scolture Sella Reggia Si Diana

3. View of Salone (unnumbered)

from earlier decades and has none of the sobriety and incipient classicism of French
architecture of the 1660s. The plan of the village of Venaria is closely related to the town
of Richelieu in France, built by the cardinal of that name in the 1630s. Yet other features,
such as the piazza in front of the palace, the parterre, grotto, and fountain designs for
the gardens are closely related to the almost contemporary features created for Louis
XIV at Versailles. As we shall see, the *retardataire* elements belong to the first stages of
construction before 1664, while those elements in more contemporary style were started
in a second building period after 1666.

Still a third influence on the design may be traced in the most original and distinctive
structures at Venaria Reale, the Teatro at the end of the upper garden, the Fountain of
Hercules, and the project for the Temple of Diana. Their designs are a product of the
lively Turinese tradition of stage design and festivity architecture. Festivities, ballets,
jousts, and other forms of entertainment were common in all the courts of Italy and the
rest of Europe at this time, and fantasy and elaboration were characteristic of the tempor-

CALISTO PVNITA

O NON PROMETT
O NON
MANCAR DI FEDE

J. Miolle Pinx.   G. B. Branbil delin.   G. Tasniere Sculps. Taur.

4. Diana and Callisto, one of Diana cycle in Salone (unnumbered)

ary architecture constructed for them. Turin's court entertainments were among the most elaborate as well as the most numerous.[11] However, while festivity architecture was entirely ephemeral elsewhere, some of the Turinese designs were translated into permanent structures. The Teatro seems to be a permanent version of the temporary structures, usually a kind of arch, built at the entrance of cities as a welcome for visiting dignitaries or as the start of ceremonial processions. The Fountain of Hercules is a replica of a scene, perhaps a backdrop, of one of the festivities in 1660 for the marriage of Margarita, Carlo Emanuele's sister, to the duke of Parma, Ranuccio Farnese. The Temple of Diana, in both form and concept, can be traced to two preceding festivities, both celebrations or invocations of Savoy dynastic ambitions.

[11] See n. 81 for a list of material about Turinese festivities. A great many of the 17th- and 18th-century descriptions of the various festivities are preserved in the Biblioteca Reale, Turin, in the collection *Miscellanea di Storia Patria*. There is a relatively complete list in Manno and Promis, *Bibliografica* (see n. 3).

The villa's influence on subsequent architecture in the area was limited. Not only does it represent the culmination of early Baroque architectural development in the Piedmont,[12] but it came at the end of an era; shortly thereafter the style was transformed and reinvigorated by the genius of Guarini and the other great architects of the late seventeenth century.[13]

1. THE FIRST BUILDING PERIOD, 1660–1665

Building History

Venaria Reale is northwest of Turin; the villa and the town were built on the site of a village called Altessano Superiore on the banks of the river Ceronda. It and another village, Altessano Inferiore, were feudal possessions of the Counts Arcore.[14] Carlo Emanuele first started buying land there in 1654, but the major purchase was in 1658 (Doc. 1). He continued to acquire land in order to enlarge the hunting park and to regularize the streets and the facades of the houses of the town through 1674.[15] Count Amedeo di Castellamonte was put in charge of the project, and some of the designs were ready before the end of 1659 (Docs. 2, 3).[16] Construction started in 1658,[17] but 1660–61 were

---

[12] This is true of other architectural commissions of Carlo Emanuele, such as the Palazzo Reale in Turin. For more information on the architecture of Carlo's reign, see n. 1 and G. Claretta, *I Reali di Savoia* (see n. 6).

[13] Earlier literature on the villa included Pamparato, *Venaria Reale*; Brino, et al., *Castellamonte*, 108–17, 130–31; A. E. Brinckmann, *Teatrum novum Pedemontii. . . .*, Dusseldorf, 1931, 82–89; R. Pommer, *Eighteenth-Century Architecture in Piedmont: The Open Structures of Juvarra, Alfieri, & Vittone*, New York, 1967, 23–35, 144–64. See also the *Mostra del barocco piemontese*, 67–80.

[14] Documents for the Venaria Reale exist in several *fondi* of the Archivio di Stato in Turin (hereafter AST). See App. I for a description of them.

A checklist of the documents I found in the archive and of those cited in earlier publications but which can no longer be traced, with a brief description of their contents, is in App. I. App. II is a transcription of the surviving *ristretti*, which are preserved in AST, Sez. Ia, Provincia di Torino. App. III has a transcription of the documents for the Temple of Diana, Castellamonte's description and other texts related to its history.

A copy of the 1565–79 *Consegnamento de' Beni posseduti dal S.r Arsimino Arcore de' SSre d' Altessano superiore* is in AST, Sez. III, Art. 810, *mazzo unico*, int. 1.

[15] Land purchases before 1666 appear in AST, Sez. III, Art. 810, *mazzo unico*, int. 33. Later purchases are recorded in AGF ¶ 18.

[16] Boggio, "Architetti Carlo ed Amedeo di Castellamonte," 52ff. Also responsible for supervision was Giorgio Turinetti, President of the Finance Council (Consiglio di Conti), the financial bureau of the government. The duke specifically authorized them to make contracts with Giovanni Battista Piscina, who was "impresaro della fabrica del detto Palazzo della Venaria Reale," for walls, roofing, and tiles. Money was paid out by him on the basis of *misure e stime* carried out by an official of the court, the *misuratore per S.A.R.*, with a second person, often Castellamonte, who also signed the documents as proof of his approval. The *Ristretti* were also signed by Oratio Gina, *Auditore*. Turinetti and Castellamonte could also contract for stone, lumber, ironworks, and "altre cose necessarie" with "Capomaestro Carlo Busso." Individual subcontractors were in charge of each construction trade (masons, carpenters, plumbers, etc.). They too were called "Capomaestro," and made estimates, signed contracts, and hired workers (the skilled workers seem to have usually been relatives). Some of them worked for cost of materials and labor, particularly the less skilled laborers, such as carters, but most contracted to do the work for a fixed sum.

[17] One of the descriptions of the wedding of Margarita of Savoy, sister of Carlo Emanuele II, to Ranuccio Farnese, duke of Parma, which took place on 12 May 1660, reports that one day of the celebrations was dedicated to Diana with a hunt which took place at Venaria Reale, "fabrica superba intrapresa da doi anni in qua ma non ancora compita da S.R.A." *Racconto Succinto delle Sollenità per le Nozze tra i Serenissimi Signori Prencipessa Margherita di Savoia e Ranuccio II, Duca di Parma e di Piacenza*, Turin, 1660, 14.

5. View of Palazzo and Gran Cortile (pl. VIII)

the years of major construction. A total of £55,800 was spent during these two years (Doc. 6),[18] evidently with pressure from the duke to complete the work.[19] Although the sum was large, the construction consisted mainly of modifications, additions, and reconstructions of the existing castle.[20] It seems likely that the original structure on the property was what is now the central block of the palace.[21] New wings or pavilions were added to this, probably the two blocks flanking the central loggia, and a half underground space visible under the loggia was excavated for kitchens (Fig. 5). Large stables were built

[18] This is the figure given in a payment authorization (Doc. 6). *Ristretto* 1 (Doc. 12 and App. II, no. 1) gives the sum of £205, 229:71:3 paid out from 1660 to July 1663.

[19] Doc. 6 includes an item paid from the duke's private purse to bring bricks from a distant kiln "per la premura dell'espeditione dell' opera."

[20] Item 39 of Doc. 6, £8700 to "Cappi M.ri da muro Giovane Christoffaro Carezano p. saldo di quello gli é dovuto p. la fabrica—[delle] due Paviglioni fatti nella fabrica vechia della [includes payments for the 'guard'arnese'] della Venaria Reale." Art. 197, Mandati, 1657–67, has a number of payments for adapting balustrades, moldings, and ceilings made for the Palazzo Reale to apartments in the palace at Venaria Reale. Also in the *Ristretto* for 1664 (App. II, no. 2, cap. 1) there is a payment for "il muraglione tra il Palazzo novo, et il vechio fatto contro la terra del gran Cortile, comprese li tre grotte et l'incamisola fatta alli due pezzi di muraglia di detto Palazzo vechio ove vi sono li due rami di scala @ £11 cad.o trab. £2665:1:1."

[21] It is also possible that a wing of the forecourt was the original building, but the design of the entrance loggia of the main building looks very quattrocento in character and detail.

6. Stables (pl. VII)

closing off the *cour d'honneur* from the other service buildings (Fig. 6), and a wing parallel to the main building built with a center tower called the Torre dell' Horologgio (Fig. 7). Wings housing the villa chapel and offices protruded east toward the entrance plaza which was separated by a walled loggia (Fig. 8).[22] A third floor was added to the central block of the building and a belvedere built over the center (Fig. 9).[23] Stables, kennels, a pheasant house, and other accessory buildings were constructed for "[le] commodità convenienti alla sua reggia persona come gran Prencipe" (See Fig. 1, nos. 7, 10–12; Fig. 2, nos. 11–13, 19–21).[24] The documents refer to the construction of a Teatro delle Commedie and locate it in the "secondo salone." Castellamonte describes a performance

[22] Item 10, Art. 179, ¶ 10, 1660 in 1661. Payment to "S.r Gio. Anto. Boggietto, M.ro Rolla, Gio. Rosso, I. Alessan.ro Pistone e Boggietto p. lavori e spese fatte p. la fabrica e coperta del Torione delle Horologgio sopra la seconda porta del Cortile della Venaria Reale nell' anno 1660 . . . £911:5." The main items of the construction can be followed in the itemized account in App. II, no. 1, which is a summary of expenses between the start of the construction and June 1663.

[23] 24 June 1663, App. II, no. 1, fol. 73r.
"Facciamo fede noi sottosignati [Turinetti and Castellamonte] che havendo l'Alt.Sua Reale stabilito di alzar un piano di più tutto il corpo del suo Palazzo della Venaria Reale oltre il primo stabil.m.to del dissegno della Med.ma Reale Alt.a signato, sopra il quale haveva il Capo M'ro Gio: Batta. Piscina impresaro di d.ta fabrica fondato il suo partito, e di più di d.to novo alzam.to havesse anco ordinato che li rialsassa un'altro corpo di fabrica nel mezzo di esso Palazzo in forma di belvedere. . . ."

[24] ¶ 18, 29 November 1660, fol. 15r, Doc. 4. This is a contract concerning a purchase of water which explains, ". . . havendo S.A.R.le del Ser.mo S.re Carlo Emanuele fattosi erreger la sua Ven.a R.le con scuderia per li cavalli nel luogo Altezzano superiore e datto principio ad un gran Pallazzo p. sua habitatione e deporto et anco fatto dessignare giardini con altre commodità convenienti alla sua reggia persona come gran Pren-

7. Forecourt and Torre dell' Horologgio (pl. V)

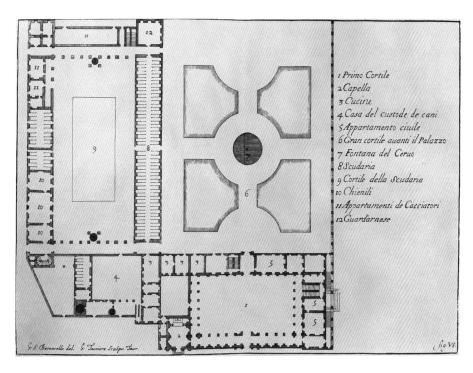

8. Plan of Forecourt, Gran Cortile, and Stables (pl. VI)

153

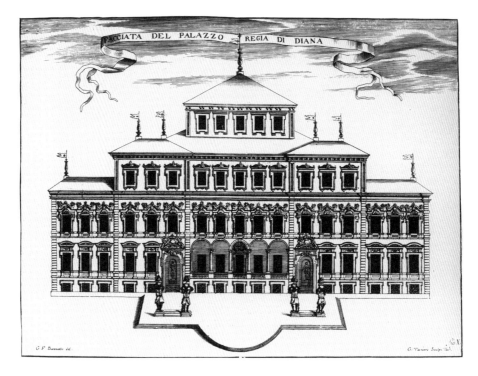

9. Facade of Palace (pl. x)

in it (p. 20), but there is no indication on the plans or in his text of its location in the palace.[25]

The gardens were also started at this time. During 1661 trees were planted in the park along rides and allées that had been leveled.[26] Land was purchased for a piazza in front of the villa chapel (See Fig. 1, no. 4; Docs. 8, 9).[27] Payments in 1662 are for adaptations for use at Venaria Reale of decorations already prepared for the Palazzo Reale in Turin (Docs. 10, 11). The palace was complete enough for the duke and his bride to stay there on their wedding trip in 1663.[28] The *ristretto* for the years 1660, 1661, 1662, and the first half of 1663 show that a total of £205,229 was spent.

---

cipe; gli sij necessario haver una balera con grande quantità d'acqua non solo per adaquare gli giardini, uso de Cavalli ma anche per le Peschiere, fontane et altri suoi dissegni."

[25] The Teatro delle Commedie appears in a *misura* of 20 November 1662 (App. II, no. 1, fol. 62r). "Primo il solaro della loggia del Teatro delle Comedie fatto a perfilo cioè nel secondo salon. Più altro solar rustico con paradossi del Teatro della Comedia."

[26] Art. 179, ¶ 10, 1660 in 1661.

Conto che rende all'Ill.mo et Ecc.mo Camera Il Sig.r Ant.o Garagno . . . nel'anni 1660, 1661 = Doc. 6.

c) #23. 2008 rovere in alee del Parco £1138.13.4.

d) #24. leveling of allée in Parco £1615.9.0.

[27] Art. 179, ¶ 10, 1660 in 1661.

e) #30. Land bought for a piazza in front of the chapel "fatta fare dal S.A.R. nella facciata del Primo Palazzo della sua Venaria Reale £67.10.

[28] May 1663, Turin, Biblioteca Reale, Miscellanea Storia Patria (hereafter BRT, Misc. St. Pat.), vol. 299, int. 1, describes the visit of Carlo Emanuele and bride at Venaria Reale.

A lull in the building activity occurred between 1662 and 1666. At this time the major additions were complete and the basic work on the gardens was done. The *ristretti* show expenditures of £47,452 in 1664 and £42,081 in 1665, while in 1666 they rose to £62,702. Documents for this period include contracts for garden maintenance and payments for the completion of decorations such as the basin of the fountain in the forecourt (Docs. 14, 15, 19, 20).[29] At the same time, however, land was being purchased to regularize the streets and facades of the buildings along the streets of the town (Docs. 17, 21, 23).

Comparison of the documents with Castellamonte's description and illustrations shows him to have been accurate in his depiction, even in the small details. Naturally, unfinished structures, such as the Temple of Diana or the village churches, which belong to the second building campaign, were represented as complete, but it is not unreasonable to suppose that Castellamonte, the architect of the project, supplied designs for these buildings to the illustrators of his book.

Tradition and Venaria Reale

The Palace   The palace of Venaria Reale is a reflection of local traditions in castle and palace design. The documents show that the major changes made at Venaria Reale consisted of the addition of wings to an original rectangular block (see Fig. 5).[30] Each of the wings held a suite of rooms or an apartment with an antechamber, reception room, a second chamber with an alcove for the bed, and a dressing room, according to Castellamonte (Fig. 10).[31] These apartments flanked the central *salone* which ran from the porticoed entrance facade to the garden loggia. The hall was more than two stories high and had a central barrel vault with groined corners and clerestory windows at each end.

These modifications and additions brought the palace into conformity with a local tradition of villa and castle design. Although few of the seventeenth-century villas have survived unaltered, there is evidence that a plan with a central block and projecting pavilions or wings was common to many of the villas and castles of the period. Racconigi, before its seventeenth-century alterations, appeared to have this form (it actually had a

---

[29] Art. 199, ¶ 1, 1657–67.

a) Fol. 126v, 16 October 1665.

Contract with Alessandro Bolier, gardener, to plant *bussini* "ne' dui giardini della Venaria Reale, piantando quello di sotto tutto di nuovo e quello di sopra dove il busso sarà morto ò mancanti."

b) Fol. 129v, 14 December 1665.

Contract for marble rondeau of fountain at Venaria Reale to follow Castellamonte design and be like fountain of the Bastion Verde [Palazzo Reale, Turin].

c) Art. 199, ¶ 1, 1657–67, fol. 146v, 15 September 1666, Doc. 25.

Contract with Roberto Chevalier del fu Mathieri di Normandie, giardiniero della Venaria Reale for maintenance of garden for next ten years. He is obligated to

a) Mantenere il Busso del Giardino Grande delle fontane

b) Per d.o giardino manterrà gli alberi fruttiferi

c) Manterrà parim.te al giardino di sopra il busso quando S.A.R. l'havrà fatto piantare [Doc. 25]

d) Manterrà gli stradone delle due giardini e del cortile del Palazzo e delle Scuderie e dei chienili

e) Muoverà li citroni alla aranciera in inverno

"Et tutto questo . . . il trav.o di £1000 d'argento annuali a parte da S.A.R."

[30] See pp. 150–55 for the building history.

[31] See Castellamonte, 33–65.

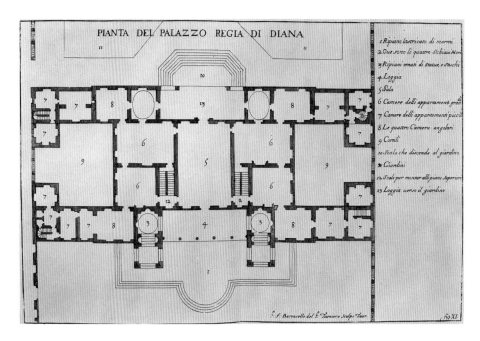

10. Ground plan of Palace (pl. XI)

central courtyard),[32] and the Vigna di Madama, the Villa della Regina, and the d'Aglié castle in the town of the same name actually did (Figs. 11, 12).[33] Even where there were no side wings or pavilions, a two-story central *salone* was common. Examples are the *salone* and *primo piano* at Valentino,[34] at the earlier Palazzo Viboccone at the Parco Regio,[35] as well as at the Villa della Regina.[36]

[32] For the early history of Racconigi, see N. Gabrielli, *Racconigi*, Turin, 1972, and A. Lange, "Disegni e documenti di Guarino Guarini," *Guarino Guarini e l'internazionalità del Barocco*, Turin, 1970, I, 130–49. The illustrations of Racconigi and the other royal villas near Turin are taken from J. Blaeu, *Novum Theatrum Pedemontii et Sabaudiae sive accurata Descriptio ipsorum Urbum Palatiorum, Templorum. . . .*, Amsterdam, 1682. See F. Rondolino, "Per la storia di un libro," *Atti del Società piemontese di archeologia e belle arti* 7 (1897), 314–59, for the dates of the different plates.

[33] The Vigna di Madama was designed by Padre Andrea Costaguta for Cristina, the mother of Carlo Emanuele II. It was begun in 1648. See R. A. Marini, "La Vigna di Madama Reale, *Atti della Società piemontese di archeologia e belle arti* 10 (1921), 57–127. The Villa della Regina (pl. x in the *Teatrum*) was acquired in 1617 by Prince Maurizio of Savoy, uncle of Carlo Emanuele II. The original construction of 1620 was enlarged in the 1640s by Lodovica, Carlo Emanuele's sister and widow of Maurizio. See Carboneri, *Ascanio Vitozzi*, 172–73. The d'Aglié castle was built between 1639 and 1645. See Brinckmann, *Teatrum novum Pedemontii . . .*, 18, pl. 6Bf.

[34] Valentino, bought by Emanuele Filiberto in 1564, came into Cristina's possession in 1630. For the history of the castle, see F. Cognasso, M. Bernardi, et al., *Il castello di Valentino*, Turin, 1949. A plan of the *primo piano*, dated ca. 1648, appears on p. 240.

[35] The Palazzo Viboccone, destroyed in 1706, was built either in the 1570s for Emanuele Filiberto I, or ca. 1605 for Carlo Emanuele I. See D. Heikamp, "I Viaggi di Federico Zuccari," *Paragone* 9 (1958), fasc. 105, 62, n. 35, for the later date, and Carboneri, *Ascanio Vitozzi*, 168–69, for arguments for the earlier date. The view in Blaeu, *Teatrum*, pl. 40, may reflect the alterations of Amedeo Castellamonte in the 1640s. See G. Zorzi, *Le ville e i teatri di Andrea Palladio*, n.p., 1969.

[36] M. Bernardo described the reception hall at the Villa della Regina as ". . . una salone centrale, il quale occupa in altezza due piani secondo uno schema consueto alle ville piemontese del seicento." *Tre palazzi a Torino*, Turin, 1963, 108.

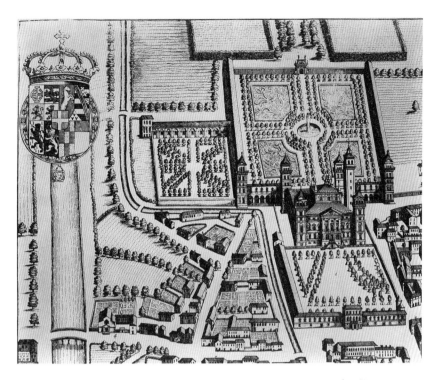

11. Bird's-eye view of the castle of Racconigi (Bleau, *Teatrum*, pl. 98)

12. Villa della Regina (Bleau, *Teatrum*, pl. 36a)

157

The exterior forms of Venaria Reale and other villas of the period seem to derive from another tradition, a type of castle built in the Renaissance with a central block and four corner towers. These in turn derived from earlier castle types, such as those with towers and screen walls. Military innovations made this castle design indefensible, and new types with the wedge-shaped protrusions familiar from sixteenth-century fortresses developed. The earlier form survived, often in the residences of rulers, with modifications that suggested their role as a residence. An example of the transition is a castle now called the Villa Gallia in Gravedona on Lake Como. It was built in the 1580s as the headquarters of the local ruler, and thus functioned as castles did originally. The traditional central block with four corner towers is retained, but the two facades have open loggias approached by wide flights of stairs.[37] Several of the royal villas originated as castles (e.g., Venaria, Valentino, and Racconigi), and their original shape was probably similar to that of the Villa Gallia. The entrance to the palace of Venaria has just such a loggia, and it appears to be a survival of the earlier castle.[38]

The use of a central two-story *salone* in villa design probably originated in the late fifteenth century,[39] but appears most frequently in the sixteenth century in the Veneto. Possibly the Turinese plan found so frequently in the seventeenth century derived from Palladian and other Venetian villas. Palladio's influence there is documented by his dedication of the third volume of the *Quattro libri* to Emanuele Filiberto in 1570.[40]

It is difficult to bring light to a central *salone* unless it is higher than its flanking wings, and there is always the problem of providing a connection between the wings at the upper level. In many buildings of this type, the room is dark and gloomy. The problem was partly solved at Venaria Reale by the construction of an upper passageway over the front loggia which, however, did not obstruct the light from the large end windows.[41] Castellamonte's solution was used in later buildings, but eventually different plans became more popular, and the central *salone* was abandoned.

[37] A. Bascapé, *Ville e parchi del lago di Como*, Como, 1966, 137–39. See also A. Peroni, "Architetti manieristi nell'Italia settentrionale: Pellegrino Tibaldi e Galeazzo Alessi," *Bollettino del Centro Internazionale di studi di architettura Andrea Palladio* 9 (1967), 272–92, fig. 185 and pl. XVI. The attribution to Tibaldi is unsupported. C. Frommel, "La Villa Madama e la tipologia della Villa Romana nel rinascimento," *Bollettino del Centro Internazionale di studi di architettura Andrea Palladio* 11 (1969), 47–64, has further discussion of this type of castle-villa.

[38] The documents suggest that the original building consisted of the rooms numbered 3–6 in Castellamonte's plan (Fig. 10). This would correspond to the conventional middle block with side towers of the earlier castle type.

[39] See, for example, the *salone* of the Medici villa at Poggio a Caiano, dated ca. 1513. Two designs by Palladio should be mentioned as Venetian examples: the Villa Godi in Malinverni and the Villa Poiana. See R. Cevese, *Ville delle provincie di Vicenza*. Ville d'Italia, Veneto 2.I, Milan, n.d., 81–96, 111–21, and pls. 87–88, 115–16. See also a Palladian project for a Mocenigo villa at Dalo on the Brenta published by Zorzi, *Palladio*, fig. 145.

[40] Despite Palladio's statement in the preface to Book III of the *Quattro Libri* that he had been called to Turin by Emanuele Filiberto, no documentation has been found for this visit. Traditionally he is supposed to have worked at the Parco Reale and Mirafiori. See Zorzi, *Palladio*, for a discussion of the problem.

[41] Brino, et al., *Castellamonte*, gives a transverse section of the building on p. 112. The garden facade of the palace was drastically altered in the 18th century, so it can no longer be determined if there was a similar passageway there.

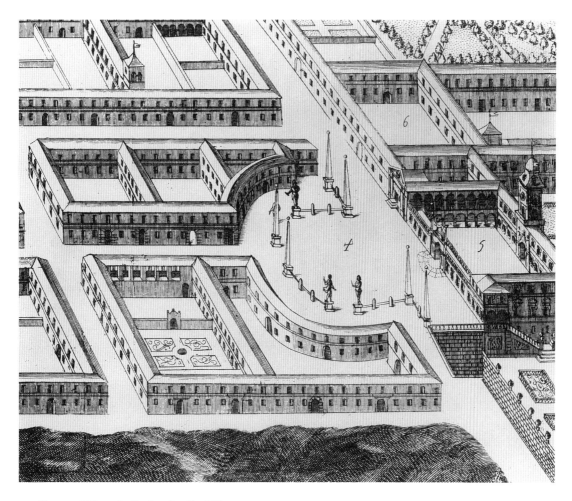

13. Piazza of Venaria Reale; detail of Fig. 1

Although, as we shall see, many aspects of Venaria were strongly influenced by the innovations created for Louis XIV at Versailles, the modifications to the palace were strictly in the local tradition. Much the same could be said of the ornament and the interior decorations.

The Town   An integral part of the overall design for Venaria Reale was the walled town, laid out in regular blocks along a central street leading from the village gate to the piazza in front of the palace. Buildings of similar design and height line this street and were planned for the side streets also (Fig. 13). A cross axis at the center of the town consists of an arcaded piazza with columns on the foci of the oval. Two churches were planned but neither was constructed exactly like the design represented in Castellamonte's views.[42]

---

[42] Although both facades were constructed, the southern church was never completed and the northern one was built in a simpler form. See Pommer, *Eighteenth-Century Architecture in Piedmont*, 143–45.

14. View of center of town of Turin
(Bleau, *Teatrum*, pl. 16)

The coordination of a village with a villa and hunting park is by no means unknown in Italian architecture. Examples include the streets laid out in the 1560s in Bagnaia connecting the village piazza to the entrance gates of the Villa Lante, and the monumental approach avenue to the Farnese palace at Caprarola.[43] The concept of streets lined by identical facades goes back at least to the fifteenth century, when they were advocated by Alberti as an important principle of urban design.[44]

The village of Venaria Reale, however, was more elaborate in its development, and its appearance reflected contemporary urban design in both Piedmont and France. Unlike the villages of Bagnaia and Caprarola where the alterations were designed only to produce a monumental approach to the villa or palace, Altessano Superiore was transformed from a rustic agricultural village to a sophisticated ambient for members of the court who were encouraged to build palaces by the donation of sites to them.[45] Thus

[43] C. Lazzaro-Bruno, "The Villa Lante at Bagnaia: An Allegory of Art and Nature," *Art Bulletin* 59 (1977), 553–60. For Caprarola see documents in M. Walcher Casotti, *Il Vignola*, n.p., 1900, II, 264–70; a discussion of the plan in L. Partridge, "The Sala d'Ercole in the Villa Farnese at Caprarola," *Art Bulletin* 53 (1971), 470–71.

[44] Leone Battista Alberti, *De Re Aedificatoria Libri Decem*, Rome, 1516, Bk. VIII, chap. 6.

[45] In the dialogue between Bernini and Castellamonte, Bernini remarks that the town gate and main avenue, ". . . mi paiono l'ingresso d'una ben ordinata Città, e non d'un picciolo Villaggio. . . ." Castellamonte

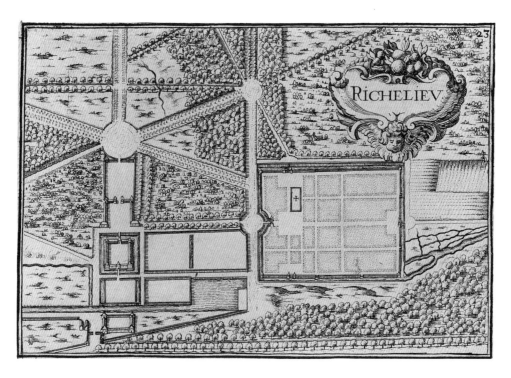

15. Town of Richelieu (Tassin, *Vues et Profils;* photo: Houghton Library, Harvard University)

Carlo Emanuele must have envisioned his use of the villa for more than an occasional sojourn or day's hunting, but rather as a site for more extended residence attended by members of his court.[46]

The design of the village on a long axis is very like the design of new streets and piazzas in Turin by Vitozzi, Carlo Castellamonte, the father of Amedeo, and Amedeo himself.[47] Early in the seventeenth century, the piazza in front of the Castello in Turin, then the center of the city and the residence of the dukes, was regularized and surrounded by arcaded buildings of identical design and height (Fig. 14). A second piazza in front of the Cathedral, now destroyed, was similarly designed by Carlo who also initiated the plans for the present Piazza San Carlo and the Via Roma, at the time of the

---

replies, ". . . che questa era una picciola Villa, e mal composta fabbricata con strade ritorte, con Case basse, e rusticali: . . . S.A.R. . . . si risolse d'abellir anco la Villa, riducendolo . . . dalla Case anco la rustichezza con riformarle in Palazzi,. . . . si mossero à gara gl'uni e gl'altri [Cavaglieri e Ministri di sua Corte] à fabbricar questi Palazzi, che danno la forma non solo à questa gran strada, ma alle Piazze ancora, . . . à quali S.A.R. fece dono de siti, e delle Case, che conveniva demolire comprate à prezzi considerabili da propri Padroni, molte delle quali sono pure state fabbricate à spese di S.A.R. . . ." (p. 5). The documents recording these purchases and donations are preserved in AST, Sez. II, Fondo, ¶ 18, vol. 1, 1632–1757. My thanks are due to Dottoressa Isabella Ricci for making this set of documents known to me.

[46] See n. 24.

[47] See Pollak, *Turin*, 134–43.

enlargement of the city which was begun in 1620.[48] As executed by Amedeo, the facades were more elaborate and elegant than the street facades of Venaria Reale, but they were organized on the same principles of congruity and continuity.

Although Italian precedents for the concept of the design can be found even in the fifteenth and sixteenth centuries, a more immediate source and a possible direct influence on Venaria Reale is the village built by Cardinal Jean Armand du Plessis de Richelieu at his chateau of the same name (Fig. 15). He ordered a whole new village built along an axis at right angles to the principal axis of the chateau, the gardens, and the park. The gate into the chateau grounds is preceded by a semicircular piazza, similar in shape to the piazza at the entrance to the palace at Venaria Reale, while the main axis of the village is interrupted by a piazza on which were built the church and Hôtel de Ville.[49] The buildings lining the main street were uniform in height and appearance; their construction was subsidized by the donation of building sites, as were the houses at Venaria Reale.

The Gardens   The original gardens at Venaria were thoroughly traditional in design and decoration. Castellamonte's views show two principal formal gardens (see Fig. 1, nos. 17, 19), a *boschetto* (no. 16), and the *Parco dei Cervi* (no. 25). Other areas shown with planting are the *cour d'honneur* (no. 8), an area behind the orangery (no. 13), and a courtyard planted with oaks (no. 11) next to the kennels.

The two ornamental gardens (see Fig. 1, no. 19; Figs. 16, 17)—on the lower level north of the palace next to the great *balera* and the terrace or parterre at the upper level behind the palace—are shown laid out in simple rectangular beds surrounded by box.[50] The corners were marked with trees in boxes, possibly some of the orange trees (*citrone*) purchased in April 1664 (Docs. 14, 16). Neither have the complicated shapes of *parterres de broderie*, which had been fashionable in both Italy and France for several decades. Castellamonte's views show curvilinear patterns within the rectangular enclosures, which may have been created by plantings of flowers but could also have been colored sand. Fountains in each garden were set in the middle of the beds; in the upper garden standing statues are shown in the center of small pools, while in the lower garden seven pools of different shapes and sizes were equally spaced along its length. The largest at

[48] See M. Passanti, ed., "Lo sviluppo urbanistica di Torino e gli architetti Carlo e Amedeo di Castellamonte," in Brino, et al., *Castellamonte*, 199–201.

[49] M. Dumolin, "La construction de la ville de Richelieu," *Bulletin de la Societé des Antiquaires de l'Ouest*, ser. 3, 10 (1934/35), 520–51; H. Wischermann, "Ein unveröffentlichter Plan der Stadt Richelieu von 1633," *Zeitschrift für Kunstgeschichte* 35 (1972), 302–6, with earlier bibliography. See also P. Francastel, *L'urbanisme de Paris et l'Europe 1600–1800. Travaux et documents inédits présentés par Pierre Francastel*, Paris, 1969, for information about other examples of urban design in France in the first half of the 17th century, especially for the article by J.-P. Babelon "L'urbanisme d'Henri IV et de Sully à Paris," pp. 47–60 in that volume. See now H. Ballon, *The Paris of Henry IV, Architecture and Urbanism*, Cambridge and London, 1991.

[50] Contract with Alessandro Bolier on 10 October 1665 to plant new box in the lower level garden and replace the dead box in the upper one (see App. I, Doc. 19).

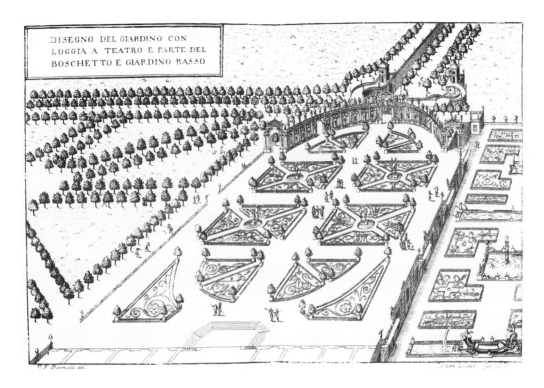

16. Perspective view of upper gardens (pl. xv)

17. Plan of upper gardens (pl. xiv)

163

18. Fountain in lower garden (pl. XVII)

19. Fountain in lower garden (pl. XVI)

the center was boat-shaped (Fig. 18); the other canal-shaped pools had figures of putti blowing horns while seated on the coils of a sea serpent's back (Fig. 19); two of the rectangular pools had standing figures of Neptune with tridents spouting water, and the other two had central spouts and figures of huntsmen at the corners (Figs. 20, 21). Only the latter differ from conventional fountain decoration types.

20. Neptune fountain in lower garden (pl. XIX)

22. Neptune grotto in lower garden
(pl. XX)

21. Third fountain type in lower garden (pl. XVIII)

The sustaining wall of the lower garden was articulated by seven niches with "giuochi d'acqua"[51] and appropriate water deities. The statue of Neptune shown in the grotto on plate XX (Fig. 22) was installed in 1665.

[51] As per contract with Celerone Franco 20 November 1664. See App. II, Doc. 2.

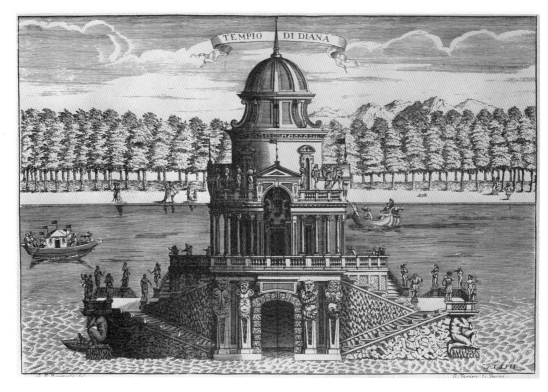

23. Temple of Diana (pl. XXVII)

2. THE SECOND BUILDING CAMPAIGN, 1666–1672

History

A whole new campaign of construction started in 1666. In the next six years, in a manner reminiscent of the contemporary activity at Versailles, the principal building was enlarged, as was the piazza in front of the palace, and new garden structures were added. I believe the additions to the palace to be the smaller wings, two on each side that are visible in the bird's-eye view (see Fig. 1).[52] Evidence that the villa had become more than the hunting lodge originally planned is given by the conversion of the former pheasantry to apartments for court officials, and the acquisition of plots in the town for members of the court.[53] The statues of nymphs and shepherds for the niches of the Teatro, construc-

[52] In the plan (Fig. 10), these are the rooms numbered 7. In a letter of 22 February 1669 to San Maurizio, his ambassador in Paris, Carlo Emanuele wrote, "Je suis à la Venerie ou je ajouste deux bras à la maison, les quels je presse pour pouvoir abiter cet hiver." Claretta, *Regno di Carlo Emanuele II*, II, 385.

[53] An account submitted by Gio. Antonio Boggetto for metalwork provided in the years 1673, 1674, and 1675 refers to supplies for "la fabricha delle stanze destinate per li SS.ri Ministri di Stato la quali s'e convertite la fasanera vecchia. . . ." Art. 207, 1672 in 1678. ¶ 18, vol. 1, fol. 55v, 29 April 1665, describes the duke's intention to have identical buildings built from the entrance to the palace buildings on the piazza and notes that he has given building sites to "alcuni de Sig.ri Cavaglieri della sua Corte" who have offered to construct them.

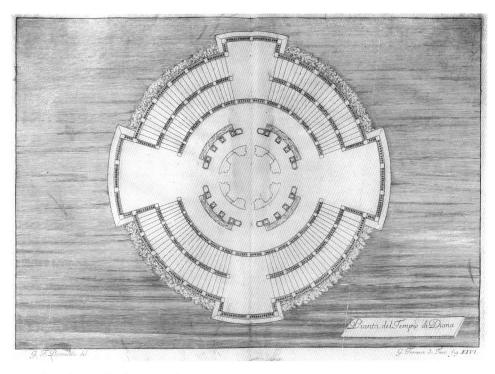

24. Plan of Temple of Diana (pl. XXVI)

tion of which had started by 1666, were ordered and installed in the same year (Fig. 16; Docs. 24, 30).

In May 1669 a design for one of the most impressive decorations at Venaria Reale, the Temple of Diana, was shown to the duchess (Figs. 23, 24).[54] Construction, however, did not start until 1673. In 1670 construction of the Fountain of Hercules, its stairs, and pavilions was paid for, and in 1671 its decoration began (Figs. 25, 26; Docs. 37, 47, and App. II, nos. 8, 9). The allée starting at the Fountain of Hercules was extended to the site of the future temple (Doc. 38); that it was not a canal despite Castellamonte's views is clear from his description and the documents (see Figs. 1, 2).[55]

After 1673 the work again slowed down at Venaria Reale, and although changes continued to be made, most of the money was spent on finishing decorations.[56] The

[54] This is described in a letter to Carlo Emanuele (see App. III, no. 1). It is not clear from the letter if this was Castellamonte's final design, but it did have a rocky base, with steps leading up to the temple.

[55] These appear in a set of documents of May and June 1678 (Docs. 63, 65) that testify to work done by Carlo Adamo before his death—work for which his heirs are petitioning for payment.

[56] The few changes are the addition of the *perspettive*, a new garden next to the new orangery, and the *fasanera*. There are contracts for maintenance of the fountains and pipes in 1678, for maintenance of the roofs in 1679, and a general contract with Pietro Rossi signed 30 May 1679 for repairs and maintenance for the next ten years.

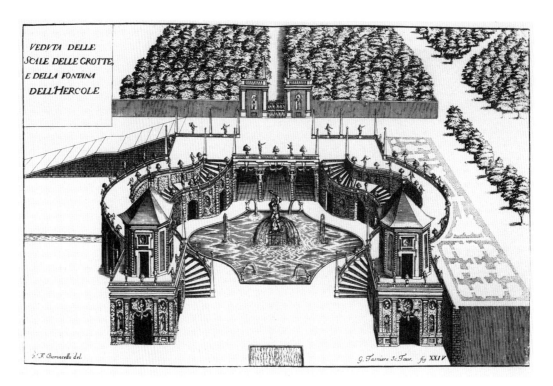

25. Fountain of Hercules (pl. XXIV)

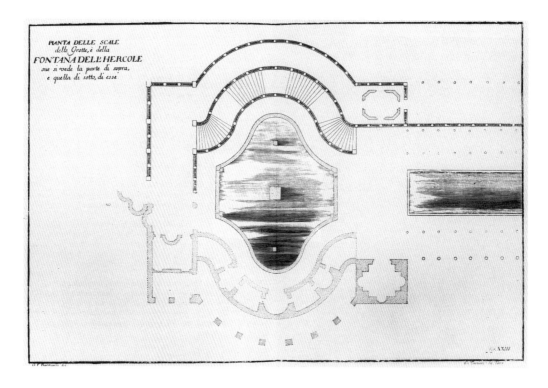

26. Plan of Fountain of Hercules (pl. XXIII)

Temple of Diana was unfinished when the duke died in 1675, and was never completed as planned. A contract for roofing the structure was drawn up in 1679, but there is no record that it was completed (App. III, nos. 5, 6). Although Carlo Emanuele's widow, Maria Giovanna Battista, preferred her villa, the Villa della Madama, Venaria Reale was scrupulously maintained as the numerous contracts for maintenance demonstrate.[57]

Venaria Reale and Versailles

The original design for the palace at Venaria Reale and its decorations, as well as the layout of the gardens, were the outgrowth of the local traditions, part Italian and part French, for villas. The modifications and additions started in 1666 were influenced by developments taking place at Versailles, where Louis XIV, starting in 1662, had initiated new construction and alterations to the hunting lodge built by Louis XIII.

Louis XIV and Carlo Emanuele II were first cousins. The dynasties were linked by several intermarriages arranged to stabilize relationships between France and the Duchy of Piedmont, which in the seventeenth century included parts of Switzerland, the present French Department, the Savoie, and extended as far south as Genoa on the Mediterranean coast of Italy.[58] The childhood of the two rulers had had many similarities.[59]

Numerous parallels in their lives must have made all the more galling to Carlo Emanuele their most important difference. Louis XIV was the ruler of one of the wealthiest and most powerful nations in Europe, while Carlo Emanuele ruled a small duchy lacking the military might and the great wealth possessed by Louis. He was in fact a "poor relation."[60] Nevertheless, his envy of Louis XIV and his desire to emulate him were important influences on his life and in his projects.[61]

A comparison of Venaria Reale with Versailles and the construction dates of their individual parts shows that Versailles was an important influence on the second stage of construction at Venaria which began in 1666. When work started at Versailles in 1662, the additions to the old castle at Venaria were nearly complete, the buildings of the *cour d'honneur* had been constructed, as well as a chapel and an entrance plaza.[62] The first

---

[57] A document of inspection, parts of which are transcribed in App. III, no. 6, suggests that the property was controlled by the "Auditore patrimoniale," and hence there may have been a requirement that the villa be maintained at least during the minority of Vittorio Amedeo.

[58] Carlo Emanuele's mother, Maria Cristina, was the daughter of King Henry IV of France and sister of Louis XIII, the father of Louis XIV.

[59] Carlo Emanuele's childhood is discussed by Claretta, *Regno di Carlo Emanuele II*, I, 12–70. For Louis XIV, see P. Erlanger, *Louis XIV*, n.p., 1965, 11–192.

[60] An example of his uneasy rivalry with Louis XIV was his request at the time of his marriage to Francesca (Françoise) d'Orléans, Louis' niece, that the French king call him by a title reserved for the sons of French kings, "Monsieur" ("trattato col titolo regio"). This was refused, but as a compromise Louis XIV agreed to address him as "fratello." G. Datta de Alberis, *Cristina di Francia. Madama Reale*, Turin, 1943, 333.

[61] "Un peu plus agé [Carlo Emanuele] que Louis XIV il le prenait pour modèle non dans les grandes choses de la politique et de la guerre, pour lesquelles il se sentait trop peu de génie et de ressources, mais dans les arts et les travaux de la paix. . . ." C. Rousset, *Histoire du Louvois et de son administration politique et militaire*, Paris, 1862–64, 4th ed., III, 58. The same author also suggests that the Venaria Reale was a reflection, "comme un souvenir lointain," of Fontainebleau.

[62] See pp. 150–55.

Veuë et perspectiue du Chasteau de Versaille, du cõsté de l'entrée

27. View of entrance to Versailles by Israel Sylvestre

construction at Versailles extended long wings in front of the *cour d'honneur* of the original U-shaped building with stables on one side and new kitchens on the other.[63] An enclosed plaza of semicircular form was constructed, delimited by a low balustrade terminating in pyramids (Fig. 27). Shortly after these were built at Versailles in 1664,[64] land was purchased at Venaria Reale to enlarge the piazza (Docs. 23, 27, 28), and the new form, as illustrated by Castellamonte (see Fig. 13), is identical to that of Versailles.

Modifications to the old gardens at Versailles were initiated at the same time as the plaza construction there. Le Nôtre replaced the rectangular *parterre de broderie* behind the palace with an elongated horseshoe-shaped terrace. Two ramps led down from the parterre to a lower level where an allée on the central axis divided the bosquets (Fig. 28).[65] This work appears to have been completed by 1663.[66] Shortly after, changes were

[63] For the early history of Versailles, see A. Marie, *La Naissance de Versailles*, Paris, 1968. The first construction is discussed on pp. 24–25, and a plan by Israël Sylvestre showing the *cour d'honneur* appears on pl. VI.

[64] The view by Sylvestre is dated 1664.

[65] The appearance of the park of Versailles ca. 1660/61 is shown in a plan in the Bibliothèque Nationale, Paris (Collection d'Anville nr. 83, Paris, Bibl. Nat. Ge DD 2987) reproduced in G. Weber, "Die Versailles-Konzepte von André Le Nôtre," *Münchner Jahrbuch der Bildenden Kunst* 20 (1969), fig. 1, and Marie, *La Naissance*, pl. III. The 1663 plan, fig. 30, is in the Bibliothèque de l'Institut, Paris, ms. 1307, fol. 68. Weber, "Versailles-Konzepte," discusses the first changes to the gardens at Versailles, pp. 208–9; Marie, op. cit., 26–29.

[66] Weber, "Versailles-Konzepte."

28. Plan of Le Nôtre parterre at rear of
chateau of Versailles (Paris, Bibliothèque
de l'Institut, ms. 1307, fol. 68;
photo: Archive photographique)

Veüe du Chasteau de Versailles, du costé
du Jardin

Versaliarum Palatij a parte horti
Prospectus

29. Garden facade and parterre at Versailles by Israel Sylvestre

initiated at Venaria Reale which involved replanting of the parterre behind the palace.[67] This area was given a similar U-shaped termination when a screen wall called the Teatro was built starting in 1666.

The chateau at Versailles sits on a ridge with the ground sloping away from it on all sides except the entrance. Among the earliest works there by Le Nôtre were the constructions that created the flat area around the chateau and the ramps or stairs leading to a leveled lower area. To the south of the chateau his design consisted of a *parterre de gazon* with two stairs at either side leading to a lower terrace.[68] Another such composition was designed for the terraces on the main east-west axis of the gardens, above and behind the Fountain of Latona. This project, never actually executed, was represented by Sylvestre in a view dated 1674 (Fig. 29). The fountain is shown surrounded by seventeen niches built under a U-shaped terrace. The center niche was to have had a rocky backdrop with two reclining figures framing a dragon.[69] On either side the niches were to contain statues of Neptune and Juno respectively (Fig. 30).[70] This project also seems to have been the source of inspiration at Venaria Reale. The Fountain of Hercules, which was completed in 1672 (Doc. 40), also had grottoes built under the upper terrace. Castellamonte describes a fountain in the center of the grotto with a statue of Neptune on a shell drawn by two sea horses, statues which appear in a *misura* of 1673 (Doc. 48).[71]

Other decorative details also appear to have been influenced by Versailles. An example is one of the fountains of the lower garden at Venaria Reale. The illustration in Castellamonte's book (see Fig. 19) shows a putto seated on the entwined tails of two nereids blowing a horn which is a waterspout. This is very similar in spirit and conception to one of the putto figures from the south parterre above the orangery, depicted by Le Pautre in 1677 (Fig. 31) and even closer to one of the rejected designs for this same pool in which a putto is shown holding up a fish from whose mouth the water spouts.[72]

There can be no doubt that Carlo Emanuele II was aware of the events at Versailles. His ambassador, Francesco Tommaso Chabò, Marchese di San Maurizio, kept him informed of everything that was happening and even sought advice and criticism on the

[67] Although the parterre had already been planted, a contract drawn up with Roberto Chevalier di Normandie for maintenance of the gardens included the item, "Manterà parim.te al giardino di sopra [= the parterre behind the palace] il busso quando S.A.R. l'havrà fatto piantare" (Doc. 25). (See n. 29, item 3, c.).

[68] Marie, *La Naissance*, 28

[69] Marie, *La Naissance*, 158. A design for this fountain is in Stockholm, Royal Museum, Cronstedt Coll. #39.

[70] An anonymous drawing of the Neptune fountain, Paris, Louvre, Cabinet du dessins, #30136–8185. For other fountains of this project, see Marie, *La Naissance*, pls. 83–84.

[71] "Sotto questa gran Loggia sostenuta da quattro grandi Termini di marmo in figura di quattro Vecchioni si vedono nelle loro grotte quattro Colossi rappresentanti quattro Deità Infernali, e più in dentro in Antro più profondo un Nettuno sopra sua concha tirata da due Cavalli Marini con due Ninfe sedenti à fianco in altri due Nicchi, quali gettano in diverse maniere copiosa quantità d'acqua." Castellamonte, 80.

[72] The drawing (Bibliothèque Nationale, Cab. des Estampes Va 362 VII, no. 51–1959 des papiers de Robert de Cotte) is illustrated in Marie, *La Naissance*, pl. x. Another project appears in a drawing in Stockholm (National Museum, Coll. Tessin, no. 7774) dated 1662. Marie, *La Naissance*, pl. IX.

30. Anonymous drawings of project for Neptune and Juno statues and grottoes at Versailles (Paris, Musée du Louvre, Cabinet des dessins, no. 30136–8185; photo: Documentation photographique; Bibliothèque Nationale, Cabinet des Estampes, B 2a; photo: Bibliothèque Nationale)

31. Cupid fountain at Versailles (Le Pautre, *Statues, fontaines . . . au Jardin de Versailles,* 1672–77)

33. Facade of the Orangery (pl. XII)

32. Hercules Fountain (pl. XXV)

designs for Venaria Reale.[73] A letter from the ambassador dated 27 September 1669 is an example of the interchange of ideas:

> La cour est à Versailles depuis le jour de Noël, le Roi veut y faire un ville fermée a l'imitation de celle que V.A.R. a fait faire à la Venerie. Je sais qu'ils n'ont pas voulu voir le plan que j'en ai decaceté; afin que l'on ne disse qu'il lui en avait fair venir la pensée, mais il est certain qu'elle l'a formé sur ce que M. de Bellefon lui a di [?] après que le Roi en eut montré le plan. Je l'ai fait voir aux ingenieurs du Roi qui l'ont trouvé superbe.[74]

The town of Versailles, however, bears no resemblance to that of Venaria.

Versailles was not the only royal French residence with influence on Venaria Reale. The unusual double reverse curve of the terraces and stairs of the Fountain of Hercules (see Figs. 25–26) is like those in the staircase called the Fer à Cheval in the Cour des Offices at Fontainebleau, built by 1634. Sometime during that same decade the island in the L'Éstang (the pond adjacent to the Jardin des Pins) was given a more regular shape and a small pavilion placed on it. A permanent architectural structure on an island in a

---

[73] See Claretta, *Regno di Carlo Emanuele II*, II, passim, for letters from San Maurizio to Carlo Emanuele.

[74] The letter goes on to report that the king's engineers found "la maison belle mais mal tourrie, les jardins petits parceque ils sont spacieux et les allées extrement larges et presqu' autant que le dit jardins. Ils trouvèrent aussi que V.A.R. en a trop borné la vue par les architectures qu'elle a fait elever au fond [the Teatro?]; ils censurent aussi le degré qui conduira dans l'allée d'eau bas, et surtout le rocher et les eaux qu'elle veut faire élever au bout." Published in Claretta, *Regno di Carlo Emanuele II*, II, 386.

garden lake was not common, and the Fontainebleau example was possibly the inspiration for siting the Temple of Diana at Venaria Reale in the center of a small lake.[75]

Thus Carlo Emanuele's building construction campaign at Venaria Reale can be traced to the influence of the new developments taking place at Versailles between 1662 and 1668. Another possible influence of Versailles is in the change in focus of the iconographical program which occurred with the construction of the Fountain of Hercules and the Temple of Diana.

The Garden Structures

The most unusual features of Venaria Reale are the garden structures which were all built or started in the second campaign. In chronological order they consist of the "Teatro," or "Loggia al Teatro," as Castellamonte titles it, that is, the semicircular screen that terminated the upper garden (see Fig. 16), the Fountain of Hercules, that is, the ensemble of stairs, pavilions, and pool with the Hercules fountain (Figs. 25, 26, 32), the facade of the "new" orangery (Fig. 33), and the Temple of Diana (see Figs. 23, 24). Although they fulfill conventional functions, their design has little or no precedent in garden structures, but are closely linked to stage design and festivity architecture.

The Teatro screen is a case in point. The U- or hippodrome-shaped garden terrace belongs to a tradition that goes back to antiquity, and can be found in numerous sixteenth- and seventeenth-century gardens in Italy, as well as in Le Nôtre's early designs for the parterre at Versailles, but the elaborately decorated screen that terminated it was an innovation.[76] It functioned very much like a backdrop on a stage, terminating and defining the space of the upper garden. The orangery facade and the screen wall of the Teatro are designed in the same vocabulary one finds in other works by Castellamonte; in the former, the wall surfaces are articulated by banded fluted pilasters, with columns flanking the major door.[77] Similar details are visible in the *Teatrum* view of the Porta del Po built by Castellamonte in 1673 (Fig. 34). It is the curvilinear shape of the facade that distinguishes it from the usually more severe designs of Castellamonte. Although curve and vocabulary are ultimately derived from Borromini, the exuberance of the shape and its decorations foretell the more extravagant later designs of Guarini and Juvarra. It was placed at the end of the walled court numbered 14 on the bird's-eye view (see Fig. 1) to shut off the view toward the pheasant house and the asymmetrically placed orangery. Thus the facade played the same role as the backdrop of a stage set and had much the same character as the temporary arches erected to welcome visitors in the customary ceremonial entries of the period.

[75] See J. Dan, *Le Trésor des merveilles de la maison royale de Fontainebleau*, Paris, 1642, 34, for a description of the stairs, and pp. 178–79 for the pavilion. See M. J. J. Champollion-Figéac, *Le Palais de Fontainebleau*, Paris, 1866, 349.

[76] This feature was considered particularly displeasing to French visitors, who objected to its interruption of the view down the long axis of the allée.

[77] I did not find any specific payment documents for the sculpture and ornaments that appear in the illustration. It is first mentioned in the *ristretto* of 1670 (App. II, no. 8).

34. Porta del Po (Bleau, *Teatrum,* pl. 30b, detail)

The only one of these four structures that remained incomplete was the Temple of Diana, a building which Castellamonte characterized "di Magnificenza sormonta tutti li già veduti" (p. 81) (see Figs. 23, 24). It appears from a document of 1679 (App. III, no. 6) that the rocky base was actually built, with stairs in two flights, and that at least a start was made on the walls of the first level of the temple.[78] This of course was barely the beginning of the ambitious design described by Castellamonte, with the perforated base for the passage of boats, the atlantes flanking the entrance to the passages. The temple itself was to have been round, its walls divided by eight pilasters and sixteen columns. This level terminated with a cornice decorated with twenty-four nymphs of Diana; above there was to be a high drum and a cupola. Both inside and out the walls between the columns were to have niches, while the interstices were to be covered with a mosaic of shells and mother of pearl.

The interior, the "Lavacro" of Diana, was to have had a statue group of Diana attended by eight nymphs whose golden cups jetted water, "giuochi d'acqua" to surprise visitors, and a fountain whose waters fell to the lake below.[79]

[78] The contract calls for a roof to cover the "piano" of the temple, to be supported on eight circumferential pillars 2.25 meters high ("piedi quatro e mezzo dal suo piano") and one higher central pier, octagonal in shape. A wood cornice on top of the outer pilasters was to support 12 rafters, each 7.7 meters long. Another roof was to cover the stairs and was to be supported by 18 rafters resting on a cornice over 12 piers built on the exterior walls of the stairs and the marble "cordone" of the Temple floor. These rafters were to be approximately 6 meters long. See App. III, no. 6.

[79] For Castellamonte's text, see App. III, no. 6. The description of the interior of the temple is notably less detailed than those of the completed parts of the villa, and I suspect that no final design had been developed.

Some idea of the dimensions of the temple and its base can be deduced from the 1679 contract for roofing what had been completed (App. III, no. 6). The temple must have been about 15 meters in diameter, sitting on a base which was approximately an additional 14 meters wide. Applying these measurements to Castellamonte's plan and elevation produces the startling dimensions of a base approximately 9 meters high and a temple height of 22 meters.

A project for a garden pavilion of such a scale was unprecedented in the 1660s. A few island structures precede it, notably the modest octagonal pavilion on the lake at Fontainebleau, and the sixteenth-century mount on an island at Castle Chatillon. Lakes with islands are more common; there is the Isolotto at the Boboli Gardens, and an island with a small pavilion at the approximately contemporary Villa Barbarigo at Valsanzibio in the Veneto.

Individual features of the design can be related to earlier precedents. The rocky base set in a body of water and with cross passages should be compared to Bernini's Four River Fountain in Rome, completed in 1645–54, while the statue group of Diana attended by nymphs is reminiscent of the Apollo and attending nymph group in the Grotto de Thétis at Versailles, constructed in 1665–66.[80]

The chief inspiration for the design, however, derives from the tradition of temporary decorations and settings created for festivities and celebrations at court in the previous decades.[81] Characteristic of the repertory of decorations are those erected in the piazza in front of the Palazzo Madama for the celebrations in 1650 of the marriage of Carlo Emanuele's sister, Henrietta Adelaide, to the son of the elector of Bavaria (Figs. 35, 36).[82] These, as were many others during the next thirty years, were designed by Amedeo Castellamonte. In the views of the event, one can see a rocky base (representing the Alps) with herms flanking a doorway, much as the atlantids at the Temple of Diana. On the opposite side of the piazza, the trees symbolizing the Erycinian (German) forest flanked a temple, whose forms are almost identical to the Temple of Diana design. There is no reason to suppose that these decorations were copies of earlier designs; they are, however, characteristic examples of the design vocabulary of court festivities.

[80] See L. Châtelet Lange, "La grotte de Thétis et le premier Versailles de Louis XIV," *Art de France* 1 (1961), 133–48, for a history of the construction of the grotto and an interpretation of its meaning.

[81] There is a large bibliography on the subject of festivities at the Savoy court in the 17th century. See, with its references to earlier publications, M. McGowan, "Les fêtes de cour en Savoie. L'oeuvre de Philippe d'Agliè," *Revue d'histoire du Théâtre* 3 (1970), 83–242 [mainly the festivities held during the Regency of Maria Cristina, 1637–62]; M. Viale Ferrero, *Le Feste delle Madama Reali di Savoia*, Turin, 1965, which also includes material on the Regency of Carlo Emanuele's widow, Maria Giovanna Battista. The former is particularly useful for its study of the illuminated manuscripts recording the festivities made by Tommaso Borgonio (see n. 83). Two treatises by Claude François Menestrier have descriptions of festivities at the court which he attended and in some cases devised the themes: *Receuil des devises et des poésies*, Lyons, 1663; *Traité des Tournois, Ioustes, Carrousels, et autres spectacles publics*, Lyons, 1669. The Biblioteca Reale in Turin's collection, Misc. St. Pat. contains several hundred pamphlets printed as descriptions or records (sometimes even exegeses of the symbolism) of the several events in the 17th-century festivities. They are listed in Manno and Promis, *Bibliografica*.

[82] The *libretto* for this tourney is in BRT, Misc. St. Pat., 298, int. 8. The illustrations are from Tommaso Borgonio's manuscript description of the tourney, BRT N13–344. See n. 81, for a description of these manuscripts.

35. View of Piazza Madama during *Ercole Domitori carosello,* illustration by Tommaso Borgonio (Turin, Biblioteca Reale, ms. N-13–344; photo: Chomon-Perino)

Finally, the source for the design of the Fountain of Hercules is the most unusual of all four of the structures. The design problem, to create a transition between two levels in a garden, was common in villas in Italy, and the solution of ramped stairways by no means uncommon—examples such as the Belvedere Court at the Vatican and the Villa Giulia in Rome readily come to mind. There are also earlier examples of placing grottoes under these connecting stairs. In this case, however, the specific design is directly derived from a stage set for a ballet performed at the celebrations for the marriage of Carlo Emanuele's sister, Margarita, to Ranuccio Farnese, duke of Parma, in 1660.

The ballet, described in an illuminated manuscript by Tommaso Borgonio, *L'Unione per la Peregrina Margherita reale . . . col Serenissimo Ranuccio Farnese, Duca di Parma,* had as its theme a myth of Hercules bringing pearls back from India; its opening scene took place in the ancient city of Babylon, which was portrayed on the backdrop.[83] At the end of the act, a curtain opened in the middle of the backdrop to reveal a view of the Temple

[83] The sets are described in a document (Art. 199, ¶ 1, 1657–67, fols. 50–67) that also has the contracts for the floats (see App. III, no. 8), arches, etc., but there are no specifications for the drop with the Temple of Hercules. The *Racconto succinto delle Solennità per le Nozze di Margherita, etc.,* Turin, 1661 (BRT, Misc. St. Pat., 304, int. 8), does not have a *libretto* of the ballet. It, however, is described and illustrated in ms. BNaz Qv 53, fol. 21, one of the illuminated manuscripts made by Tommaso Borgonio to record court festivities. See McGowan, "Les fêtes," for information about Borgonio. Twelve of these manuscripts survive, dating between 1640 and 1667. Three are in the Biblioteca Reale and the rest in the Biblioteca Nazionale, Turin.

36. Scenery representing Piedmont and the Alps from *Ercole Domitori carosello* (Turin, Biblioteca Reale, ms. N-13–344; photo: Chomon-Perino)

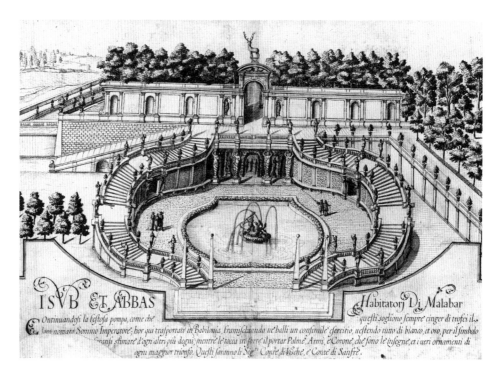

ISVB ET ABBAS

Habitatorj Di Malabar

37. Temple of Hercules by Tommaso Borgonio, illustration in *L'unione per la Peregrina.* . . .
(Turin, Biblioteca Nazionale, ms. QV 53, fol. 21; photo: Chomon-Perino)

of Hercules (Fig. 37). The painting is on part of a folio with descriptive text; there is no possibility that it was bound in at a later time.

A comparison of the Borgonio illustration with Castellamonte's plate reveals some differences: there are no pavilions in the stage set; the gates at the top are different; there are fewer grottoes; and the Hercules fountain is placed on a low rocky base, instead of being raised on a pedestal. Nevertheless, they clearly are only variants on one design. Castellamonte was also responsible for the designs for these festivities; given their date (1660), it is possible that the set is also a record of an early project for decorations at Venaria Reale.[84]

There is also a link between the fountain at the base of the stairway (see Fig. 32) and these festivities. The *carosello*, or tourney, also called a *balletto a cavallo*—a traditional event in court festivities—was preceded by a procession in which there were four floats, representing, one might even say symbolizing, Savoy, France, Parma, and Florence, the four nationalities of the couple's parents. The Florentine float carried a rocky mount with a painted cascade of water flowing down it. At the top was a figure of Hercules fighting a Hydra with seven heads, clearly anticipating the statue in the Fountain of Hercules.[85]

[84] The festivity scenarios, including the one for the ballet, were by Filippo di San Martino, Count d'Agliè, who for many years had been the chief divisor of the themes for the celebrations, the tourneys, dramas, and processions as well as the ballets. G. Tani, "Le Comte d'Agliè et le ballet de cour en Italie," *Les Fêtes de la Renaissance*, ed. J. Jacquot, Paris, 1956, 221–34, and McGowan, "Les fêtes" (see n. 81).

[85] The contracts for the construction of the floats and some of the other temporary decorations are preserved in AST, Art. 199, ¶ 1, 1657–67. See App. III, no. 8.

Castellamonte's designs for the garden buildings at Venaria Reale reveal a hitherto unparalleled relationship between festivity and garden architecture. It was not uncommon for the former to reflect or even represent in smaller scale actual structures. Here the garden structures perpetuated in masonry the ephemeral festivity decorations. Might one even propose that the succession of the structures was intended to emulate the conventional succession of scenes in theatrical performances at this time?[86] An opening pastoral act (such as supplied by the nymphs and shepherds in the Teatro screen) or a scene on the front curtain was common. This would part to reveal an architectural set (the Fountain of Hercules), and the performance would culminate with some sort of distant view of a temple or city (the Temple of Diana).

3. THE ICONOGRAPHICAL PROGRAM, FESTIVITIES, AND THE THEATER

The second building campaign, which included the construction of the Fountain of Hercules and the design and initial construction of the Temple of Diana, brought important modifications in the iconographical program at Venaria Reale. The original decorations of the palace depicted myths of Diana and the activities of the hunt to create a Kingdom of Diana, the goddess of the hunt, and thus the appropriate focus of decorations for a hunting lodge.[87] As we have seen, these decorations on the interior of the palace were closely linked with earlier decorations in the other royal villas near Turin.[88] The myths of Diana and the scenes of hunting in the several apartments were designed by Tesauro, Castellamonte tells us, to teach "il vivere humano, e civile."[89]

Fountains in the original gardens were decorated with the familiar array of ancient deities but with no explicit theme.[90] One cannot detect any personification of the ruler or his wife in the program, nor any allegorical reference to actual events as in the fountains at Versailles. There seems to have been little French influence in the early decorations, with the possible exception of motifs borrowed from Anet, the chateau Henry III built for Diane de Poitiers, where the decorations were also based on the myths of Diana the huntress.[91]

[86] Per Björstrom, *Giacomo Torelli and Baroque Stage Design*, Figura, n.s. 2, Stockholm, 1961, 15–28.

[87] The facade of the palace carried an inscription: "Questo à un Genio Guerrier gradito hostello / Delle Caccie Regali / Fondò il secondo CARLO EMANUELO / Per avezzar gli strali / Della Dea delle Caccie à quei di Marte, / Che la Caccia, e la Guerra è un'istess' arte" Castellamonte, p. 8.

[88] See n. 10.

[89] "Hà perciò il Gran Conte Tesauro . . . Autore di tutte queste Compositioni intitolato questo Palazzo la REGGIA DI DIANA, e sotto allegorici Documenti de' fatti favolosi di questa Dea delle Caccie, c'insegna con Motti, & Inscrittioni in lingua Italiana il vivere humano, e civile. . . ." Castellamonte, p. 24. In another place, Castellamonte explains that in the ten paintings in the *salone* representing Diana's myths, ". . . sono spiegate le Attioni principali di Diana accomodate all'uso delle Corti" (p. 26). These mottoes are the most moralizing and didactic.

[90] The grottoes under the steps of the Fountain of Hercules had four statues of the gods of the underworld, and one of Neptune standing on a shell drawn by sea horses (Castellamonte, p. 80). Another Neptune was in one of the eight grottoes of the lower garden (Fig. 22).

[91] Anet also had a bronze deer over the gateway and motifs related to the hunt in its decorations. See A. Blunt, *Philibert de l'Orme*, London, 1958.

However, the new constructions are certainly intended to personify Carlo Emanuele and Maria Cristina. The pavilions of the Fountain of Hercules (see Figs. 25, 26) contained decorations representing the deeds of Hercules with Diana presiding over them.[92] A statue of Hercules and the Hydra, twice life-size, was erected in the pool at the base of the stairs of the fountain (see Fig. 32). Its pedestal had reliefs depicting four of the deeds of Hercules, one of which appears in Castellamonte's illustration.

Personification of rulers as heroes and ancient deities in decorations and in garden statues was neither new nor unusual, and the use of Hercules myths to personify rulers and their virtues belongs to a long iconographic tradition. This had been particularly strong in Turin in the earlier part of the century, where a number of examples made the identification very specific. Events of special dynastic importance were usually celebrated with ballets or tourneys using the theme of Hercules conquering monsters. These include a celebration of the birth of Prince Francesco Giacinto in 1632[93] by a performance in the piazza in front of the palace of a tourney between noblemen of the court and the Herculean monsters. The theme recurred at the marriage of Henrietta Adelaide, Carlo Emanuele's sister, in 1650 to the son of the elector of Bavaria and the marriage of his other sister, Margarita, to Duke Ranuccio Farnese of Parma in 1660. Even closer was the parallel made between Hercules and Hebe and Carlo Emanuele and his first wife, Françoise d'Orléans, in the decorations erected to welcome them at their entrance to Turin after their marriage in 1663.[94] The identification of the ruler with Hercules was particularly strong in the 1650 tourney, *Gli Hercoli Domatori de' Mostri, et Amore domatore degli Hercoli* (see Figs. 35, 36). The four Hercules represented the nationalities of the bride's parents, Duke Vittorio Amedeo of Savoy and Maria Cristina, daughter of the king of France, and the bridegroom's, Maximilian, elector of Bavaria and Maria Anna, daughter of the Holy Roman Emperor, Ferdinand II. Examples abound of this personification in palace decorations as well as the more ephemeral festivity decorations.[95]

[92] Each pavilion, according to Castellamonte (p. 76), had a vaulted octagonal room. Niches in the walls contained marble busts and mirrored panels. The vaults were divided into eight compartments, with a central one at the top representing Diana and two nymphs sending a celestial lion to combat the Greeks. Four of the ceiling compartments were mirrored and the other four contained scenes of Hercules fighting the Nemean Lion, the serpents which attacked him in the cradle, the Nubian giants, and the Dragon guarding the Gardens of the Hesperides. In each of these scenes the animals were depicted as fountains with water rather than blood flowing from their mouths. The second pavilion's central panel showed Diana sending a boar to attack the Erimantheans, and in the other panels Hercules was depicted conquering the boar, fighting Anteaus, and killing King Augeus and the Cretan Bull. Again the animals were depicted in the form of fountains.

[93] The older brother of Carlo Emanuele II, heir to the throne until the death of his father in 1637, and ruler under the regency of his mother until his death in 1638.

[94] Described in the *libretto* by V. Castiglione, *Le feste nuttiale delli R. Altezze di Savoia, Carlo Emanuele II e Francesca Borbone di Valois*, BRT, Misc. St. Pat., 299, II, int. 1, and in *Dichiaratione architettonica degli archi trionfali, ...per l'entrata di Carlo Emanuel II e Francesca di Valois*, Turin, 1663, BRT, Misc. St. Pat., 303, int. 3.

[95] For instance, the theme of Hercules, conqueror of monsters, also appeared in the vault of the room in the Castello in which Carlo Emanuele received the Bavarian ambassador in 1650. See V. Castiglione, *LI REALI HIMENEI De' Serenissimi Principi Sposi HENRIETTA ADELAIDE di Savoia, E FERDINANDO MARIA Di Baviera*, 1651, 19 (BRT, Misc. St. Pat., vol. 298, int. 11).

38. Scene of festivity at Savigliano with Bath of Diana from Emanuele Panealbo,
Relazione della solenne entrata. . . . , Turin, 1668 (photo: Chomon-Perino)

The identification of the ruler's spouse with Diana was not as traditional in Turinese iconography, although common elsewhere, but the events leading up to the commission of the temple show that the goddess of the hunt was intended to personify Maria Giovanna Battista.[96]

The origins of the Temple of Diana can be traced to a specific event. Castellamonte in his description says that the temple is really a "Bath of Diana," and the interior of the structure was to have had fountains and the nymphs of Diana's entourage. A Bath of Diana had been the major feature of the decorations erected to welcome the duke and duchess to Savigliano, a small town south of Turin in July 1668. They passed through on their way to Valdieri (south of Cuneo), renowned for the curative properties of its springs.[97] It was hoped that the pilgrimage would result in a pregnancy, for the couple had had only one child, who was sickly, and who, indeed, had been close to death several times in the previous winter.[98]

---

[96] The identification is affirmed by the plate in Castellamonte representing her as Diana.

[97] The entry is described by Emanuele Filiberto Panealbo in *Relazione della solenne entrata fatta nella città di Savigliano delle Reali Altezze Carlo Emanuel II e Maria Giovanna Battista di Nemours il primo di luglio 1668*, Turin, 1668. See App. III, no. 1. He states, "Essendo M.R. Maria Giovanna Battista di Nemours stata consigliata da Signori Medici di prender li Bagni di Vaudier [Valdieri] per disporsi con la salubrità di quell'acque à consolar con un Secondo Principe gli suoi fedelissimi Popoli. . . ."

[98] No other child was born to the couple, but ironically their son, Vittorio Amedeo II, lived to the age of 64, dying in 1730, while Carlo Emanuele died at the early age of 41.

183

The main piazza of Savigliano was laid out as a garden with a fountain 6 meters high and 1 meter wide (Fig. 38). At the rear was a loggia which the narrator of the *Relazaione* calls "il Bagno di Diana." It had a porticoed facade that opened on a grotto with a seated figure of Diana. Herms on the portico piers represented Diana's nymphs.

Although the visit to Valdieri did not have the desired result, the idea of a permanent "Bagno di Diana" clearly was retained in the design of the Temple of Diana at Venaria Reale, just as its round form came from a traditional pavilion type used in festivities. However, we must assume that there is more to these decorations than the simple ornamentation of the garden and recreation of stage designs. Tesauro said festivities and jousts were "imprese vive e metafore animate";[99] and this is so of painting cycles and other art forms in this period.

The Labors of Hercules had become traditional metaphors for a ruler's conquest of vice or his enemies. Diana, the maiden huntress, personified the virtues of female rulers, while a round temple form was resonant with allusions to virtue and chastity. But the key to the interpretation lies in yet another quotation from Tesauro, his description of a festivity in celebration of the birthday of the duchess, Maria Cristina, in 1660: he describes the piazza where the tourney took place as a garden decorated with greens and flowers but peopled with "stranissime e monstruosissime fiere." He commends the *concetto*, "ingegnossima e nobilissima l'Inventione perochè il Giardino metaforicamente rappresenta il Piemonte . . . la chiusura figurava le Alpi. . . . I mostri finalmente dinotavano i detrattori e gll'individiosi."[100] That this is the metaphor of the iconographical program at Venaria Reale is shown by a *libretto* dedicated to Madama Reale, Maria Giovanna Battista, by Pietro Antonio Arnoldo, *Il Giardino di Piemonte Hoggi vivente nell' Anno 1673*.[101] It describes the "Giuochi e Feste fattesi in Carnevale nella Piazza Reale di Torino." The subject was the "Trionfo de' Vitij et al sostegno delle Virtù." It opens:

> Al' Armi, al'armi, ò Gran Giovanna, a VOI
> I più augusti Trionfi il Ciel riserba;
> Isvenata da voi l'Hidra superba
> Pur hoggi ammireran gli Alpini Heroici.

In another verse Madama Reale is described as "nata a produrre intrepidi campioni" and that her virtues

> Non a scoppiar contro de Vitij i Tuoni
> Ne à far de Mostri glorioso spoglio
> Ma pur de l'Hidra infami a gran cordoglio
> Quelle distruggi, e le virtù incoroni.

---

[99] Tesauro, *Cannocchiale*, quoted by Viale Ferrero, *Feste*, 67.
[100] Quoted in Viale Ferrero, *Feste*, 12, and from Tesauro, *Cannocchiale*, 1670 edition, no page given.
[101] Arnoldo's poem was published in Turin, 1673.

Further on, a section, an "Ode Pindarica," is dedicated to Carlo Emanuele and praises his achievements as a ruler. Another section apostrophizes Venaria Reale itself, "de suo [Carlo Emanuele] Genio Regal fulgida Prole / ove in vece di Cintia il Toro cole / la Gra. Giovanna à più gran numi equale."

> Tu sei pur Quella in cui l' Architettura
> Vince se stessa ove l'HERCULEO FONTE
> con vaghi scherzi, e con delizie pronte
> In arca i Cigli l' Arte e ala Natura.

A final poem is addressed to "Madama Reale, Vera Diana della Real Venaria," and says:

> Cedan le finte [the performers] à una Real Sovrana
> E di mia Venaria per Essa eretta
> Giovanna sol sia l'Immortal Diana

Written at the time that construction was just about to start on the Temple of Diana,[102] this *libretto*, which is not a description but the record of the actual script of the celebration, ties the themes of the conquest of vices by Hercules to the virtuous rule of Maria Giovanna and provides the interpretation of the new iconography at Venaria. Its garden is the Garden of the Piedmont, a common allegory in seventeenth-century festivities, and it is governed by the two virtuous rulers. Hercules, at one end of the long allée, has conquered the detractors and the vices represented by the Hydra and the other monsters on the statue pedestal. Diana at the other end rules from the Temple of Virtue, and their joint beneficence assures the wealth and well-being of the state. Just as the garden architecture is the permanent record of the festivities and their decorations, the iconography perpetuates the *concetto* of a festivity which honored the reigning couple. Once again the transitory celebration has been made concrete and permanent.

4. THE AFTERMATH

History

The first plans for alterations to the villa after Carlo Emanuele's death occurred when his son, Vittorio Amedeo II, made plans for changes at the end of the century.[103] Damages sustained during the French attack in 1693 may have been the impetus, but a letter by his court architect, Michelangelo Garove, suggests Vittorio Amedeo's motivation was similar to his father's original one—he wanted to make it suitable for the use of royalty.[104] Major additions to the palace were designed by Garove, and a plan for the

---

[102] The contract for its construction is dated July 1673. See App. III, no. 3.

[103] See D. Carutti, *Storia del regno di Vittorio Amedeo II*, 3rd ed., Turin, 1897, and G. Symcox, *Victor Amedeus II: Absolutism in the Savoyard State, 1675–1730*, Berkeley, 1983.

[104] A letter from the superintendent, Fabrizio Maulandi, dated 2 October 1693 and published by Pamparato (*Venaria Reale*, 19–23) describes the damage, which was not heavy. However, a letter by Garove suggests the motivation was to improve rather than restore. "S.A.R. ayant trouvé le bâtiment de la Venerie manquant de toutes sortes de commodités, et de tout ce qui se requiert pour la majesté d'une maison royale. . . ." published by Pommer, *Eighteenth-Century Architecture in Piedmont*, App. III, no. 2, 146.

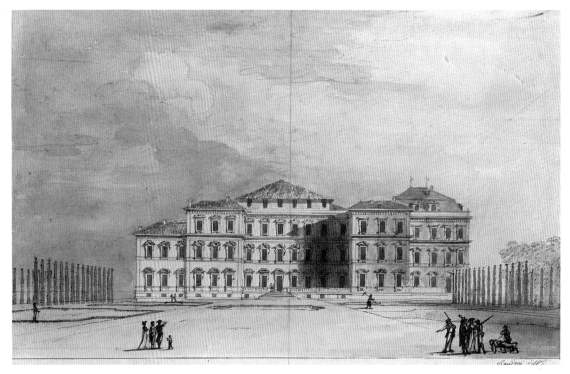

39. View of garden side of Palace at Venaria Reale after Garove addition, drawing by Carlo Randoni (Turin, Biblioteca Nazionale, V.I. 74, no. 5034; photo: Chomon-Perino)

complete reconstruction of the gardens was made; only minor alterations to the palace were actually carried out. These included the addition of a new pavilion to the south (Fig. 39), the side away from the river, and a gallery projecting to the east toward the town.[105] Repairs were carried out at the Fountain of Hercules, although the duke had been advised to demolish it.[106] The allée from the fountain to the incomplete Temple of Diana was widened, and the latter was demolished. All work came to a halt about 1704 with the gallery and eastern pavilion still incomplete.[107] Ten years later Juvarra contributed plans for their completion, and in 1716 construction began on the chapel he designed. Its consecration in 1732 marked the end of construction at Venaria Reale.[108]

The history of the villa since then is one of gradual decay and destruction. Renewed attacks by French armies in the nineteenth century caused the destruction of what remained of the gardens.[109] The buildings, used as a military barracks in the nineteenth

[105] For a discussion of this period and a summary of the documents, see Pommer, *Eighteenth-Century Architecture in Piedmont*, 143–49.

[106] See n. 104.

[107] Pommer, *Eighteenth-Century Architecture in Piedmont*. See n. 103.

[108] Ibid., 149–76. Columns from the Temple of Diana were used in the Juvarra chapel. Documents in AST, Sez. IV, Bilanci Fabbriche e Fortificazioni . . . 1718. Bilancio per Fabbriche Civile. Venaria Reale. Capella, and Sez. III, Tesoria delle Fabbriche, Fortificazioni ed Artiglieria. 1721. Cap. 357. Thanks to the late Richard Pommer for sending me the information and document citations.

[109] Pamparato, *Venaria Reale*, 24.

century, have been in ruinous condition since World War II. Although a restoration of the *salone* was undertaken in the 1960s, today the roof has become so weak that the whole central edifice is endangered. No trace of the gardens remains, nor of the Fountain of Hercules, and the surviving buildings stand isolated among the weeds of the neglected fields. A few of the paintings from the Salone, as well as a fragment of the Hercules and Hydra statue from the Fountain of Hercules, are in the Palazzo Madama. Nothing else seems to have survived.[110]

Later Influence

Venaria Reale marks the culmination of a villa style that had begun in the previous century and which had determined the form and decorations of the ring of royal and aristocratic villas that encircled the city of Turin. It was, however, also the end of the tradition. For the rest of the century, villa building consisted of modification and enlargement of older castles already in the royal domain. The next villa with similar function and location, the hunting lodge at Stupinigi initiated in 1729 following designs by Juvarra for Vittorio Amedeo II was based on an entirely different principle of design.[111] Except for some unexecuted designs by Guarini for stairs at Racconigi with shapes derived from the Fountain of Hercules (Figs. 40, 41),[112] none of the distinctive and inventive garden structures at Venaria were copied elsewhere. However, they continued to form part of the vocabulary of stage and festivity decorations in Turin until the Napoleonic era. We will never know what inspired this unique transformation of that fantastic, ephemeral style into solid, three-dimensional form nor why it has remained unique in the history of garden architecture.

[110] See n. 8.

[111] Plans were sent to Munich at Henrietta Adelaide's request in the early 1660s for a hunting lodge which she planned at Nymphenburg; ultimately they were not used, but the decorations, planned by Tesauro, also were based on the *concetto* of Diana's Kingdom. G. Claretta, *Adelaide di Savoia, duchessa di Baviera e i suoi tempi*, Turin, 1877, 137. See also L. Berghoff, "Emanuele Tesauro und seine Concetti unter besonderen Berücksichtigung von Schloss Nymphenburg," Ph.D. diss., Munich, 1971.

[112] Published by Lange, "Documenti di Guarini," catalogue nos. 38 and 36 respectively, pp. 251–52.

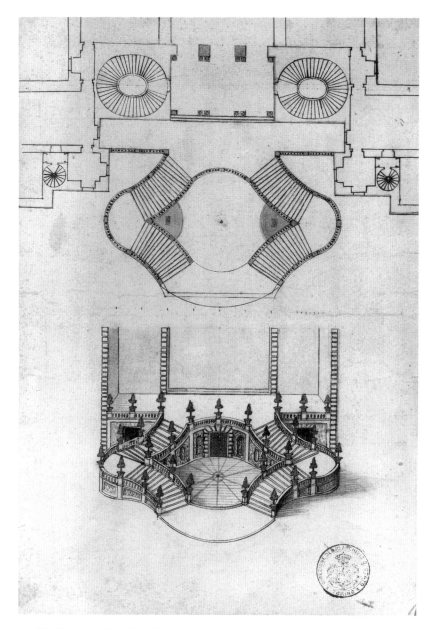

40. "Scallone a collo d'oca." Perspective drawing and plan of Guarini
project for garden stairs at Racconigi (Turin, Archivo di Stato,
Finanze, "Az.Sav.Car." Cat. 43, m.o 1, n.o 6/7; photo: Laboratorio
Fotographico Rampazzi)

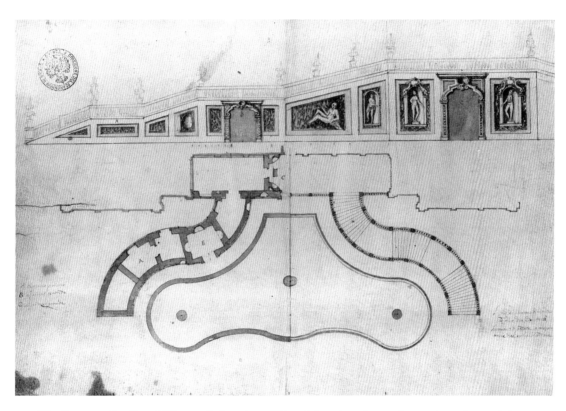

41. "Scallone a collo d'oca." Plan and elevation of Guarini project for garden stairs at Racconigi (Turin, Archivo di Stato, Finanze, "Az.Sav.Car." Cat. 43, m.o 1, n.o 6/9; photo: Laboratorio Fotographico Rampazzi)

TABLE OF MEASUREMENTS FOUND IN THESE DOCUMENTS

Measurements for construction
Trabucco = 6 piedi liprando = 3.08 meters
Piede liprando o di Piemonte = 12 oncie = 0.51 meter
Oncia = .043 meter

Distance and area measurements
Giornata = 100 tavole = 3,800 square meters
Tavola = 4 trabucchi quadrati = 38 square meters

Monetary
Livre = 20 soldi
Soldo = 12 denari

The documents I have used are in the Archivio di Stato in Turin (hereafter AST), in the following *fondi* (= registers) Sez. III, Art. 179, *Conti delle fabbriche di S.A.R.;* Art. 197, *Mandati;* Art. 199, *Registri delle sessioni del Consiglio;* Art 207, *Fabrica di Venaria Reale;* Art. 108, *Recapiti per Venaria Reale.* Documents pertaining to land acquisition are in Sez. III, Aziende Generale R. Finanze. ¶ 18. *Istromenti d'acquisiti fatti da S.M. di beni e terrimenti alla Venaria negli anni 1632 al 1717* (hereafter AGF, ¶ 18). The *ristretti* for the years 1663 (includes 1660–62) to 1672 for the documents preserved in the *fondi* listed above are in AST, Sez. I, Provincia Torino, *Mazzi* 32–35. I am grateful to Mirka Beneš for informing me of the existence of these documents in Sez. I and to Chiara Passanti for checking my transcriptions and making several new ones. My thanks are due to Dott. Isabella Ricci of the AST for calling my attention to the documents of AGF ¶ 18.

A *fondo* is the name for an individual register or independent account. They were cross-referenced, so the bills presented for payment and recorded in the *Conti* or other registers were referred to in the *misure* and *stime* (measurements of work completed and estimates of value of materials) and again in the *mandati* (orders for payment). These in turn were summarized in the year end *ristretti.* For some projects, a register was also kept with lists of payments to individual workmen and for categories of materials.

Each *fondo* contains separate *busti,* or folders (also referred to as *mazzi*), each usually containing the records of one or more years, and within each *busto,* individual fascicles were referred to as *interni.* Where the *interno* numbers were not written on the fascicle, I have assigned my own, according to the sequence in which I found them. This was done for my own records—the fascicles are rarely in the same sequence on later consultation.

APPENDIX I

DOCUMENT CHECK LIST, 1658–1700

1. 1658 July—Art. 810, Venaria Reale, int. 33.
   List of owners who sold houses and property in Altessano Superiore in 1654, 1657, and 1658, docs. in ¶ 18.
2. 1659 20 April—Art. 179, ¶ 10, 1660 in 1661.
   Authorization for payment of expenses at Altessano to go through Camera dei Conti, with signature of Abbate Don Paulo Grom Ternengo, Governatore of Palazzo and Fabrica—*Misure* to be verified by Castellamonte.
3. 1659 26 September—Pamparato Doc. 3, no source given.
   Authority to the Council, its president, Giorgio Turinetti and to Castellamonte to contract prices for construction at Venaria. Accounts to be paid from rents at Stupinigi.
4. 1660 29 November—¶ 18, vol. 1, 1632–1757, fol. 15r.
   Purchase of water for Venaria in return of remission of taxes to town and population of Druent.
5. 1660 10 December—Art. 179—Mandati 1651–64, fol. 108r.
   Payment to Secondo Gratapaglia for gilding a balustrade made for the Palazzo Reale and sent to Venaria Reale.
6. 1660–61—Art. 179, ¶ 10.
   "Conto che rende all'Ill.mo et Ecc.mo Camera Il Sig.r Anto Garagno Cons.r e Tes.re della Casa di S. A. R. per la spesa fatta nella fabriche e dependenti da quella della Venaria Reale negl' anni 1600 & 1662."
   Authorization for payments for work done in 1660–61 according to *misure* made at several dates during the two years.
   Total cost   £55892:5
7. 1661 11 October—¶ 18, fol. 20.
   Purchase of land "ove comincia la cinta del detta [Venaria Reale] parco."
8. 1661 16 October—¶ 18, fol. 26.
   Survey of land purchased on 20 April 1660.
9. 1661–64—¶ 18, fols. 20, 37, 39, 43, 45, 49.
   Purchases of land to enlarge park.
10. 1662 10 February—Art. 199, ¶ 1, 1657–67, fol. 88v.
    Contract for gilding and painting with grisaille a ceiling originally intended for the Palazzo Reale and now to be used in the *gabinetto verso il nuovo parco* at Venaria Reale.
11. 1662 February–July—Art. 197, 1651–64, fols. 144v–148r.
    Payments for decorations on ceiling moved to Venaria Reale from Palazzo Reale.
12. 1663 24 June—Sez. I, Fondo Provincia Torino, Mazzo 32, int. 1.
    Ristretto of expenditures at Venaria Reale for years 1660–June 1663. See App. II, no. 1.
13. 1664 14 February—Art. 197, 1651–64, fol. 153v.
    Payment for stuccoes in *gabinetto* at Venaria Reale.
14. 1664 2 April—Art. 197—Mandati 1651–64, fol. 186v.
    Payment for vases for orange trees for garden of Venaria Reale.
15. 1665 11 April—Art. 207, 1664–65.
    Record of survey of sites to purchase for plaza in front of palace.

16. 1664 14 April—Art. 197—Mandati 1651–64, fol. 186v.
    Payment for 100 cases of orange trees (*citrone*).
17. 1664–67—¶ 18, fols. 52, 55, 59, 65, 70, 74, 78.
    Purchases of land opposite church of San Rocco and to enlarge plaza in front of palace.
18. 1665 15 January—Sez. I, Fondo Provincia Torino, Mazzo 32, int. 2.
    Ristretto of expenditures at Venaria Reale in 1664. See App. II, no. 2.
19. 1665 10 October—Art. 199, ¶ 1, 1657–67, fol. 126v.
    Contract with Alessandro Bolier, gardener, to plant new box in lower garden and replace dead box in upper garden.
20. 1665 14 December—Art. 199, fol. 129v.
    Contract for marble for "Rondeau" of a fountain at Venaria Reale to be made according to design of Castellamonte and to be similar to fountain at the Bastion Verde of Palazzo Reale.
21. 1665 3 December—Art. 810, int. 33.
    Purchase of land and six houses for plaza.
22. 1666—Sez. I, Fondo Provincia Torino, Mazzo 32, int. 3.
    Ristretto of expenditures at Venaria Reale in 1665. See App. II, no. 3.
23. 1666 26 May—¶ 18, fol. 71r.
    Purchase of houses to be demolished and replaced with new ones with identical facades on the plaza.
24. 1666 13 June—Pamparato, p. 36, n. 17.
    Contract with Giuseppe Maria Carlone and Francesco Pozzo for sixteen busts (eight nymphs, eight shepherds for the "Teatro").
25. 1666 15 September—Art. 199, Registri, ¶ 1, 1657–67, fol. 146v.
    Ten year contract with Roberto Chevalier del fu Mathieri di Normandia, gardener at Venaria Reale for maintaining the gardens.
26. 1667 28 April—Sez. I, Fondo Provincia Torino, Mazzo 33, int. 1.
    Ristretto of expenditures at Venaria Reale in 1666. See App. II, no. 4.
27. 1667 12 May—¶ 18, fol. 78r.
    S.A.R. has decided to enlarge piazza and construct houses on it and along main street with similar symmetrical facades.
28. 1667–71—¶ 18, fols. 84–109, 117–28.
    Purchases of property for piazza and main street.
29. 1668 8 October—Sez. I, Fondo Provincia Torino, Mazzo 33, int. 2.
    Ristretto of expenditures at Venaria Reale in 1667. See App. II, no. 5.
30. 1668 8 October—Pamparato, p. 36, n. 17.
    Receipt for payment of 150 ducati (£ 4:10 ca.) for statue of Diane for the Teatro of Giardino Grande by Bernardino Quadri.
31. 1668 1 August—Pamparato, p. 36, n. 17.
    Payment to Carlone and Pozzo for sixteen busts for "Teatro."
32. 1669—Sez. I, Fondo Provincia Torino, Mazzo 33, int. 3.
    Ristretto of expenditures at Venaria Reale in 1668. See App. II, no. 6.
33. 1669 26 June—Pamparato, Doc. 11.
    Contract for stuccoes for rooms "che sono nelli due appartamenti novi della Veneria Reale verso il giardino."
34. 1670—Sez. I, Fondo Provincia Torino, Mazzo 34, int. 1.
    Ristretto of expenditures at Venaria Reale in 1669. See App. II, no. 7.
35. 1671—Sez. I, Fondo Provincia Torino, Mazzo 34, int. 2.
    Ristretto of expenditures at Venaria Reale in 1670. See App. II, no. 8.
36. 1672—Sez. I, Fondo Provincia Torino, Mazzo 35, int. 1.
    Ristretto of expenditures at Venaria Reale in 1671. See App. II, no. 9.

37. 1672—Art. 207, Mazzo Venaria Reale, (Hereafter Art. 207, fascicle nos. are mine), int. 1.
   Contract with Carlo Adamo for the terrace, grotto, and fountain of the Fountain of Hercules, and second one for his work on the pavilions at the Fountain.

38. 1672–73 April–February—Art. 207, int. 4.
   Account of Pietro and Domenico Adamo and Madalena Adamo, widow of the late C.po M.ro Carlo Adamo, for the work at Venaria Reale between these dates. [Note these and other requests for payment by the heirs of Carlo Adamo are in the *busto* containing the certification by Garove and Castellamonte that the work had been done. See Docs. 63, 65, 72. I have placed the requests in the years when the work was contracted for or done.]

39. 1673 3 July—Art. 207, int. 1b.
   Contract of Carlo Adamo for construction of rocky base for Temple of Diana.

40. 22 October 1673—Art. 207, int. 3.
   Misura made by Fabrizio Maulandi with assistance of Castellamonte and *Auditore* Oratio Gina of work done by Carlo Adamo in 1672.

41. 1673—Art. 207, int. 1a.
   Account of Giuseppe Andrea, son and heir of the late Carlo Adamo, for work at Venaria Reale in 1673.

42. 1673 10 Jan and 6 April—Art. 207, int. 1e.
   Misure of leveling in park next to the *gran alea.*

43. 1673 24 April—Art. 207, int. 1c.
   Contract with Carlo Adamo for *scuderia grande* on "contrada principale per compir la linea delle case verso Ceronda paralella all'altre."

44. 1673 14 June—Art. 207, int. 1d.
   Contract with Adamo for *nuovo forno* "in linea della contrada della Venaria Reale."

45. 1673 2 July—Art. 207, int. 1b.
   Directions for construction of foundations and rocky base for Temple of Diana. See App. III, no. 3.

46. 1673 20 October—Art. 207, int. 1f.
   List of horses rented for work.

47. 1673 22 October—Art. 207, int. g, h.
   Two accounts of Carlo Adamo for labor and materials supplied at Venaria Reale in park and Fountain of Hercules.

48. 1673 22 October—Art. 207, int. 5d.
   Misura by Amedeo Castellamonte and *Auditore* Oratio Gino of construction, supplies, and costs of work carried out at Venaria Reale under the supervision of Capo Maestro Carlo Adamo in 1673. Includes work on the *gran alea,* walls in park, Casa di Sto. Spirito, and Temple of Diana. Signed by Fabritio Maulandi, Aiutante di Camera, and Capitano della Venaria. See App. III, nos. 4, 5 for *misura* of Temple of Diana.

49. 1673–75—Art. 207, int. 3.
   Account of Sig. Gio. Antonio Boggetto for *ferramente* provided at Venaria Reale in 1673, 1674, and 1675.

50. 1674 21 May—Art. 207, int 6.
   Verification of *ristretto* of *ferramenti* supplied by Ant. Bog[g]lieto for *il giardino delle fontane* and Fountain of Hercules. Signed by Fabritio Maulandi.

51. 1674 15 October—Art. 207, int. 5c.
   Misura made with Amedeo Castellamonte and *Auditore* Oratio Gina, signed by Gio:Eusebio Mozzo Ag.re and Antonio Bettini Ingegn.re. Miscellaneous masonry work in gardens and at Fountain of Hercules.

52. 1674–75—Art. 207, int. 5a.
   Account of heirs and widow of Carlo Adamo for work at Venaria Reale in 1674–75—mainly small construction in town.

53. 1675 20 February—Art. 207, 1674–75.
    Account of work supervised and paid for by the late Capo Maestro Carlo Adamo in 1673 and 1674 for elongation of *gran alea,* work on Temple of Diana.
54. 1675 2 May—Art. 207, int. 5e.
    Contract for work by Carlo Adamo followed by a *misura* dated 25 June for construction of walls for "tre prospettive del nuovo giardino de frutti avanti la fasanera," and other minor construction.
55. 1675 2 May—Art. 207, int. 5c.
    Bill for work contracted for in Doc. 42.
56. 1675 25 June and 4 August—Art. 207, int. 3.
    Stima of construction for the "tre prospettive" built by Carlo Adamo and authorization of payment by Gina.
57. 1676—Art. 810, Mazzo unico, int. 3.
    Request by S.r Fabrizio Maulandi for repayment of £1067 for payments made by him per order of S.A.R. in 1675–76.
58. 1676 9 April—Art. 207, int. 5d.
    Misura of work by Carlo Adamo at Temple of Diana signed by Gazano Ferrero Misura.re di S.A.R. and Gio: Eu: Mozzo for work listed in Doc. 41.
59. 1678 6 February—Art. 810, int. 5.
    Deed of donation of land to S.r Maulandi at Venaria Reale as payment for his expenditures in the chapel of San Giuseppe and concession of an altar and burial places for himself and his heirs.
60. 1678 17 December—Art. 810, int. 4.
    Contract with Mons. Nicolas Royer (da Pariggi), "direttore d'acque e fontane" at Venaria Reale to maintain fountains and pipes made by Conte e Cavag.e Gran Croce Gio. Battista Truchi, minister of state, head of finances, director of affairs at Venaria Reale.
61. 1679—Art. 810, int. 2.
    Contract with Antonio Battagliero, *ricopritore,* for maintenance and repairs of roofs on buildings constructed after the original contract of 1664. It lists the "Citronera. Fasanera, Palazzo tenuto da Madama la Prencipessa, le Scuderie che sono nel luogo, le case nuente [word?] del Giudice, Soldati giustitia, e dell'hoste Trincotto, Casa del Parco, li due Pavaglioni coperti à lose che sono vicini alla fontana [Fountain of Hercules]."
62. 1679 7 May—Art. 810, int. 62, 63.
    Two copies of contracts for repairs and upkeep at Venaria Reale with Pietro Rosso.
63. 1679 30 May—Art. 207, int. 5d.
    Signed testimony by Michele Angelo Garove that work by late Carlo Adamo on the *gran alea* at Venaria Reale, first to level it and then to raise its level because water stood in it, was by express order of the late S.A.R.
64. 1679 30 May—Art. 810, int. 6.
    Contract with Pietro Rosso to do all repairs at Venaria Reale itemized by the S.ri Aud.ri Gen.le with assistance of S.r Conte Castellammonte and *agrimensori* after their visits of 5, 6, and 7 April to Venaria Reale. Includes instructions for roofing the Temple of Diana. See App. III, no. 6.
65. 1679 8 June—Art. 207, int. 5d.
    Testimony of Amedeo Castellamonte concerning excavation and refilling of *gran alea,* and other signed statements by Maulandi and Scaracello.
66. 1679–80—Art. 207, int. 6.
    Accounts for repairs to roof of orangery.
67. 1679–81—Art. 207, int. 7.
    Account of M.ro Pietro Rosso for work commissioned at Venaria Reale, includes repairs to the pond and pipes on the river.

68. 1680—Art. 207, int. 8.
    Account of M.ro Pietro Rosso for repairs made to Casa di Caval Bianco for damages made by students from the Collegio di Savoia on vacation.
69. 1680—Art. 207, int. 9.
    Account of M.ro Pietro Rosso for routine repairs made at Venaria Reale in preparation for a visit by the court.
70. 1681—Art. 810, int. 63, fol. 70.
    Inspection of the walls, roofs, and marble at Temple of Diana.
71. 1681 7 December—Art. 810, int. 7.
    Agreement to rent to S.r Ramma, a tenant at Venaria Reale, for four years at £4000 per year.
72. 1682 18 January—Art. 207, int. 17.
    Signed testimony by Amedeo Castellamonte that Capo Maestro Carlo Adamo in work done at Temple of Diana in 1672–75 had followed his instructions and the designs, especially for its rocky base.
73. 1682 18 January—Art. 207, int. 19.
    Request by heirs of Carlo Adamo and his widow for extra payments for work on Fountain of Hercules and other construction at Venaria Reale.
74. 1683—Art. 207, int. 11.
    Account of M.o Pietro Francesco Rosso for routine repairs at Venaria Reale.
75. 1684 19 July—Art. 207, int. 12.
    Bill for work done at Venaria Reale by Gio. Batt.a Genoa *Serragliere*.
76. n.d.(1684?)—Art. 207, int. 13.
    Account by M.o Pietro Rosso for work at Venaria Reale for visit by Cort.o cola.
77. 1684—Art. 207, int. 14.
    Account of M.ro Pietro Rosso for work done at Venaria Reale, includes repairs to old stables near the Ceronda which were falling in ruins.
78. 1685–87—Art. 207, int. 15.
    Account of *Fonditore* S.re Francesco Amoneto for repairs to pipes of fountains at Venaria Reale. Includes repairs to the Fountain of Hercules and a bridge made of oak to the Temple of Diana.
79. 1686—Art. 207, int. 16, 17.
    Accounts by M.ro Pietro Francesco Rosso for plumbing repairs at Venaria Reale.
80. 1687 4 April—Art. 810, int. 9.
    Consignment of part of income of Venaria Reale.
81. 1687 2 November—Art. 810, int. 11.
    Request of citizens of Venaria Reale to be allowed to cut wood in the land adjacent to the royal park.
82. 1687 22 December—Art. 810, int. 8.
    Request for payment of repairs done to fountains at Venaria Reale in 1685–86.
83. 1687–88—Art. 810, int. 10.
    List of carriage horses at Venaria Reale and loan of them.
84. 1687–88—Art. 207, int. 22.
    Account of M.o Pietro Francesco Rosso for repairs to roofs, Fountain of Hercules, and rebuilding loggia of houses for officials of Madama Reale.
85. 1688 21 June—Art. 810, int. 13.
    Bill by Ramma for expenses incurred for quarters occupied by soldiers and huntsmen of S.A.R.
86. 1688—Art. 207, int. 18.
    Account of Gio. Antonio for leveling ground for pastures for imported horses of S.A.R.

87. 1688 April—Art. 810, int. 14, 15.
   Agreement with town of Venaria Reale on boundaries of the "Bosco" at Venaria Reale and itemized contract for repairs.

88. 1689 1 April—Art. 810, int. 17.
   Contract with Ant. Bongiovanni for maintenance of channels and water level of *balera*.

89. 1689 9 April—Art. 810, int. 12.
   Ramma's rent (see Doc. 71) for next three years raised to £5600 per annum with a prepayment of £2800, a total of £19,600.

90. 1689—Art. 810, int. 18.
   Renewal of 1679 contract with Pietro Francesco Rosso to make repairs and maintain the palace and other buildings at Venaria Reale.

91. 1689 17 May—Art. 810, int. 19.
   Printed notice of public meeting to rent Venaria Reale, "Case, Cassine, Molini, Beni, e Redditi," as they are now rented to Sig. Gio. Domenico Ramma.

92. 1689—Art. 810, int. 20.
   Contract to rent Venaria Reale to Ramma, 1690–93.

93. 1693 11 September—Art. 810, int. 30, 31, and 32.
   Concession of *redditi* to Giuseppe Antonio Boetto for six years and two copies of contract for same.

94. 1693 19 September—Art. 810, int. 27.
   Renewal of contract for *redditi* of Venaria Reale as of last six years.

95. 1693 2 October—Pamparato, pp. 19–23.
   Letter of Fabrizio Maulandi describing the attack by the French and the extent of the damage.

96. n.d. (after French attack)—Art. 810, int. 28, 29.
   List of repairs to be made at Venaria Reale and a *ristretto* of same.

97. 1695—Art. 810, int. 34.
   Bill of repairs to municipal laundry house.

98. 1696—Art. 810, int. 35.
   Contract for cleaning *balera*.

99. 1699 August—Art. 810, int. 37.
   Measurement of *beni* at Venaria Reale. Total is *giornate* 116, *tavole* 70 (ca. 450,000 m. sq. or 45 hectares).

100. 1699 18 November—Art. 810, int. 40.
    Contract to rent *beni* and water of park for six years starting in 1700.

101. 1699—Pommer, *18th Century*, p. 146; Brinckmann, *Teatrum*, pp. 86–87.
    Description by Michele Angelo Garove of plans and elevations showing alterations projected for Venaria Reale and a letter by the Count de Sales describing improvements not mentioned by Garove, including a critique of the Fountain of Hercules.

102. 1700 31 July—Art. 810, int. 40.
    Contract with M.ri Pietro, Gaija, Eusebio Bello detto Giacolone, and Deffendente Fontana to build a pavilion onto the palace at Venaria Reale according to instructions of Michele Angelo Garove. To use material from part of palace to be demolished. Pavilion to have facade on south towards the orangery and to west toward the grand allée that divides the garden from the *bosco*.

APPENDIX II

RISTRETTI (YEAR-END BUILDING ACCOUNTS), 1660–1668

All documents transcribed here are from AST Sezione I unless otherwise noted.[1]

1) Fondo Provincia Torino, Mazzo 32, int. 1.

Conto della Spesa del Palazzo della Venaria Reale

Caricamento del present.o conto della fabrica del Palazzo della Venaria Reale per li fondi che lo medemo ha havuti fondatto su le spese infrascritt.o, et aligatt., col ristretto del costo d'essa.

Et primo deve la fabbrica di detto Palazzo della Venaria Reale livre cento venticinque milla trecento da soldi venti caduna che S.A.R. ha fatt.o pagare come sotto nelle anni 1660, 1661, 1662 et corrent. 1663 per tutto giugno, come s'e degnato la mede'mo R.A. a scrire per suo biglietto a me sotto Aud.re diretto delli 12 giugno corrente sigillato, et sotto scritto Meyner, posto a d.o del presente conto

dico	£ 125,300
Nov. e Dic. 1659	20,000

Received from Sig.r Torelli Aiutant.o di Camera di S.A.R

1660 £   24,300 del denaro de minuti piaceri = 1800 doppie a £13, soldi 10

1661 £   32,400 del denaro de minuti piaceri = doppie 2400 a £13:10 ca

1662 £   32,400 del denaro de minuti piaceri = doppie 2400 at £13:10 ca

1663 £   16,200 = doppie 1200 @ 13:10 ca

Più livre dieci milla ottocento venti tre soldi diec'otto e denari dieci d'argento che sono stat.o pagat.o al Capo Mastro Gio Batista Piscina

Impresaro della sudetta fabrica	£ 10,823:18:10

An additional £ 59,097:16:19 to be paid to Piscina from other sources

Account of all expenses up to June 1663

Le opere da muri, e da bosco, le opere di marmi et altre pietre a carico del capo m.re piccopietre Carlo Bussa	£ 24,714:17: 3
Canalli di tolle d'op.e e fatture diverse e opere di Piombo a carico di Matteo Caviglio	£ 2,076: 8: 8
Ferri provisti dal Riva, Boggietto et altri	£ 14,633:11: 4
Bagliature ferri	343: : 4
Costo quadrettoni straordinari [word?] comprati per li sternità del salone e galeria £ 736:14	
Lavori diversi di terra	481: 8
Lavori diversi di bosco fatti dal fu M.r Giannotto Valone	£ 1,008
Per quattro fornelli di pietre d'Ars, oltre li sei provisti da Piscina	£ 486

[1] The existence of the Venaria documents in Sezione I were brought to my attention by Mirka Beneš, and I would like to express my thanks to her for sharing this information. When I consulted them in the spring of 1980, I was only able to spend a short time in Turin. As a result, some of the notes were made in English. I have indicated this by italics in the documents. At this writing I have not been able to return to Turin to amplify the transcription nor to check it. Some of the documents were copied for me by Chiara Passanti, whom I also want to thank. I will indicate which she transcribed at the specific documents.

Porte e chiasure fatti da M.ro Antonio Battaglieri	£ 1,039:16
Vitriaio fatto dalli vitrieri Baudino e Peletta	£ 3,589: 8
Lavori minuti diversi	701:14: 4
	£ 205,229: 7: 3

La fabrica rileva	£ 205,229: 7:3
La fondi havuti	£ 195,220:15:7
Resta	£ 10,008:11:8

£ = S.20, d 12
Order for payment of amount owing from account of "minuti piaceri"
Mandati and receipts, and accounting of sources of money paid out

Conto del costo del Palazzo della Venaria Reale che S.A.R. ha fatto fabricare nelli anni 1660, 1661, 1662 et part.e del corrente 1663 fondato sopra le capitolazioni, misure, fedi, quittanze, et altre pezze infra mentionati, designati, et aligati.

Et primo livre cento quaranta sei milla cincquecento dicisette, so. 15:&[denari]8–da soldi venti cadu'na che sono stati pagati al Capo Mastro Gio' Battista Piscina Impresaro della fabrica del detto Palazzo della Venaria Reale, cioè le lavori di muro, e di bosco nelli anni 1659, '60, '61, '62 et corrente 1663. . . . somma alla quale come sotto rilevano, le muraglie, cave di terra, ornamenti, coperti, solari, travi armati, stabilitiure, sterniti et altri lavori dal sudetto fatti fare per le costruzioni di detto Palazzo ne' sudetti anni, come consta dalle misure di S.e Antonio Borrione, misurature per S.A.R. delli 16 Nov. 1660 et 20 mede'mo mese, 1662 . . . approvato dal S. Conte Amedeo Castellamonte   £ 146,517:15: 8

The following is an itemized list of the individual accounts which make up the total above.

Cap. 1. Muraglie tr[abuchi] 4410:3:1 come alli capi 3 & 4 della misura delli 16 9bre dell' anno 1660, et 20 9bre 1662,
compreso tra. 156:3:1 che rilevano quelle del infernet.o fatto fuori del Palazzo   £ 78,785: 1: 4

Cap. 2. Tra. 3423:1:3 muraglie dalle fondamento sino al primo cornicione ove terminano li due piani conforme al primo disegno.   £ 58,194:10:10

Cap. 3. Tr.605 muraglione dal primo cornisone ove terminano detti due piani sino al secondo cornitione ch'è il terzo piano come a capo 4 del detta misura agiustati dalli dietro nominati 58.ri a £ 19:10 cad.o trab. che sono £ 2:10 di piu del prezzo capitolato rispetto al mag.re altezza
                                                      £ 11,797:10

Cap. 4. Tr 382:1:10 à che ascendono le muraglie del belvedere . . .   £ 8,793: 0: 1

Tra 4410:3:1   £ 78,785: 1:16
Coperti
Tra 222:2:2 coperti di coppa di tutto detto Palazzo.   £ 4,827: 5: 2

Cap. 5. Tra 28:4:8 delli due appartamenti bassi a due piani come a Capo 5 della misura (che conforme al primo disegno dovevano esser galerie aperte a £ 20 caduni trabucco . . .
                                                      £ 575:11: 1

Cap. 6. Tra 133:4:10 coperti delli quattri pavaglioni et galeria tra li due pavaglioni verso il cortile . . . di più . . . per esser sta. fatti un piano più alto di quello . . .   £ 2,876:16: 4

Cap. 7. Tra 59:4:8 Coperta del belvedere. . . .   £ 1,374:17: 9

Cap. 8. Tra 29:5 Coperto fatto de due lati del belvedere indi disfatti per mutatione del disegno . . .   £ 238:13: 4

Cavi di Terra
Cap. 9. Cavi di terra di tutti li officij del Palazzo tra 368:2:8 . . . da quali detratti tr. 66:2:6 del

cavo della fondamento entrato nella misura . . . che l'Impresaro Piscina restava tenuto fare, restano

tr 294:0:2 . . . £ 2,352: 4: 5

Esportazioni terra fomdam.
Cap. 10. Esportationi de sudetto tr 66:2:6 detratti dalli officij alla rippa verso Ceronda

£ 265:13: 4

Solari a profilo
Cap. 11. Solari a profilo, e qualche parti di rustichi fatti alle stanze di detto Palazzo
Tr 394:1: 11 £ 8,529: 2: 2
Tra 238:2:5 come a capo 9 della misura sud.a £ 5,244:15: 2
Cap. 12. Tra 80: 2: 9 Solari fatti al terzo piano £ 1,850:10:10
Cap. 13. Tra 77:2:9 In tre solari a profilo fatti sopra il salone come alli capi ondeci di detta misura . . . il secondo de quali solari doppo quello è sopra la volta d.a S.A. ha fatto disfare ultimatam.e per render più svelto quello del salone . . . £ 1,433:14: 2

tra 394:7:11 £ 8,529: 2: 2
Cap. 14. Per numero dieci someri armati dal Piscina fatti provedere e mess' in opra à due de solari sovra il Salone a pretiati. . . . .
Armature someri
Per l'armature di n.o 58 someri che sono in opera alli solari del secondo e terzo piano . . .

£ 2,544:15
N.o 5 al solaro rustico sopra la volta del salone
Cap. 16. Tra 4:1:9 Soffitto £ 64: 7: 6
Cap. 17. Tra 31:1:5 Pavimenti d'assi fatti al salon del belvedere et ai gabinetti laterali d'esso

£ 374:16: 8
Cap. 18. Tra 3:4:4 di stibij d'assi £ 55:16: 8
Cap. 19. Tra 73:1:8 stibij di listelli con paradossi e renne fatti per divisione delle quattro grandi camere del terzo piano per tutta l'altezza d'essa, e sotto alli arconi del belvedere, e scaletta dell' appartamento di Madama la Prencipessa . . . £ 1,099: 3: 4
Cap. 20. Tra 184:2:6 di cornicione rustici e stabiliti incl. tra 86:2:10 lineali di cornicioni fatti a dentelli che gira attorno al Palazzo
&
Cap. 21. Tra 69:1:2 di Cornicione fatto a modiglione attorno a detto Palazzo sotto al coperto
&
Cap. 22. Tra 28:4:6 di cornicioni al belvedere £ 477:15:10
Cap. 23. Tra 92: di cornici rustiche incl. Tra 39:5 di cornici grandi fatti attorno del salone stuccata à due ordini
Tra 18:4 di Cornici fatti sotto alle volte ovate de due gabinetti nelli Paviglioni verso la terrazza
Tra 34 Cornici fatti attorno alle quattro volte stuccate de Paviglioni al piano nobile
Dadi
Cap. 24. Tra 324:2:6 di dadi fatti dentro e fuori di detto Palazzo £ 395:21: 1
Ornamenti finestre
Ornamenti di rustico e stabiliti di num.o 201 tra finestre grandi o picoli comprese due porte fatti a detto Pallazzo £ 4,410
60 grandi incl. 2 porte di gabinetti verso terrazza per 2 piani nobili 30 piccoli . . . per offizij
28 per 2 piani dei appartamenti bassi che dovevano esser gallerie e 10 in più
13 piccoli per 13 finestre piccole degli offitij sotto à quelle de sud.i appartm.ti bassi che dovevano esser gallerie
40 ornamenti alle 40 finestre del terzo piano
18 ornamenti di n.o 18 finestre del belvedere
2 ornamenti delle due porte del Salone cioè una verso la galeria, l'altro verso la terrazza

Bugne

Cap. 26. Per n.o 566 Bugne doppie rustiche e stabiliti . . . fatti alli cantoni d'esso Palazzo

£   724:15

Cap. 27. Lesene fatti a 16 cantoni del Palazzo cioè 12 al terzo piano et 8 al belvedere à due lesene per caduno

Stabiliture

Cap. 28. Tra 2247:3:2 interne & esterne   £   8,990: 2: 2

- - - - - - - - ²

Infrascadure

Cap. 32. Tra 173:4:1 di Infrascadure delle volti del salone, de quatro pavaglioni, gabinetti, infernetto et altre   £   347: 7: 2

Cap. 33. Tra 190:4:3 sterniti di quadretoni stilati delle camere del primo, e secondo piano escluso il salone   £   3,814: 3: 4

Cap. 34. Fattura, calcina e sabia per tr 40:0:4 à che rilevano li sterniti di quadretoni straordinari del salone, galeria del piano nobile et due antri   £   721

Cap. 35. Sternito della galaria al secondo piano di tr 11:1:6

- - - - - - - -

Cap. 38. Tra 94:5 Sterniti di mattone in piano fatti nell'officij   £   1,138

Cap. 39. Fattura calcina e sabia per tr 49:5:8 di sterniti di lose delle ripiani delle scale esteriori verso il gran cortile e bosco   £   199:15: 6

Cap. 40. Tra 116:5:2 Sterniti di pietre con luoro guidone di mattoni fatti sotto del salone al piano delli officij, sotto alla terrazza nel infernetto, al cortile verso Ceronda et altrove

£   467: 8: 0

Cap. 41. Sterniti di pietre con sue guidone di mattoni fatto in calcina al cortilato verso mezo giorno acio l'acqua non penetri nel infernetto ivi contiguo   £   227:11: 3

- - - - - - - -

Cap. 43. Per haver messo in opera tutti li scalini si di marmore che di sarisso 410 scalini alle due scale laterali al salone

84 scalini di sarisso alla scala à lumaga attinent.e alla appartam.o di M.R. 33 scalini di scrizzo alla scala che va al infernetto

Tra 225 di scalini di marmore, e di sarisso messo in opera all due scale esteriori delle due ingressi o siano soliti verso il gran cortile e giardino

- - - - - - - -

Cap. 45. No. 16 Telari di fornelli di stucco fatti alla francese con luoro cornici e folgolai[?] di quadretoni alle camere del secondo e terzo piano   £   288

Cap. 46. Per n.o sei fornelli di Pietra d'Ars. . . .   £   675

- - - - - - - -

Cap. 49. Per li sei pozzi   £   724: 6

  3 in cucina che sono d'acqua viva

  1 d'acqua viva nel inferneto

  2 morti—1 in guard'arnese, l'altro in cortiletto verso Ceronda

Cap. 50. Per tra 34 architravi rustici fatti nelle quattro camere del Paviglione indi disfatti per mutatione di disegno   £   34

- - - - - - - -

Più livre venti'un milla sette cento trenta una, soldi dieci otto, et denari sei che sono pagati al Capo M'ro Picca pietre, Carlo Busso nelli anni 1659, 1660, 1662 &1663 per li mani d'opra . . .

---

² The dotted lines indicate a part of the document has not been included. Many of the recorded items were for details unnecessary for the building history.

sono per pagamento delle colone con luoro basi, e capitelli balaustrada, piedestali, tutti lavori di marmori di forent[?], scalini et altre opere di sarisso seguenti. . . . £ 21,731:18

Cap. 64. Et primo quatro colone con loro capitelli intagliati, e basi di marmore di forese che sono in opera alla galeria verso il gran cortile £ 2,160

- - - - - - - -

Cap. 66. Tra 7:3:1 balistrada di marmore compita messa in opera all cinque arcade della sudetta galeria, et alla terrazza verso il bosco £ 1,352:10

Cap. 69. Tra 43:4:8 Scalini di moroe d'un trab. caduno messi alle due scale avanti archi or siano post.i stucat.i della facciata verso il cortile grande et a quelle che sono sotto alli arconi ove sono le nichie, e alli repiani della galeria sud.a £ 2,561

- - - - - - - -

Telaro di scrisso no. 5, cioè uno ch'è attorno all'occhio della volta che da lume alla scala del infernetto

- - - - - - - -

Cap. 83. Per numero due scalini di sarisso messi uno alla ferrata del Parco, cioè alla porta d'essa et l'altra ad altra Porto di d.o Parco verso mezogiorno £ 31:10

Per marmore non usati per la variatione del disegno £ 3,090

- - - - - - - -

Pagati alli picca pietre Domenico Gallo livre cento novanta tre . . . per n.o 35 scalini . . . per la scale del infernetto £ 193: 6

Pagati ai piccapietri Domenico, Giovanni Maria & Gio.Francesco fratelli Galli per opere minore di pietra

Pagato al Capo M'ro piccapietre Deodato Ramello per opere minore di pietra Pagato al piccapietre Bramante Pietro Antonio Mariora & Gio Maria Gallo per tra.34, piedi tre et oncie quatro di sterniti di lose . . . fatti nel repiani e gran platea delle scalle esteriori della facciata verso il gran cortile £ 1,400: 2: 9

- - - - - - - -

Più pagato al Tolaro Matteo Caveglie . . . per il prezzo delli canali di tolle doppie et canoni di tolle semplici da esso provisto . . . £ 2,076: 8: 8

- - - - - - - -

Pagati alli mercanti di ferri Gio Tomaso Rivo, et Gio Antonio Gobbietto e Carlo e Domenico Galliciani. . . . £ 14,633:11: 4

- - - - - - - -

Pagati alli seraglieri Simeone Chiambreto, Gio Matteo Bertrami et Guglielmo Manassero . . . per le bogliture delle chiavi lamoni et altre fatture £ 343: 4

- - - - - - - -

Pagato al lavaterra Domenico Kans detto Salvaij
for earth filling £ 295: 8
Pagato a Gio Antonio Langasco *for earth leveling* £ 186:10

- - - - - - - -

Justification of total cost £ 205,229: 7: 3
Signed Gina [?] Aud.e
     30 Giugno 1663

18 Novembre 1659 *First contract with Piscina, the Capomaestro. Includes specifications*
Autorità concesssa da S.A.R. alli SSi Conti P.e Giorgio Turinetti et Cont. di Castellamonte. . . .
Havendo S.A.R. risoluto di far fabricare il suo Palazzo d'Altezzano ne due anni venturi 1660, e 1661 conforme alli disegni che ne sono fatti dal Conte Amedeo de Castellamonte vuole S.A.R che la sovrintendenza di tal fabrica sia appoggiata alla cura delli Presid.te Turinetti, e Conte di Castellamonte. . . .
Signed 26 Settembre 1659

Misure

Misura di 6 Giugno 1663 fatto da Conte Castellamonte, Sig.re Gina, etc.

Prima il cavo di terra della nave della fabbrica compreso quello di quatro pavag.ni e valanche

fori dette muraglie	tra	204: 5:0

Più quella della galleria verso Sironda compreso quello

delle valanche	tra	18: 1: 0
Più il cavo dell'infernetto compreso quello della scala in tutto	tra	73: 0: 0
Più il Cavo della galleria verso la scuderia ossia guarda arnesi	tra	19: 2: 0
Più con pezzo di cavo di terra cavato nell'offitio sotto il terrapiano	tra	0: 4: 4
Più quello fatto avanti l'usci della galleria verso Sirando	tra	21: 4: 0
Piu quello fatto avanti il murag.ne del cortoletto verso Sirando: 4		22: 4:4
		————
	trab	360: 2: 8

Da quali trab 360:2:8 di cavo di terra cubi si dedure il cavo delle

fondam.te delle muraglie di d.to pallazzo solam.te assend.te a	trab	66:26
dico	tra	66: 3: 6
		————
		294:0:2

For the following misura *the individual measurements were not transcribed.*

Muraglie cioè quelle dalla fond.to desso Palazzo sino al primo Cornison

Fondam.to della faciada della paviglione verso il giardino e boschetto

Muraglie della paviglione verso li officij paralella allo sud.ta fond.ta

Muraglia della Testa del Paviglione

Muraglia che divide il pavag.ne dal gabinetto del giardino

Muraglia che divide d.to gabinetto dalla galleria verso il giardino

paralella alla sud.ta e della med.a misura

Muraglia della testa della stanza verso mezzo giorno et infernetto tra un pavag.ne e l'altra

Muraglia della faciada del pavag.ne verso la scud.a e gran cortile [*This is the same size as the facade of the pavilion on the garden side.*]

la muraglia del pavag.ne paralella alla sud.ta verso il scaletta

la testa del pavag.ne sud.to verso la scuderia garande della med.a misura dell' altra pavag.ne

Muraglia parallela all sud.ta che divide il pavag.ner dal gabinetto

Muraglia che divide le d.to gabinetto dalla galleria verso il cortile

Muraglia che divide le due Anticamere verso l'infernetto dalla scaletta

Muraglia che divide d.te due Anticamere verso l'infernetto dal salon

Muraglia parallela che divide d.to salon dalle Anticamere verso Seronda

Muraglia della testa del Salon verso la galleria e giardino

Più quella desso Salon verso la galleria e gran cortile parallela alla sud.ta

Muraglia della galleria verso il giardino tra li due pavag.ni

Muraglia della galleria verso il gran cortile

La muraglia della faciada verso il gran cortile tra li doi pavag.ne sopra le colone dall' imposto delli archi sino per tutto d.o p.o cornison

- - - - - - - -

La murag.ne della faciada del pavag.ne verso Ceronda

Muraglia parallela alla sud.to della misura dell'altro pavag.ne verso il boschetto

Muraglia che divide d.to pavag.ne verso Sironda dal gabinetto

Muraglia che divide d.to gabinetto dalla galleria

Più quella della faciada delle due Anticamere

Più quella che divide d.te Anticamere verso Sironda dalla scala verso il gran Cortile

Più quella della testa desso Pavag.ne verso Sironda

Più quella della faciada del Pavag.ne verso d.to Cortile e Sironda

Più quella che divide d.to pavag.ne dal gabinetto del med.ma
Più altra paralella all sud.ta che divide il gabinetto dalla galleria
Più quella che divide d.to gabinetto e galleria verso il cortle delle Anticamere e scaletta
Più le tre muraglie della entrada dessa scala fori della faciada e verso il cortile
Più altra paralella alla sud.ta verso il gran cortile

Total Tra 2,232: 0: 0

Misura di 16 Nov 1660
Muraglia dell'infernetto tutta attorno che si da nodo per pieno attesi lintamisada al di dentro e
pillastri che sono di mattoni fond.to sino ove termina   tra   72: 5: 4
La volta desso infernotto d'un mattone di ponta e una testa di pietra   20: 4: 0
Più le muraglia fatta sopra essa volta per suo diametro compreso le muraglie a dritura della
faciada della gran scud.a e fasanera qual murag.a termina il cortiletto avanti il palazzo
- - - - - - - -

[Misura] 20 Novembre 1662
Primo il solaro della loggia del Teatro delle comedie fatto a perfil cioè ne secondo salon
Più altro solar rustico con paradossi del Teatro della Comedia
- - - - - - - -

Facciamo fede noi sottosignati che havendo l'Alt.Sua Reale stabilito di alzar un piano di più
tutto il corpo del suo Palazzo della Venaria Reale oltre il primo stabil.m.to del dissegno della
Med.ma Reale Alt.a signato, sopra il quale haveva il Capo M'ro Gio: Batta. Piscina impresaro di
d.ta fabrica fondato il suo partito, e di più di d.to novo alzam.to havesse anco ordinato che li
rialsassa un'altro corpo di fabrica nel mezzo di esso Palazzo in forma di belvedere
- - - - - - - -

Agreement to raise cost of construction over 1st contract by £ 2: 10 per trabuco *for new story and £6 per*
trabuco *for the belvedere.*
Signed by Turinetti and Castellamonte, 24 June 1663

2) Fondo Provincia Torino, Mazzo 32, int. 2.[3]

Conto della spesa per la fabriche e opere fatte fare alla Venaria Reale l'anno 1664 ascendenti à
£47,452.S.di 4.d.1
Sommario della spesa delle fabriche e lavori contenuti nel prnt. conto somes.to

fog.1 pagina 2.a	£	30,967:	3:	7
fog.5 pagina p.ma	£	8,131:17		
detta pagina 2.a	£	51		
fog.7 pagina p.ma	£	1,232:17		
detto pagina 2.a	£	2,066:	7:	6
fog.8 pag.a prima	£	4,922:19		
Tutta la spesa rileva	£	47,482:	4:	1

Il fondo havuto, et partite poste in
carigamento a fog.uno pag.a prima in quatro
partite rilev.o   £   35,369

Resta S.A.R. in debito di dette £ 12,113:4 fanno Dop.e 897 £3:14   £   12,113: 4: 1

---

[3] Chiara Passanti transcribed the summary of expenses of this document and the balance sheet, and I
the *capitolazioni*. I have included only the items in the *capitolazioni* and *misure* that give information on the
date of construction of individual parts of the villa, or about building methods and practices.

La spesa delle fabriche de muraglioni, portico con stanze sopra, alsamento de chienili, e stanze, casino attinente alla Chiesa, cavi di terra, spianamento del giardino, lavori di pietre, canali di tola, et altre opere fatte fare nell'anno hor scorso di comando di S.A.R. alla sua Venaria R.le contenute in cap.61 de. presen.e conto rilevano alla somma di livre quaranta sette milla quattrocento ottanta due soldi quatro, e un denaro, da soldi venti cad.a, et il fondo previsto e pagato, e partite mese in quatro cappi del carigam.to ascende à livre trenta cinque milla trecento sesanta nove simili [word?] essendo mag.re la spesa del fondo sud.o di £12,113 di questa somma resta S.A.R. debitrice del Sig.r Presidente Turineti che hà pagato gli operarij con dn. suo proprio. . . . In fede Torino li 15 Gennaro 1665

Signed Gina Aud.e

S.A.R. hà pagato il sudetto resto

Signed Giorgio Turineti

f.1r

Conto della spesa fatta nell'anno hor scorso 1664: alla Venaria Reale per le fabriche de muraglioni de'giardini, delle muraglie del alsamento delle stanze sovra li chienili, scuderie e appartam.ti attinenti, delle stanze e portico fatto in fondo al cortile rusticho tra la grande scudaria et detti chienili del casino attinenti alla chiesa fatto per li SS.ri elemosinarij et Cappellani, per li cavi di terra, lavori di pietre et altre opere in fra espresse fondata su le misure, capitolazioni, et pezzi qui gionti:[4]

f.1f

Muraglie

Cap. 1. Tr 242:1:8 à quali ascende il muraglione tra il Palazzo novo, et il vechio fatto contro la terra del gran Cortile, comprese li tre grotte et l'incamisola fatta alli due pezzi di muraglia di detto Palazzo vechio ove si sono li due rami di scala a £11 cad.o trab.   £   2,665: 1:

Cap. 2. Tr 576:3 à quali rileva il muraglione del giardino da basso cominciando dalla testa congionta al Pavag.le del Pallazzo vecchio verso il luogho et Ceronda, et che continua verso Ceronda, et va terminare et congiongersi al piccolo pezzo che si fece fare l'anno compreso il perapetto di Mattoni, che e à cad   £   6,341:10

Cap. 3. Tr 391:3:2 à quali ascende il muraglione fatto nel angolo in fondo al giardino grande che risvolta parte verso mezanotte, comprese anche le fondamenti de tre portali et del Teatro ove va la balaustrado   £   4,306:16: 1

Cap. 4. Tr 12:3 muraglie del rondò inmezo al gran Cortile . . .   £   162:10

- - - - - - - -

f. 2v Incamisato di mattoni fatta alli due Paviglioni del Pall.o vecchio verso Ceronda, et al pezzo di muraglione attinente al Paviglione del Palazzo novo verso il gran Cortile, e Ceronda.

- - - - - - - -

Cap. 58. Più livre milla quattro cento cinquanta pagato al Cappo M.ro Piscina per haver fatto il riempim.to di terra tutto allongo del muraglione del giardino basso in larghezza di trab. tre indi spianato et ridotto a livello tutto il piano di d.o giardino, fatto purgar et esportar la terra cattive da quadri d'esso et fatto portar altra buona per la profondità di un piede liprande dello giardino cominciando dalla testa del muraglione verso levante et luogho della Venaria et terminando al patto a rettalinea al paviglione verso il gran cortile e Ceronda del palazzo novo . . .   £   1,450

Cap. 59. Più pagato al Andrea Celerone et à Sebastiano, et Pietro padre e figlio de Francone . . . per trab. n.o 445:1 di cavo e esport.ne di terra e spianamento d'essa per la continuatione del

---

[4] The summary pages of this document were transcribed by Chiara Passanti, the rest by me.

giardino basso et per poter fare il muraglione che deve sostener la terra del gran giardino alto cominciando dallo cavo del pavaglione del Palazzo novo verso il gran Cortile et Ceronda et terminando alla testa del arco ò sia volta ch'è nel muragl.e fatto nel angolo di detto giardino

£ 1,891:19

Total	£	47,482: 4: 1
Sums Provided		35,369

Amount owed by S.A.R. 12,113: 4: 1

Signed 15 Gennaio 1665

S.A.R. ha pagato il sudetto resto

Signed Giorgio Turineti

Misura fatta il 26 Novembre 1664 par Antonio Borrione

P.o ho misurato al murag.ne del giardino da basso che resta tra il pallzo novo, e vechio dalla fond.ta sine ove termine compreso le murag.e delle tre grotte osia nichie volte sop.a esse grotte muraglie del recipiente e n.o sei di speroni di detto il bifalco d'esse tre grotte rileva in tutto à

trab 229: 0: 0

Contract with Piscina per spianamento a lievello del giardino..17 Sept. 1664

- - - - - - - -

Più promette di far spiano tutto il sito di detta [basso] giardino. . . . per tutta la sua larghezza . . . et dove si faranno li quadri per piantam.to de bussi, e fiori . . .

Le alee di detto giardino tanto di longo che di traverso promette spianar a livello come sopra, e di far porta in essa Terra à sabia pargata di giara dandole [word?] in modo che rieschino piane e belle come sono quelle de giardini.

Contract with Celerone Franco e Francone for excavation for extension of lower garden 20 Nov. 1664

. . . spianam.to et esportatione della terra che resta ancor ad esportarsi, et spianarsi dal novo Palazzo della Venaria R.le esso compreso sino per tutta la fuga del giardino alto ad effetto di porter far siguitar il muraglione alto dove si fanno li grotte per i giochi d'acqua et indi quello di sotto necessario per sostegno della detta terra da esportarsi tra d.i due muraglioni per far li giardini bassi . . .

Fare il sito tra li detti due muraglioni da farsi . . . in modo che dal piano del giardino alto a quello basso vi resti dieci piedi liprandi d'altezza.

3) Fondo Provincia Torino, Mazzo 32, int. 36.[5]

Spesa delle Fabriche fatte alla Veneria R.le

l'Anno 1665 rilevanti £ 42,081:16:8

Sommario del credito ò sia spesa della fabrica e lavori fatti d.e £461

primo fo. faccia prima	£	19,003: 6: 3
fog.3 faccia 2.a	£	20,788: 6: 5
fog. 4 faccia p.ma	£	1,829: 4
	£	42,081:16: 8

La spesa fatta nell'anno hor scorso per la fabrica de' restanti muraglioni de giardini per l'ucelara, cason per il guardaboscho, baulustrade di marmore, piramidi simili, scalini di serizzo

[5] Transcribed by Chiara Passanti.

ferramente, et altre opere contenute in cap.46 di questo conto, rilevano alla sud.a somma di livre quaranta due milla ottanta soldi sedici, e denari otto, et il pagato à conto d'esse per un sol cap. rileva alla somma di livre trenta cinque milla, e cento, siche essendo mag.re la spesa di £6,9881:16: 8 de pagato di questa somma di livre sei mila nove cento ottanta s.13:8 si dechiara S.A.R. debitrice In fede Torino li 8 dell'anno 1666. fanno d.[oppi]e. 517 £2:6
Signed Gina Aud.e
S.A.R. hà pagato il sudetto resto
Signed Giorgio Turineti

4) Fondo Provincia Torino, Mazzo 33, int. 1.[6]

Conto spese fabriche Venaria Reale 1666
Ascendente a £ 62,702:14:11
Sommario de' lavori fatti nell'anno 1666 alla Venaria Reale descritti ne cappi di discarimento del qui gionto Conto

Riempimento e spianamento del restanti giardino delle fontane	£	3,294
Casa et Scudarie per servitio dela Ser.ma Principessa compreso il casino ivi attenta per l'hoste	£	20,018:17:10
Ottangolo del Ucelera da primo Cornicione in su comprese le arre de ferro. e tavelle per il coperto	£	2,718:12
Li due archi in fondo al grande Giardino escluso li quatro cavie stabiliture da farsi	£	16,182:11: 4
Balaustrata trab 63:1:4	£	9,957:10
Piramidi di num.o diece a Duca.ti 80 l'uno	£	3,600
Poggioli quattro di tavoloni di scrizzo comprese li ferri, boblittura d'essi	£	2,067
Tellari fontane	£	54
Lavori diversi, cioè per metter in opra li Piramidi, balaustri, tavolini. . . .	£	373: 1: 6
Forno fatto al Casino per il Guarda boscho	£	113:14
Casa per il Sig.r marchese di Parella	£	3,926: 5: 6
Esportazione terra dalla Piazza del Teatro	£	240: 6: 8
Spese cibarie in occasione della misure nel corso dell'anno pas.o	£	116: 8
Canali per li coperti fatti sovra le due picole Terrasse della Torre del horologio	£	40:16: 1

Li lavori importano	£	62,702:14:11
Il denaro		54,368
Resta S.A.R. debitore		8,334:14:11

Signed Gina Aud 28 Aprile 1667
Si son ricevute le £8,334:14:11 mancanti
hoggi li 28 Aprile 1667 dalle proprie mani
di S.A.R.
Signed Georgio Turineti

---

[6] My transcription checked by Chiara Passanti.

5) Fondo Provincia Torino, Mazzo 33, int. 2.[7]

Spese per le Fabriche della Venaria Reale nel 1667

Ascendenti a livre 75,404:13:4

Sommario delle fabriche, et opere fatte alla Venaria Reale l'anno 1667 esp.e questo Conto

Fabrica della Cassina	£	7,202: 6
Lavori fatti alla Piazza primo Palazzo	£	5,010:18: 9
Quelli fatti alla Terrazza	£	9,014:10: 9
Alla Casa Madama la Prencipessa	£	750: 4: 6
A quella tenuta dal Trateur	£	78: 6:11
Fertonadura muraglione delle Grotte	£	1,178:16
Grotta attinenti al Pavag.le primo Palazzo	£	311: 2
Teatro et Arco di mezo con tutti li lavori marm.re	£	49,323: 9: 5
Pozzo del gran Cortile	£	296
Lavori di terra	£	109:12
Spianamento Piazza primo Palazzo	£	200
Lavori fatti alla Torre del horologgio	£	91: 0:10
Sternito di mattoni della grande Scuderia	£	307: 8: 8
Minuti lavori Parco	£	219
Lavori Ucelare	£	137:10: 6
Ferramente minute	£	53:10
Porta pavaglione Palazzo vechio	£	35
Vitriate racomodate et parti fatti di nuovo	£	373: 9
Minuti lavori del seragliero	£	30:12
Pozzo Casa S.r March.e Parella, e sottomura.ne	£	135
Aggionte fatte dal S Conte Castellamonte alli estimi	£	322:10
Lavori minuti da boscho, e spese cibarie	£	244: 6
	£	75,404:13: 4

Le fabriche et lavori fatti fare alla Venaria Reale nell'anno scorso 1667, rilevano come dal controscritto Sommario à livre settanta cinque milla quatro cento quatro soldi tredici, e denari quatro   dico £ 75,404:13: 4

Li pagamenti fatti da S.A.R. à conto rilevano livre sessanta quatro milla, et ottocento   dico £ 64,800

- - - - - - - -

Resta S.A.R. debitrice di   £ 10,604:13

Le fabriche et lavori fatti fare alla Venaria Reale nell'anno da S.A.R., espressi in cap. 114 del presente conto rilevano alla somma di livre settanta cinque milla quatrocento quatro s.13:4 et li pagamenti fatti à conto d'essi, à livre sessanta quatro milla e ottocento, siche essendo maggior il speso del ricevuto di livre dieci milla seicento quatro s. 13:4 di questa somma di £10,605:13:4 si dichiara S.A.R. debitrice del sig.r Conte, et Presidente Turineti, al qual conto hò proceduto per comando del A.S.R., de qual nel suo biglietto à me diretto in datta 15 giugno scorso, qui giunto In fede Torino

li 24 8.bre 1668

Signed Gina Aud.e

Note in left margin of manuscript Le £10,604:13:4 si portano nel conto Fab.a 1668

---

[7] Summary transcribed by Chiara Passanti, caps. by me.

Cap. 23. Pagato al Carlo Busso e Deodatto Ramello per marmore, Soccoli, piedestalli delle quattro statue e li soccoli delle sei Piramidi £ 1,004:11: 9

Piramidi a bugno num.o sei con . . . piedastalli e balle £ 2,160

Collonette n.o 73 £ 1,149:15

Due soccoletti fatti per metter sotto alle due statue nelle nichie della porta che non si son poi messi, anzi ritirati nel magazeno £ 16

tr 10:30 muraglio sotto alle collonette [*sc. the "teatro"*]

Cap. 70 Pagato al Carlo Busso per marmore per soccoli, piedestalli, cimase, cornicioni, cornici, freggio, vasi delli archi, anzi balle sovra questi, cartelle di d.o Teatro et Archi di mezo, et li soccoli provisti e datti travagliati, che son sotto alle sedici statue delle nichie £ 18,338

Cap. 71. Baulastrata £ 3,430

Cap. 72. 4 Collone al Archo di mezo con basi e capitali £ 2,160

Cap. 73. Piramidi n.o quatro. . . . . £ 1,440

Cap. 74. Quatro mezo basi delli Termini £ 124

Cap. 75. Quatro mezo basi e quatro mezi capitelli al archo di mezo verso il boscho £ 360

Cap. 76. Nove balle sovra li tre archi £ 558

Cap. 77. Otto grandi vasi travagliati a fiori e frutti che sono sovra li piedestalli della balaustrata £ 1,620

- - - - - - - -

Cap. 79. Quatro Termini grandi da marmore messi in opera alle due Porte del Teatro et quatro cani pur di marmore che sono sovra li Archi £ 3,063

- - - - - - - -

Pagato al Piccapietro Gio. Batt. Casella per Lavori di muro Tra 174:3 £ 4,714: 2

Ornamenti di lesene, cornici, 8 ochi di 8 nichie, 10 capitelli e base *1/2 cost, other half paid to Busso* £ 804:10: 9

- - - - - - - -

Cap. 91. Pagato a Bernardo Falconi, scultore, per n.o 30 statue di marmore bianco di frabosa £ 8,100

Cap. 92. Pagato al Bernardino Quadro per una statua di Diana di marmore bianco che resta in opra sovra il frontispicio del Arco di Mezo del Teatro £ 675

Cap. 93. Pagato al Giuseppe Maria Carlone n.o 16 busti di marmore bianco di frabosa con luoro peducci. . . . nelli ochi di detto teatro £ 1,290

(6) Fondo Provincia Torino, Mazzo 32, int. 3.

Spesa delle Fabriche fatte alla Veneria R.lel'Anno 1668

Ascendente al £ 53,742:15: 2

Sommario del Presente Conto

Che sono dovuti al Sig.re Presidente Turinetti per resto conto

1667 qui portati £ 10,604:14: 4

Costo Fabrica Trincotta £ 10,787:19

Costo casa attiguo a detto Trincotto £ 10,968:15: 2

Forno del Comune, con stanza e boteghino £ 765:15

Diversi lavori di muro et altri £ 2,102:15: 8

Balaustrata cordoni piramidi[8] £ 6,640:11: 3

---

[8] These were placed along the side of the "gran giardino" = lower garden on the park side.

Statue n.o 4 et 16 busti rondò condotto[9]	£	2,180
Lavori di muro	£	616:11: 8
Sterniti di pietre nove et altri rifatti	£	1,094: 6: 2
Lavori minuti di marmore e fatture	£	240

(7) Fondo Provincia Torino, Mazzo 34, int. 1.

Conto delle spesa fatta per le fabriche della Venaria Reale nell'anno 1669
Ascendenti al £ 72,157: 4:10

This ristretto has no summary page like the others.

Conto delli due brachi di fabrica aggionto al Pallazzo della Venaria Reale verso il grande giardino,[10] de pagamenti fatti a conto de lavori di muro et di pietre della grande scalla della fontana del Hercole, et d'altri minuti lavori fatti fare nell' anno prossimo scorso 1669 respettivamente dalli Capi M.ro Gio.Batta' Piscina et da [picca]pietre Carlo Busso e Deodato Ramello et da altri. . . . . .[11]

£ 14, 032: 9: 3 pagato a Capo M.ro Piscina per le muraglie, coperti, solari, stabiliture, sterniti, ornamenti et altri lavori . . . per la fabrica de due brachi o sieno corpi di fabriche ch S.A.R. ha fatto aggiongere al Palazzo della Venaria Reale verso il gran Giardino.

Cap. 31 Pagato al Bernardino Quadro per li stuchi che ha fatto alli anticamere Camere Alcove e gabinetti delli piani nobili d'essi due brachi di fabriche

Cap. 69. Pagato al Bernardo Falcone £1380 per la statua di Hercole di marmore biancho di frabosa (havendo S.A.R. fatto venir la pietra) d'altezza un trabucho et per il gietto del Fora[?] Clava e pella di bronzo.

Cap. 83. Pagato al Bernardo FAlconi £1800 (400 ducattoni) per quattro statue rapresentanti quatro schiavi mori, che a fatti di marmore nere di frabose quanto alla testa brachi gambi e il resto del corpo di pietra d'Ars, che sono in opra sovra li piede.li della scalla esteriore del Palazzo di d.a Venaria verso il gran cortile.

Included in this account book are contracts for statues. These were for 1) the four Moorish statues of the front courtyard and 2) for herms for the Fountain of Hercules: 1) "d'altezza piedi quatro liprandi in atto di portar sopra le spalle vase di citroni quali reggerano con le due mani."
2) "due di donne e due di huomini attempati con barbe in atto di sostener con le mani che se li metter sopra il capo, d'altezza piedi quatro liprandi"

(8) Fondo Provincia Torino, Mazzo 34, int. 2.

Conto spese fabriche Veneria Reale 1670
Ascendenti a £ 110,255:19: 8
Conto delle muraglie lavori di marmore di scrizzo che li Capi M.ri da muro Gio Battista Piscina e da pietro Carlo Busso e Deodato Ramello hanno respettivamente fatti fare nelli anni 1669 et

---

[9] This is a payment for putting the statues in place. In Cap. 86 Bernardino Quadri is paid £2,160 for the statues and sixteen busts to be placed in the fourth rondeau of the "gran giardino" = the lower garden.

[10] The misura of 19 November 1669 refers to the new construction as "P.ma Paviglione verso Seronda" and the other wing as "Braccio verso l'ucceliere o sia à mezzodi."

[11] From Caps. 63, 65 Piscina was paid £14,385 for the walls and ornaments of the stairway and Busso £15,136 for marble decorations (balaustrati, soccoli, piedestali, pilastri, cornicioni, etc.).

1670 per la construtione della grande scalla grotto Terrassa e Paviglioni della Fontana del Hercole della Venaria Reale, della Citronera fatta fare . . . de due corpi di casa à teatro . . . attinente alla nova Chiese su la Piazza della villa. . . .

(9) Fondo Provincia Torino, Mazzo 35, int. 1.0.
Conto delle Spese per la Fabrica della Veneria Reale
Ascendenti à livre 111, 664: 6: 9
Conto delle spese fatti nell'anno scorso 1671 di com'ando di S.A.R. per li lavori di marmore et altri attorno alle Grotte, e grande scala della fontana d'Hercole della Venaria Reale, del cavo et esportatione di terra fatto per formar la grande alea ivi, muraglione al longo d'esso per sostegno della terra, per le fabriche della nova fasanera, de quatro paviglionetti aggionti al Palazzo, de due Corpi di Casa attigui alla Chiesa della communità, de mollini da seda, del follone et altre . . . . [12]
Sommario, ò sia ristretto del presente Conto de lavori fatti alla Venaria R.le nel 1671
Primo £ 1,677:14, che S.A.R. resta debitrice per saldo del Conto lavori 1670, remesso al A.S.R.
dico £ 1,677:14
A m.ro Carlo Adamo per tra 1039:2:6 cavo, et esporta.e di terra per formar la grand alea della fontana d'Hercole £ 7,275:17: 8
Muraglione, che sostiene il terreno al longo di detta Alea che hà fatto fare detto Adamo, rilevante tra 39992:1:10 £ 3,138: 8:10
Lavori fatti far l'istesso Adamo, alle grotte grande scalla e due Paviglionetti della fontana d'Hercole, compreso il recipiente, condotti, et altri lavor'in ordine ad esse £ 4,394:12
Giornali Traggi à pestar machiaferro £ 213
Al Scultore Falconi per statue n.o 63 di marmore di Carrara, ed due di Frabosa che hà proviste,di num.o—Busti e 24 bassi rilevi pur di marmore Carrara, ed à conto di cinque altre statue che deve proveder per le grotte, et per altri lavori,e cause espresso nel conto
£ 16,517: 2: 6
Alli Capi m.ri piccap.e Busso e Ramello, per li lavori di marmore fatti alle grotte, grande scalla, e Pavaglionetti della fontana d'Hercole £ 11,531: 3:10
Saldadura bornelli piombo, e cimento di quelli di terra al fontanero Bridel £ 984:15
Murci pagati al Governa.re di Susa Baijotti £ 3,500
Altri murci al Oggiero £ 97:16
Al s Fabriccio Maulandi per impiegar nel pagamento condotto murci sud.i £ 3,000
Al fornasaro Bello per limbesi £ 139:13
Al lottonero Verna per robinetti, e scaricadori di bronzo £ 753
Condotta Bovari, delle Statue, Busti, e bassirilevi £ 136
Fatture ferri, come al capo 56 del conto £ 92
Spesa cibaria P.P. S.Carlo à capo 57 £ 216
Alli Stuca.ri Tencalla, Gianollo, Scalla,et altri per li ornamenti di murci, e mosaichi delle grotte, et muraglie interne grande scala, come alli Cap. 58, 59, 60, 61, 62, 63, 64 et 65 del conto
£ 1,896: 9: 3
Cochiglie d'arselle pagate à Pietro Rosso £ 201
Giornali pagati à fachini £ 102

---

[12] The rest of this document was transcribed by Chiara Passanti.

Due bassi rileve di marmore frabosa	£	348
Al Padre Tadeo per 60 casse cochiglie, come alli cap. 69 et 70 del conto	£	2,038
Ucelli di boscho al Intag.re Quirico	£	18
Saccaria per condurre machiaferro	£	6: 5
Calcina, con quale si sono mess'in opra li murci come à cap. 73 et 74 del conto	£	670:16: 8
Macchiaferro pagato al Cittadino	£	57
Giornali di piccapietre,come à d.o 78 del conto	£	109:10
Fattura mascaroni di marmore	£	94:10
Chiodi, fillo di l'ottone, machiaferro, et altro pag.to al Boggietto come à d.o 78 del conto		
	£	2,501:11: 6
Nolito e condotta di n.o 56 casse cochiglie al s. Duchene	£	591:11
Boglitture, e fatture ferri al Barra	£	66: 9
Lavori minuti di boscho dal Garella	£	48:16
Cavo de quatro grandi fossi, e riempim.to di terra grassa per piantamento Alea, fontana d'Hercole fatto far dal Adamo	£	1,504: 2
Cavo, et esporta.ne di terra per l'abassam.to di dett'Alea fatta far dal mede.o	£	887: 4: 4
	£	64,808: 7: 7

S'aggiongono qui livre duecento due, e meza pagate al piccapietre Carlone, per due Statue di marmore, che à fatte rappresentanti, cio una, Cleopatra, et l'altra Amore, valut.e dal s Conte Castellamone ducate 45 come per sua fede, et quitta. di detto Carlone qui giunte

	£	202:10
Li lavori fatti alla scalla, grotte, et Alea fontana d'Hercole ril.o	£	65,010:17: 7

Fabrica della fasanera fatta dal Adamo £ 5,400 del prezzo fatto, et £ 615: 2: 8 per lavori fatti di più di suo obligo

	£	6,015: 2: 8
Lavori fatti dal mede.mo alla fasanera vechia, come dalli cap.96 sino à 100 del conto		
	£	343:13:11

Fabrica de dui Corpi di Case, attigui alla Chiesa Parochiale della Venaria R.e fatti da m.ro Carlo Righinoi £ 13,500 cioè £ 13/m di prezzo fatto, et £ 500 di donativo acord.li da S.A.R.

	£	13,500

Fabrica de quatro Pavaglionetti aggionto al Palazzo fatti dal Adamo £13,867:4 cioè £12,150 valuta di dop.e 900 Italia di prezzo agiustato et £1,717:4 per lavori di più di suo obligo

	£	13,867: 4: 5
Altri lavori sequenti fatti alli med.mi	£	1,706: 7
Stuc.ra soffitta à cap. 115 del conto	£	135
Stuc.ra volta gabinetto à cap,116	£	94:10
Soffita d'intaglio e doradura d'essa à cap.117 e 118 del conto	£	432
Parchetto di noce à cap.119	£	100:10
Finestre di pittura, e rabeschi	£	181
Fornello di marmore interciato	£	108
Vitriate à cap. 122	£	235: 1
Ferramente à cap. 123	£	231: 6
Scallini di marmore à cap.124	£	54
Pitture fatte dal Rechi à cap, 125	£	135
	£	1,706: 7
Li lavori fatti alle facciate delle due Chiese rilevano come s.to	£	2,459:16: 3
Stuca.ra e quadrattura d'esse come al cap. 126	£	750
Li due quadri di pittura a fresco	£	270
Due croci	£	38:10
Alsamento delle due Porte, et altri lavori à cap. 129	£	210: 4: 5

Lavori di marmore fatti dalli piccapietre Busso e Ramello
come al cap. 130 del conto   £   1,191: 1:10

     £   2,459:16: 3
Lavori fatti dal Adamo ove sono li mollini da seda come nelli cap. 132 successivam.te sino à 137
del conto   £   1,530: 9: 8
Fabrica del follone fatto dal med.mo, come nelli cap. 138
succes.e sino à 145
Cavo fosso che porta l'acqua à mollini da seda   £   68: 4
Ferramente per essa fab.a, et quella del follone à cap. 147   £   225:12: 9
Lavori fatti attorno del infernetto descritti nelli cap. 148
sino à 152 del conto   £   277: 1: 6
Tellari à carta fatti alle finestre Case del cavalbianco, et della Panatteria, come à cap. 153 del
conto   £   185: 4
Lavori fatti alla facciata della Citronera come sotto   £   2,042:14: 8
quelli di marmore e di lose fatti dal Busso et Ramello espressino nelli cap. 155, sino à cap. 161
del conto   £   1,907:14: 8
quadro di pittura fatto dal Rechi, à cap.16   £   135

     £   2,042:14: 8
Lavori diversi contenuti in lista fatti dal Adamo   £   286:11
Stipendio Sovrastante Garrove   £   365
Ferramente diverse, come al cap. 167 del conto   £   597
Diverse, come . . . ali cap. 165, 166, et 168, 169   £   277:15
Ligattura del Conto   £   3

     £ 111,664: 6: 9

Le spese delle fabriche, fatte fare nell'anno scorso 1671 alla Venaria R.le, cioe per il cavo ed esportatione di terra ad effetto di formar la grande Alea, muraglione d'essa per le Grotte, Statue, Busti, bassi rilievi et altri lavori di marmore, fasanera, per li due Corpi di Case attigui alla Chiesa Parochiale del sud.o luogo, de quatro Pavaglionetti aggionti al Pallazzo novo, del folone, mollini da seda, et altre, come consta da. cap. 170 del presente Conto, arilevano livre cento ondeci milla sei cento sessantquatro, soldi sei, e denari nove d'argento à soldi venti caduna, et il denaro provisto e fatto pagare da S.A.R. à conto d'esse, ascende à livre ottanta milla simili, come in un solo capo del Caricamento, si ch'essendo mag.r la spesa di livra trenta milla seicento sessanta quatro soldi sei, denari nove, del come s.ra provisto, et fatto pagare d'essa somma di £ 30,664:6:9 si dechiara S.A.R. debitrice del sig. Conte, Primo Presidente et Capo del consiglio delle Finanze della medesima Georgio Turineti per saldo di detto Conto, al quale hò proeceduto, io Aud.e sottos.to per commando della med.ma R.A., portato dal suo biglietto qui gionto delli 30 x.mbre scorso In fede Torino li 18 Aprile 1672
Signed Horatio Gina Aud.e
Per Pagamento delle £30,664.6.9 che S.A.R. resta debittore del Presidente Turineti da Lui esposte per compir alle spese fatte alla Venaria Reale l'anno passato 1671 son statti assignati li minuti piaceri di S.A.R. p. le mesate sottos.te, quali son statte pagate dalli Chioattero e Bagnolo[13] ogni mesata cioè

[13] Bagnolo is a small village southwest of Turin at the base of the foothills. I have been unable to locate Chioattero, but from the context of the reference I assume it was also a village, and the amounts referred to are taxes or other payments rendered to the rulers of Piedmont.

£ 2,700 dal Bagnolo, et £1350 dal Chioatero, et così resta questo conto saldatto, In fede Torino
li 27 Luglio 1672

Mesata Genaro 1672	£ 4,050
Febraro	£ 4,050
Marzo	£ 4,050
Aprile	£ 4,050
Maggio	£ 4,050
Giugno	£ 4,050
Luglio	£ 4,050
Agosto à con. di £ 4,050 il resto	£ 2,314. 6. 9
	£30,664. 6. 9

Signed Georgio Turineti

APPENDIX III

DOCUMENTS FOR THE TEMPLE OF DIANA

1. E. F. Panealbo, *Relazione della solenne entrata fatta nella città di Savigliano delle Reali Altezze Carlo Emanuel II e Maria Giovanna Battista di Nemours il primo di luglio 1668,* Turin, 1668.
"Videro in faccia al giardino, in forma di teatro, varie termini dipinti che rappresentavano le Ninfe, qua le Napee, la le Druidi, da un canto e dall' altro le Amadriadi e le Oreadi, in mezzo delle quali stava Diana tutta festosa nel fonte di una Grotta, riquadrata in altezza di tre trabucchi che per finime.to havea la figura di Chiarezza; leggendosi sopra i termini delle Ninfe in altezza di due trabucchi posta à modo d'un gran freggio per tutta la larghezza del Teatro quest' Epigrafe CHIAREZZA ACCRESCE SPLENDORE, & al di sopra di tutto il Teatro & in tanta quantità ch'emulavano le selve di Creta, e Frigia.

2. 30 May 1669, AST, Corte, "Lettere di Particolari" C, Mazzo 34. As published by A. Lange, "Disegni e Dcumenti di Guarino Guarini," *Guarino Guarini e l'Internazionalità del Barocca.* Atti del Convegno internazionale promosso dall' Accademia delle Scienze di Torino, 30 Settembre–5 Ottobre 1968, Turin, 1970, I, 205. Letter of Carlo Giuseppe Vittorio, Conte di Buttigliera to Carlo Emanuele II.
Je fis voir hier au soir le dessain du Temple de Diana à M.R. [the Duchess], et luy dis ce que V.A.R. m'avoit commandé. L'absence des Marquis de Saint Germain, de Saint Damien, et du General Gontery a rendu la compagnie des plus capables en matière de bastiments, ou comme on dit, des crittiques, beaucoup moindre; il s'y trouva pourtant Madame la Princesse, les Marquis de Livourne, Ville, del Marro, le Comte de Verrue e l'abbé Scaglie: tous au premier abort admirerent le dessain susdit, mais comme une bonne partie de la science consiste à trouver a redire, on s'ingenia a treuver quelque chose pour cela, et affin que chacun ouvrit son sentiment, il dis que le Bettin avoit fait ce petit projet pour la Temple di Diane que V.A.R.veut faire faire.
Madame la Princesse trouve le degré incomode et jugeroit plus à propos, qu'on fit en derriere le temple, bien ayssé, qui alla respondre au deux costés du premier rang de balustrades: peutestre qu'elle prevoit qu'entra cy et la bastiment du Temple le desgre entre les rochers sera trop petit pour elle.
Le Conte de Verrua trouve que le rocher n'est pas une bas assez noble pour dit temple qui sera au dessus, l'abbé respond que non, et allegue l'example de ce pallais de Rome, ce qui est bien plus a propos dans un bois, et a une Venerie.
C'est tout que c'est dit sur ce sujet. Madame la Princesse m'a commandé en suite de dire à V.A.R. de sa part, que comme V.A.R. avoit appreuvé le dessain de sa vigne, qu'elle apreuvoit aussy celuy du Temple.
[Rest of letter on different subject.]
Signed
Buttilieres

3. Art. 207, Mazzo Venaria Reale, 3 July 1673.
Istruttione per le fondam.te e Muraglie del Roccio sopra quale dovea fabbricarsi il Tempio di Diana.
Si osserverà per le misure il disegno che sarà rimesso, tanto nella pianta, le profile

Li quattro pilastroni si farano tutti di pietra di caccia, ò di fiume grosse più che si potrà, che nodino bene in calcino tutta forte, cioè che la calcina sormonti le pietre, perciò si farà più tosto liquida che dura, la sabbia sarà tutta grisa e ben purgata, e li. . . . .serano le pietre con giarrone di fiume, e la muraglia tutta . . . li batterà ugualm.te con pistone di legno.

Li d.ti pilastri s'incamisarano di mattoni di Valdoc ò Vialbere ben stagionati di gross.a di oncie dieci

Le volte de' canali, e del nodo di mezo si faranno parimente di mattoni della sud.ta qualità, et di gross.a di oncie dieci

Io sotto.to Carlo Adamo ho promesso à S.A.R. di far le muraglie contenute nella sovra.ta Instruttione, cioè tutte quelle che si dovranno far di pietra per la construttione del d.to Tempio e scale sino al piano di esso per il prezzo di livre sei soldi dieci per ogni trab. di gross.a di oncie dieci,e quelli di mattone e [?] per il prezzo di livre nove il trab. di gross.a d'on.e sei per le quale muraglie tanto di pietra che di mattoni la calcina si provederà a spese di S.A.R.

Più di esporta la terra che si cavarà dalli fondam.ti fuori della muraglia del parco nella Ceronda per il prezzo di livre cinque per ogni trabuco cubo.

Torino 2 lug.o 1673

      Carlo Adamo

    4.   Art. 207, Mazzo Venaria Reale, 22 October 1673.

Misura and stima of work of Carlo Adamo including the foundations of the Tempio di Diana, work on the grand allée, and at the Fountain of Hercules

f. 2r Tempio Diana

Segue la Misura del Tempio di Diana

Muraglie ordinarie in tutto trabuchi trecento quaranta cinque p 3, on. 5   Tr 345:3:5

[Next lines almost illegible but they refer to mortaring the wall, restoration of a part of the wall that had fallen, excavation for foundations of the wall and the removal of the excavated earth.]

Più il Cop.to fatto sopra d.ta Tempia da d.o Adamo, e poi e stata levato—calculo in tutto venticinque tr.

Il sudetto coperto e stato construito di boschami e coppi che per fatura e disfatura e guastamen.te de' boschami e coppi si estima livre sei cad.o trab.

    5.   Art. 207, Mazzo Venaria Reale, int. 18, (= 1674–75) 9 April 1676.

Part of an account submitted by the heirs of Carlo Adamo.

             - - - - - - - -

Segue la misura del Tempio di Diana

Primo tutte le muraglie di pietra senza cintura fatte dopo l'altra misura generale tra.bi duecento setanta quatro piedi uno Tr 274:1

Muraglie tutte di matoni pervenute dalla cintura et incamisata delle muraglie tutte di pietre per l'augmento della misura trab. otanta sette piedi quadri oncie nona Tr 87:4:9

Muraglie volte di matoni trab.i cinquecento quatro piedi cinque oncie nove–incluse le quatro trombe delle scale dico Tr 54:5:4

Muraglie per l'augmento del preza del valor di tutto pietra a mattoni la quale entrata già per pietre e solo per il sbalza de prezzo trab.i setanta uno Tr 71

Primo n.o 14 lesene alteza cad.no tr. 1:2:0 larg à piedi 13 gross p 1 1/2/ Tr 21

Più per tr 8 di dado di due soc.i rustico

Tr 2:16

Più per n.o 22 bugne altez p 8 per le due porte a [?] 12 cad.no

Tr 324

Lavori d'estimo ascend.i à

Tr 13:4

Benna per piccapl.e

Muraglie di n.o dieci pilastri che sostengono il coperto della bena' per li picapietre trab due piedi
tre dico à £14

Tr 2:3

Coperto sopra essi trab.i dieci piedi quattro

Tr 10:4

Signed Gazano ferrero misura.e di S.A.R.

      Gio: Mozzi

      Torino 9 Aprile 1676

      6.   Art. 810, int. 63, 30 May 1679.

Per la manutenazione della fabrica della Venaria Reale data M. Pietro Rosso

- - - - - - - -

Al Tempio di Diana si deve coprir tutto cioè pilastri di muraglia scoperto & si calcola la spesa in
tutto [Blank]

- - - - - - - -

Istruttione a chi dovrà far le reparationi della fabriche della Venaria Reale

- - - - - - - -

Il coperto del Tempio di Diana si farà in due pezzi, il primo pezzo coprirà tutto il Piano del
Tempio e sarà portato da nove Pillastri, cioè p otto ripartite attorno la circonferenze e uno nel
mezzo, quelli attorno la circonferenze saranno alti piedi quatro e mezzo dal suo piano e grosse
oncie quindeci cioè due mattoni a Testa et quello di mezzo oncie ventiquattro, cioè quattro mattoni e si farà di figura ottangola tutti di mattoni buoni e fatti con Calcina forte e questo sarà alto
piu delli altri tutta monta del coperto sopra li pilastri della circonferenza correrà tutto attorno
una banchetta di legno di rovere, o maletto di grosezza d'oncie sette in quadro o sij sei per traverso
e sette per l'altro Dal pilastro di mezzo faranno cader sopra detta banchetta dodici legni di rovere
o maleto di grosezza d'oncie cinque in sei, e saranno longhi trabucchi due e mezzo sopra quale
poseranno le [renne] distanti l'una dall' altra oncie nove sopra esse [?] li listelli e coppi
Il secondo pezzo coprirà in giro tutte le scale e poserà all' infuori sopra dodici pilastri da farsi
sopra la muraglia esteriore delle scale in altezza di più, che meno, e grossezza ognuno di tre
mattoni di ponte & all' indentro posarà sopra il Cordone di marmo del Piano di d.o Tempio
attorno li detti pilastri correrà la banchetta di rovere ò malesto d'oncie sei di larghezza e sette
d'altezza sopra quale caderanno diciotto legni di rovere o maleto di grosezza d'oncie cinque in sei
e longhezza trabucchi due circa e sopra essi le remi listelli et coppi come sopra quali coppi saranno
di moneaglieri ben staggionati e cavalcavanno oncie due l'uno sopra l'altro e metteranno ad ognuno di detti legni e banchetti le sue aguscie di legni sufficienti contro de Pilastri
Li due ripiani alti delle scale si copriranno a frontespicio con quattro pilastri a due per piano della
qualità di sud.i del primo pezzo di coperto & il boscami parimente della medema qualità.

- - - - - - - -

Turin, 7 May 1679

Signed C. Amadeo Castellamonte

      7.   Art. 810, int. 63, 12 April 1680.

Inspection visit of the Auditore Patrimoniale to verify repairs.

- - - - - - - -

Più si sono visitate le muraglie, coperti, & marmi che sono in opera al Tempio di Diana e ritrovato
il tutto in buon stato. . . . . .

8. 1 March 1660—Art. 199, 1 1657–67, fols. 50r, 54v–56v.
Biglietto di S.A.R. al Consiglio
delle finanze per il regolam.
delle spese delle da farsi
in occasione delle Nozze di Mad.ma
La Princip.a Violante Marg.ta di
Sav.a col Ser.mo Duca Ranutio di Parma
Cap.ne de gli Intag.ri Castelli e p le 4 Carri trionfali

Per la prnte noi sotto scritti Quirico Castelli, e Gio Bta Botto intagliatori residenti nella p.nte Citta Promettiamo, e si oblighiamo verso S.A.R. et avanti il Cons.o delle finanze di dett' A.R. di fare li quattro Carri Trionfali, che hanno da servire p la festa a Cavallo da farsi in Piazza Castello in occasione delle Nozze della S.ma P.a Mad.a Margarita di Savoia et di osservare la seguente is-trutt.ne

Instrut.ne a chi dovrà fare li 4 Carri Trionfali

Li quattro Carri li saranno dati da S.A.R. nel stato nel quale si trovan, à quale agiongeranno quello che sarà di bisogna p slongarli et alagarli all misura del dissegno, detti quattro Carri devono esser longhi un trabl. e mezo in tutte, e largh. un trab. nella maggior larghezza, et altezza di due trabuchi dal piano di Terra compreso ogni ornam.to vi faranno in Tavolate sopra di essi p la sudetta longhezza, et longhezza ben chiodato, et sicuro p piantarvi sopra à ogn'uno di essi li ornamenti, che si vedon de dissegni.

- -

Carro di fiorenza

Il Girello di questo carro sarà di tella dipinto, et argentato, come si vede nel dissegno attorno vi cor-rerà la ballaustrata con base, cimasa, e piedestalli di legno, e li ballaustri di Cartone, il tutto argentato sovra li piedestalli vi saranno vasi di verdura argentati, e tra essi quantita di gigli rossi.

Il piano del Carro sarà compartito a quadri di Giardino piena di fiori e gigli rossi.

La rocca, o sia fontana, si formarà di listelli e telle, e sopra essi quantità di murti[?] di pastume argen-tate e di parti, e ove si vedono le cascate d'acqua si farà il fondo argentato, e sopra vi si dipingeranno le dette cascate.

Attorno il piede di detta rocca vi saranno n.o otto gran cochilie fatte di centeni listelli, e tella tutte argentate, e dipinte e dentro esse vi saranno otto figure di Deità fatte di carta pista argentate e finte d'oro

Nella sommitá della rocca vi sarà un Hercole di pastume di oncie 20 circa di altezza combatta con la mazza, un Idra di sette capi fatti di legno, il tutto argentato e finto d'oro.

Sarà ornato d.o Carro con qualche rami di verdura, e quantità di coralli finti, e si procurerà di osser-var più che si potrà il dissegno.

- -

Promettono li sudetti di fare li detti Carri conforme alli dissegni et Istrutioni red.e, e darli fatti fra li 28 del prossimo mese d'Aprile p il prezzo di livre mille ottocento d'arg.a @ 326 l'una da pagarsi cioè livre seicento simili anticipatam.e et restante, come si andarà avanzando il lavoro, et li sudetti quattro carri con luoro ornamenti restaran.o di S.A.R. e p osservanza di quanto sopra si sono Sotto Scritti Torino li 19 Marzo 1660
Amadeo Castellamonte Ingignero
Quirico Castelli Prometto come Sopra
Io Gio Bat.a Botto prometto come Sopra

9. Description of the Temple of Diana, Castellamonte, pp. 81–83.

Vede dunque in mezzo à questo Lago sorger un Scoglio con macigni di monte formato in modo dall' Arte, che la Natura istessa non lo ricusarebbe per proprio parto, se quei Mostri impietriti (che da ogni parte si scorgono) col loro tacere non la mentissero.

E sforato in croce lo Scoglio con canali di larghezza capace al passaggio delle Barche. Sono le entrate de' canali ornate, & arricchite di grande Colossi di marmo, quelle che scontrano la retta linea della grande Allea hanno nella fronte ogn'una quattro gran Termini di marmo rappresentanti Deità maritime, con capelli, e barbe rabbuffate, e fatte di scoglio, e questi sostengono li due ripiani delle Scale, che posano al Tempio.

Ornano le altre due diametrali alle sudette, due Atlanti di marmo per caduna, quali condannati à reggere li primi Ripiani di dette Scale, s'abbassano sopra un ginocchio, e curuati in se medesimi fanno forza con le spalle al sostegno del peso di mezzo un Monte.

Raggirano circolarmente tutto lo Scoglio otto salite di Scale di marmo per l'ascesa al Tempio, con sponde parimente di marmo fatte con tal' arte che dalla sommità dello Scoglio cadono à salti per dette sponde cannaletti d'acque, che bagnano d'alto in basso.

Sopra questo dunque s'erge il superbo Edificio di forma perfettamente rotonda, sostenuto da otto Pilastroni di candidissimo marmo, e da sedici Colonne del medesimo, che riposando sopra altretanti Piedestalli reggono un Corniccione abbellito di tutti quelli ornamenti, con quali la Greca Architettura hà saputo arricchirne l'ordine Corinthio.

Sopra questo volgesi una Ballaustrata, sopra quale posano ventiquattro Ninfe del Choro di Diana, che danno finimento alla parte esteriore del Tempio.

Li Muri della Cella di questo Tempio tanto al di dentro, che al di fuori, sono alternativamente ripartiti in aperture per il lume, & in Nicchi per altre Statue, che rispondono agl' intervalli delle Colonne, abbelliti di ricchi ornamenti di marmo, e tutto quello che sopravanza a' Marmi vien ricoperto da quel bel Musaico di Conchiglie, e Madriperle.

Finisce la Cella in una proportionata Cupola coperta di lastre di piombo, costeggiata da otto Cartelloni di rame dorato, che supportano un' Aguglia parimente di rame dorato.

Il di dentro del Tempio si conuerte nel Lauacro di Diana, ove ella assisa in luogo eminente vien servita da otto Ninfe, quali scherzando trà loro si gettano addosso l'acqua con tazze dorate, e in medesimo tempo riuolgono gli loro dardi d'acqua contro gl' incauti, e troppo curiosi Spettatori. Da che tutto ne vien formato un bellissimo Fonte, le acque del quale uscendo dalla Cella danno l'essere ad un Riuolo, che girando attorno al bassamento del Tempio, e passando per la bocca di diversi Mostri ricadono precipitose, e scoperte nel Lago, dal quale per nascosti canali, montarono al Tempio, e rompendosi frà le punte dello Scoglio, e nella discesa delle Scale rendono col biancheggiarsi all'occhio, e co'l mormorio all' orecchio non sprezzabile meraviglia.

A Cardinal's Bulb Garden:
A *Giardino Segreto* at the Palazzo Barberini in Rome

Introduction

1. The Inventory and a Reconstruction of the Garden

2. The Horticultural Treatise—How the Plants were Grown

3. The Flower Album

4. Identification of the Plants in the Garden and Conclusions

Appendix I The Inventory, Biblioteca Apostolica Vaticana, Ms. Barb. Lat. 4265

Appendix II Horticultural Treatise and English Translation, Biblioteca Apostolica Vaticana, Ms. Barb. Lat. 4278

Appendix III Catalogue of the Flower Album, Biblioteca Apostolica Vaticana, Ms. Barb. Lat. 4326

Appendix IV Plant Lists
1. Alphabetical list of plants in the inventory and their location in the garden
2. Alphabetical index to plants in the horticultural treatise
3. Modern botanical names of plants in the flower album listed alphabetically

Appendix V Glossary of terms in the inventory, treatise, and flower album

Dedication

To the memory of Georgina Masson,
or as her friends were privileged to call her,
Babs Johnson
I could not have done this study without her pioneering work

INTRODUCTION

For almost two centuries flowers have been considered the essential and most important feature of a garden, but this was not always true. In earlier eras priority was given
to trees planted in informal settings, or to the creation of elaborate patterns with evergreen shrubs and trees trimmed in precise geometric forms; from this grew the misconception that these earlier gardens were totally devoid of flowering plants. The illusion is
particularly strong in the case of Italian gardens of the sixteenth and seventeenth centuries, yet it is easy to demonstrate that such was not the case. Contemporary descriptions
often refer to flowers and flower gardens, and views show areas called *Giardino di Semplici*.
The term *semplici* was understood by foreign travelers to mean "simples," or medicinal
and culinary herbs, but in Italy the term also meant ornamental plants.[1] The misconception could not be corrected by a visit to the gardens, because flowers were usually found
only in the *giardino segreto*. The *giardini segreti* were walled areas reserved for the personal
use of the patron and family adjacent to the palace or villa building. Thus travelers'
accounts of their visits to villas were limited to areas accessible to the casual visitor, the
larger areas of garden and park, where indeed the plantings were usually green trees
and shrubs.[2]

The *giardino segreto* appeared early in the history of Italian Renaissance gardens. It
probably derived from the small enclosed gardens found in medieval castles and the
cloister gardens of monasteries, and as in the earlier prototypes, it was often the place
where rare and valuable plants were grown. In fact, one might say that the true innovation in Renaissance villa design was the addition of large parterres and parks to the
traditional enclosed garden adjacent to the residence. *Giardini segreti* were a particularly
important feature of gardens in Rome in the sixteenth and seventeenth centuries, a
period when many villas were built on the periphery of the densely occupied center.
Perhaps the pressure of visitors in that center for pilgrims and tourists created more need
for a private enclosure than in the more out-of-the-way rural villas. The late seventeenth-
century views of villas in Rome by Falda give an idea of the appearance of those *giardini
segreti* (Figs. 1, 2) and their simple geometric planting plans.[3] An even more detailed idea

[1] This misconception was first pointed out by G. Masson, "Italian Flower Collectors' Gardens," *The
Italian Garden*, Dumbarton Oaks Colloquium on the History of Landscape Architecture 1, ed. David R. Coffin, Washington, D.C., 1972, 61–80. Reference to different meanings of the word "simplici," 67.

[2] English travelers to Italy in the period with which we are concerned published many travel books.
For a short title list of these reports and a discussion of English visitors to Italian gardens, see J. D. Hunt,
Garden and Grove, London, 1987, 223–24. David Coffin has suggested that the *giardino segreto* was developed
for the personal use of the patron because the rest of the gardens were usually accessible to the public. See
"The '*Lex Hortorum*' and Access to Gardens in Latium during the Renaissance," *Journal of Garden History* 2
(1982), 201–32. A revised and enlarged version of this article appears in D. Coffin, *Gardens and Gardening in
Papal Rome*, Princeton, 1991, 244–57.

[3] The bird's-eye views in Giovanni Battista Falda, *Li giardini di Roma. . . .*, Rome, [1680?], are the best
evidence for the placement and appearance of the Roman *giardini segreti*.

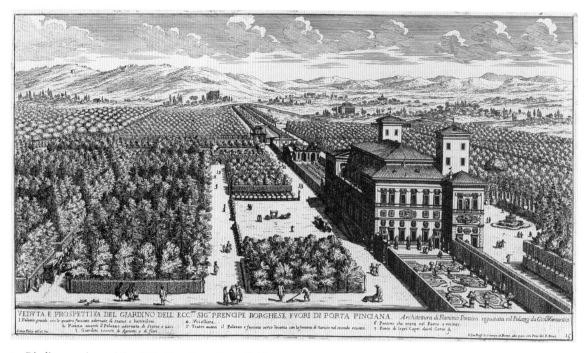

VEDVTA E PROSPETTIVA DEL GIARDINO DELL' ECC.^{MO} SIG.^{RE} PRENCIPE BORGHESE, FVORI DI PORTA PINCIANA.   Architettura di Flaminio Pontico seguitata col Palazzo da Giou.Vansantio.

1. Bird's-eye view of the Villa Borghese from Falda, *Li giardini di Roma,* pl. 15 (photo: Dumbarton Oaks)

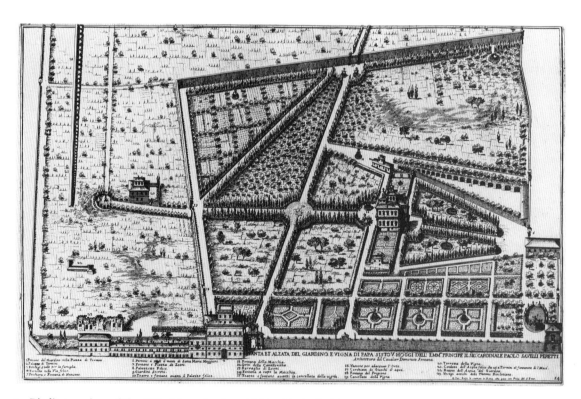

2. Bird's-eye view of the Villa Montalto from Falda, *Li giardini di Roma,* pl. 14 (photo: Dumbarton Oaks)

222

of their appearance can be derived from a detail from an Italian altar frontal (Fig. 3) which shows all the features known from descriptions of individual villas and building accounts—fountains, seats, and loggias or pergolas to provide shade, walls covered with vines or espaliered plants chosen for their fragrance. Descriptions rarely, however, gave the names of flowers in the gardens,[4] and even lists and inventories usually listed only the genera and not specific varieties or cultivars of plants. In addition, none of the surviving gardens have their original plants or layouts, and documents usually give no information about planting patterns or methods of cultivation.

Identification of plants presents the greatest problem in any attempt to reconstruct the appearance of these gardens. The nomenclature used in plant names in the pre-Linnaean era was based on such externals of form as leaf width and color (the latter particularly susceptible to changes due to climate and soil), and some of the physical characteristics of the flower. It is not always possible to correlate a seventeenth-century flower name with its modern binomial classification, which is based on the reproductive parts of the flower. In addition, many of the plants found in the seventeenth-century gardens, especially the exotic importations from Asia and the Americas, were mistakenly named after traditional genera, others are no longer in cultivation, and modern developments in hybridization have drastically altered the form, color, and growth habits of plants identifiable with those grown in the past. For that reason, a group of three manuscripts in the Biblioteca Apostolica Vaticana are unique in the information that they provide about the herbaceous plants in one *giardino segreto,* planting patterns, horticultural practices at the time, and the appearance of many of the flowers in the garden. The first, Vat. Barb. Lat. 4265, is titled "Giardinetto Secreto Dell' Em.mo Sig.r Card.le Antonio." Its vellum binding is stamped with a cardinal's coat of arms and a shield with the Barberini bees.[5] This particular crest identifies the cardinal as Antonio Barberini (1607–71), the nephew of Pope Urban VIII, and the *giardino segreto* as the small garden (approximately 18 × 10 meters) visible in seventeenth-century views to the northeast of a wing of the Barberini Palace on the Quirinal hill in Rome.[6] It is an inventory of the plants in

[4] Descriptions of the *giardini segreti* of the Villa Borghese in Rome in D. Montelatici, *Villa Borghese fuori di Porta Pinciana,* Rome, 1700, are typical of the usual information given about plants. ". . . si vede un giardino, posto lungo l'muro della strada maestra, chiuso dagl' altri lati con tavole, e cancelli di legno ricoperti al di fuori con verdeggiante spalliera di lauro regio; il quale vien diviso in più scompartimenti piantati di più sorti di fiori, cioè d'Anemoni, Tulipani, Giunchiglie, Giacinti & altri" (p. 65). ". . . una scalinata di quattro gradini, [dove] s'espone alla vista sopra di essi un gran numero di vasi, e cassette piene di fiori, quando d'Anemoni, e Giacinti, quando di Tulipani, di Garofali, ed altri, de' più rari . . ." (p. 315). In 1650, the two *giardini segreti* also contained orange trees. *Villa Borghese fuori di Porta Pinciana descritto da Iacomo Manilli Romano guardarobba di detta villa,* Rome, 1650, 115–17.

[5] I am grateful to Marilyn Aronberg Lavin for calling my attention to this manuscript which she discovered in the research that led to her publication, *Seventeenth-Century Barberini Documents and Inventories of Art,* New York, 1975. The inventory manuscript has recently been cited by Lucia Tongiorgi Tomasi in "Francesco Mingucci 'Giardiniere' e pittore naturalistica. Un aspetto della committenza Barberiniana della Roma seicentesca," *Atti del convegno celebrativo Cesi, ottobre 1985,* Rome, 1987, 296–97.

[6] The location of the garden was determined by Francesca Consagra in a report given in a seminar on 17th-century gardens in Italy, France, and England held at Dumbarton Oaks in 1982. Its size (ca. 18 × 10 m) was estimated by comparison of the scaled plans (figs. 101–2) in Waddy's *Roman Palaces.* See n. 9 for full citation.

3. A *giardino segreto,* seventeenth-century Italian altar frontal (photo: The Metropolitan Museum of Art, Rogers Fund, 1907 [07.2])

the garden, listed by location as was customary in inventories at this time. The planting beds and rows are given numbers, and the compartments indicated on the accompanying plan of the garden is numbered to correspond.

A second manuscript, Vat. Barb. Lat. 4278, is listed in the manuscript catalogue of the archive as "Trattatino della coltivazione di alcuni fiori cioè degli Anemoni, dei Giacinti, de Narcisi, de Tulipani, de Garofali."[7] It is unillustrated. It contains specific instructions for the cultivation and propagation of the flowers listed in the title, all of which also appear in the inventory.

The third manuscript, a florilegium or flower painting album, Vat. Barb. Lat. 4326, signed by Francesco Mingucci and dated 21 August 1639,[8] is dedicated to Cardinal Francesco Barberini (1597–1679), the elder brother of Cardinal Antonio, nephew of Urban VIII and ultimately vice-chancellor of Rome.[9] It has eighty-one pages of flower paintings, a single plant, or species on all but two pages.

Many are the same genera and species that appear in the inventory and are discussed in the horticultural treatise. These manuscripts and their contents are discussed in the following pages, and the appendices will bring together information about the ornamental plants named or depicted in the manuscripts. The text of the inventory has been transcribed and appears in Appendix I. Appendix II is a transcription of the horticultural treatise with a translation of the text on the facing page. The translation was done by Peter Armour and has been emended by me. The flower album is illustrated in Appendix III with an identification in modern botanical nomenclature of the plants and a commentary on the history of their introduction or their earliest known uses by Carla Teune of the Botanical Garden of the University of Leiden. Appendix IV contains plant lists arranged alphabetically, and Appendix V is a glossary of words found in the inventory and treatise.

Each of the manuscripts makes a significant contribution to our knowledge of the several disciplines or arts represented in them. Together they offer a unique compilation of knowledge about horticultural practice in seventeenth-century Rome.

However, one must also ask how the garden, its flowers, and the flower album are related to other aspects of art patronage at this time. There can be no doubt that flower collecting and gardens were important to the Barberini family, and that their interest involved more than a simple visual pleasure in plants. Urban VIII's library contained a large collection of botanical books, as did his nephew's, Cardinal Francesco.[10] Barberini

---

[7] Cited by Tongiorgi Tomasi, "Mingucci," 287 and n. 31. She refers there to another manuscript in the Biblioteca Apostolica Vaticana (hereafter Bibl. Apost. Vat.), Barb. Lat. 4283, listed in the inventory as "Del Gelsomini e delle Rose." See n. 43.

[8] First cited by G. Vaccai, "Francesco Mingucci pittore pesarese e i tre codici della Biblioteca Vaticana," *Rassegna Marchigiana* I (1822–23), 452–58. Some of the flowers depicted in this album are discussed by Masson, "Italian Flower Collectors," 74–78, and Tongiorgi Tomasi, "Mingucci," 293–96.

[9] See P. Waddy, *Seventeenth-Century Roman Palaces: Use and the Art of the Plan*, New York, 1990, chap. 10, 128–31, for the dates of the members of the Barberini family and of their positions.

[10] "L. Holstein" (Francesco Barberini), *Index Bibliothecae qua Franciscus Barberinus. . . . Magnificentissimas Suas Familiae ad Quirinalem Aedes Magnificentiores Reddidit*, Rome, 1681, 2 vols.

account books show that the latter paid for the illustrations, designed by such important artists as Pietro Cortona, Andrea Sacchi, and Guido Reni, in *De florum cultura libri IV,* whose author, the Jesuit priest Giovanni Battista Ferrari (1584–1655) was a member of their household. One may assume that the Barberini subsidized its publication as well as that of Ferrari's *Hesperides*,[11] if they did not commission them. The Barberini were not alone in their interest in flowers and botany—this was a period when the nobility and monarchs all over Europe were avidly collecting and growing exotic plant importations[12]—and cut flowers in elaborate arrangements were used at banquets and to decorate rooms, as Ferrari's illustrations show. Flowers were also the most popular form of decoration for fabrics, porcelain and silverware, and many other valuable objects.[13]

I would like to express my warmest thanks to the two Prefects of the Biblioteca Apostolica Vaticana, Monsignor Alfonso Stickler and Leonard Boyle who granted permission to publish these three manuscripts.

1. THE INVENTORY AND A RECONSTRUCTION OF THE GARDEN
MS. BARB. LAT. 4265

The inventory manuscript, Barb. Lat. 4265, is a small booklet, 20.6 × 14 cm, bound in vellum with the Barberini coat of arms on the front cover but no title or date. The first page of the inventory is headed with the title, "Giardinetto Secreto Dell' Em.mo Sig.r Card.le Antonio"; the folio numbering begins there with number one, although it is actually the fourth page of the manuscript. The inventory occupies twenty-one folios of the manuscript, and there are an additional four empty folios.[14]

---

[11] Giovanni Battista Ferrari's treatise, *Flora, seu de florum cultura libri IV,* Rome, 1633, is discussed by I. Belli Barsali, "Il trattato di Giovan Battisti Ferrari." It is dedicated to Cardinal Francesco. An Italian edition with the title *Flora, overo, cultura di fiori* (hereafter *Flora 1638*) appeared in 1638 dedicated to Donna Anna Colonna Barberini, sister-in-law of Cardinal Francesco, and the wife of Prince Taddeo Barberini, and a second Latin edition was printed in Amsterdam in 1646. My citations are to the Italian edition unless the citation reads *Florum 1633.* Payments for plates by Greuter made from designs by Pietro da Cortona are recorded in Cardinal Francesco's *Mastro de' Casa* accounts. M. Lavin, *Barberini Documents,* 12, 20 (docs. 98, 160), respectively. See I. Belli Barsali, "Una fonte per i giardini del Seicento: Il trattato di Giovan Battista Ferrari," *Il giardino storico italiano,* ed. G. Ragionieri, Florence, 1981, 221–34. G. B. Ferrari, *Hesperides sive De Malorum Aureorum Cultura et Usu Libri Quatuor,* Rome, 1646. The latter contains plates and descriptions of citrus plants, especially the inedible but ornamental varieties that were so popular for use on espaliers and in vases.

[12] See Masson, "Italian Flower Collectors," 61–80, and idem, "Italian Flower Connoisseurs," *Apollo* 88 (1968), 164–71.

[13] Ferrari, *Flora 1638,* discusses flower arrangements and bouquets in Book 4. Flower vases, boxes to transport cut flowers are illustrated on pp. 399, 405, 411, 415, 419, 421, 431. Note that some authors of florilegia, especially Flemish and French, call themselves embroiderers or say their plates are for silversmiths. See C. van de Passe, *Hortus floridus . . . ,* Arnheim, 1614–16, who says his plates are for silversmiths, and P. Vallet, *Le iardin du roy tres chrestien Henry IV roy de France, . . . ,* Paris, 1608 and *Le iardin du roy tres chrestien Loys, roy de France, . . . ,* Paris, 1623. Vallet calls himself "brodeur du Roy."

[14] The text of the inventory appears in App. I. A table with an alphabetical list of the plants named and their locations in the parterres, planting beds, and vases is in App. IV.

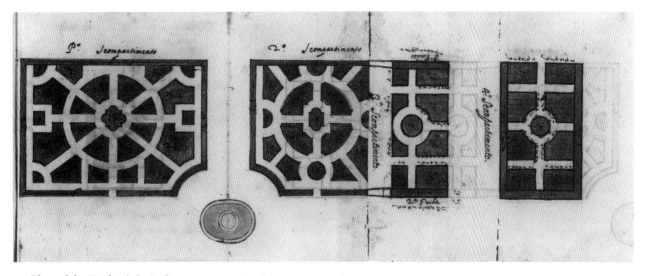

4. Plan of the Barberini *giardino segreto,* ms. Barb. Lat. 4265 (photo: Biblioteca Apostolica Vaticana)

A plan of the planting beds inventoried is bound in the front, with a blank sheet between it and the first inventory page (Fig. 4). It consists of two sheets pasted together; the second sheet is folded over to fit within the edges of the binding (see also Pl. I).

Neither the location of the garden nor the date of the inventory are given, but it has been identified as the small walled garden located behind and north of the main body of the Palazzo Barberini in Rome.[15] Falda's bird's-eye view (Fig. 5) shows a portion of the garden and the small oval pool that appears in the inventory plan. Its site is part of a triangular piece of land acquired by the Barberini in 1628,[16] north of the palace wing that was a survival from the earlier Villa Sforza. It is possible that the garden was created in 1632 at the time the structure to its north was built to house the tapestry weaving workshop, but it is more likely that the garden was not built until Cardinal Antonio rented the palace from his brother Taddeo in 1635.[17]

[15] See n. 6.

[16] The cardinal's walled garden should not be confused with the *giardino segreto* built for Donna Anna Barberini on the south side of the Sforza wing and just visible in Falda's bird's-eye view (Fig. 5). For the history of the acquisitions of the various pieces that ultimately comprised the palace and gardens, see P. Waddy, "The Design and Designers of the Palazzo Barberini," *Journal of the Society of Architectural Historians* 35 (1976), 154.

[17] "1632 Misura e Stima . . . in fare il Casino vicino a S.to Niccola di Tolentino, quale si è fatto quelli che tessono li Razzi." See Lavin, *Barberini Documents,* 48. The document appears in a volume of *Giustificazioni* of Cardinal Francesco Barberini. Gifts of marble pieces (a capital and other fragments) by Cardinal Francesco for the "termini del Giardino Del Emm.mo Sig.r Cardinale Antonio" are recorded in 1638, 1639, and 1640. Lavin, op. cit., 142, 144, and 149. It is described briefly in H. Tetius, *Aedes Barberinae,* 23–25. I would like to thank Patricia Waddy for her help with these dates, communicated to me by letter prior to the publication of her book, *Roman Palaces.* The history of the Barberini palace is traced in chap. 12, 174–271. Cardinal Antonio's residence there and his alterations and additions are discussed on pp. 244–51. Cardinal Antonio paid his brother Taddeo 3,000 scudi rent a year for the north half of the palace.

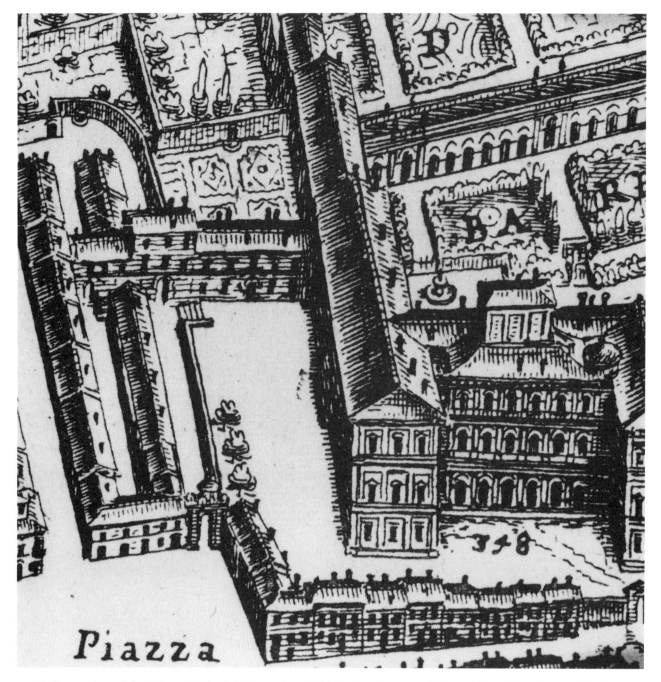

Piazza

5. Bird's-eye view of the Palazzo Barberini, Rome, from Falda's 1675–85 map of Rome (photo: Dumbarton Oaks)

The inventory must postdate the structure that bounds the garden's western side. Referred to in the inventory as the "*Stanze*," payments for its construction appear in 1641.[18] The most likely date of the inventory is 1644 either when an inventory of all Cardinal Antonio's possessions was made or in July when he fled to France after the death of his uncle, Pope Urban VIII.[19] After his return in 1653, he lived in the Giubbonari palace, and the Quirinale palace was occupied by younger members of the family.[20]

Like most inventories of the period, the lists of plants are arranged by location (parterre, planting bed, and row) rather than by item, and they are keyed to the numbers on the plan.

The plan (see Fig. 4) shows four individual parterres, *scompartimenti*, each divided into geometrically shaped planting beds, *cassettoni*, which are numbered consecutively in each unit. Within the planting beds each row is given a number, and the plants in that row are named. Sometimes the location of individual plants is given, particularly the tulips, to which special attention is drawn throughout,[21] and the anemones on the edges of the beds nearest the *Stanze*, the building at the west end of the garden. The borders, *guide*, of each planting bed are also numbered, and the rows in each border described. They were edged with bricks, *mattoni*, or tiles, *pianelle*.

The first parterre had borders on all four sides, the fourth had three, and the second and third each had them on two sides only. In addition to the plants in the beds, the inventory lists the contents of the twenty-eight flower vases in the *giardino segreto*.[22] Indications of directions in the inventory show how the parterres were placed within the walled space of the garden. It was enclosed on all four sides. On one end were the *Stanze*, the Cardinal's suite that opened to the Theater to its west; at the other there was a small oval pond and fountain. The two larger *scompartimenti* (I, II) were placed between the *Stanze* and the path, called the *viale di mezzo* or center path, in front of the fountain. The wall on the palace side of the garden had a loggia, while the other wall had espaliered evergreen citrus plants, *spalliera d'agrumi*. Two small rectangular parterres (III, IV) were on this side of the garden. Although the plan in the inventory has been cut and pasted, suggesting that part of the original sheet is missing, the plant lists follow the numbers on the plan almost exactly. Only one discrepancy between plan and inventory was found—the inventory lists (fol. 14v) a second round bed in Compartment III which does not appear on the plan. Thus one can be sure that the layout of the garden was only partially axial and symmetrical, and that the borders missing in the second and third parterres did not exist, at least at the time of the inventory. In appearance, the garden must have been very similar to the *giardino segreto* depicted in Ferrari's *Hesperides* (Fig. 6),[23] but with

[18] Payments for their construction appear in records dating 30 January 1641. Waddy, *Roman Palaces*, 396, n. 304.

[19] A complete inventory of all Cardinal Antonio's possessions was made in early 1644, when his uncle, the pope, was ill and not expected to live. In fact, the pope died in July 1644. Lavin, *Barberini Documents*, 157.

[20] Waddy, *Roman Palaces*, 250–51.

[21] References to the plan are given here as follows: Roman numeral for the compartment, second numeral (arabic) for a planting bed in the compartment, third number (arabic) for the row in the planting bed. I.25.2, ". . . sette Tulipani pennacchiati . . . de' quali si tiene nota particolare," (fol. 7v).

[22] Hereafter vases are referred to as V plus number.

[23] Ferrari, *Hesperides*, pl. opp. p. 342.

6. *Giardino segreto,* Ferrari, *Hesperides* . . . , pl. opp. p. 342 (photo: Dumbarton Oaks)

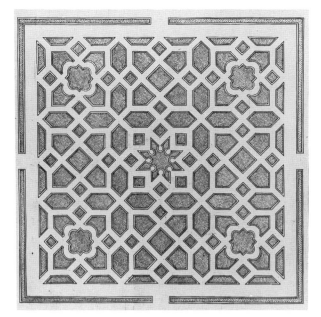

7. Garden parterre design, Ferrari, *De florum cultura*, pl. 25 (photo: Dumbarton Oaks)

8. Garden parterre design, Ferrari, *De florum cultura*, pl. 31 (photo: Dumbarton Oaks)

flowers rather than orange trees in the vases. Each parterre had different shaped planting beds. In the two larger they were rectangular or curved in shape and arranged around a curvilinear center bed. The two smaller parterres (III, IV) were simple rectangles with circular beds at the center. Geometric layouts were typical of the small urban gardens of the period and of the preceding century as well.[24] Ferrari's designs published in *Florum 1633* follow the same principles of geometric and axial planning even though they are clearly plans for very large gardens (Figs. 7, 8).

Although we know the shapes of planting beds of the period, there is little evidence for the positioning of plants. Printed views, such as a plate from Crispin van de Passe's *Hortus floridus* (Fig. 9) or Furttenbach's *Architectura recreationis* (Fig. 10),[25] suggest that it was the normal practice for the plants in ornamental gardens to be in straight rows the way vegetable and cutting gardens are planted today. The inventory, which provides almost the only documented evidence for the placement of plants in the beds for this period,[26] establishes that in the two large parterres the plants followed the shapes of the beds. In the two smaller parterres (III, IV), where the rows are indicated on the plan, the end beds, with two exceptions, have rows running east and west, while all the others

[24] See the 16th-century designs published by D. Coffin, *Gardens*, figs. 108–11. Lucia Tongiorgi Tomasi has discussed layouts of this type in "Projects for Botanical and Other Gardens: A 16th-Century Manual," *Journal of Garden History* 3 (1983), 1–34. The persistence of this kind of design is documented by the plates with views of gardens of the Veneto in J. C. Volkamer, *Flora noribergensis. . . .*, Nürenberg, 1706 and *Continuation der Nürnbergischen Hesperidum*, Nürenberg, 1714.

[25] Van de Passe, *Hortus floridus*, frontispiece to Parts I, III; J. Furttenbach, *Architectura recreationis*, Augsburg, 1640, frontispiece.

[26] The plan and inventory published by Masson, "Italian Flower Collectors," pl. III, fig. 6 shows the same planting style.

9. Spring Garden, Van de Passe, *Hortus floridus* . . . , frontispiece, Part I
(photo: Dumbarton Oaks)

10. Garden, Furttenbach, *Architectura recreationis,* fol. 15 (photo: Dumbarton Oaks)

run north and south. The borders of all four parterres were planted along their length, but with occasional cross rows of different kinds of flowers.

Parterres I and II were planted symmetrically around the central bed and along an axis that ran across the width of the garden parallel to the *viale di mezzo*. The schematized reconstruction of Parterre I shows that the beds were, with two exceptions, planted symmetrically around the long axis (north-south) of the parterre (Pl. IIA). Parterres III and IV, which were in line with and to the side of the two large parterres, were planted symmetrically with respect to their central axis.

Although the plants listed in the inventory would naturally bloom over a period of several months, the horticultural practice of the period was to force or retard bloom so that all the plants would blossom at one time.[27] Only then were they placed in flower beds in the garden. Instructions in the treatise describe a process by which plants were lifted after their bloom was finished and repotted or replanted in late autumn and protected in sheds during the winter.[28] This custom of bedding out plants that were all in bloom made the creation of patterns of color feasible; the total effect would have been like a carpet or tapestry, with massed colors highlighted by contrasts of the individually spaced single plants.[29]

Within each bed variations in color, texture, and shape were created by the selection of different genera or cultivars. Most rows had only one or two kinds of flowers in them. Although it has not been possible to determine the colors of all of the plants listed, it is safe to say that the garden was predominantly in shades of yellow and white ranging from the pure white of the poetica and tazetta narcissus and the hyacinths to the golden and sulfur yellows of the trumpet narcissus (Pl. IIB). Color accents were supplied by the varying shades of blue and violet hyacinths. Bed 8 of Compartment I is an example of a typical mixed bed. The corners had gold-colored narcissi, there were three rows of blue or violet hyacinths, with a gold narcissus in the center, a row of white trumpet narcissi, and in the last row, on the edge of the path, three specimen tulips.

Reds, pinks, and blues were supplied by the single-colored tulips; they were planted in solid rows.[30] Flamed tulips added accents of strong color when planted as single specimens in the beds and in the borders (i.e., the areas nearest the walkways, or in the flower vases). Twenty-two different flamed tulips, *tulipani pennacchiati,* appear in the inventory; those with color descriptions include: white and red; white with red flames; *persichino,* an intense pink; striped in white; red and sulfur yellow; red and yellow with flames the shape of deer horns, to name but a few. The anemones, planted singly as specimens in borders and vases, also provided strong color accents of pinks, deep reds, and blues.

---

[27] Ferrari describes what he calls the "stazione arbitraria di fiori. . . . il fiore sia pronto d'ogni tempo; sì che hora con l'anticipare, hora del differire la maturità, hora col continuarla, ci faccia godere in qualunque tempo, e a voglia nostra la primavera." He follows with specific directions how to force a rose to be the first plant to flower in the spring. *Flora 1638,* 444–45.

[28] See chap. 2, "The Horticultural Treatise," for a discussion of the practice and App. II, for an example of specific instructions, in this case, for anemones, in I.1,20,22,24,26, etc. Ferrari, *Flora 1638,* 944–45, also describes how to force or retard bloom.

[29] Masson, "Italian Flower Collectors," 71, quotes Ferrari as saying the way flowers were planted gave "the effect of an 'orderly carpet of flowers.'" *Flora 1638,* 215.

[30] See below, App. I, IV.1.

All the plants, with the exception of dianthus (*garofani*, III.9.2), were bulbs, tubers, or corms, and all were spring flowers. Clearly they were chosen to provide a mass of bloom and color over a relatively short period of time. The question is what was done to the garden during the rest of the year? Unfortunately the treatise only describes how to grow plants; there are no instructions for the care of the planting beds. Were the spring plants overplanted with summer annuals as we do today? Were the beds left bare, since the cardinal did not spend summers in Rome? Possibly colored sand was spread in decorative patterns as was done in early seventeenth-century parterres in France.

A more detailed look at the inventory shows that although a great many species or varieties were named, seventy-seven in all, only six genera were represented, namely *Anemone, Dianthus, Hyacinthus, Narcissus, Ranunculus,* and *Tulipa.* There were two species of anemone, one dianthus, seven varieties of hyacinths, five species and sixteen varieties of narcissus, two ranunculus, and twenty-nine varieties of tulips, most of them cultivars.[31] These genera appear with the same relative frequency in other gardens or florilegia of this period. Narcissus predominated in this garden: they are also numerous in Ferrari's *Florum 1633* and the early florilegia, such as Sweerts' *Florilegium* and Rabel's *Theatrum florae.*[32] They occupy three folios (10r–13r) in the horticultural treatise and eleven of the folios of the flower album (fols. 3–11, 72). Few of them were exotics, although a plant name like *Narciso Constantinopolitano* (single, IV.3.4; double, I.2.5) or *Narciso Gentilini* (I.10.5) suggest an imported and a specimen plant respectively.

The number of individually planted anemones and tulips reflect their importance to garden owners of the time.[33] For example, in the three rows of the border of Parterre III (III.10.1–3), one was planted with three double anemones (*A. persichino doppia*),[34] three ranunculi (*R. a foglia di Ruta*), and three single anemones (*A. rosso con fiocco lionato*). The middle row had nine different tulips, all flamed.[35] The third and innermost row was planted with double trumpet narcissus (*Trombone doppij*). Similarly, each of the vases held only two to four plants, almost without exception anemones and tulips, with a few hyacinths and narcissi for color contrast. All the flamed tulips were planted singly (III.10.2, 11.2.; V.25–28); only the plain colored were planted as rows (*T. coloretti,* II.14.4; there were twenty-six rows in all of this kind of tulip).

Tulips were treated similarly in a garden of the same period, one at Cisterna owned by the duke of Sermoneta, Francesco Caetani. In a list discovered by Georgina Masson in the Caetani archives in Rome, there are seven different varieties of tulips, either

---

[31] In App. IV.1, the plants are listed alphabetically and their locations given.

[32] Ferrari, *Florum 1633;* E. Sweerts, *Florilegium . . . tractans de variis florib[us] . . . ,* Frankfurt a. M., 1612; D. Rabel, *Theatrum florae in quo ex toto orbe selecti . . . proferuntur . . . ,* Paris, 1633.

[33] The treatise notes that "tulips do not like the company of other flowers near them" (IV.1), but the less valuable solid colored tulips, the *coloretti,* were planted in rows. Only the flamed, *pennacchiati,* were placed individually as specimen plants.

[34] The treatise advises planting anemones near the tiles that customarily edged the beds (I.25).

[35] *T. rosso e giallo con fiamme a corno di cervo; T. de' SS.i Lani; T. detto Brachettone; T. bianco candido e rosso, stamine nere fondo turchino; T. persichino e bianco; T. candido e rosso acceso; T. persichino rigato di bianco; T. giallo e rosso; T. Agatha detta del P.re Savelli.*

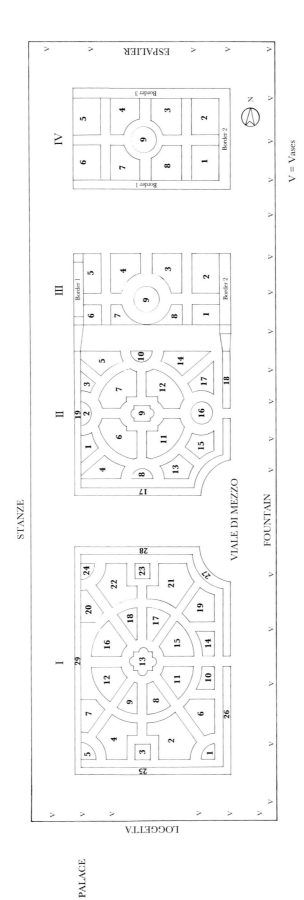

1. Plan of the Barberini *giardino segreto* showing its location in the palace grounds and identifying the compartments and planting beds by number

IIA. Color-coded reconstruction of the planting bed relationships in Compartment I

Narcissus, Tazettas, Jonquils, Trumpets

Hyacinth

Tulip

IIB. Color-coded reconstruction of the planting plan of Compartment I

III. *Giunchiglia* (*Narcissus jonquilla* L.), fol. 9

(all the following color illustrations from ms. Barb Lat. 4326;
photo: Biblioteca Apostolica Vaticana)

6.

IV. *Trombone, (Narcissus poeticus* L. or *N. pseudonarcissus*), fol. 6

V. *Narciso Constantinopolitano doppio,* (*N. poeticus* L.), fol. 5

VI. *Tazzetta della gran sorte* (*N. tazetta* L.), fol. 3

34.

VII. *Giacinto* (*Hyacinthus orientalis* L.), fol. 34

VIII. *Anemone (A. coronaria* L.), fol. 55

IX. *Argemone* (*Anemone pavonina* Lam.), fol. 44

X. *Ranunculi a foglia di Ruta* (*R. asiaticus* L.), fol. 70

XI. *Tulipano pennacchiato* (*T. sylvestris* L.), fol. 17

XII. *Tuliipano coloretto* (*T. gesneriana* L. ?), fol. 31

24.

XIII. *Tulipano di Persia* (T. clusiana DC), fol. 24

XIV. *Punica Granatum* L., fol. 46

named or described by color. There were small quantities of each tulip variety, and each was given an individual numbered location on the plan.[36] Planting them singly, as was done in the Barberini and the Caetani gardens, emphasized the differences in the appearance of the individual specimen tulips.

Hyacinths were used in fewer numbers than narcissus, but much more frequently than either tulips or anemones. Most frequently they were planted in rows by themselves (I.3.1; II.9.1), but they were also mixed in rows with narcissi (II.1.1). Both single and double forms were used, and most were blue and violet, although there were a few whites (*Giacinti bianchi,* III.3.1; IV.7.6; *Giacinti bianchi orientali,* II.26.3).

Nevertheless, some of the plants in the garden were extremely valuable. The decade of the 1630s marked the height of the tulip craze in western Europe, so a garden with seventy-three individual tulip bulbs and thirty-four rows of *tulipani coloretti* was worth a fortune. Anemones were also highly prized at this period; once again it seems that a plant inventoried individually, as were the anemones in the vases and rows by the loggia, was especially rare and valuable.

One cannot say if this garden is a typical *giardino segreto* for there is too little information about other gardens of the period. Its site, walled off from the main garden and with the only access a door from a private apartment in the palace, is similar to others known, and contemporary florilegia all have the plants listed here. However, in this garden the plants were grouped more densely, and they dominated the enclosure in a manner not found in the few other *giardini segreti* for which there is evidence. The principles of axiality and symmetry followed in the disposition of the plants are in accord with designs for other art forms of the period, but there is more irregularity. The garden's function is also unclear. The plants are neither a collection of exotica like the Horti Farnesiani on the Palatine nor a scientific display as found in the botanic gardens of that era. Nor could it have served as a laboratory for the propagation of new hybrids, like the enormous Caetani garden at Caserta. So the garden remains something of an enigma in its design and in its function, yet better documented than any other garden of the period.

2. THE HORTICULTURAL TREATISE—HOW THE PLANTS WERE GROWN
MS. BARB. LAT. 4278

The horticultural treatise, Barb. Lat. 4278, is a small volume, 21.5 × 15.5 cm, bound in vellum. Like the inventory, there is no title or author's name on the cover—only the coat of arms of Cardinal Francesco Barberini—nor is there a title page within. Folio 1r starts with the heading "Of broad-leaved Anemones and narrow-leaved Anemones, known as Tenuifolii and Latifolii."[37] There is no indication of date or author's name, nor

---

[36] Masson, "Italian Flower Collectors," pl. III, fig. 6. Masson discusses the archival material and the garden, 70–78.

[37] "Dell'Anemoni a fronda larga, et delli Ane[mo]ni a fronda stretta detti Tenuifolij & Latifolij." For the Italian text and the English translation, see App. II.

is there a dedication.[38] The text has been attributed to the Francesco Mingucci who wrote the dedication and claims to have made the flower paintings of the third manuscript (Barb. Lat. 4326),[39] but there is no evidence, internal or external, for this attribution, and I am not convinced of it. As we shall see, the author is a knowledgeable and experienced gardener. His instructions are practical and would still be useful today. The language of the text is awkward and not very learned, but the writer shows a familiarity with the botanical terminology of the period, and with the nomenclature in use by scientists. In contrast, the contemporary treatise also associated with the Barberini family, Ferrari's *Florum 1633* (Italian edition, *Flora 1638*), has many fantastic and impractical instructions, and was clearly written by a scholar acquainted with earlier writings (with occasionally equally fantastic horticultural lore) but with little or no actual experience.[40] We know little about Mingucci, but could he have been both a trained, and from the evidence of his other work, expert painter and an experienced gardener?

In the text, the author discusses methods of growing a number of different plants. In addition to those found in Cardinal Antonio's garden (narcissi, hyacinths, anemones, ranunculi, tulips, and dianthus), he gives instructions for the cultivation of plants such as iris, fritillaries, grape hyacinths, and ornithogalums. There are also directions for growing a number of exotics, most of them recent importations. These include *Scilla peruviana* L. ("Giacinto Peruano"), the so-called Narcissus of the Virginia Islands, *Zephyranthes atamasco* (L.) Herb ("Narciso dell' Isole Virginie"), *Yucca gloriosa* L., ("Yucca"), Peonies ("Peonie"), Martagon Lilies ("Martagoni"), *Amaryllis* ("Lilio Narciso Indico 'Belladonna'"), *Haemanthus coccineus* ("Narciso scaglioso 'bifolio' o 'Suersio'").[41] These plants are all bulbous, tuberous, rhizomous, or cormous, with the exception of the dianthus.[42]

The horticultural directions are organized by genus, species, and varieties. For each the author discusses the appropriate soil or soils to use. Many different kinds of soils are

[38] Francesco was made cardinal in 1623, which gives a terminus post quem for the manuscript. Although he lived until 1679, I think it likely that the treatise, like the inventory, was composed before the death of Urban VIII in 1644. A second volume with instructions on growing roses and jasmine, Barb. Lat. 4283, was written after the publication of the Latin edition of Ferrari's *Florum 1633*.

[39] See nn. 7, 8.

[40] See pp. 223–24 for a fuller discussion of Ferrari's treatise.

[41] These plants were identified by Masson, "Italian Flower Collectors," 78. Masson quotes the Caetani inventory as calling the *Zephyranthes atamasco* from the "Virgin Islands" (p. 78). Ferrari and the Horticultural Treatise say "Virginia Islands." Masson also notes that Ferrari named the *Haemanthus coccineus* the "Narciso . . . Suertio" after its Dutch grower whom she identifies as Emanuel Sweerts, a Dutch botanist and plant grower. Ferrari also refers to Sweerts in his introduction, "Emanuel Suertius Batavus in praefatione per brevi, quam Florilegio suo, suo nudis florum imaginibus praescribit . . ."*Florum 1633*, 73. He is referring to Sweerts' *Florilegium*. See n. 33.

[42] It is interesting that the dianthus, which was extremely popular and widely planted in France at this period (see chap. 4), was relatively rare in Roman gardens and flower paintings of the seventeenth and eighteenth centuries. Another manuscript horticultural treatise, Vat. Barb. Lat. 4283, which is in the same hand as Barb. Lat. 4278 we are discussing, gives instructions for growing roses and jasmine. This will not be published here because the main focus of this study is the Cardinal's *giardino segreto*, and neither of those plants were listed in the inventory.

recommended—a greater variety than we call for today.[43] If we assume that it was the practice to mix different flowering plants in the individual rows, as was recorded in the inventory,[44] then each individual plant may have been placed in a pocket of its own specific type of soil.

He gives instructions for the annual cycle of maintenance for the different varieties. Many plants were considered best grown in vases or pots—these include anemones, some varieties of hyacinths, and especially some of the exotics, such as the tuberoses, Indian ornithogalums, and *Zephyranthes atamasco*. Others were started in pots and then bedded out, and still others were left in the ground over several seasons. Planting time for almost all the plants was in September. Even the narcissi, many of which were left in the ground for two or three years, were started in pots. All the potted plants were given protection from rain, sun, and the tender plants had protection from frost. Once the cold season is over the author describes how best to bring the plant into flower, and when to plant it in a vase or bed it out.

Finally, bedded out plants and those in vases were lifted after they had finished flowering or their stalks had withered, usually in July, and they were allowed to dry before being stored until the new planting season. Plants left in the beds, however, were only lifted for division and propagation, usually after two or three years. Propagation methods for each genus is given. Tubers were divided and offsets of bulbs were separated from the older bulb at this time. Both were usually started in pots and kept there until they reached flowering size. Particular attention is given to the need for cover and protection of the plants and tubers during the period when they are forming their roots and developing stalks, as well as the period when they are stored out of the ground. Damp, wet, and cold situations are to be avoided, as well as exposure to very hot sun. In the former, the plant stock would rot or wither; in the latter, they would be stewed or baked. Instructions are also given for collecting seed and starting plants from seed. Again pots are the favored environment for starting plants. Emphasis is put on methods of selecting the strongest or most vigorous plants for seed sources. Since hybridizing by cross pollination was unknown, methods for preserving a spontaneous mutation or chance cross pollination are given, and the author points out that some plants do not produce sports ("non varia"). Some genera are characterized as not setting seed, such as the "Lilio Narciso Indico," yucca, or double ranunculus.[45] Presumably, these plants were dead headed as soon as the flowers withered, so that the seed pods never developed.

[43] Named are: composted (*terra fatta di frondi d'arbori*), sandy (*arenosa*), friable or lean (*magra*), exhausted (*sfruttata*), field or unfertilized soil (*vergome*), orchard (*terreno d'horto*), rich (*grassa*), open (*larga*), light (*leggiera*), purged (*purgata*), and lean (magra).

[44] See especially the vases where anemones, tulips, and narcissi were planted together. Ferrari, *Flora 1638*, 217, recommends placing tiles between different genera planted together, ". . . seperare i fiori diversi l'uno dal l'altro con tramezzi di pianelle fitte in terra."

[45] III, 15, 19, 26 (fols. 12v, 13v, and 15v respectively). The Roman numerals refer to the sections of the treatise in both the original and the translation, the arabic numbers are to the paragraphs. Folio numbers are given in parentheses.

The depth to plant the roots and/or bulb, or tuber or corm, is specified for each variety discussed and sometimes the spacing between plants. The depths are considerably shallower than those usually recommended today, ranging from 1½ to 4 inches (2 to 5 *dite*) even for very large bulbs like the trumpet narcissus. Possibly the fact that the ground does not freeze in Rome, and hard frosts are rare, made shallow planting practical. Also plants that were to be taken up at the end of the flowering season would not need the depth for roots that plants left in the ground require. Usually it is recommended that plants have ample space around them to promote air circulation and allow adequate light. This practice explains the spacing one sees in garden depictions of the period—massing of plants in clumps and irregular groups was neither aesthetically pleasing nor horticulturally recommended.

The seasons for planting, growing on, planting out, and taking up are much the same for all the plants. September is the most common time for planting or potting—a favored date just before and after the full moon. Varying times, from early to late winter are recommended for beginning to force the potted plants, depending on their hardiness, while July is most frequently mentioned as the time to lift plants.

To any experienced gardener, the *accorto giardiniere* the author refers to so often, it will be surprising that there is no mention of plant diseases. Methods for ridding the soil of grubs (I.12, fol. 2v) and warnings about the dangers of caterpillar and worm damage to hyacinth corms (II.4, fol. 7v) are his only references to disease or insect infestation.[46] Instructions for the cultivation of the soil are minimal, too. The author warns against damaging shallow roots by too deep cultivation, against breaking the crust of soil which forms around the stalks, and gives recommendations for the placement of vases where they can absorb moisture from tiles. He is most concerned with the amount of water in the soil, especially at times when the plant has just finished flowering, or has just been set out or potted.

In fact, the organization of the treatise and the kinds of instructions given suggest that it was written to acquaint the owner with requirements for growing a special group of plants, many of which were recent importations. The ordinary gardening skills of weeding, watering, prevention of damage by insects, etc., are taken for granted, but the novelty of the plants and of this kind of garden in Rome made the precision and the detail of the instructions necessary. The owner could consult this manual and use it to instruct the gardener in tasks requiring a knowledge of the growth and reproductive habits of plants.

The treatise represents an innovation in horticultural writing, and this perhaps explains its existence in manuscript rather than printed form.[47] It differs in important ways from the two types of treatises that survived from antiquity and were used as models throughout the Middle Ages and the Renaissance. For general instruction on the culti-

---

[46] Ferrari, *Flora 1638*, in contrast, devotes two chapters to diseases and pests. See pp. 240–41.

[47] There is no internal evidence for the date in the manuscript; while the companion manuscript, Barb. Lat. 4283, the treatise on growing roses and jasmine, was written after the publication of the Latin edition of Ferrari's text, *Florum 1633*.

vation of plants, agricultural treatises, such as those by Virgil, Cato, Varro, Columella, and Palladius continued to be consulted in this period, as well as Crescentius' manual, *Liber ruralium commodorum*, which was written in the early fourteenth century and circulated in many manuscript copies. It was first printed in 1471.[48] These treatises contained information about the selection of sites, analysis of types of soil, general instructions on growing crops, and usually chapters on animal husbandry as well. Little if any material was included on pleasure and ornamental gardens, although Crescentius included some descriptions of sites, layout, and appropriate plants in his chapters on three kinds of country estates.[49] By the sixteenth century some space in agricultural treatises was devoted to the pleasure garden, but such a section never occupied more than a small part of the more general text. An example of this may be found in Olivier de Serres' treatise, *Le théatre d'agriculture et message des champs*. A section of de Serres' Book Six is on the *boquetier*, a term for a pleasure garden planted with trees and shrubs as well as flowers.[50] Of the writers of the period only de Serres included instructions for growing specific plants, but never with the detail found in the Barberini manuscript.

A second kind of plant book that had come down from antiquity was the herbal, in which the appearance and the properties of medicinal and in some cases culinary herbs were described. The most influential in the Renaissance was Dioscorides' first-century treatise[51] which was translated as *De Materia medica libri sex,* and used as a starting point and model for new treatises on herbs.[52] Other important sources from antiquity are Theophrastos' *Historia plantarum* and Pliny the Elder's *Natural History*.[53] Renaissance herbals followed these models; their texts were confined to the description of the appearance of plants, the methods of their preparation as medicine, and their curative properties. The earliest botanical books, written with the purpose of classifying plants into systems

[48] Virgil, *Eclogues, Georgics;* Cato, *De re rustica;* Varro, *De re rustica;* Palladius, *De re rustica libri xiiii;* Columella, *De re rustica.* For a brief history of the Crescentius text, the manuscript copies, early printed versions, and earlier bibliography, see R. Calkins, "Piero de' Crescenzi and the Medieval Garden," *Medieval Gardens,* Dumbarton Oaks Colloquium on the History of Landscape Architecture 9, ed. E. B. MacDougall, Washington, D.C., 1986, 155–74.

[49] Book VIII, chaps. 1–3, on small herb gardens, gardens for people of moderate means and gardens of kings and aristocrats.

[50] Published in Paris in 1605. Book VI, chap. 10, 550–609. Book VI has the subtitle, "Des Iardinages, Pour Avoir des Herbes & Fruits Potagers: des Herbes & Fleurs odorantes: des Herbes medecinales, des Fruits des Arbres, etc." He discusses shrubs such as roses, jasmine, and box, trees such as cypress and laurel, plants for borders of beds, herbs like lavender and thyme, and flowering plants: dianthus, wallflowers, violets, cock's-comb, lilies, anemones, crown imperials, and even some tulips.

[51] A 6th-century illustrated manuscript was brought to Vienna by Ogier Ghiselain de Busbecq, who was also responsible for the first recorded importation of tulips from Turkey. It is in the National Library in Vienna, Cod. med. gr. 1.

[52] Typical examples are Mattioli's publications, *Commentarii in libros sex Pedacii Dioscorides de medica materia,* Venice, 1554, with many subsequent Latin as well as Italian editions and *Compendium de plantis omnibus una cum earum iconibus de quibus scripsit suis in commentariis in Dioscoridem editis,* Venice, 1571. Editions of the *Commentarii* and the *Compendium* appeared in Germany, France, and Poland in Latin and the vernacular languages.

[53] Theophrastos, ed. prin., Venice, 1495–98, ed. prin., Latin, Treviso, 1483, Pliny, ed. prin., Venice, 1469. Pliny's Books 24–27 are about trees and plants, their appearance and medicinal properties.

of relationships, took their organization and form from the herbal. Rembert Dodoens, for instance, in *stirpium historiae pemptades sex sive Libri XXX* (1583), describes plants following the Aristotelian division of plant matter into trees, shrubs, and flowering plants. He describes each plant and the location where it grows, when it flowers, gives its name in other languages, cites earlier authorities, but gives no horticultural information. Dodoens and other early botanists are cited by Ferrari as authorities for the latter's identification of plants.

In the sixteenth century in France a new genre, the garden design treatise, appeared. An example is Claude Mollet's, *Théatre des plans et iardinages contenant des secrets et des inventions. . . .* [54] Primarily a design theory and pattern book, a few chapters list flowers and plants appropriate for gardens. They also have no horticultural information.

If compared to these traditional types of writings, it can be seen that the Barberini treatise is an almost complete novelty. Its contents are totally devoted to ornamental plants, with no consideration of any possible medicinal or culinary use.[55] In addition, the instructions for growing are incomparably more specific, and include more detailed information about the plants' requirements (soil, moisture, exposure) than is found in other horticultural or agricultural books of this period.

A comparison to the contemporary horticultural treatise by Ferrari, *Flora, seu de florum cultura libri IV,* will clarify the function of the manuscript treatise. The former was published in 1633, dedicated to Cardinal Francesco, and at least partially financed by him.[56] It too has extended instructions for growing the plants which are discussed in the manuscript; in addition a whole section of the book is devoted to the description of each type of plant, including the appearance of the roots, bulbs, and other root forms. Illustrations of the most exotic plants are included.

Ferrari's text starts with a traditional section on selection of sites and garden plans, garden staff, and garden tools. Book Two describes the appearance of a number of ornamental plants, many of which are listed in the inventory of the plants in the bulb garden, and it also includes a number of exotics that appear in the treatise but not the inventory. Book Three has instructions for their culture and propagation. Unlike the manuscript treatise, there are extended instructions to prevent damage by pests, insects, etc. (In the Italian edition these instructions are in two chapters with the titles "Guerra di Giardini contra gli animali maggiori" and "Ordigni contra gli animali minutia.") The final book describes the use of cut flowers for decorations and fantastic methods for changing colors and odors in plants. The arrangement of chapters and, in fact, the physical layout of the book are closely related to Olivier de Serres' *Théatre d'agriculture,* which was the most recent publication of an agricultural-horticultural treatise.[57] The kinds of instructions

[54] Paris, 1652.

[55] Many plants we now consider purely ornamental were used for medicinal purposes in the Renaissance, and some, especially bulbous plants, were used for food.

[56] Payments for engravings of designs by Pietro da Cortona for the book were made in 1630 and 1632 (see Lavin, *Barberini Documents,* 12, 20).

[57] See p. 239 and n. 50.

given for the ornamental plants are similar too, so in this respect one could include Ferrari's treatise in the traditional literature on gardening. Some of the information is also traditional, and certainly not the product of a practicing gardener's experience. An example is Ferrari's instructions for changing the odor of a plant (in this case a skunk cabbage) by making cuts in the root or bulb and drenching it with perfume. He claims that after several seasons the cabbage smelled as sweet as a rose. A similar process, this time using colored inks, is recommended for changing a flower's color.[58]

However, Ferrari's treatise also differs in important respects from traditional writing. The inclusion of long allegorical passages, unusual in subject matter, but with the purpose of glorifying his patrons, the Barberini, is an innovation as is the tone of encomiastic hyperbole in all but the most practical parts of the book. Also new is the limitation of the discussion to purely ornamental plants, with no information of their possible medical or even culinary properties.

Both the treatise and Ferrari's book were clearly prepared for the owners of a new type of pleasure garden that had become popular in Rome and Italy at the end of the sixteenth century.[59] Unlike the plants in earlier gardens, which included herbs, food plants, and fruit trees, plants were now selected solely for their aesthetic appeal or their rarity, and culinary or medicinal plants were consigned to a separate kitchen garden. Thus the kind of instructions and descriptions found in the earlier manuals were unnecessary. Because the plants in these gardens were often unfamiliar, either new importations, newly domesticated indigenous plants, or new varieties of older plants, new kinds of information were needed. The most popular plants in these gardens were bulbous, rhizomatus, and cormous, unlike the perennials popular earlier.[60] Not only were many of them novelties, but they required different methods of culture and propagation. Perennials can be moved, divided, and propagated while their foliage is still recognizable, but the new kinds of plants must be handled in a dormant stage when they are difficult to identify. Ferrari's detailed description of the appearance of the tubers and bulbs provided a means of identification.[61] Finally, one can say that the treatise clarifies how it was possible to maintain a garden such as the one owned by Cardinal Antonio. Judicious planning of the planting, dividing, and lifting schedules, at which the treatise hints but does not specify, would have made it possible to bring all the plants into bloom at one time. Presumably the controlling factor would have been those plants left in the ground

[58] Ferrari, *Florum 1633*, 457–503. As I have already pointed out, hybridizing or the process used today of cross-pollination was not known, so growers were dependent on chance cross-pollination and mutation for new colors and forms.

[59] See C. Lazzaro, *The Italian Renaissance Garden: From the Conventions of Planting, Design and Ornament to the Grand Gardens of Sixteenth-Century Central Italy*, New Haven and London, 1990, chap. 2, "The Planting Reconstructed," especially 27–28.

[60] The numerical dominance of these plants in the Barberini bulb garden, the treatise and Ferrari, and as we shall see in the flower album, is an indication of their popularity.

[61] See p. 240 and the lists in App. V.

for several years at a time, while the ones routinely lifted at the end of their bloom could have been manipulated to come into bloom simultaneously.

3. THE FLOWER ALBUM
MS. BARB. LAT. 4326

The flower album, Barb. Lat. 4326, is the largest of the three manuscripts under discussion. It too is bound in vellum with the cardinal's coat of arms on the front. Measuring 26.8 × 20.9, it contains a title page with a miniature of the Barberini castle at Castel Gondolfo, and on the facing page a dedication to Cardinal Francesco Barberini signed Francesco Mingucci da Pesaro, and dated 21 August 1634. The rest of the volume consists of eighty-two folios of blue paper; eight-one have a tempera and gouache painting of one or two flowers, and one is blank.[62] All the genera listed in the inventory of Cardinal Antonio's *giardino segreto* are represented in this album and in roughly the same proportion. There are eleven narcissi (fols. 3–11, 72, 77), twelve anemones (fols. 41, 43–45, 48–55), eight hyacinths (fols. 33–40, 51, 53), and twenty tulips (fols. 13–20, 21–32).[63] There are also ranunculi (fols. 47, 67, 70) and one dianthus (fol. 12), both of which were planted in the garden, seventeen other genera, as well as two which have not been positively identified. Unfortunately no plant names are given in the album.

It is the least unusual of the three Barberini manuscripts, for flower illustration books, that is, florilegia, which first began to appear in the mid-sixteenth century, existed in numerous printed and manuscript copies by this time. Among the printed books, and almost certainly known to the Barberini circle, were Crispin van de Passe's *Hortus floridus* of 1614, two French publications by Pierre Vallet, *Le iardin du roy tres chrestien Henry IV . . .* of 1608 and the 1624 edition dedicated to Louis XIII, and Emanuel Sweerts' *Florilegium*.[64] Perhaps more relevant for this manuscript is the tradition of animal and plant

---

[62] There is a companion volume, Bibl. Apos. Vat., Barb. Lat. 4327, with paintings of birds also dedicated to Cardinal Francesco and signed by Mingucci. The manuscript is smaller (26 × 20.5 cm) than the flower album, but its leaves have been trimmed on two sides. The illustrations are by several different hands and all are inferior in quality to the flower paintings. For information about Mingucci and earlier bibliography, see Tongiorgi Tomasi, "Mingucci." Another manuscript by Mingucci, "Stati Domini citta terre e castelle dei Serenissimi Duchi e Principi della Rovere," dated 2 April 1626 and dedicated to Urban VIII is preserved in the Bibl. Apos. Vat., ms. Barb. Lat. 4434. It also is not of as high artistic quality as the flower album. Mingucci refers to the manuscript of the della Rovere possessions and his plans for the album of bird paintings in his dedication of the flower album, as well as to one of the "Stato & Dominio della felicissima, & nobilissima Casa Barberini," also in the Barberini archive at the Vatican. I have not examined it.

[63] The contents are listed in App. III by folio number with their modern botanical name, an English name, and a brief description. The identifications were made by Carla Teune of the Leiden Botanical Garden and translated into English by Vanessa Bezemer Sellars. I am extremely grateful to them both. A small photograph is placed by each entry, and examples of the most prevalent genera are reproduced in color in the text.

[64] See E. Caprotti, "Illustrazioni botaniche nell' Italia del seicento," *L'Esopo* 2 (June 1979), 17–29. I could not find either in the "Holstenius" catalogue of Cardinal Francesco's library. Ferrari refers to Sweerts, but the other authorities he refers to for plant identifications were botanists, such as Clusius and Mattioli, or ancient writers. See nn. 9 and 29 respectively.

painting fostered by rulers and aristocracy throughout Europe in the sixteenth century.[65] While some commissions by royal or aristocratic patrons had a scientific purpose,[66] the emphasis in the depictions was on the beauty of the flowers and plants, and the images were large, even life-size at times.

The realistic style of flower representation in these florilegia derived from the tradition of flower depiction in illuminated manuscripts and late medieval paintings, especially in Flanders and Germany. In contrast, the earliest illustrated herbals were often not botanically accurate, for the plates, usually small in size, were made to accompany a descriptive text. Only when botanists began to make observations directly from nature and assemble floras of plants in their surroundings did the need for accurate representation become essential. This led, by the beginning of the seventeenth century, to the adoption of the realistic style already common in flower books to scientific botanical illustration while botanical accuracy became a requirement in florilegia.[67]

If we class the Mingucci manuscript among the florilegia of the period, then we must ask what purpose it served. Earlier examples recorded the plants in a specific garden, such as Basilius Besler's *Hortus Eystettensis* (1613) and possibly Vallet's two editions of his *Le iardin du roy*.[68] Others were nursery men's records of their plants for sale, for example, Emanuel Sweerts' *Florilegium* (1612), while some seem to have been intended simply as compendia of ornamental flowers. An example is Daniel Rabel's *Theatrum Florae* (Paris, 1633). Still others, such as Ligozzi's paintings both for Francesco de' Medici and for Aldrovandi, were made to serve as scientific records.

The flower album does not fit any of the usual categories. One presumes that Mingucci's dedication would have named the specific garden if he was illustrating its plants, and a serious scientific record would need plant names as well as depictions.[69] Unlike Rabel's and other books that illustrate ornamental plants, Mingucci's album includes wild plants (*Valeriana officinalis* L. [Valerian], fol. 60; *Filipendula vulgaris* Moench [Meadow Sweet], fol. 80), but only a few rare plants. There are none of the Indian/African or American importations featured in Ferrari's *Florum 1633*, and in the horticultural treatise. In the proportion of plates allotted to the different flowers, and especially in the variety of tulips depicted, it most closely resembles the collection in Cardinal Antonio's bulb garden. Yet even here there are differences, for the garden contained no colum-

---

[65] See Tongiorgio Tomasi, "L'Immagine naturalistica a Firenze tra XVI e XVII secolo, contributo al rapporto 'Arte-Natura' tra manierismo e prima età barocca," *Immagini anatomiche e naturalistiche nei disegni degli Uffizi, Secc. XVI e XVII*, Gabinetto Disegni e Stampe degli Uffizi 60, eds. R. Ciardi, L. Tongiorgio Tomasi, Florence, 1984, 37–67, especially 46–49.

[66] As, for instance, the paintings done for the noted Bolognese naturalist, Ulisse Aldrovandi, by Jacopo Ligozzi, court painter for Francesco I de Medici. Tongiorgio Tomasi, op. cit., 47.

[67] For a history of botanical illustration of this period, see A. Arber, *Herbals. Their Origin and Evolution. A Chapter in the History of Botany, 1470–1670*, 2nd ed., Cambridge, 1953, chap. 7; W. Blunt, *The Art of Botanical Illustration*, London, 1950, chaps. 4–10; C. Nissen, *Die Botanische Buchillustration, ihre Geschichte und Bibliographie*, 2nd ed., Stuttgart, 1966, 37–74.

[68] Nevertheless Vallet's designation as "brodeur du Roy" and the dedication of the first edition to Marie de Medici shows that the prints were also intended for use as embroidery patterns.

[69] In the companion album of birds (Barb. Lat. 4327; see n. 62) the original paintings of birds are unnamed; only the pages copied from earlier publications or manuscripts have names.

bines, chrysanthemums, or delphinium, for example. Ultimately, it would seem, the selection is simply one of plants that appealed to Mingucci (or to Cardinal Francesco?), assembled for their visual appeal, and presented to the cardinal for his enjoyment. Their botanical accuracy was to be expected at this period—one can compare a small early publication, the *Fiori Diversi* (Rome, 1640), of Nicolas Robert, the French artist later renowned for his *vélins* of flowers in the Jardin des Plantes of Louis XIV.[70]

Stylistically, the flower paintings most closely resemble the Ligozzi paintings made for the duke of Tuscany, either for his personal collection or for the Aldrovandi botanical collection in Bologna.[71] As Ligozzi's, they combine a botanical exactitude, which has enabled botanists to identify them by modern nomenclature, with a highly sophisticated mode of representation. The flowers, set against the pale blue of the paper on which they are painted, are depicted in luminous colors enclosed by firm linear outlines. The vivid colors, the highlights in white, and the dark shadowing give a startling three-dimensionality to the flowers, which are usually centered on the page.[72] The paintings are done with a skill only surpassed in the earlier Ligozzi paintings. Many of the sheets, although not all, also represent the bulbs as well as the flowering plant—a mode also used by Ligozzi and in a number of the early seventeenth-century printed florilegia.[73] Except for the tulips, most are shown in full bloom with their leaves, stems, and characteristic mature growth. A few tulips are depicted in overblown or dying phases of bloom and are most similar in style to flower paintings of the period, primarily Dutch, in which flowers of all stages, from bud to decay, were common.

Most of this era's conventions of flower representation are followed; that is, the placement of the flower and its stem to capture its most characteristic appearance at maturity, as, for example, the two martagon lilies (fols. 1, 2) and the lily of the valley (fol. 69). However, despite similarities in style to Ligozzi's work and to contemporary conventions of portrayal, the album's paintings are not copied from or even closely based on printed or painted prototypes. At a time when printing plates were frequently reused in other publications, and printed pages copied for new plates, or used as pattern books by flower painters, the originality of these images is striking.

With the exception of the two lilies on the first two folios, the succession of plants in the album roughly follows the natural order of bloom. Narcissi are followed by tulips and they by hyacinths, anemones, and ranunculi. Roses come next and then a number

[70] For Robert's *vélins*, paintings on parchment of specimen flowers, made first for Gaston d'Orléans to record plants in his garden at Blois in the 1630s, and later for Louis XIV of flowers in the Jardin des Plantes in Paris, see L. Vezin, *Les artistes au Jardin des Plantes*, Paris, 1990, 19–22. Given the close connections between the Barberinis and the French court, the *vélins* might have been the inspiration for the flower album.

[71] For Ligozzi, see *Floralia: florilegio dalle collezioni fiorentine del sei-settecento*, eds. Marilena Mosco, Milena Rizzotto, Florence, 1988, and *"Flora e Pomona": L'orticultura nei disegni e nelle incisioni dei secoli XVI-XIX*, Gabinetto Disegni e Stampe degli Uffizi 72, Florence, 1990. Essays by Lucia Tongiorgio Tomasi, Alessandro Tosi, and Leo S. Olschki.

[72] The paintings and their colors are remarkably well preserved. One wonders whether the cardinal ever looked at it or whether, like a Christmas tie, it was immediately put away and forgotten.

[73] Van de Passe, *Hortus floridus;* Sweerts, *Florilegium;* Rabel, *Theatrum Florae.*

of summer flowers, such as clematis and columbine. Stock and delphinium end the series. The succession is not strictly followed, for some narcissi appear toward the end of the album, and in fact, hyacinths usually precede all but species tulips. This seasonal arrangement is typical of most florilegia. Besler and van de Passe separate the plants of each season by title pages and the other florilegia usually follow a seasonal order.

For the purposes of this study, the value of the album lies in its botanical accuracy. This has allowed the plants to be identified by modern botanical names. At the same time comparison of the paintings to contemporary florilegia, whose plants are named, have permitted an identification of many of the plants listed in the inventory and discussed in the horticultural treatise with the flowers. Thus it is possible to visualize not just the larger color patterns of plants in the cardinal's garden but also their variety and subtlety of their hues, shapes, and even patterns of growth.

4. IDENTIFICATION OF THE PLANTS IN THE GARDEN AND CONCLUSIONS

The greatest difficulty in reconstructing the appearance of an older garden that is known only by a list of its plants is to correlate the names with modern botanical nomenclature or with images that can be identified by modern names. Even relatively recent gardens present difficulties, since cultivars go out of fashion and hybridizing alters the colors and growth habits of varieties that retain the older names. The identification of plants in the pre-Linnaean era is made even more difficult by the lack of a standardized nomenclature or taxonomic identification. Often identical names were given to plants that appear to be botanically separate genera, species, or varieties—this is particularly true of plants imported from Asia and the Americas.

Almost all the names and identifications in use in the seventeenth century were based on earlier sixteenth-century publications by Clusius (L'Ecluse), Dodoens, Fuchs, or Mattioli.[74] Some of these earlier books were illustrated with small woodcuts, which were neither detailed nor, with a few exceptions, accurate enough to allow for a positive identification. Others were devoted to medicinal plants rather than the new or traditional ornamentals.

I have attempted to relate the plants listed in the inventory and named in the horticultural treatise with the flowers depicted in the flower album. This was made more difficult by the fact that the names used by the list maker do not always correspond with those used by botanists or scientifically knowledgeable patrons of the period. Some identifications have been made, however, by matching Ferrari's descriptions and plant names with some of the printed florilegia of the period and the images with those in the flower album.[75] These will be discussed below, starting with the most numerous plants, the narcissi. Some of the narcissi in the inventory are represented in the flower album—

---

[74] The most frequently cited publications are: C. de L'Ecluse [Clusius], *Exoticorum libri decem: . . .* , Antwerp, 1605; R. Dodoens, *. . . Stirpium historiae pemptades sex. . . .* , Antwerp, 1616; L. Fuchs, *De historia stirpium commentarii insignes . . .* , Basel, 1542 et seq.; P. Andrea Mattioli, *Commentarii, Compendium.*

[75] The most useful for this purpose have been D. Rabel, *Theatrum Florae . . .* , Paris, 1633; Vallet, *Le jardin du roy;* Basilius Besler, *Hortus Eystettensis . . .* , Eichstätt, 1613.

if not the specific cultivar or species, at least the subgenera. Ferrari discusses the difficulty of identifying all the different narcissi known, saying that they have, ". . . a countless variety of colors, shapes, and sizes . . . nature and art combining to make novelties daily."[76] Four species, the *giunchiglia*, the *narciso*, the *tazetta*, and the *trombone*, are named in the inventory, and each of these species include several varieties or cultivars. Ferrari also used these same terms, identifying the *trombone* with Clusius' *N. pseudonarcissus* of Spain and Dodoens' *narcissus salvaticus*. These names still survive in modern classifications of narcissus, although their relationships have been redefined.[77] The section, Jonquilleae, includes *N. juncifolius* and *N. jonquilla*. Both are included in the inventory lists and from the album illustrations (fol. 9 [Pl. III]); we can see that they had the long reed-like leaves of *N. jonquilla* with the corona shorter than the perianth and the strong yellow color found in modern varieties. Many of the tazettas in the inventory are called poeticas today. True tazettas are usually multi-flowered, often yellow, and with a short corona, while poeticas are usually single-flowered, white, and with an even shorter corona.[78] Examples of tazettas are depicted on folios 3 (Pl. VI), 4, 7, and 8.

The *trombone* today called a trumpet narcissus is most probably the *pseudonarcissus* in folio 6 (Pl. IV), while the *Narciso di Constantinapolo doppio* (fol. 5, Pl. V) in the inventory and Ferrari is a poeticus. The *narciso non ha pari*, whose name at least is the ancestor of *N. x incomparabilis*, cannot be identified with any of the other narcissi in the album, most of which are tazettas (Pl. VI) and poeticas. The *collo di camello* planted throughout the garden may be a variety of trumpet narcissus, but I have not been able to identify it with an album painting or with a modern name.

The second most numerous plant in the inventory is the hyacinth. They were also planted in rows, not singly. Although a number of different names are listed, all belong to the species, *H. orientalis* L. It is usually believed that hybridization of hyacinths did not begin until the eighteenth century but the presence of named varieties (*Giacinto doppio detto Januario* [Double hyacinth named after Januario], *G. detto del Cornaro* [Cornaro's Hyacinth], and *G. polianto da Brescia* [Multi-stemmed Brescian Hyacinth]) suggest that several different cultivars were available in the seventeenth century. Several of these appear in Ferrari's descriptions but none can be matched with the hyacinths in the album. None of the flowers depicted in the album are double, only two possibly are white and none can be correlated with hyacinths depicted in other florilegia of the period. However, these hyacinths give an idea of the variety of hyacinth colors available; they range from whites and pale blues and lavenders through to deeper colors of blue (fols. 34 [Pl. VII], 40).

---

[76] ". . . varietà innumerabili de' colori, delle figure e delle grandezza . . . concorrendo la natura insieme con la cultura giornalmente a far novità," Ferrari, *Flora 1638*, 102–3.

[77] See the discussion of *Narcissi* in L. H. Bailey, E. Z. Bailey, *Hortus third*, rev. and exp. ed., New York, 1976, 754–56.

[78] "Pheasant's eye" is a popular modern poeticus; "paper white," commonly used for forcing indoors, is a tazetta.

The inventory divides the genus *Anemone* into two separate groups: one, called simply *anemone*, is Ferrari's *A. tenuifolia*.[79] Both single and double forms are listed. The anemones of this type (fols. 49, 50, 52, 54, and 55 [Pl. VIII]) have been identified by the modern botanical name, *A. coronaria* L. The colors of the flowers in the album correspond to the inventory's double anemones (*A. sanguigno doppio* or *A. rosso col fiocco lionato*). The two *A. rosso vellutato* in vases 3 and 6 are a popular cultivar called velvet or *plucheé*. Examples are to be seen in folios 41, 49, and 55 of the album.[80]

The second group of anemones, the *argemone*, can be identified with the modern *A. pavonina* Lam., and Ferrari's *A. latifolia*. Several of these appear in the flower album (fols. 43, 44 [Pl. IX], 48, and 53). Both types of anemone were extremely popular in the seventeenth century.[81] A number of anemones in the bulb garden cannot be identified (*A. la Guascogna; A. Madre della Celeste; A. la Palidetta*), but such names indicate that they were selections grown as prized specimen plants.

Two ranunculi appear in the inventory, in vases 24 and 28. One, a *ranuncula a foglia di ruta* (Rue-leaved ranunculus) may be the flower Ferrari describes as having a yellow double flower. A ranunculus like this is depicted in folio 70 of the album (Pl. X). It has been identified as a *R. acris* L. 'Flore Pleno.' The semidouble ranunculus (*R. asiaticus* L.) of folio 67 has a white blossom with red blotches and stripes; it could be *ranunculus scritta*, the second type of ranunculus listed in the inventory.

Only one row of dianthus (*garofano*) appears in the inventory, and there is no indication of color. It was placed in the center of a circular bed of Parterre IV (9.2). A pink carnation (*D. caryophyllus* L.) is represented in folio 12 of the album.

Of all the flowers in the inventory, the tulips have been the most difficult to relate to other sources of the period. A large group, twenty-two in all, are called *tulipani pennacchiati*, or flamed tulips. Several of these are named varieties (*T. de' Signor Lani; T. detto il cugino di Bosuelt; T. detto Agata di Tre Colori del S.r Fabri*). Others in this group are described by color (*T. bianca e rossa; T. candido rosso acceso come fiamme in tutte le foglie; T. aranciato; T. pennacchiato di bianco e giallo*). They may be compared to the tulips in the album on folios 13, 14, 17 (Pl. XI), 18, 19, 22, 23, 27, and 29, that have flowers of red and yellow. Similar tulip colors are to be found in several florilegia of the period, but with no identifying names, they cannot be cross related.

A second group are the *tulipani coloretti*. These appear in greater numbers than the flamed tulips and were planted in rows rather than singly. They can be identified with the tulips of one color, or those with colored edges to the petals (fols. 15, 16, 21, 25, 28, 31 [Pl. XII]). In the album, tulips of this kind have all been identified as early cultivars, probably developed from the first tulips brought into western Europe in the sixteenth century. The inventory also includes a *tulipano di Persia*, which Ferrari describes as having

---

[79] *Tenuifolia* and *Latifolia* were used to refer to leaves as well as to petals. The horticultural treatise uses *fronda* for leaf most of the time, but occasionally it is also used as a term for petal. See the glossary in App. V.

[80] See Masson, "Italian Flower Collectors," 75–76, for a history of this cultivar and its popularity.

[81] See Masson, op. cit., 74–78, for a discussion of their popularity and the numbers of anemones grown in the Caetani garden at Sermoneta.

reddish petals with white borders;[82] I believe it to be the tulip on folio 30 (Pl. XIII) of the album which is usually called a *T. clusiana,* after the director of the Leiden Botanical Garden who was the first successful propagator of this species imported to Austria in 1568. The inventory also refers to a *tulipano di seme,* that is, a plant raised from seed rather than propagated by division of the bulb.

This completes the list of plants in the inventory. A comparison to the plants named in the horticultural treatise and by Ferrari, or depicted in the flower album, shows that Cardinal Antonio's garden did not have as varied a group of plants as other gardens at this time.[83] The treatise and Ferrari also discuss iris, roses, lilies, and peonies, all of which appear in the flower album, and recent exotic importations such as yucca, jasmine, cardinal flower, and others from Asia and the Americas.

Tetius tells us that exotics were planted in the larger part of the Barberini garden, behind the main part of the palace, and Ferrari describes fourteen "Indian" plants there.[84] An example of such an exotic is depicted in the album, the first known representation of a double flowered pomegranate, *Punica Granatum* (fol. 46, Pl. XIV). The Farnese garden on the Palatine had at least twelve very rare importations, such as a passion flower, a yucca, and an *Amaryllis belladonna* L., and the Caetani garden at Sermoneta had many rarities from different parts of the world.[85]

While many of the plants included in the manuscript treatise and Ferrari's text were in common use, even if originally importations, like the hyacinths and tulips, or new hybridizations of native plants, like some of the anemones and narcissus, both texts include descriptions, instructions, and in the case of Ferrari, illustrations of unusual exotics. The most unusual are a group called "Indian" although many were in fact from South Africa. Three such, the *Lilio Narciso Indico* 'Belladonna,' tentatively identified by Masson as an Amaryllis (*A. belladonna L.*),[86] the *Narciso 'Jacobeo'* and the *Narciso scaglioso*

---

[82] Ferrari, *Flora 1638,* 150.

[83] Although tulips, hyacinths, anemones, and ranunculi are not indigenous, they all had been imported in the 16th century and were in common use. Tulips were first listed in Europe in 1554, hyacinths, 1562, ranunculi, 1580. Some of the Barberini narcissus were also importations, some native, and this is true for the anemones too.

[84] The main garden behind the palace, which is divided in two sections by a loggia or retaining wall, is visible in Falda's map of Rome. Payments for plants in 1627 listed in an account book of Cardinal Francesco are probably for this garden. They included 1000 junipers, 1400 hollies, 3400 myrtles, 800 laurels, cedars, cypresses, olive and nut trees. Lavin, *Barberini Documents,* 198. The first four genera presumably were used for edging the planting beds and to line the walls, while the others would have been set in the planting beds. In 1633, Ferrari named only the exotica in the large garden. Some are from East Asia, South Africa, and some from America. They include the *Narciso Jacobeo, Narciso detto Suertio, Iacinto tuberoso, Iuca indiana, Fragole Canadane, Trachelio Americano, Gelsomino indiano dal fior vermiglio, Granadiglia, Vite Canadane, Lauro indiano, l'Ulivastro forestiero, albero delle vite, acacia, Musa indiana* identified by Ferrari as Pliny's *Pala* or banana tree, *Papiro di Egitto. Flora 1638,* 377–78.

[85] The Farnese garden collection of rarities is described in T. Aldini (also attributed to Pietro Castelli), *Exactissima descriptio rariorum quarundam plantarum . . .* , Rome, 1625. See *The Age of the Marvelous,* 383. There were also aloes, and what Ferrari calls a "coral tree," *Flora 1638,* 379. See Masson, "Italian Flower Collectors," 74–78, for rarities at Sermoneta.

[86] Masson, "Italian Flower Collectors," 79.

'bifolio' or 'Suersio' appear in both.[87] Specifically Western Hemisphere plants are the *Giacinto Peruano* (*Scilla peruviana L.*) and the *Narciso dell' Isole Virginie*.[88] Both the treatise author and Ferrari refer to their novelty and to difficulties experienced in growing them. The inclusion of these true exotics is further proof that the treatise was created for the purpose of providing information and instruction for new introductions to Roman gardens, introductions that were avidly collected by the aristocrats and nobility of Rome.[89]

The treatise also casts light on the nature of the collection in Cardinal Antonio's garden. None of the unusual plants, the importations from Asia and the Americas, appear in the inventory. The balance of text occupied by the commoner plants, anemones, hyacinths, narcissi, is roughly the same in the treatise and the inventory. A major difference is in the treatment of the tulips. The treatise mentions only a few types, milk-white, veined, *coloretti*, and Persian, and not much space is devoted to their culture or propagation. Ferrari describes only two, the *bambagina* and the *Persiano di due colori*, again a relatively small proportion of the total. In contrast, the inventory, in addition to the *coloretti*, the Persian, the *Tulipani di seme*, and several others described by their colors, lists twenty-one broken or veined tulips specifically by name. These tulips occupied a prominent place in the garden, planted individually in a row or in vases, and the less special ones were massed in many rows. One might say that the purpose of the design and planting was to display the collection of tulips, which was enormously valuable, and anemones against the background created by the narcissi and hyacinths.

The function of a *giardino segreto* was very different from the larger gardens where the exotica were to be found. The main gardens of the Barberini palace and Farnese gardens on the Palatine were for display to the large circle of Roman society. These gardens were an index of the owner's wealth and power, their collections inspired by the same motives that generated the vast collections of paintings, sculpture, silver, gold, and objects made of precious stones. A *giardino segreto* was for the personal use of its owner, family, and close personal friends, a place for peace, reflection, and repose. The fountain cooled the air and provided a background of musical sounds and the scented plants supplied fragrance to the air. The loggia created a shady place to sit, while the massed plantings in the planting beds made a colorful carpet at one's feet and the background against which the individual tulips and anemones could be admired and treasured, just as the gems and natural wonders in the secluded studies inside the palaces.

[87] The latter has been identified as *Haemanthus coccineus* by Masson, "Italian Flower Collectors," 80. "Suersio" is an Italianization of "Sweerts" and refers to the Dutch plantsman, Emanuel Sweerts.

[88] Identified as the *Zephyranthes atamasco* by Masson, "Italian Flower Collectors," 78.

[89] Cardinal Alessandro Farnese grew a collection of exotics in his garden, the Horti Farnesiani, on the Palatine in Rome, as attested in Aldini, *Exactissima descriptio*. Another important collection was formed by Prince Francesco Caetani. See Masson, "Italian Flower Collectors," passim.

APPENDIX I

THE INVENTORY

BIBLIOTECA APOSTOLICA VATICANA, MS. BARB. LAT. 4265

20.6 × 14 cm

fols. 1r,v [Blank]
fol. 2r Plan of the planting beds (Fig. 4)
fol. 2v [Blank]
fols. 3r,v [Blank]
fol. 4r   Giardinetto Secreto
                    Dell' Em.mo Sig.r Card.le Antonio
                         P.mo Scompartimento
                         contiguo alla Loggia
P.mo Cassettone segnato col suo num.o: come nella figura precedente
p:ma fila dalli Capi, et in mezzo della fila Narcisi gialli in oro, tramezzati da Tazzette della gran
sorte.
2.a fila Giunchiglia dalla foglia unita
3.a Tromboni bianchi
4.a Narcisi non ha pari solferini
    e Nell'angolo un Narciso Solferino

                         2.o Casettone
P.a fila, 2.a, 3.a, e 4.a Tazzette della gran sorte mescolate con Tazzette della foglia unita
5.a, 6.a, 7.a, et 8.a fila, Narcisi Constantinopolitani dopij
fol. 4v   P:mo Scomp.to
                         3.o Cassettone
P:ma fila Giacinti detti del Cornaro, et alli capi due Tazette della gran sorte.
2.a Alli capi Tazzette d'Olanda dico Non ha pari gialli, et in mezzo una Tazzetta d'Olanda.
3.a Tazzette d'Olanda stellate

                         4.o Cassett.e
P.ma fila, 2.a e 3.a Tazzette della gran sorte
5:a, e 6:a Narcisi Doppij Constantinop.ni

                         5:o Cassett.e
P.ma fila tazzette della gran sorte, et alli capi Gialli in oro
2.a Giunchiglia Unita
3.a Tromboni bianchi

fol. 5r   P.mo Scomp.to
                         6.o Cassettone
Ne gl'Angoli Gialli in oro n.o 5
P.a fila, e 2.a Giacinti Polianti
3.a Tazzette della gran sorte dalla foglia unita, et in mezzo un Narciso massimo d'Olanda detto
del Gaetano

                         7.o Cassettone

In tutto conforme al 6.o cassettone precedente

8.o Cassettone

Negl'Angoli Gialli in oro num.o 4
P.a fila Giacinti odoratiss.i et in mezzo un Giall'in oro
2.a, e 3.a Giacinti similm.te odoratiss.i
4.a Tromboni Bianchi
5.a Tre Tulipani d.i Duchi Primotici

9.o Cassettone

In tutto conforme all'8.o precedente
fol. 5v

P.mo Scomp.to
x.o Cassettone

P:a fila: Alli capi Gialli in oro, et in mezzo tre Tulipani Primotici Buoni.
2.a Giunchiglia di Spagna
3.a Giacinti d:i del Cornaro, et in mezzo un Tazzetta d'Olanda stellata
4.a Tromboni della gran Tromba con l'ale solforine
5.a Alli capi Gialli in oro, et in mezzo due Narcisi Gentilini

xi:o Cassett.e

Alle punte Tazzette della gran sorte
P.a fila vicino al Circolo Tazzette dela gran sorte
Tutte l'altre fila [sic] Giunchiglia grossa di Spagna, eccetto la fila di mezzo, nella q.le sono 4 gialli in oro, et in mezzo un Narciso massimo d'Olanda d.o del Gaetano.
fol. 6r

P:mo Scomp:to
xii.o Cassettone

In tutto conforme al precedente Cassett: xi.o

xiii.o Cassettone

P.a fila Non ha' pari Gialli
2.a Giacinti Polianti di Brescia
3.a Tazzette della gran sorte, et in mezzo un Narciso massimo d'Olanda d.o del Gaetano.
4.a Giacinti odoratissimi
5.a Tromboni Bianchi et attorno un Circolo di Tulipani Coloretti

xiiii.o Cassettone

In tutte conforme al Cassettone x.o eccetto l'ord.e della fila, che è al contrario

xv.o, e xvi.o Cassettone

Conforme al Cassettone xi:o e xii:o

xvii.o e xviii:o Cassett.e

Conforme al Cassettone 8:o e 9:o
fol. 6v

P:mo Scomp:to
19:o Cassettone

Nelli contorni Gialli in oro n.o 5
P:ma fila Tromboni bianchi
2:a Giacinti di Brescia
3.a Giacinti come sopra
4.a Tazzette della gran sorte dalla foglia unita, et in mezzo Narciso mass.o d'Olanda d:o del Gaetano

20.o Cassettone

Conforme al soprascritto Cassettone 19:o

21:o, e 22:o Cassettone

Conforme al 2.o Cassett.e

23:o Cassettone

Conforme al 3:o Cassettone

24:o Cassettone

Conforme al Cassettone 5:o

fol. 7r   P.mo Scomparim.to

P.ma Guida, ò l'Cassettone segnato n:o 25: vicino alla Loggetta

Alli capi Gialli in oro, in mezzo a due Tazzette della gran sorte. Segue una fila di Giunch:a di Spagna, di poi per linea retta in mezzo Tulipani di seme, tramezzati da Tromboni della gran tromba con l'ale Solferine. In mezzo un Giallo in oro di quà, e di là due Tazzette d'Olanda stellate. Vicino alli mattoni dalla parte di dentro Giunchiglia di Spagna, e Tulipani di Persia.

fol. 7v   P:mo Scomp:to

2:a Guida

O'vero Cassett:e segnato n:26 che è il p:o contiguo al viale di mezzo. Alli capi et in mezzo gialli in oro tramezzati da due tazzette della gran sorte, e vicino una fila per traverso di Giunchiglia di Spagna. Di poi una fila per lo lungo, in mezzo Giacinti Bianchi orientali, tramezzato da sette Tulipani pennacchiati di diversi colori, de quali si tiene nota particolare. Vicino alli mattoni dalla parte di dentro una fila per lo lungo di Giunchiglia di Spagna e Tulipani di Persia

fol. 8r   P:mo Scomp.to

3.a Guida

O'vero Cassettone segnato n:o 27. Alli capi Gialli in oro, tramezzati da due Tazzette della gran sorte come sopra nella predette Guide. Di poi una fila per lo lungo, in mezza di Giacinti bianchi, e Tulipani Pennacchiati n.o 4 de quali si tiene nota. Vicino alli Mattoni di dentro una fila di Giunchiglia di Spagna, e Tulip.i di Persia: come in tutte l'altre sequenti Guide.

Dove cominci la Guida a'voltare vicino alla Fontana, in mezzo per lo lungo Giacinti Polianti, e Tulipani di Seme, et un Tulipano Pennacchiato buono di contro al mattone segnato.

fol. 8v   P.mo Scomp:to

4.a Guida

Segnato n.o 28, che sequita immeditam.te alla precedente come l'istessa, cioè in mezzo per lo lungo Giacinti Polianti, e Tulipani di Seme e Coloretti. Vicino alli Mattoni Giunchiglia di Spagna, e Tulipani di Persia, et alli capi Gialli in oro in mezzo a due Tazzette

5.a Guida

Segnato n.o 29 vicino alle Stanze, è conforme alla Guida 2:a dirimpetto, eccetto nel mezzo non vi sono Narcisi Gialli, per causa de Pilastretti, ma ben si a'tutti li Capi tra l'un Pilastretto, e l'altro, e vi sono cinque Tulip:i Penn:i Buoni all'incontro de mattoni segnato con q:o Segno ˆ.

In tutte le sudette Guide, a i Cantoni, e per lo lungo vicino alle Pianelle, vi sono diverse Radiche d'Anemoni, et Argemoni &

fol. 9r   2.o Sco'partimento

P.mo Cassettone

P.ma fila Giacinti buoni tramezzati da Tromboni bianchi

2:a Tromboni Doppij

3:a Alli capi due Tazzette d'Olanda stellate, in mezzo delle quali due dalla foglia unita

2.o Cassettone

In mezzo un Narciso massimo d'Olanda d:o del Gaetano

P.mo circolo piccolo Giacinti di Cornaro

2.o circolo grande Giunchiglia di Spagna tramezzata da Tulipani Coloretti

3.o Cassettone

Conforme in tutto al Cassettone P:mo

fol. 9v   2.o Scomp.to

4.o Cassettone

P.ma fila Tazzette della gran sorte

2.a Tromboni doppij.

3.a Giacinti Polianti di Brescia, et alli capi due Gialli in oro.

4.a Tulipani tela d'oro.

5.o Cassettone

In tutto simile al 4.o precedente.

6.o Cassettone
P:ma fila circolare Tazzette della gran sorte, et alli capi Tazzette d' Olanda dalla foglia unita.
2:a Non ha' pari Solfarini.
3:a Giunchiglia di Spagna, in mezzo di q.le Gialli in oro.
4.o Colli di Camello doppij, e nella punta dell'Angolo perfetto una Tazzetta d'Olanda stellata.

fol. 10r   2.o Scomp.to

7:o Cassettone
In tutto simile al 6:o precedente

8:o Casettone
P:ma fila alli cappi, et in mezzo Gialli in paglia tramezzati da Colli di Camello Doppij.
2:a Giunchiglia unita, e Tromboni bianchi

9.o Cassettone
P:ma fila Giacinti Polianti, et alli capi due Gialli in oro.
Il tutto tramezzati da Giunchiglia unita.

10.o Cassettone
In tutto simile al Cassettone 8.o precedente eccetto che in cambio di Gialli in paglia, son G. in oro

ii.o e 12:o Cassettone
In tutto simile al Cassettone 6:o

fol. 10v   2:o Scomp:to

13:o Cassettone
P,ma fila Tulipani Rossi, e gialli
2:a Giacinti, et in mezzo due Gialli in oro
3:a Tromboni doppij
4:a Tazzette della gran sorte.

14.o Cassettone
Simile al Cassettone quinto cioè
P:ma fila Tazzette della gran sorte.
2:a Tromboni Doppij.
3:a Giacinti Polianti, in mezzo de' q.li 2 Gialli in oro.
4:a Tulipani Coloretti.

15:o Cassettone
P:ma fila Giacinti di Cornaro.
2:a alli capi due Gialli, et in mezzo tre Tazzette Massime &.
3:a Tromboni Bianchi
4:a Tulipani Coloretti d:i Porpore

fol. 11r   2.o Scomp:to

16:o Cassetone.
Come il Cassettone 2:o

17:o Cassettone.
P:ma fila Tazzette della gran Sorte.
2:a Giacinti di Cornaro, et alli Capi due Narcisi Gialli.
3:a Giunchiglia di Spagna.
4:a Colli di Camello tramezzati da no. ha pari solfarini.

fol. 11v   2.o Scomp:to

P:ma Guida.
Segnato n.o 17: Alli Capi, et in mezzo Narcisi Gialli, Gialli [sic], tramezzati da due Tazzette della gran sorte, seguita una fila per traverso di Giunch:i di Spagna, Dipoi una fila lo lungo in mezzo di Giacinti di Brescia, e Tulipani Penn:i Buoni n:o 20 de quale si tiene nota. Alla svolta della Guida, sin che finisce, alli capi, Gialli in oro tramezzatti da due Tazzette della gran sorte, con la fila per tramezzo di Giunch:a di Spagna, e con la solita fila in mezzo di Tulipani Coloretti. Vicino

alli matoni dalla parte di dentro Giunchiglia di Spagna, e Tulipano Coloretti.

fol. 12r   2.o Scomp.to
                                                  2:a Guida

Segnato n:o 18 contigua al Viale di mezzo. Alli capi Tromboni dall gran Tromba grande, Solfarini, tramezzati da due Tazzete, Di poi per la lungo in mezzo Narcisi non ha' pari Gialli, e Tulipani Coloretti.

Vicino Matoni dalla parte di dentro una fila di Giunchiglia di Spagna, e Tulipani Coloretti.

                                                  3:a Guida

Segnato n:o 19 verso le stanze. Alli capi Gialli in oro. In mezzo Tazzette della gran sorte. Poi una filetta di Giunchiglia di Spagna, et i Gialli sono in capo a' tutti li quattro tramezzi. Poi per lungo in mezzo Giacinti, e Tulipani Pennacchiati n:o 4 de quali si tien nota.

Vicino alli mattoni dalla parte di dentro una fila di Giunchiglia di Spagna, e Tulipane di Persia.

fol. 12v   2.o Scomp:to

In tutte le retroscritte Guide del sud:o Scomp:to, alli Cantoni e per lo lungo vi sono diverse radiche d'Anemoni, e d'Argemoni &.

fol. 13r   3:o Scompartim:to
                                                  Cassettone p:mo

P:ma fila Narcisi Costantinopolitani dopij
2:a Giacinti in mezzo del quale Gialli in oro
3:a Tazzette della gran sorte

                                                  2.o Cassettone

P:ma fila Tulip:i Coloretti, et in mezzo un Giall' in oro
2:a Giunchiglia dalla foglia unita
3.a Tazzete della gran sorte
4.a Giacinti di Brescia
5.a Tromboni Dopij
6.a Tulipani coloretti et in mezzo un Narciso Massimo d'Olanda d:o di Gaetano

fol. 13v   3.o Scomp.to
                                                  Cassettone 3:o

P:ma fila Giacinti bianchi
2:a Tromboni Solfarini
3:a Narcisi Tela d'Olanda.
4:a Tromboni doppij
5:a Tazzette della gran sorte.
6:a Tulipani coloretti
7:a Guinchiglia dalla foglia unita
8:a Tulipani coloretti.

                                                  Cassettone 4:o

In tutto come il 3:o Cassettone preced.te

                                                  Cassettone 5:o

P:ma fila un Narciso Giallo in mezzo da due Giacinti buoni
2:a l'istesso
3:a l'istesso
4:a l'istesso
5:a l'istesso
6:a Tulipani coloretti
7:a et 8:a l'istesso.

fol. 14r   3.o Scomp:to
                                                  6:o Cassettone

P:ma fila Narcisi Costantinopolitani
2:a Tazzette della gran sorte.

                                                  7:o Cassettone

P:a fila Giacinti buoni.

2:a Tazzette della gran Sorte.

3:a Gialli in oro

4:a Collo di Camello Dopij

Ultimo un Narciso Massimo d'Olanda d:o del Gaetano.

8:o Cassettone

Simile al precedente 8:o [sic] Cassettone ma con ordine al rinverso.

9:o Cassettone Tondo

P:ma fila circolare contigua alli mattoni Giacinti tramezzati di Narcisi Gialli in Oro, cioè due Giacinti, et un Giallo in oro.

2:a fila circolare tramezzata da Garofani, cioè verso le stanze di sua Em.za due Giacinti,

fol. 14v   3.o Scomp.to

Segue l'ultimo Cassettone Tondo. con un Giall' in oro in mezzo, e verso il Viale del mezzo del Giardino, due altri Giacinti con un Giall' in oro in mezzo.

Ultimo in mezzo tre Narcisi Massimi d'Olanda detti del Gaetano, posti in triangolo

In d.o Scompartimento vi sono due Guide ò vero Cassettoni, uno verso le stanze dell' Em.mo Pro're., e l'altra verso il viale del mezzo del Giard.o, et ogni Guida hà tre fila per lo lungo la p.a contigua alli mattoni *alli mattoni* [sic] di fuora tutta di radiche diverse, la 2.a fila in mezzo alle guide tutta di Tulipani Pennacchiati diversi. La 3.a fila contigua alli mattoni, di dentro tutta di Tromboni Doppij, come più distintamente di sotto.

fol. 15r   3:o Scomp:to

P:ma Guida.

P:ma fila di Radiche contigua alli mattoni di fuora, cominciando la fila dal Pilastro verso la Portella di d:e Stanze, e dal segno di questa figura ˆ che si troverà nel mattone contiguo à d:o Pilastro, qual segno in ogni Guida di questo Scomp:to mostra il sito delle radiche e cipolle

P:ma Radica Anemone Persichino Doppia

2.a l'istesso

3.a l'istesso

4:a Ranunculi a' foglia di Ruta

5:a l'istesso

6:a l'isteso

7:a Anemone Rosso col fiocco lionato

8:a l'istesso

9:a l'istesso

fol. 15v   3:o Scomp:to

P:ma Guida

2:a fila di mezzo di Tulipani Pennachiati cominciando dal segno del mattone contiguo Pilastro come sopra, e seguitando ad ogni segno.ˆ.

P:mo Tulipano, Pennacchiate Rosso, e Giallo, con fiam.e à corno di Cervo

2.o T.o Penn.o de SS.i Lani

3.o T: Pennacchiato d:o Bracchettone

4:o T: Penn.o Bianco Candido, e rosso stamine nere fondo turchino

5:o T: Penn:o persichino, e bianco

6:o Tulip:o Penn:o Candido, e rosso acceso, come fiam.e in tutte le foglie Bellissimo.

7:o T: Penn:o persichino rigato di bianco.

8:o T: Penn:o Giallo e Rosso Bello.

9:o T: Penn: Agata detta del P're Savelli.

3:a Fila contigua alli mattoni di dentro dal principio della Guida sin' al fine, all' incontro delli Segni come sopra, Tromboni doppij.

fol. 16r   3:o Scomp.to

2:a Guida

La 2:a Guida ha' tre fila per lo lu.ngo come la p:ma di Radiche e cipolle situate come sopra all'incontro delli segni di mattoni ˆ

P:ma fila di Radiche contigua alli mattoni di fuora hà il suo princ:o all'incontro dell'ultimo cantone del Pilastro, che sta fra il 2:o, e 3:o scompartim:to

P:ma Radica Anemone dal fiocc.o verde.

2:a l'istesso

3:a l'istesso

4:a Ranunculi a foglia di Ruta

5:a l'istesso

6:o l'istesso

7:a Anemoni Rossi col fiocco Lionato

8:a l'istesso

9:a l'istesso

10:a Anemone persichino Doppio

ii:a Anemone persichino doppio.

fol. 16v   3:o Scomp:to

2:a fila della 2:a Guida contigua al Viale ha' il suo principio dal sudetto Pilastro, come la fila delle Radiche, camina per il mezzo della Guida per lo lungo et è di Tulipani Pennacchiati posti all' incontro de segni, com sop. .ˆ.

P:mo Tulipano Pennacchiato bianco, e Rosso.

2:o Tulip:o Penn:o d:o Colonna Ardente.

3:o T: Penn:o Giallo, e Rosso bello.

4:o T: Penn:o Rosso oscuro fiammate di bianco.

5:o T: Penn:o d:o Agata di tre colori del S.r Fabr.o

6:o T: Penn:o Bianco, e Rosso bello.

7:o T: Penn:o Marmorino

8:o T: Penn:o Rosso, e Solfarino

9:o T: Penn:o Agata

10:o T: Penn:o detto il Cugino del Bosuelt [?]

11:o T: Penn:o Giallo e Rosso.

3:a Fila contigua alli mattoni di dentro dal principio sin' al fine Tromboni doppij situati all'incontro de segni come sopra, &.

fol. 17r   40 Scompartimento.
                                          P:mo Casettone

P:ma fila Tulipani Coloretti.

2:a Narcisi non ha pari

3:a Tazette delle gran sorte

4:a Tromboni dopij

5:a Giacinti buoni et in mezzo un Narciso Massimo d'Olanda d:o del Gaetano.

6:a Tromboni bianchi

                                          2:o Cassettone

Conforme al precedente Cassettone P:o

                                          3:o Cassettone

P:ma fila Tulipani Coloretti

2.a Narcisi no' ha pari.

3:a Tazzette della gran sorte

4:a Narcisi Costantinopolitani

5:a Giacinti di Brescia, et in mezzo un Narciso massimo d'Olando d.o del Gaetano

6:a Tromboni Solfarini

fol. 17v   4:o Scomp:to
                                          4:o Cassettone

Come il Precedente Cassettone 3.o ma co' le file al rinverso.

5:o Casettone.

P:ma fila Colli di Camello, et in mezzo un Giall' in oro.

2:a Giunchiglia dalla foglia unita, et in mezzo un Narciso d'Olanda minore

3:a Narcisi Gialli, et alli capi una Tazzetta della gran sorte.

4:a Tazzette della gran sorte

5:a Giacinti buoni

6:a Tulipani Coloretti.

6:o Cassettone.

In tutto simile al precedente Cassetone 5:o

7:o Cassettone

P:ma fila Tulipani coloretti et in mezzo un Giallo in oro

2:a Giacinti di Brescia, in mezzo Narciso Mass.o de Gaet:o

3:a Tazzette della gran sorte.

4:a Tromboni Solfarini.

5:a Narcisi di Costantinop.i, alli capi Narcisi d'Olanda minori.

6:a Giacinti bianchi

fol. 18r   4:o Scomp:to

8:o Cassettone

Conforme al precedente cassettone 7:o eccetto l'ordine della fila che è al rinverso, et in cambio di tromboni Solferini, vi sono non hà pari.

9:o Cassettone, Tondo.

P:ma fila circolare contigua alli mattoni, un Narciso Massimo d'Olanda d:o di Gaetano, et un Giall' in oro, et così segue tutta la fila dentro il Tondo.

2:a fila circolare tutta di tromboni Doppij

Ultimo in mezzo un Pianta di [blank]

Seguitano tre guide che circondano d:o Scomp:to

fol. 18v   4:o Scomp:to

P:ma Guida.

La P.a Guida di questo Scomp:to è quella, che è contigua al Viale che divida il 3:o scomp:to dal 4.o ha la fila per lo lungo, e tutte di Tulipani Coloretti

2:a Guida contigua

Al Viale di mezzo, è tutta di Tulipani Coloretti come sopra

3:a Guida

Contigua al d.o verso la spalliera d'Agrumi, ha le file come sopra tutte di Tulipani Coloretti diversi.

fols. 19r,v [Blank]

fol. 20r   Vasi di Fiori
del Giardino Secreto dell' Em:mo Sig:re
Card:le Antonio Barberini

P:mo Vaso. In mezzo Anemone Orlato, attorno tre Anemone Rossini.

2.o Vaso. In mezzo Orlato.

        Attorno Rad.e Anemoni Rossi col fiocco lionato

3.o V. In mezzo Orlato.

        Attorno Anemone Rossi col fiocco lionato n:o 3

4.o V. Anemone Sanguigno Dopii

        Attorno Anemone di cinque Colori n:o 3

5:o V. Anemone Sanguigno sud:o

        Attorno Anemoni persichino n:o 3.

6:o V. In mezzo Anem. Sanguigno d.o

        Attorno Anemoni Rossino n.o 3.

7:o V. In mezzo Anem:e Solfarino fiammato rosso doppio. Attorno Anem.i dal fiocco Verde.3.

8.o V. In Mezzo Anem:e Solfarino sudetto

fol. 20v   Vasi di Fiori
        Attorno Anemoni Rossi Vellutati. n.o 3

9:o Vaso In mezzo Anem:e Solfarino fiammata Rosso Doppio. Attorno P:o Argemone Colombino acceso, 2:o Argemone Violace. 3:o Argemino Cremesino.

10.o Vaso in mezzo Anem.e bianco fiammato d'Incarnato doppio
        Attorno Argemone buoni n.o 3.

ii.o V: An: Bianco sudetto. Attorno Argemone
        P:o Il bel tenerino, 2.o Palombino acceso, 3.o Rosso Cremesino

12:o V: in mezzo bianco fiammato sudetto.
        Attorno Arg:e
        n.o. p.o la Massima Paonazza
        n.o 2.o Il bel Tenerino
        n.o 3.o La Madre della Celeste

13.o V. in mezzo Anem. scritto buono, attorno Argem:i n.o p:p Cremesino bello, 2.o e 3.o Madre della Celeste.

14: V: in mezzo Anemone scritto buono; attorno Argemoni n.o p:o Cremesino bello, 2.o Carneo, e 3:o Palombino

15. V. in me. Anem: scritto buono n.o p.o, 2.o, e 3.o Argemoni Madre della Celeste.

fol. 21r   Vasi di fiori

16:o Vaso In mezzo, et attorno Argemoni n.o 4

17:o V: in mezzo In mezzo Incarnato di limone gello.
        Attorno Anemoni dal fiocco lionato n.o 3e

18:o V: In mezzo Carneo massimo, attorno Argemoni
        n.o p.o la Guascogna, 2.o la Paldetta
        n.o 3:o Rosso oscuro.

19:o V: In mezzo Argem. Rosino tre Argemoni buoni tramezzati da tre Giungchiglie [sic] *solfarine* [sic] Riflesse n:o 8.

20.o V: in mezo Argemone cremesino, tre Anemoni buoni tramezzati da tre Giunchiglie

21:o V: In mezzo Argemone Rosso cremesino,
        Attorno tre Argemoni buoni, tramezzati da cinque Giungifogli

22.o V: in Mezzo Giacinto Doppio detto Januario.
        Attorno tre Argemoni buoni.

23.o V: in mezzo Giacinto sud.o Attorno Argemoni buoni nn.o.3.

fol. 21v   Vasi di fiori

24:o Vaso. in mezzo Giunchiglie Doppie n.o 6
        Attorno Ranunculi à foglia di Ruta.

25.o V: In mezzo un Non ha pari Doppio.
        n.o p.o Tulipano Pennachiato, bianco candido, e Rosso, stamine nere, fondo
        Turchino, belliss.mo.
        n.o 2.o Giunchiglia di Spagna
        n.o 3.o Tulipano Penn:o Cera di Spagna Pennacchiato di bianco.
        n.o 4.o Giunchiglia di Spagna

26. V: in mezzo, un Giacinto Stradoppio
        n.o p.o Tulp. Penn: persichino Aranciato, pennacchiato di bianco, e giallo.
        n.o 2.o Giunchiglia di Spagn.a
        n.o 3.o T: Penn:o detto Colonna Ardente.
        n.o 4.o Giunchiglia di Spagna.

27. V: in mezzo Giacinto Verde
        n.o p.o Tulip.o Penn.o d:o il Generoso Belliss:o
        n.o 2.o Giunchiglia di Spagna.
        n.o 3.o T: P:o Rosso oscuro, e solfarino chiaro.
        n.o 4.o Giunchiglia di Spagna.

fol. 22r   Vasi di Fiori

28.o Vaso in mezzo Ranunculo scritto

      n.o p.o Tulipano Pennacchiato, violacea oscura, Paonazzo, e bianco staminea, e fondo Turchino

      n.o 2.o Giunchiglia di Spagna

      n.o 3.o Tulip.o Pennacchiato, d.o il Cugino del Bosuelt.

      n.o 4.o Giunchiglia di Spagna

fols. 22v, 23, 24, 25r,v [Blank]

APPENDIX II

HORTICULTURAL TREATISE

BIBLIOTECA APOSTOLICA VATICANA, MS. BARB. LAT. 4278

21.5 × 15.5 cm

Note: In the English translation each division of the text has been given a Roman numeral, and each paragraph has been given an Arabic numeral. The numbers of the Italian text match those in the translation.

[I] (fol. 1r)   Dell'Anemoni à Fronda larga, et delli
Ane[mo]ni à fronda stretta detti Tenuifolij,
& Latifolij.

[I.1] L'Anemone Latifolio deve esser' piantato prima del Tenuifolio, stenta più à nascere tarda più à far fiori, et ci vuol più tempo à far il moltiplico, talche è bene piantarlo alla Luna di Settembre tre giorni avanti il plenilunio.

[I.2] Deve esser' piantato in Vaso per far meglio, si il moltiplico, come maggior quantità di fior, & anco per custodirlo più, & dal gelo, & dalla soverchia aqua.

[I.3] In tutti li Vasi dove si piantaranno le radice, ò altre cipolle si deve fare il buco del Vaso grande almeno qua[n]to una piastra fiorentina, con ponervi sopra tre, ò quattro cocciole grandi, che coprino detto buco, & sopra le cocciole tanti sassetti della grossezza d'una nocchia, che riempia il Vaso per quattro buone dita, & poi finirlo d'empire di terra della qualità, che ricercano le piante.

[I.4] Richiede terra grassa, leggiera, et purgata, che non (fol. 1v) renda fetore, ne calore, avvertendo però, che dove si piantarà la radica vi è necessaro la terra magra, e leggiera, dalla quale deve esser' circondata detta radica per ogni intorno due grosse dita, & questo si fà, acciò che la radica, quale è asciutta nel ripigliar, che fà d'humore naturale della terra da un'estremo all'altro non s'imbeva d'humore più tosto alterato che mediocre, con pericolo manifesto di marcirsi.

[I.5] Piantata, che sarà quattro dita sotto terra, ò poco più, perche calando la terra restarà tre dita sotto, che è il suo dovere, non si ponga al sole per evitare il soverchio caldo, che suol essere alle volte nel mese di Settembre, qual potrebbe cagionare subollimento alle radiche, che ancora non hanno preso vigore con le sue radice.

[I]   Of broad-leaved Anemones and narrow-leaved Anemones,
                                    called Tenuifolij,
                                      & Latifolij.
                        [*Anemone coronaria L.* and *A. pavonina L.*]

[I.1] The broad-leaved Anemone *(Anemone latifolio)* must be planted earlier than the narrow-leaved, because it is slower to start growing, later to flower, and needs more time to produce the propagation stock; it is, therefore, advisable to plant it in the month of September three days before the full moon.

[I.2] It should be planted in a pot so that it will both propagate better and produce a greater number of flowers, and also so that one can more easily protect it from frost and from excessive rain.

[I.3] In all the pots in which the roots or other bulbs are to be planted, one should make a hole in the pot at least as big as a Florentine *piastra,* putting over it three or four large sherds to cover the said hole, and over the sherds enough pebbles the size of a hazelnut to fill the pot to a depth of a good four fingers, and then filling it up with soil of the quality the plants require.

[I.4] It needs composted, purged, well-drained soil, which does not give off a smell or heat. Note, however, that where the rootstock is to be planted crumbly, light soil is necessary, which should be laid all around the said root for a good two fingers' distance.[1] This is done so that, the rootstock which is dry, in the absorption of the natural moisture of the soil, does not go from one extreme to the other and does not absorb a greater than average amount of moisture, with the obvious danger of rotting.

[I.5] Once it is planted at a depth of four fingers below ground, or a little more, so that as the soil settles it will still be three fingers deep, as it needs to be, it should not be put out in the sun, for one should ensure it is not exposed to too much heat, which sometimes occurs in the month of September, and which could cook the rootstock, as it has not yet become strong enough with its roots.

---

[1] A *dita* is approximately 5 cm.

[I.6] Fatte, che haveranno le radici, et cominciato à metter fuori frondi con ogni sicurezza si possono esponere al sole, avvertendo, che sotto il Vaso vi si metta un mattone, acciò che per la soverchia acqua, che potrebbe piovere, non venisse à marcirsi, perche si suole serrare il buco che è sotto il Vaso, restando in terra senza detto mattone.

[I.7] Desidera sole assai, luogo caldo, & quel che più importa larga, che non sia occupato, perche per esser naturale alle (fol. 2r) piante il crescere in alto, questa sorte di pianta quando alza le sue frondi assai, perde il suo vigore, & tutta se ne và in fronde, con far pochi fiore, et sfiatati per non esser la virtù unita, il che avviene quando si pone in luogo stretto, et occupato, che l'aria non ci possi giuocare, come per esperienza si vede.

[I.8] L'altra ragione è, che alzando le frondi l'Anemone, qual suol fare i pedicozzi sottili, arrivandoli un freddo, ò vento addosso più facilmente li secca ritrovandosi di fuori, che sotto terra, & seccandosi viene à esser offesa la radica con notabili patimento.

[I.9] S'humetti ogni volta, che vederassi la terra non esser nera, mà quasi polvere intorno il Vaso senza bagnar le frondi, sì per schivare l'offesa del sole, come del gelo, & questo si facci la mattina più tosto, che la sera nel tempo dell'Inverno, et nel tempo di primavera si deve far la sera.

[I.10] Mai (il che molti sogliono inconsideratamente fare) si tocchi ne con Zeppi, ne con ferri, la superficie della terra scalzandolo, perche toccandola, et rimovendola si viene à rompere quel suo coio, ò crosta, & così adacquandosi con maggior facilità scende, & percuote la radica, quale ama l'humidità temperata, & non soverchia, & violenta et (fol. 2v) per questo effetto quando si pianta si suole sopra à detta radica in mezzo del Vaso mettervi più terra à guisa di monticello affinche l'acqua scoli meglio intorna al Vaso, & non muoia sopra la pianta.

[I.11] Avanti della primavera i fiori, che produrranno dette radiche per l'ordinario saranno perfetti, però si devono tagliare radente la terra, acciò che non sfogando la sua virtù in quelli aborti resti con maggior vigore, & à suo tempo possi far la dimostratione, che deve, & ciò si deve rimettere al giuditio dell'accorto Giardiniero, quale vedendo il fiore sfiatato lo tagli, et lassi il pieno, avvertendo però, che tutti i fiori si devono tagliar con forbicette, perche rompendoli con le dita facilmente si smove la radica, la quale stà debolmente attaccata, come anche haver riguardo, che una pianta quando haverà ridotto à perfettione una dozzina di fiori si può contentare, essendo assai più piccola d'una pianta di garofoli, de'quali più oltre si parlerà.

[I.12] Suole ancora occorrere, che alcune volte la terra produce certo vermetti, che il volgo chiama bruchi, qual nascondendosi in quella trà le radici, & trà le frondi la notte uscendo fuori, & cibandosi delli pedicozzi delle frondi, & del gambo de fiori li tagliano, & rodono cagionando perciò malatia (fol. 3r) notabile alla radica si per esser animali, che per natura loro abbrugiano, si anco per le sopradette ragioni, che nascondendosi nella terra la tengono di continuo smossa, come anco per il rodimento delle frondi, et delli fiori.

[I.13] Sogliono alcuni poco accorti Giardinieri per liberar la radica dal nemico andar con diligenza rimovendo la terra con un Zeppo per ritrovare il bruco, quale benchè trovi, et ammazzi, ad ogni modo evidentemente si scorge, che la radica riceve notabili danno per esserli levata quella prima crostola, con la quale si reparava, & defendeva dalli sopradetti contrarij, & quel che più importa sempre dove stà il principale bruco de lì interno devono esser altri figli piccoli, che per la piccolezza, & per il colore simile alla terra non si scorgono.

[I.6] When they have formed roots and begun to put forth leaves, they can be exposed to the sun in complete safety. Note that a tile should be placed under the pot to ensure that the plant does not start to rot because of excessive rain which might fall, since the hole in the base of the pot often becomes blocked up if it stands on the ground without the aforesaid tile.

[I.7] It needs plenty of sun and a position which is warm and, most importantly, open and not occupied by other plants to grow tall, and when the stalks of this type of plant grow very high, all its strength goes into growing leaves, only a few flowers are produced and they are weak because its strength has been dispersed—this happens when it is set in a cramped and crowded position, where the air cannot flow freely, as one sees through experience.

[I.8] The other reason is that when the stalks of the anemone, which has slender pedicles, have grown tall, any cold or wind which might assail it can more easily wither them since they are outside rather than underground, and, as the plant withers, the rootstock comes to suffer considerable damage.

[I.9] Whenever the soil seems dusty rather than dark, one should water all around the pot, without wetting the leaves, in order to avoid damage from both sun and frost, and this should be done in the morning rather than in the evening during the winter, and in the spring it should be done in the evening.

[I.10] Though many do so unthinkingly, one should never cultivate the soil with hoes or other garden tools in order to break it up, because, disturbing the surface breaks its skin or crust; as a result, when it is watered, the water filters down more easily to the rootstock, which likes moderate, not excessive and intense, humidity—to achieve this, when planting, put more soil over the said rootstock in the middle of the pot in the form of a little mound, so that the water can better drain away around the pot, and the plant above does not die.

[I.11] The flowers which the said rootstock produces before spring will not normally be perfect, and so they should be cut back at ground level so that the plant does not spend its strength on these premature flowers but is left stronger and can make its due show in its own time. This must be left to the judgment of the discerning gardener who, seeing an unhealthy flower, should cut it off and leave the full one. Note, however, that the flowers should always be cut with small secateurs, because, if one breaks them off with one's fingers, the rootstock, which is only lightly attached to them, can easily be disturbed. One should also bear in mind that, once a plant has brought a dozen flowers to perfect bloom, one should be satisfied, since it is a much smaller plant than the dianthus, which will be discussed later on.

[I.12] Also, it may happen, moreover, that the soil produces certain little worms, popularly called grubs, which hide in it among the roots and among the leaves; at night they come out and feed on the leaf stalks and the flower stems, cutting them through and nibbling them, and thus causing considerable damage to the rootstock, in that they are animals whose very nature it is to graze in this way, and also for the aforementioned reasons, that by hiding in the soil they disturb it constantly, and because they nibble the leaves and flowers.

[I.13] To preserve the rootstock from the attacks of this enemy, some undiscerning gardeners go around turning up the soil carefully with a hoe in order to find the grub, but even if they find and kill it, it is patently obvious that in any case the rootstock suffers considerable damage because the outer skin, which screened and protected it from the abovementioned hostile forces, has been taken from it; more importantly also,

[I.14] Deve dunque il Custode di esso eleggere rimedio il meno dannnoso, che sia per liberarla, è prender detto Vaso mettendolo tutto sotto l'acqua, lasciandolo stare sotto di essa un mezzo quarto d'hora in circa, & così si vedranno uscir fuori tutti li bruchi, che vi sono per non affogarsi, quali ammazzati si caverà il Vaso dall'acqua riponendolo al suo luogo, acciò si scoli, & così non viene ad esser rimossa quella superficie della terra, (fol. 3v) riserrandosi li buchi, dalli quali sono usciti detti animali, anzi in tal guisa resta la terra più ristretta insieme.

[I.15] Nè osta quello mi si potrebbe opponere che havendo detto di sopra, che questa radica è nemica della soverchia humidità hora dica, che si debba metter sotto l'acqua, perchè l'esperienza lunghissima hà mostrata, che l'acqua in tal modo data al Vaso non gli hà per lo più nociuto, & all'incontro cava fuori il nemico, qual manifestamente fà mori la radica.

[I.16] Restano ancora offese le radiche per negligenza de' Giardinieri, & è come per esperienza si vede, che si trovano alcuni Vasi, quali sono di terra mal cotta, ò fatti di terra rossa, quali due sogliono per natura loro tener la terra più humida, che non fanno gl'altri, & di terra bianca, onde per la continua humidità rendono sempre inferme le radiche, talche si deve haver gran riguardo in eleggere li Vasi ben cotti & di terra bianca.

[I.17] Per il moltiplico è d'avvertire, che non si devono spezzar le radiche se non si vedono apertamente divisibili, ovvero quando sono d'una certa grossezza (in che molti s'ingannano) quali vedendo una sì bella & grossa radica non la spezzano, spe-(fol. 4r)rando, che produchi maggior numero di fiori, et grandi, il che succede tutto al contrario, perche quando una radica è gionta à una certa grossezza, che si giudichi esorbitante se gli deve dare una zeccata per sentire si è vacua di dentro; perche essendo vota piantandola senza romperla, tutto quel vacuo si riempirebbe d'humidità, et acqua, & manifestamente perisce, dove si devono spezzare, & alli tagli di esso si deve mettere un poco di cera termentinata per preserverla dall'humidità, che imbeverebbe se si piantasse co'l taglio aperto.

[I.18] Il tempo di spezzarle è meglio otto giorni doppo cavate, si per esser più tenere, et facili al dividersi, che doppo risecche, essendo durissime, come anco giova al taglio, che in quel tempo restando aperto s'indurisce, & resiste più à marcirsi, si deve fare il taglio con il coltello, acciò venga più polito.

[I.19] Per il moltiplico della varietà è necessario il seminare, & il seme si debba raccogliere dalli fiori li più pieni, che si possana havere, che facendo in mezzo del fiore un globo con alcuni schiacciati granelli vestiti di sottil lana, si devono raccogliere nel mezzo giorno asciutti, & quando sono fatti, si conosce, che comincia la sommità di esso globo ad allargarsi, si raccoglie con un poco di gambo, acciò possi finire di perfettionarsi, con metterlo dentro una scatola all'asciutto.

[I.20] (fol. 4v) Nel tempo di Settembre quattro giorni avanti il plenilunio si seminarà in un Vaso, ò Catino in terra grassa leggiera, et purgata, & la terra dove si ponerà il seme deve esser crivellata minutissimamente con Setaccio, poi si vada spandendo il seme sopra quella terra con diligenza à usanza di pizza, et coperta, che sarà la terra del seme si deve ricoprire dell'istessa terra alla grossezza d'una costa di cortello, ò poco più, et inaffiarla con diligenza con una scopetta, affinchè bene imbeverata non venga à esser scoperto il seme, & così si deve continuare sin tanto, che haveran fatta le terza fronda, & secondo, che vanno nascendo si devono ricoprire gentilissimamente con l'istessa terra, setacciandola sopra sin tanto che veranno le radiche à star sotto un dito.

round about the place where the main grub is, there are of necessity always other little grubs, its offspring, which because of their smallness and their color, which resembles the earth, cannot be seen.

[I.14] The custodian must therefore choose the least damaging remedy possible to save the plant. This is to take the said pot and immerse it entirely in water, leaving it underwater for about half of a quarter of an hour. Thus one will see all the grubs that are there coming out so as not to be drowned. After killing them, one must take the pot out of the water and put it back in its place to drain. In this way, the surface of the soil is preserved and the holes from which the said animals emerged are sealed up; indeed, this method leaves the soil more closely packed.

[I.15] There is no obstacle in the objection that might be made here, namely, that I said above that this rootstock is averse to excessive moisture, whereas now I say that it should be put under water, for very long experience has shown that when the pot has been watered in this way it has generally done it no harm; on the contrary, it brings out the enemy, which obviously would kill the rootstock.

[I.16] The rootstock can also be damaged by negligence on the part of the gardeners, and this, as experience shows, is because there are pots of poorly-baked or of red clay, and these two types naturally keep the soil more humid than do the other pots of well-baked and white clay, thus constantly damaging the health of the rootstock through continual humidity; one must therefore take great care to select pots which are well-baked and of white clay.

[I.17] As regards propagation, one should note that the rootstock should not be divided unless it is clearly seen to be divisible, or when it has reached a certain size. Many people go wrong here when they see a really fine, large root and they do not divide it because they hope it will produce a greater number of flowers, and big ones too. What happens is exactly the opposite, because, when a root has reached a certain size, such that it could be considered over-large, one should give it a tap to hear if it is hollow inside, for, if it is empty and is planted without being divided, the hollow inside fills up with moisture and water, and obviously it will die. Instead, it should be divided and a little wax mixed with turpentine should be applied to the cuts to protect the root from the moisture it would absorb if it were planted with the cut still open.

[I.18] The best time to divide them is eight days after they have been dug up, because then they are softer and more easy to divide than after they have dried up and become very hard; this is also good for the cut which, if it is left open then, becomes hard and more resistant to rotting. The cut should be made with a knife so that it is cleaner.

[I.19] To propagate the variety, sowing is necessary. The seed should be collected from the most mature flowers one can get, when in the middle of the flower a globe has been formed with some flat little seeds covered in light down. These should be collected at midday when they are dry, and one can see when they are ready, for the top of this globe begins to swell. It should be collected with a bit of the stem so that it can complete its development to the full, and it should be put in a box in a dry place.

[I.20] In September, four days before the full moon, the seed should be sown in a pot or bowl, in composted, well-drained soil, and the soil in which the seed is to be planted must be sifted very fine with a sieve. Then one should scatter the seed over the soil carefully and in pinches. When the soil is covered with seed, it must be covered over with the same sort of soil to the thickness of the back of a knife-blade or a little more, and carefully watered with a watering pot so that it receives a good soaking without the seed being exposed. One should carry on in this way until they have produced their third leaf, and concurrently, as they come up, one should add very gently the same sort of soil, sieving it over them until the rootstock is a finger's depth below ground.

[I.21] Alcuni fioraranno in capo à otto mesi se saranno ben custoditi esponendoli al Sole in luogo caldissimo, con defenderli dal freddo, & giaccio della notte, perche per essere piccoli non havendo fatto molte radiche il giaccio alzando il terreno le suole buttar fuori, et così periscono.

[I.22] Seccate le frondi, si devono mettere in luogo fresco, che non vi piova, né si devono cavare se non à mezzo Settembre, perche cavandosi prima, essendo troppo piccioli, patirebbono dal soverchio caldo. Dipoi si devono scieglere li piccoli dalli (fol. 5r) grandi, così, & li grandi metterli in terra, & li piccioli repiantarli nelli Catini, ò Vasi, che così si vedrà la varietà di essi ò semplice, ò doppia.

[I.23] Avvertendo, che subito seminati si devono metter all'ombra, acciò co'l tempo si vadino ingrossando li granelli, tra otto giorni si devono esporre al sole, havendo però riguardo, che la terra sia sempre humida, et bagnata, acciò che per il calore del sole non venghino à esser offese le pianticelle tenerissime, che spontano, & à questo modo nasceranno più presto.

[I.24] Quelle radiche, che si piantaranno in terra vogliono pur luogo largo, et aprico terra d'horto meno grassa di quella che si pone in Vasi, devono esser piantate sotto due dita distanti un palmo l'una dal'altra, & se à sorte per l'impeto della troppo acqua restassero scoperte le radiche si devono ricoprire, si devono cavare ogni doi anni per levare il moltiplico & per il calor dell'estate se li deve crescere la terra di sopra per defenderli, quale alle prime acque se gli levarà, lasciandoli la terra di prima.

[I.25] Et perche dette radiche amano il fresco, & humido temperato, si devono sempre piantare più accosto, che si puote alli mattoni, perche mettendo fuori le sue radiche abbracciano con quella sua capigliara tutto quel fresco de mattoni (fol. 5v) dal quale come esperienza si vede ricevono tanto notrimento, che fanno gran quantità di moltiplico, con maggior copia di fiori, et vigorosi, et si conservano meglio.

[I.26] Si devono spiantare alla fine di Giugno con metterli in luogo asciutto conservandoli insieme con la terra, che verrà attaccata à dette radiche per spatio di otto giorni con nettarli, et partirle, acciò che così in un subito venendo dall'humidità essendo l'aria calda non si corrughino, perche poi nel piantarle le dette rughe, ò crespe si gonfiarebbono, & empirebbono d'acqua, con pericolo di marcir la radica.

[I.27] Le radiche delli Vasi si devono conservare in questo modo finiti, che haveranno i fiori si devono ponere in luogo, che non habbino più acqua nè sole, mà aria, perche essendo all'hora la staggione, che retirano in se l'humore naturale, tanto delle frondi, come delle radiche, percuotendoli il Sole con la soverchia humidità, & acqua, che suol venire dal Cielo, li potrebbe subollire, se potranno cavare alla fine di Giugno, che saranno ben mature con usarvi la sopradetta regola, et quelle che non si vorranno cavare si possano lasciar stare un'altro anno, con ponervi al Settembre sopra il Vaso un dito di terra grassa per darli un poco di ristoro et esporle come sopra.

[I.28] (fol. 6r) Se bene alcuni sogliono per conservarle porvi sopra della terra à guisa di cuppola, credendosi in questo modo renderli sicure da detto pericolo, s'ingannano, perche la vehemenza del calor del Sole, et dell'humidità, che penetra sotto patiscono l'istesso del subollirsi.

[I.29] Avvertimento, che alle volte da un'istessa pianta d'Anemone si vedono fiorire fiori semplici & doppi, deve l'accurato Giardiniero ligar con diligenza con filo quel gambo di quel fiore doppio, affinche quando cavarà detta radica possa riconoscere l'occhio, che haverà il fiore doppio, et quello con diligenza separare dalli altri occhi, qual occhio sempre farà il medemo.

[I.21] Some will flower after eight months if they are well looked after, being exposed to the sun in a very warm place and protected from the cold and frost by night, for since they are small and have not yet produced much rootstock, the frost, by lifting up the soil, exposes them to the open air, and so they die.

[I.22] When the leaves have withered, the plants should be put in a cool place, where they cannot be rained on. They should not be dug up before the middle of September because they are very small, and if they are dug up earlier they will be damaged by excessive heat. One should then sort the small from the large, planting the large ones in the ground and replanting the small ones in the bowls or pots, for in this way one will be able to see whether they are the single or double variety.

[I.23] Note that as soon as they have been sown they should be placed in the shade so that the seeds may grow bigger with time; after eight days they should be exposed to the sun, but one should make sure that the soil is always moist and saturated so that the heat of the sun will not damage the very tender, little plants which appear, and in this way they will come up more quickly.

[I.24] The rootstock which is to be planted in the ground also needs a spacious, sunny position and garden soil [*terra d'horto* loam?] less rich than that used in pots. They should be planted two fingers deep and a handsbreadth apart from each other, and, if the rootstock should happen to become exposed by the force of very heavy rain, they should be covered up again. They should be dug up every two years for division. To protect them from the heat of the summer, extra soil should be laid over them, but at the first rains this should be removed, leaving the same soil as before.

[I.25] Also, because these roots like coolness and moderate humidity, they should always be planted as close as possible to tiles, for, as their roots enlarge, the capillaries spread round the coolness of the bricks, and from this, as experience shows, they draw in so much nourishment that they produce a large amount of propagation stock and a greater abundance of healthy flowers that last longer.

[I.26] They should be taken up at the end of June and put in a dry place, being kept together with the soil which will be attached to the said rootstock for the space of eight days, and then cleaned and divided, lest, being taken so suddenly from a moist environment while the weather is hot, they should wrinkle, for, if they were then planted, the said wrinkles or creases would swell and fill with water, with the risk of rotting the rootstock.

[I.27] The rootstock in the pots should be preserved in the following way. When they have finished flowering, they should be put in a place where they will get no more water or sunlight, but air instead, for this is the period in which they gather in again their natural humors both of the leaves and of the rootstock and if the sunlight should fall on them at the same time as excessive humidity or rain comes down, as happens, it might cook them. They may be dug up at the end of June, when they will be fully mature, following the rules described above, and those one does not want to dig up one can leave for another year, putting a finger's thickness of compost over the pot in September, to give them a little extra nourishment, and exposing them as indicated above.

[I.28] Though some people, in order to preserve them, lay the soil over them in the form of a dome, thinking in this way to protect them from the above danger, they are mistaken, for the fierceness of the sun's heat and the moisture which penetrates down to them bring the same risk that they will be stewed.

[I.29] Note that sometimes both single and double flowers appear on the same anemone plant. The assiduous gardener should carefully tie some string round the stalk of the dou-

[I.30] Et à questo modo è ritrovato l'Anemone Tenuifolio detto l'orlato, che havendo una radica d'Anemone rigata di bianco detta la scritta fatto molti fiori, uno ne produsse con le frondi bianche orlato di rosso, qual occhio fù diligentemente osservato con spartirlo dagl'altri, & à questo modo è stato moltiplicato, & in ciò fù il primo Mons[ign]or Vescovo di Nola.

[I.31] Delli Anemoni Tenuifolio non ne discorrerò stante che vogliono l'istessa cultura resta solo, che per essere un' poco più resintiti delli Latifolij si possino piantare un' (fol. 6v) mese doppo, acciò che riservandosi in se il vigore, che facilmente potrebbe sfogare in fiori abortivi, et inutili nell'Inverno verso la primavera produchino fiori più belli, e maggiori, come anco si possono piantare nel mese di Novembre, et Dicembre.

[I.32] Avvertimento, che le terre, che servono per Vasi vogliono esser crivellate più minutamente, che quelle, che si adoprano in terra.

[I.33] L'Anemoni non temono il freddo, mà si à sorte venisse neve grande insieme con gran ghiaccio non saria mal fatto per qualche giorno retirarli sotto tetto, ò loggia esposta al sole per lassar passare quell'impeto repentino.

[II] (fol. 7r)   Delli Giacinti

[II.1] Essendo grandissima varietà di Giacinti non gli fà mestieri differente coltura, però brevemente parlarò della natura, et cultura loro.

[II.2] Nel Giacinto si deve solo desidare numero di campanelle, et la conservatione della cipolla.

[II.3] La terra, che universalmente tutti li Giacinti turchini tanto doppii, come semplici ricercano, deve essere magra non molto leggiera, mà mediocremente tenace, non sfruttata, & sogliono far miracoli nella terra vergine magrissima che sia. Devono stare un palmo sotto terra, & altreta[n]to lontano l'uno dal'altro, in luogo aperto, et esposto al sole, per esser' nemicissimi dell'ombra, nè amano altra compagnia di fiori; Non si devono rimuovere dal luogo loro, quelli che non faranno moltiplico, se non ogni quattro anni, perche restando la terra in tanto tempo sfruttata, se gli dà terra nuova per ristorarli. Mà quando faranno moltiplico si mutaranno, e partiranno non il primo anno, per esser li figli piccioli, quali meglio ingrossano co'l notrimento, che ricevano dalla madre, mà il 2.o anno si devono cavare, che (fol. 7v) saranno ingrossati, & piantarli co'l detto ordine, & quando la cipolla sarà tondata, il che sarà in fine del 3.o anno, tornarà nel suo vigore.

[II.4] Mà perche il Giacinto bianco, et quello detto del collo incarnato sono molto differenti dal turchino nella natura della cipolla; poiche sogliono patire nella corona (tenendo io ciò avvenga, perche sijno più dolci, ò tenere) per cagione d'alcuni animali, che le rodono, onde poi si tarlano, e marciscono. Per ovviare à questo male si devono porre la metà meno sotto terra dell'altre, acciò ricevino meno humidità, cavandole ogn'anno per poterle meglio governare prima del solito, che sarà subito perdute le frondi. La ragione è, che mentre la cipolla stà in vigore, difficilmente è tormentata da tarli, e bruchi, mà quando hà riconcentrato in se il suo humore diventa più sugosa, & amabile, et all'hora comincia correre pericolo d'esser guasta, & però cavandosi per tempo, più facilmente si salverà, benche dell'istessa natura pare sia il Giacinto detto fogliato, al quale si può applicare la medema cura, et diligenza.

ble flower so that, when he digs up the rootstock, he can identify the eye which has produced the double flower and separate it carefully from the other eyes, for this eye will always produce the same.

[I.30] It was in this way that the narrow-leaved anemone (*Anemone tenuifolia*) known as the 'bordered' (orlato) variety was discovered. The root of a red anemone with white stripes, known as the 'striped' (*scritto*) variety, had produced many flowers and put forth one with white petals edged with red. The eye was carefully noted and separated from the other, and in this way it was propagated. The first to do this was my lord, the bishop of Nola.

[I.31] I shall not deal at length with the narrow-leaved Anemones (*Anemoni tenuifolij*), since they need growing in the same way. It remains only to note that, since they are a little hardier than the broad-leaved, they may be planted a month later so that they will retain within themselves the strength which otherwise might well be expended on premature and useless flowers in winter, and towards the spring they will produce larger and more beautiful flowers; so they may be planted in the month of November or December.

[I.32] Note that the soils for use in pots need to be sieved more finely than those used for planting in the ground.

[I.33] Anemones do not fear the cold, but if there should happen to be a heavy snowfall with severe frost, it would not be a bad idea to bring them indoors or put them on a balcony exposed to the sun for a few days until the sudden onslaught is over.

[II]   Of Hyacinths. (*Giacinti, Iacinti*)
                                    [*Hyacinthis orientalis L.*]

[II.1] Since there are very many varieties of Hyacinth which need to be grown in the same way, I shall just deal briefly with their nature and how to grow them.

[II.2] With the Hyacinth one should aim just to obtain a large number of bells [racemes] and to preserve the bulb.

[II.3] The type of soil which all blue hyacinths [*H. orientalis L.*, 'Flore Coeruleo'], both double and single, universally require should be sandy, not very loose but moderately clinging, and not exhausted; they often produce miraculous results in virgin soil, however sandy. They should be a handsbreadth deep in the earth and the same distance apart from each other, in an open position exposed to the sun, since they are very hostile to shade and do not like the company of other flowers. Those which are not to be propagated should not be moved from their position except every four years, for after that length of time the soil will have been exhausted, and they should be given fresh soil to revive them. But when they are to be propagated, they should not be moved and divided in the first year, for the offspring [offsets] are still small and it is better for them to grow larger with the nourishment they receive from the mother-bulb, but they should be dug up in the second year, when they will have grown larger, and planted in the aforesaid way, and when the bulb has rounded out, which will be at the end of the third year, it will regain its former strength.

[II.4] The white hyacinth, however, and the variety called the 'pink-necked' [*detto del collo incarnato*] have very different types of bulb from the blue, for their crowns are often damaged—and I believe this happens because they are sweeter or more tender— by certain animals which nibble them, so that they are blighted and rot. To avoid this bane, half should be planted less deep in the soil than the others, so that they receive less moisture, and they should be dug up every year so that they can be

[II.5] Il tempo per piantar li Giacinti in queste nostre parti è quando sarà temperato nel mese di Settembre, & di cavarli quando havranno perdute affatto le frondi, & ra-(fol. 8r) diche, che saranno ben mature, che suol esser à mezzo Luglio, mà come ho detto di sopra, quanto meno staranno cavati, meglio sarà.

[II.6] Vi sono li Giacinti Belgici, Hispanici, & Ossoleti [obsoleti?], che vogliono terra più vigoroso, per esser cipolle differenti, quali amano più il fresco, & devono esser piantati sotto terra tre dita, per esser cipolle piccole, lontana quattro dita l'una dal'altra & quando si rimuovono, si devono rimuovere per levar il moltiplico poco prima, che si ripiantino, per esser'ignude, & questo si farà nel principio di Settembre, vogliono sole moderato, fanno seme, mà non degererano.

[II.7] Il Giacinto Cipressina vuol terra grassa, sole moderato, et deve piantarsi sotto terra tre dita, luogo competentemente allegro, quattro dita lontano l'uno dal'altro, rimuovendolo ogni tre anni per cagione del moltiplico, non fà seme.

[II.8] Il Giacinto detto Tuberosa Radice, altrimente Asfodelo, deve esser posto in terra à primavera, amando più tosto esser posto in Vaso, che in terra, come per esperienza si vede. Vuole terra d'horto, piantandolo sotto tre ditta un palmo lontano l'uno dal'altro. Ama sole, & acqua assai, si deve cavare alli primi freddi subito, che perde le frondi, & conservasi come gl'altri, che si dirà appresso. Teme il (fol. 8v) gielo, desidera luogo caldo, & ogni doi anni si deve cavare per il gran moltiplico che produce, fà seme, mà non degenera, & si deve seminare la primavera con la regola degl'altri Giacinti.

[II.9] Tutte sorte di Moschi Grechi vogliono terra d'horto vigorosa, luogo competentemente assolato, piantati sotto terra cinque dita, un palmo lontano l'uno dal'altro, non si devono rimuovere se non quando si vuole il moltiplico, perche non perdono mai, le radiche si spiantano di Settembre, & se ripiantano nell'istesso tempo, fanno seme, mà non variano.

[II.10] Tutte le quattro spetie delli Giacinti Peruani assieme con il Narciso terzo del Matthiolo, per esser cipolle grosse e gagliarde vogliono terra d'horto assai piena, piantandoli quattro dita sotto, & un palmo lontano l'uno dal'altro, & si rimuovono ogni tre anni, si spiantano alla fine di Luglio, et ripiantano di Settembre, vogliono luogo competentemente allegro, fanno seme, mà non degenerano.

[II.11] Si deve anco avvertire, che quando la cipolla havrà secche tutte le frondi, resta un buco nella terra dove erano le frondi & fusto del Giacinto, per il quale venendo pioggia, entra senza dubbio quantità d'acqua, che và à trovare la cipolla, quale già hà retirato in se tutto il suo humore, (fol. 9r) et stà maturandosi, onde con evidente pericolo corre rischio marcirsi, mentre havendo bisogno di siccità, viene opressa da soverchia humidità. Pertanto il accurato Giardiniero si devono atturare tutti li detti buchi per assicurarsi. Si deve anco cercare varietà di colori quale si guadagnano seminandoli.

looked after better and earlier than usual, immediately after they have shed their leaves. The reason is that, as long as the bulb is strong, it is hard for the worms and caterpillars to hurt it, but when it has gathered all its humors into itself again, it becomes more succulent and sweet and then begins to run the risk of being damaged. Thus, if it is dug up in time, it will be easier to save it. The hyacinth known as the 'leaved' [*fogliate*] variety seems to be the same in its nature, and to it the same attention and care may be applied.

[II.5] The time for planting hyacinths in our part of the world is in the month of September when it is mild, and the time for digging them up is when they have shed their leaves completely and the rootstock is fully mature which is generally in mid-July, but, as I have stated above, the less they are dug up, the better.

[II.6] There are Belgian, Spanish, and Ossoleti [*obsoleti*?] hyacinths [not identifiable] which require richer soil because their bulbs are different and like coolness more; they should be planted three fingers deep, as their bulbs are small, and four fingers apart. When they are taken up, they should be taken up for the bulblets to be removed and then replanted soon afterward, since the bulbs are naked, and this should be done at the beginning of September. They need moderate sunlight. They produce seed but do not degenerate.

[II.7] The Cypressine Hyacinth [*Giacinto cipressino*] [*Muscari Comosus* (L.) Mill.] needs composted soil and moderate sunlight and should be planted three fingers deep in a sufficiently bright position, four fingers apart. It should be taken up every three years for propagation and increase. It does not produce seed.

[II.8] The hyacinth known as 'Tuber-root', or alternatively "Asphodel" (*Giacinto detto tuberosa* o *Asfodela*) [*Asphodelus ramosus L.*? identified by Masson as a tuberose *Polianthos tuberosa L.*], should be planted in the soil in spring, and it prefers to be put in a pot rather than in the ground, as experience has shown. It needs garden soil and should be planted three fingers deep and a handsbreadth apart. It likes sunlight and plenty of water. It should be dug up at the first cold weather as soon as it has shed its leaves and should be preserved in the same way as the others, as will be described shortly. It fears the frost and likes a warm position, and every two years it should be dug up for the large amount of propagation stock it yields. It produces seeds but does not generate new varieties, and it should be sown in spring, following the instructions for the other types of hyacinth.

[II.9] All the varieties of Greek musk-hyacinth (*Moschi Grechi*) [*Muscari* Mill.] need strong garden soil and a sufficiently sunny position; they should be planted five fingers deep and a handsbreadth apart. They should not be taken up except when one wants the propagation stock, for the rootstock is permanent. They are taken up in September and replanted in the same period. They produce seed but do not change.

[II.10] All four varieties of Peruvian hyacinth [*Scilla peruviana* L.], together with the third Mattioli narcissus [one described by Galen] have large, strong bulbs and so need very rich garden soil; they should be planted four fingers deep and a handsbreadth apart, and they should be taken up every three years. They are dug up at the end of July and replanted in September. They need a sufficiently light position. They set seed but do not degenerate.

[II.11] It must be noted that, when all the leaves of the bulb have withered, there remains an open hole in the ground where the leaves and stem of the hyacinth were, and when it rains a certain amount of water will inevitably enter through this and reach the bulb, which has already regathered all its humors back into itself and is maturing; thus there is the obvious danger that it runs the risk of rotting, for in the period when it needs dryness it is being afflicted by excessive humidity. So, to be safe, the attentive gardener should stop up all the aforesaid holes. One can also try to produce a variety of colors, which are obtained by sowing the seeds.

[II.12] Avvertimento si deve sempre raccogliere il seme da un'Giacinto il più di campanelle, quale non habbia moltiplico, et il 2.o et 3.o fusto, che fà, si devono tagliare, lasciando solo il p[rim]o, et quando il fiore sarà passato, si devono tagliare tutte le campanelle, che sono nella sommità, lasciando tre ò quattro le più basse, acciò tutto il vigore vada in esse, & mature, che saranno, si vedranno seccare, et aprire, rimanendo li granelli negri, quali si conservaranno sino à Settembre, con seminarli in vaso di buona terra d'horto, & adacquarli à suo tempo, secondo che n'havranno di bisogno, con esporli al sole in luogo caldo. Perdute, che havranno le frondi, sempre è bene mantenere la terra alquanto humida, perche per esser' cipolle picciole con poco humore, facilmente trovandosi in terra arido patiscono, così agiutate d'un poco d'humidità si (fol. 9v) mantengono meglio; avvertando tanto di questa, come di altra semenza, che tutte siano seminate rade competentemente, perche dovendo star' tre anni senza esser' rimosse è necessario habbino loco da poter' crescere. con aggiungervi ogn'anno alquanto di terra grassa sopra, acciò che quella terra, che resta sfruttata di cipolle si vada rinfrancando, et riceva maggior notrimento.

[II.13] In capo alli tre anni sogliono esser' cresciute quanto una noce, et si cavaranno quando si voranno piantare, avvertendo di non tenerle spiantate fuori della terra, acciò non patischino per il soverchio caldo, che à quel tempo suol essere, per la loro picciolezza si devono mettere sotto terra nel sopradetto modo, sinche si veda la riuscita, la quale sarà in capo alli quattro anni, & quella quantità di campanelle, che all'hora non haverà fatte, non si deve dipoi aspettar' più.

[II.14] Quando si cavano le cipolle si devono metter per spatio di doi giorni in luogo dove si possano asciugare; avvertendo di non porre al sole, perche si suboliscono, mà in luogo dove possino ricever' calda, in modo che restino asciutte. Dopò si devono conservare in luogo fresco (fol. 10r) mà non humido, come nel mattonata d'una stanza, più tosto esposta à Tramontana, che à mezzo giorno.

[III]   De' Narcisi

[III.1] Tutti li Narcisi per lo più vogliono terra magra larga, et casalina (intendendo sempre per magra, non sfruttata), si devono piantare sotto terra cinque dita incirca, et lontano l'una da l'altro un palma, in luogo aperto, & esposto al sole, nel mese di Settembre quando sarà temperato.

[III.2] Devono star' in terra tre anni per il moltiplico, & quando si cavaranno, si cavino à mezzo Luglio, & le cipolle come saranno cavate si governaranno come quelle de Giacinti, & per Narciso intendo, sì il doppio, come il semplice, come anco le Tazzette, li simplici, che fanno seme non mette conto il seminarli, perche poca varietà fanno, et di poca considerazione.

[III.3] (fol. 10v) Sono due sorti di Narcisi più doppi dell'ordinarij, uno detto del Boncori, & uno del Cucù, novamente venuto; quali per la quantità delle frondi, che sì uniscono nel fiore sogliono esser' pieni d'humidità, & per conseque[n]za più facile, si al marcirsi, come al gelarsi; Malamente vengono in luce, essendo offesi dal freddo, di modo che poterli godere è necessario ogn'anno spiantarli alla sua stagione, & non ripiantarli se non alla fine di Gennaio, conservandoli all'asciutto, acciò non germiglino, perche essendo passato il rigore dell'Inverno più facilmente fioriranno à Marzo.

[II.12] Note: One should always collect the seed from the hyacinth with the greatest number of bells but no offsets. One should cut off the second and third stem which it produces, leaving only the first, and, when the flower has faded, one should cut off all the bells at the top, leaving three or four of the lower ones, so that all the plant's strength goes in them. When they are mature, they will be seen to become dry and to open out, leaving little black seeds, which should be kept until September and then sown in a pot of good garden soil, watered at the time when they need it, and exposed to the sun in a warm place. When they have shed their leaves, it is good always to keep the soil somewhat moist, for the bulbs are small and contain only a small amount of natural humors, and so they are easily damaged if the earth they are set in is dry, and hence they can be better preserved with the addition of a little moisture. One should note that, these, as other types of seed, should all be sown fairly sparsely since they have to stay there for three years without being taken up, and so they must have room to grow; also, every year an additional amount of compost should be put over them so that the soil which has been exhausted by bulbs will be reinvigorated and take in more nourishment.

[II.13] By the end of three years they have generally grown to the size of a walnut, and they can be dug up when one wants to plant them. Note that, after taking them up, one should not leave them out of the ground, lest they are damaged by excessive heat, which is common at that time of the year, because they are small; they should be planted in the ground in the way described above until the result can be seen, which will be by the end of four years, and if by then a plant has not produced a certain number of bells, one should give up expecting any more.

[II.14] When they have been dug up, the bulbs should be kept for a period of two days in a place where they can dry out. Note that they should not be exposed to the sun, because they will cook, but put in a place where they can receive enough warmth to dry them out. Afterwards, they should be kept in a place which is cool but not humid, such as on the brick floor of a room which preferably faces North rather than South.

[III]   Of Narcissi. [*Narcissus* L.]

[III.1] All Narcissi generally need sandy and loose plain earth ("thin" should never be taken to mean "exhausted"). They should be planted about five fingers deep and a handsbreadth apart, in an open position exposed to the sun, in the month of September when it is mild.

[III.2] They must be left in the earth for three years for them to multiply and when they are dug up, they should be dug up in mid-July. When they have been dug up, the bulbs should be treated like those of the hyacinth. By Narcissus I mean both the double [*N. tazetta* 'Flore pleno'] and the single, as well as the Tazetta [*N. Tazetta* L.]. The single flowers which produce seed are not worth sowing, for the variations they produce are small and without value.

[III.3] There are two sorts of Narcissus which are more double than the standard ones; one is called the 'Boncori' and the other, which has only recently been introduced, the 'Cucu.' Because of the large number of petals found on the flower these often become full of moisture and as a result are more likely to rot or freeze. They are reluctant to sprout, since they are badly affected by cold, so that, if one wants to enjoy them, one must take them up every year at the appropriate time and not replant them until the end of January, keeping them in a dry place lest they should start to sprout, for once the rigors of winter have passed they will then more readily flower in March.

[III.4] Vogliono l'istessa coltura che gl'ordinarij.

[III.5] Tutte le sorti di Tromboni, Giunchiglie, dell'Arena, del gran Calice unite benche tutte siano specie di Narciso, voglion nondimeno terra migliore, o più vigorosa cioè d'horto (come l'esperienza n'hà insegnato).

[III.6] Devono piantarsi quattro dita sotto terra, mezzo palmo lontano l'uno dall'altro, in luogo largo, et esposto al sole, si piantano, spiantano, & governano nell'istesso modo, che li sopradetti.

[III.7] Le Giunchiglie di Spagna doppie, semplici, riflesse, (fol. 11r) bianche, solfarine, Tromboncini doppi, Narcisi Frasei, Narcisetti gialli doppi, Iuncifoli, fanno meglio in Vaso, che in terra. Amano terra d'horto sotto, e sopra, ma nel letto dove giacciono per d'intorno un grosso dito vogliono terra magra, essendo soggetti facilmente à guastarsi, perche la Giunchiglia per esser cipolla piccola, fà un fusto grosso, & in particolare la doppia, rispetto al suo corpo, per il che rimane la cipolla smunta & molle, atta à ricevere humidità, che ritrovandosi circondata dalla terra magra, benche riceva humidità, la riceve però più purgata, & meno grassa di quella, che riceverrebe dalla p[rim]a. che è più pulposa, & vigorosa, & participando del'una dal'altra, si rimpie, & meglio si conserva, come per esperienza si vede. Si adacqui ogni volta che si vedrà la terra haverne bisogno.

[III.8] Non si devono mai cavare se non per il moltiplico; devono star sotto terra due dita, e tre lontano l'una dal'altra, in luogo larga, & dominato dal sole. Il tempo di piantarle è à Settembre. Avvertendo di non tenerle quando si cavono fuori di terra più di quattro, ò sei giorni, perche per esser' cipolle picciole patiscono dal caldo, fanno seme le semplici, & si devono seminare, facendo meglio le allevate in queste n[ost]re parti.

[III.9] (fol. 11v) La coltura del seminarli è simile al Giacinto, amando un poco più l'humidità.

[III.10] L'Ornitocoli vogliono la coltura de' Narcisi, mà perche l'Ornitocolo Indico è differente; dirò brevemente la natura di esso, ama esser' piantato in vaso, vuole terra d'horto assai vigoroso, si piantano nel modo sopradetto delle Giunchiglie di Spagna, doppie, vuol sole, e luogo aperto, non ama esser' rimosso, mà quando si vuol cavare, si facci subito, che haverà fatto il seme, perche in un medemo tempo perde, et riacquista le radiche, si ripianta nel mese di Settembre, teme il soverchio freddo. Però quando è violente si deve rimettere al coperto, il seme si semina, et custodisce come quelli della Giunchiglia.

[III.11] Il Collo di Camello doppio, Narciso Musarto, di Narbona, Valdenech, Non Ha Pari di tutte le sorti, vogliono terra d'horto competentemente vigorosa, si piantano sotto terra quattro dita mezzo palmo lontano l'una da l'altro, si devono spiantare ogni tre anni, per levare il moltiplico, li semplici difficilmente fanno seme, amano sole et luogo temperato, si cavano, et custodiscono conforme gl'altri Narcisi.

[III.12] Il Narciso detto Jacobeo vuole terra magrissima, deve esser piantato in vaso nel mese di Maggio due dita sotto terra, di-(fol. 12r) feso da Novembre sino à mezzo Maggio dal freddo, et acqua, à mezzo Maggio, si deve scalzare la terra del Vaso con diligenza senza muovere la cipolla, perche mai perde le radici sinche si trova la cipolla, et diligentemente se gli distaccheranno tutti li figliuoli col riempire il Vaso dell'istessa terra, esponendolo al sole, et aria, havendoli dato una buona imbeverato d'acqua, et continuando mantener' la terra fresca facilmente trà un mese fiorisce, & mai si deve cavare, fatto che haverà il fiore se li manterrà la terra fresca, lasciandolo stare al sole sino al soprad[ett]o tempo.

[III.4] They need to be grown in the same way as the standard types.

[III.5] All sorts of Trumpets [*N. pseudonarcissus* L.], Jonquils [*N. jonquilla* L.?], and the dell' Arena large cupped-types, although they are all species of Narcissus, nevertheless, need better or richer soil, that is, garden soil (as experience has taught us).

[III.6] They should be planted four fingers deep and half a handsbreadth apart, in a spacious position exposed to the sun. They are planted, taken up, and looked after in the same way as the above.

[III.7] Spanish Jonquils [*N. x incomparibilis* L.], double, single, reflex, white and sulphur-yellow, small double daffodils, *Narcissi Fraseo,* small double yellow narcissi, and juncifolia [*N. juncifolius* Lag.] do better in pots than in the ground. They like garden soil beneath them and over them, but all around them in the bed where they lie they need a thumb's depth of sandy soil, for they are very prone to decay. This is because the jonquil has a small bulb but—and this applies particularly to the double variety—produces a thick stem in proportion to its size, so that the bulb is left drained and soft and ready to take in moisture. However, if it is surrounded by this soil, although it takes in moisture, it takes in a purer and less rich moisture than the fattier and stronger sort which it would take in from the former type of soil. By filling up with measures of both, it is more easily preserved, as experience has shown. It should be watered every time the soil is seen to need it.

[III.8] They should never be dug up except for propagation. They should lie two fingers deep and three apart, in a spacious position with strong sunlight. The time to plant them is in September. Note that when they are dug up they should not be kept out of the earth for more than four or six days, because the bulbs, being small, are damaged by heat. The single varieties produce seed and should be sown, as those bred in our part of the world do better.

[III.9] The way to grow them from seed is similar to that for the hyacinth, but they like a little more moisture.

[III.10] The Ornithogalum [*Ornithogalum* L.] needs to be grown in the same way as the Narcissus, but since the Indian Ornithogalum is different, I shall deal briefly with its nature. It likes to be planted in a pot and needs fairly rich loam. They should be planted in the way described above for the double Spanish Jonquils. It needs sun and an open position. It does not like to be taken up, but when one wants to dig it up, one should do so immediately it has produced its seed, because its rootstock dies and regrows at the same time. It is replanted in the month of September. It is afraid of excessive cold, and so when this is severe, it should be brought inside. The seed is sown and looked after as are those of the Jonquil.

[III.11] The 'camel-neck' [*N. pseudonarcissus* L. 'collo di camello'], double *Narcissus Musarto,* [narcissi] of Narbonne, Valdenech, and all types of "non ha pari" need sufficiently rich garden soil. They are planted four fingers deep and half a handsbreadth apart. They should be taken up every three years for the propagation stock to be removed. The single flowers do not readily produce seed. They like sun and a temperate position. They are dug up and taken care of in the same way as the other Narcissi.

[III.12] The Narcissus known as 'Jacobean' [*Amaryllis formosissima,* now *Sprokelia formossima* (L.) Herb.] needs very lean soil. It should be planted in a pot in the month of May, two fingers deep, and protected from November to mid-May from cold and rain. In mid-May one should scoop away the soil in the pot carefully without moving the bulb, for the roots last as long as the bulb does, and the offsets should be carefully detached. The pot should then be filled again with the same soil and exposed to sun and air after being given a good watering. If the soil is kept constantly cool, the

[III.13] Il Narciso detto dell' Isole Virginie ama il Vaso, vuol terra d'horto, sole mediocremente, deve stare sotto terra due dita, nè deve esser rimosso solo quando si cava il molti-plico, si pianta, et si spianta d'Autumno.

[III.14] Sono alcuni Narcisi d'India, quali con diverse esperie[n]ze (per non esser' à noi nota la qualità del clima donde son venuti) hò provato in più modi di farli fiorire. Sogliono questi Narcisi prima, che si addomestichino à questa n[ost]re terre consumarsi à poco à poco, & alcuni per lo più muoiono doppò consumati sin' all'anima (fol. 12v) cominciano à poco à poco à rivestirsi di nuove toniche, et assuegarsi à queste nostre terre, le quali devono esser' più tosto arenose, che altrimenti, & così ritornano nel primiero stato, & all'hora si può sperare, che facilmente fiorischino.

[III.15] Il Lilio Narciso Indico, detto Belladonna, vuole terra mediocre larga alquanto arenosa, luogo aperto, & dominato dal sole, non vuol essere mutato se non per moltiplico, non vuol stare più di tre dita sotto terra, perche mettendosi più sotto slonga il collo, & tutta la virtù, che dovrebbe unirsi nel corpo del cipolla, si dilata nel collo, & viene à perdere il vigore, et stenta poi à fiorire, non perde mai radiche. Quando si trapianta, si deve trapiantare nel fine di Luglio, quì non fà seme.

[III.16] Il Narciso scaglioso detto Bifolio, & d'altri Suersio vuol terra magra arenosa, & deve piantarsi tre dita sotto, in luogo largo, et che habbi sole, essendo nemicissimo del-l'humidità, per esser la cipolla vestita di grosse, et humide scaglie pericolose di mar-cirsi, & perciò si deve ponere in Vaso per difenderlo più facilm[en]te (fol. 13r) dall'acqua. Mai si deve cavare, come anco tutti gl'altri Narcisi d'India, perche patis-cono grandemente nel rimuoverli. Perse, che haverà le frondi, che sarà di Maggio, ò poco prima, si deve difendere dall'acqua, lasciando esposto il Vaso al calore del sole per tutta l'estate, & al principio di Settembre se gli deve dare una buona inaffi-ata, acciò si risenta, et in questa maniera io l'hò fatto fiorire ogn'anno alla sua sta-gione d'Autumno. Si potrebbe per avventura trovare altro modo migliore di questo, fà seme, mà non sò se varij, perche ancora non s'è fatta l'esperienza, si moltiplica ancora, distaccando dalla madre le scaglie, & ponendole in terra.

[III.17] Sonovi alcune altre sorti di Narcisi d'India, quali hanno abbracciato l'istessa coltura, mà non sono ancor fioriti, ò che ciò avvenga, perche la cipolla non sia arrivata alla sua perfettione di grossezza, che richiede, acciò fiorischino, ò perche ancora non si sijno ben rihavuti [word?].

[III.18] Le Fritellarie vogliono luogo ombroso, terra leggiera, et grassa, et la terra fatta di frondi d'arbori (potendosi havere) saria migliore, vogliono esser piantate (fol. 13v) sotto terra tre dita, distanti l'una dall'altra altretanto, amano il vaso per poterle meglio governare, non vogliono esser rimosse, perche patiscono, sì per la piccolezza, come anco per esser quasi ignude, fanno seme, mà non variano, quando si trapiantano si devono trapiantare subito spiantate, acciò non patischino, il che si farà nel principio di Settembre.

plant will readily flower within a month and should never be dug up; once it has flowered, the soil should be kept cool, and it should be left in the sun until the aforesaid time.

[III.13] The *Narcissus* known as "Virginia Islands" [identified by Masson as *Zephyranthis atamasco* L.] likes to be in a pot. It needs loam and average sunlight. It should be two fingers deep and should not be taken up except when the offsets are removed. It is planted and dug up in autumn.

[III.14] There are some Indian Narcissi which I have tried to make flower in several ways with different experiments (since we do not know the sort of climate they come from). Before they adapt to our types of soil, these Narcissi tend to waste away gradually, and generally some die. After wasting away to their very core, they begin gradually to grow new layers of scales to cover them, and to become accustomed to our soil, which should be more sandy than otherwise; so that they return to their original state, and then one may hope they will readily flower.

[III.15] The Indian Narcissus Lily known as 'Belladonna' [*Amaryllis belladonna* L.] needs moderately loose and somewhat sandy soil and an open position with strong sunlight. It should not be moved except for propagation. It should not be more than three fingers deep in the earth, because if it is deeper it grows a longer neck, and all the power which should be concentrated in the body of the bulb is dispersed throughout the neck; so it begins to lose its strength and then has difficulty in flowering. Its rootstock is permanent. When it is replanted, it should be replanted at the end of July. Here, it does not produce seed.

[III.16] The scaly Narcissus, known as 'bifoliate' and by others as 'Suersio' [="Sweerts," identified by Masson as *Haemanthus coccineus* L.] needs lean, sandy soil and should be planted three fingers deep, in a spacious position where it can receive sunlight, for it is very hostile to humidity, as the bulb is covered with large, moist scales which are very prone to the danger of rotting; it should therefore be put in a pot for easier protection from the rain. Like all the other Indian Narcissi, it should never be dug up, for they suffer much damage when they are taken up. When it has shed its leaves, which will be in May or a little earlier, it should be protected from the rain and the pot left exposed to the warmth of the sun for the whole summer. At the beginning of September it should be given a good watering to revive it. In this way I have made it flower every year at its proper time in autumn. It might be possible to find another, better method than this. It produces seed, but I do not know if it produces variants, since I have no experience of this as yet. One can also propagate it by detaching the scales from the mother-bulb and putting them in soil.

[III.17] There are some other sorts of Indian Narcissus [Masson, *Cybistebes longifolium* (L.) Milne-Redh., and others] which have taken to the same growing method, but they have not yet flowered, either because the bulb has not reached the full size which is needed for it to produce flowers, or because it has not yet fully recovered its health.

[III.18] Fritillaries [*Fritillaria* L., *F. meleagris* L.?] need a shady position and composted, friable soil, and, if it can be obtained, compost made of tree leaves would be best. They need to be planted three fingers deep and the same distance apart. They like to be in pots, where they can be cared for better. They should not be taken up because this damages them, both because they are small and because they are almost naked. They produce seed but not new varieties. When they are replanted, they should be replanted immediately after they have been dug up, lest they should suffer damage, and this should be done at the beginning of September.

[III.19] La Iucca vuole terreno d'horto vigoroso, luogo mediocrem[en]te assolato, si moltiplica per occhi, perche sotto terra genera alcuni occhi come quelli della canna, quali alla primavera, staccandosi dalla madre si piantano in vasi, perche crescono più presto, et si custodiscono meglio, & cresciuti si possono mettere in terra con tutta la terra attaccata, vogliono per crescere presto acqua, et sole l'estate, la madre non si deve mai muovere, nè meno li figli doppo, che saranno posti in terra, mettendovi però ogn'anno due, ò tre dita di terra grassa attorno alla pianta per reficiarla. Quando si piantano gl'occhi devono ponersi sotto terra tanto, che la sommità dell'occhio sia una costa di cortello sotto, perche più facilm[en]te germoglia, non fà seme, nè teme il freddo.

[III.20] Li Martagoni vogliono terra d'horto molto piena, luogo (fol. 14r) non molto dominato dal sole, amando il freddo, & perciò non fanno bene in questa n[ost]re parti, si piantano sotto un palmo, et altretanto distanti l'uno dal'altro. Non si devono mai muovere se non per il moltiplico. Il caldo dell'Estate gli fà gran danno; onde si deve mettere sopra la terra dove è piantato qualche cosa, che li difenda, & mantenghi la terra fresca. Il tempo del trapiantarli è poco dopo, che hanno fatto il fiore, perche all'hora hanno perse le radiche. Si moltiplicano ancora per quelle sue scagliette, distaccandole dalla madre, fanno seme, mà non varia.

[III.21] La Corona Imperiale vuole terra d'horto, luogo largo, & esposto al sole, sotto terra cinque dita, un palmo lontano l'uno dal'altra. Non si deve muovere se non per moltiplico, perche patisce, essendo la cipolla mal vestita. Si spianta, e trapianta di Settembre, fà seme, mà non varia.

[III.22] Le Peonie vogliono terra d'horto, luogo mediocremente assolato, si devono piantare sotto terra tre dita, non si rimuovono se non ogni tre anni, partendole per il moltiplico, il che si farà alla fine di Febraro, & non prima, perche non facendo prima radiche nuove vanno à pericolo di gelarsi gl'occhi. Acciò si dipartiscono più facilmente per non (fol. 14v) tagliare le loro salsiccie, che sono intrecciate insieme con la terra, che stà trà di esse, si devono mettere nell'acqua & lavarla ben bene, affinche levatali quella terra, più facilmente si possino separare alle dette salsiccie, che sono intrecci-ate trà di loro, scorgendosi meglio il luogo dove si debba tagliare, qual taglio si farà con coltello, lasciando tre, ò quattro occhi per pianta con le sue salsiccie, che si saranno più, ò meno secondo si vorrà la pianta maggiore.

[III.23] Nel piantarle poi non si devono mettere giù le salsiccie, come si trovano perche trovandosi l'una con l'altra, non solo ciascuna d'esse participa della sostanza della terra, mà conglobate insieme corrono rischio di marcirsi. Però si deve fare aggiustatamente un monticello di terra à proposito, acciò che venghino à star' gl'occhi, ricoperta, che sarà la pianta tre dita sotto. Doppò si pigli la pianta, & si vadino allargando quelle salsiccie, con ricoprire intorno intorno il monte, così ciascuna di esse hà luogo di crescere, & ricever' particolare notrimento senza pericolo di marcirsi. Ricoperta si adacqui, acciò che la terra si unischi con la pianta, non fà seme la doppia, le semplice fà seme mà non muta.

[III.19] The Yucca [*Yucca gloriosa* L.] needs strong garden soil [*terreno d'horto vigoroso,* heavy] and a moderately sunny position. It is propagated by eyes, for underground it produces eyes like those of the cane-plant [*Arundo donax* L.], and these should be detached from the mother in spring and planted in pots so that they will grow more quickly and be better looked after. When grown, they can be put in the ground with all the soil attached to them. For quick growth they need water and sun in summer. The mother-bulb should never be moved; nor should the offspring after they have been planted in the ground; but every year two or three fingers of compost should be laid around the plant for nourishment. When they are planted, the eyes should be placed at such a depth that the top of each eye is the thickness of the back of a knife below the surface, so that it sprouts more readily. It does not produce seed, nor does it fear the cold.

[III.20] Martagones [*Lilium martagon* L.] need very full garden soil and a position where the sun is not too strong, for they like the cold, and so they do not do well in our part of the world. They are planted a handsbreadth deep and the same distance apart. They should never be taken up except for propagation. The heat of summer does them great damage, and so over the ground where they are planted one should put something to protect them, and one should keep the soil cool. The time to replant them is shortly after they have flowered, because then they have lost their rootstock. They can also be propagated by means of their little scales, by detaching them from the mother. They produce seed, but do not vary.

[III.21] The Crown Imperial [*Fritillaria imperialis* L.] needs garden soil and an open position exposed to the sun, being planted five fingers deep and a handsbreadth apart. It should not be moved except for propagation, for the bulb is not well-covered and thus gets damaged. It is taken up and replanted in September. It produces seed, but does not vary.

[III.22] Peonies [*Paeonia* spp.] need garden soil and a moderately sunny position. They should be planted three fingers deep. They should not be taken up except every three years, when they are divided for propagation, which should be done at the end of February and no earlier, since they do not produce new rootstock until then, and so the eyes do not run the risk of being damaged by frost. So that they can be divided more easily without cutting through their roots [*salsicie,* also tubers], which are mixed up together with the soil which is between them, they should be put in water and washed thoroughly; thus, with the soil removed, these roots, which are mixed up together, can more easily be separated, and one can better distinguish the place where it should be cut. The cut should be made with a knife, leaving three or four eyes per plant together with the thick roots, a greater or lesser number according to the size one wants the plant to be.

[III.23] When planting them, one should not put the tubers in just as one finds them, because, when they are very close together, not only does each one have to share the same nourishment from the soil, but also, when bunched together, they run the risk of rotting. One should therefore make a little mound of earth for this purpose, so designed that, when the plant is covered over, the eyes will be three fingers deep. Then one should take the plant and proceed to spread out the roots over and all round the mound; in this way, each of them has room to grow and receive its own nourishment without the danger of rotting. When covered over, the plant should be watered so that the soil is mixed in with it. The double flower does not produce seed; the single produces seed, but does not vary.

[III.24] (fol. 15r) L'Iride prima del Clusio, et l'Iride detta di Persia vogliono terra d'horto, si piantano tre dita sotto terra, avvertendo quando si piantano slargare bene quelle sue radiche essendo differenti dall'altre per esser' di grossezza un dito picciolo, et mai si seccano. Ricevano notabil danna qua[n]do se gli distaccano. Amano sole, & luogo aperto, piantandosi un palmo lontane l'una dal'altra. Non si devono muovere se non per il moltiplico, & questo deve farsi nel mese di Settembre, tanto nel piantarle, quanto nel spiantarle, perche patiscono le loro salsiccie, fanno seme mà non varia.

[III.25] L'Iride Bulbose vogliono terra d'horto, piantandole sotto terra tre dita in luogo mediocremente dominato dal sole, quattro dita lontane l'una dal'altra, ogni tre anni si devono cavare, fanno seme, mà non varia, & quando si cavano si possano cavare nella fine di Luglio, & ripiantarle di Settembre, con conservarle come li Giacinti.

[III.26] Il Ranunculo bianco doppio ama il Vaso, vuole terra d'horto, si pianti due dita sotto in luogo mediocrem[en]te assolato, non deve rimuoversi se non per il moltiplico, & si deve rimuovere alla fine di Febraro, accomo-(fol. 15v)dando le sue radiche quando si pianta nel modo detto di sopra, come la Peonia, sfiorito, che sarà vuole il fresco; non fà seme.

[III.27] Tutti li Ranuncoli doppi si piantano di Settembre tre di avanti il Plenilunio, vogliono terra grassa, mà la migliore si stima quella, che si fà di stabbio humano benissimo macerato, luogo assolato, & acqua, fanno meglio in Vaso, che in terra, si piantano due dita sotto terra. Quando saranno fioriti, si deve mettere il Vaso all'ombra per godere i fiori, acciò che il Sole non li disfaccia subito, secchi che saranno i fusti si devono cavare, perche la terra li consuma, & riporli come sopra, non fanno seme.

[III.28] Avvertimento, che prima di piantarli, si debbano porre nell'acqua per 24. hore, acciò si gonfino un poco, perche più presto nascono; devono esser' messi lontano l'uno dal'altro tre dita, perche moltiplicano assaissimo.

[III.29] Tutte le sorti di Ranuncoli semplici vogliono luogo mediocremente assolato, terra d'horto, piantati sotto terra tre dita, fanno seme, si seminano come l'Anemone, & fanno varietà di colore, mà non riescono doppi, si ca- (fol. 16r) vano, & si piantano ogn'anno riservandosi nel modo sopradetto.

[III.30] Li Ranuncoli di Tubero vogliono sole mediocremente piantati quattro dita sotto, lontano l'uno dal'altro mezo palmo, con terreno d'horto, & amano star' in terra senza cavarsi se non per moltiplico, quali si cavano alla fine d'Agosto, & subito si ripiantano, non fanno seme.

[III.31] Li Ranuncoli, ò foglia di Ruta si piantano sotto terra due dita in Vaso d'horto vigorosa, luogo solivo, tre dita lontano l'uno dal'altro. Quando hanno secche le frondi non si cavino, perche patiscono per esser ignudi, mà si mettino in luogo fresco, difeso dal sole. Al mese di Settembre si spiantino, & si ripiantino, avvertendo, che non piova sopra il Vaso nel mese d'Agosto, perche risentendosi fanno radiche nuove, talche meglio assicurarsi, sarà bene quando havranno perse le frondi cavarli, & repiantarli, con metterli in luogo fresco, perche piovendo si trovino piantati, non fanno seme.

[III.32] Vi è un'altra sorte di Ranuncolo giallo de[tto] di (fol. 16v) Sanesio, che il volgo lo chiama Peonina gialla doppia, per far' le radiche differenti dalli altri, deve esser' piantato in terra d'horto buona con slargar à guisa di Peonia le sue radiche attorno la terra, si pianta un dito sotto, affinche l'occhio si veda apparire sopra la terra, non si deve mai si spiantare se non per moltiplico, & si spianta, & ripianta nella primavera. Vuole acqua, sole temperato. Ama il Vaso, & la terra, tanto d'Estate, quanto d'Inverno, vuol stare fresca, fà seme, mà non varia.

[III.24] Clusius' first iris [Iris spp., *I. latifolia* Clusius] and the Iris called 'Persian' [*Iris persica* L.] need garden soil. They are planted three fingers deep, and one should be careful, when planting them, to space out the tubers well, for they differ from the others by being only the size of a little finger. They never wither. They suffer considerable damage when they are divided. They like sun and an open position and should be planted at a distance of a handsbreadth from each other. They should not be moved except for propagation, and this—both the digging up and the planting—should be done in September, as the tubers are easily damaged. They produce seed, but no new varieties.

[III.25] Bulbous Irises [*Xiphium* (Mill.) spach] need garden soil and should be planted three fingers deep, in a position with moderately strong sunlight, four fingers apart from each other. Every three years they should be dug up. They produce seed, but no varieties. When they are taken up, they may be dug up at the end of July and replanted in September, being kept in the same way as Hyacinths.

[III.26] The double white Ranunculus [*R. asiaticus* L.] likes to be in a pot. It needs garden soil and should be planted two fingers deep in a moderately sunny position. It should not be taken up except for propagation, and this should be done at the end of February. When it is planted, its tuber should be planted in the way described above for the Peony. When its flowers have died, it needs coolness. It does not produce seed.

[III.27] All double Ranunculi are planted in September three days before the full moon. They need compost, though the best is considered to be that made of human dung, thoroughly steeped, and a sunny position and water. They do better in a pot than in the ground. They are planted two fingers deep. When they have flowered, one should put the pot in the shade if one wants to enjoy the flowers, for otherwise the sun will destroy them immediately. When the stems have withered, they should be dug up, as the soil rots them, and then replace as above. They do not produce seed.

[III.28] Note that before they are planted they should be placed in water for twenty-four hours so that they swell a little, for they then start to grow more quickly. They should be set three fingers apart because they reproduce very abundantly.

[III.29] All sorts of single Ranunculi need a moderately sunny position and garden soil, and should be planted three fingers deep. They produce seed and are sown as Anemones are. They produce color variants but not double flowers. They are lifted and planted every year and kept in the aforesaid manner.

[III.30] Tuberous-rooted Ranunculus need moderate sun and are planted four fingers deep and half a handsbreadth apart, in garden soil, and they like to be in the ground and not to be lifted except for propagation. They are dug at the end of August and replanted immediately. They do not produce seed.

[III.31] The Ranunculus known as 'Rue-Leaf' [*Callianthemum rutifolium* (L.) C. A. Mey] are planted two fingers deep in a pot with strong garden soil, in a sunny position, three fingers apart. When their leaves have withered, they should not be dug up, as they are naked and can be damaged, but they should be put in a cool place, sheltered from the sun. In the month of September they should be dug up and replanted. Note that one should not let it rain on the pot in the month of August, because as they revive they produce new roots, and so for safety's sake it is good to dig them up when they have shed their leaves and replant them, putting them in a cool place, so that if it should rain they will already have been planted. They do not produce seed.

[III.32] There is another sort of yellow Ranunculus, called Sanesio's, which the common folk call the little double yellow Peony. Because it produces a different rootstock from the others, it should be planted in good garden soil and its roots spread out around the soil like those of the Peony. It is planted one finger deep so that the eye can just be

[III.33] Li Ciclamini amano il Vaso, mà spatioso, perche fanno più fiori, & si conservano meglio, vogliono terra leggiera, mà non sfruttata, patono l'Inverno dal freddo, cio è li fiori, & le frondi. Vogliono luogo mediocremente assolato li Autumnali, mà quelli di prima-vera luogo solivo assai, perche comincian à fiorire d'Inverno. Non si devono mu-tare, se non si vede il Vaso quando fiorisce esser' pieno di frondi, che la persona giudichi, che la terra non li possa dar' più notrimento, quando si mutano se li deve lasciar stare attaccata tutta la terra, che stà involta alla capigliara delle radiche, (fol. 17r) altrimente levandola resta una massa di capigliara, che per qualsivoglia dilig-enza nel ripiantarli non si può spandere per la terra, mà restando in massa si mar-cino, con manifesto pericolo di far marcire anco il pane. La terra magra, che resta involta nella capigliara và repigliando il sugo, et humore di quell'altra terra grassa, che se li pone intorno. Secondariamente è cosa più sicura il non levar' la sopradetta terra, perche levandola, oltre il pericolo sopradetto di marcirsi il pane, che di sua natura è humidissimo, restando involto nella terra nuova, ch'è più della prima più facilmente marcisce.

[III.34] Si moltiplicano in doi modi. Il p[rim]o è, che quando havranno perse le frondi, e l'humore si sarà reconcentrato nel suo pane, si cavarà con diligenza il detto pane, con tagliarlo politamente per il mezzo. Avvertendo lasciare per chiascheduna parte li suoi occhi, doppò si metteranno con il taglio aperto in luogo asciutto, per tanto spatio di tempo, che asciuttandosi il taglio facci una crostola per tutta la superficie di esso, quale si coprirà con cera termentinata, che p[rim]a non si sarebbe attaccata per l'humidità; poi si porrà in vaso con la sop[radet]ta terra; avvertendo, che il taglio sia posto per sguincio più tosto verso il centro del vaso, (fol. 17v) che altrimenti, acciò l'acqua non se li fermi sopra, et l'offenda, come ancora intorno al taglio mettervi terra magra per renderlo più sicuro del marcirsi.

[III.35] Il 2.o modo è segnarli. Mà il seme non si deve raccorre p[rim]a, che non siano perse tutte le frondi del Vaso, & il bocciolo, che resta sia crepato; quale aperto, che sarà, si potrà cogliere, et serbarlo per seminare. Se i Ciclamine sarà Autumnale, si sementerà nel principio di Settembre; se sarà di primavera, si sementerà di Febraro. Deve esser' seminato in terra grassa, & purgata due dita sotto terra. Vuol sole, et acqua, non si deve rimuovere prima di tre anni, varia di colore di bianco in rosso, mà di rosso in bianco rare volte, intendendo, tanto di questo, quanto di qualsivoglia altro seme, debbano sementarsi in Vasi per custodirli meglio.

[III.36] Avvertimento, che quando saranno piantati li Ciclamini spartiti, non se li deve dar'subito l'acqua, mà in capo a quattro giorni, acciò che non così presto si riempino d'humid-ità, perche essendo il taglio fatto di fresco la subita humidità potrebbe nuocerli.

[IV] (fol. 18r)   Delli Tulipani

[IV.1] Tutti li Tulipani vogliono luogo aprico, e largo assolato, non appresso se altra compagnia di fiori, vuol terreno d'horto, leggiero, e vigoroso, mà dove si pone la corona del Tulipane deve esser' terreno magro per esser cipolla molto gentile, & deve ricoprirsi quasi tutta la cipolla con l'istesso magro, ricoprendola poi dalla sop[radet]ta terra per tre dita ò poco più, lontano l'uno dal'altro cinque dita, & questo si fà, acciò in un subito non s'imbeva di quel sugo men purgato, & corra rischio facilmente di patire.

seen above the ground. It should never be dug up except for propagation and is taken up and replanted in the spring. It needs water and moderate sun. It likes to be in a pot and both in summer and in winter that soil needs to be kept cool. It produces seed, but does not vary.

[III.33] Cyclamens [*Cyclamen* spp.] like to be in a pot, but a spacious one, because they produce many flowers and can be preserved better. They need soil which is light but not exhausted. In the winter, they can be damaged, both the flowers and leaves, by the cold. The autumn variety [*C. hederfolium* AIT.] need a moderately sunny position, but the spring variety [*C. persicum*] a very sunny position, because they start to flower in winter. They should not be moved except when one sees that, when they are in flower, the pot is so full of leaves that one judges the soil no longer capable of giving them nourishment. When they are moved, one should leave attached to them all the soil which is wrapped round the capillaries [*capigliari*] of the rootstock; otherwise, if it is removed, there remains a bunch of capillaries which, however carefully they are replanted, cannot be spread around the soil but remain in a bunch and so rot, with the obvious risk they will make the clod of soil moldy too. The exhausted soil which remains wrapped up in the capillaries takes in the nutrients and moisture of the compost which is put around them. Secondly, it is safer not to remove the aforesaid soil, because if it is removed, in addition to the aforementioned danger of rotting, the clod, which is naturally very moist, is surrounded by the new soil which is moister than the original, and so rots more easily.

[III.34] They are propagated in two ways. The first is when they have shed their leaves and the humors are concentrated again in the clump, which should be carefully dug up and cut cleanly in half. Note that eyes should be left on each side. Then, with the cut still exposed, they should be put in a dry place for enough time for the cut to dry and a thin crust to form over its entire surface; this should be covered with wax mixed with turpentine, which would not have adhered earlier because of the moisture; then it should be put in a pot with the type of soil described above. Note that the cut should be made obliquely, more towards the center of the pot than away from it, to prevent the water settling over it and damaging it; similarly, sandy soil should be placed around the cut to make it safer from rotting.

[III.35] The second way is to sow them. However, the seed should not be collected until all the leaves in the pot have been shed and the remaining bud has split; when this latter has opened up, the seed can be collected and kept for sowing. If it is an autumn cyclamen, it should be sown at the beginning of September; if a spring variety, it should be sown in February. It should be sown in rich, purged [*purgata*, cleansed] soil, two fingers deep. It needs sun and water. It should not be taken up for three years. Its colors vary from white to red, but rarely from red to white. One should take it as read that the seeds, like all other types, should be sown in pots for better conservation.

[III.36] Note that when divided cyclamens have been planted, they should not be watered immediately, but after four days, lest they should fill up with moisture too quickly, for the cut is still fresh and so sudden humidity could harm them.

[IV]   Of Tulips. [*Tulipa* spp.]

[IV.1] All Tulips need a warm, open, and sunny position; they do not like the company of other flowers near them. They need friable, rich garden soil, but where the crown of the tulip is placed there should be sandy soil, for it is a very tender bulb; the bulb should be covered almost entirely with the same sandy soil, and then covered over with the first-mentioned type of soil to a depth of three fingers or a little more; they should

[IV.2] Si piantano il mese di Settembre, temperato, che sarà, & si cavano subito perse le frondi per conservarli meglio del tempo d'Estate, subito cavati non si devono nettare dalla sua terra, nè polire delle sue scorze, solo ponerli in luogo aperto, che si asciughino per quattro giorni. Asciutti, che saranno, si devono involgere in carta, et metterli in luogo fresco, mà non humido. Quando sarà tempo di piantarli, all'hora si potranno nettare dalla terra, con levarli quella scorza secca, che non stà attac-(fol. 18v)cata alla cipolla, che si trovaranno li figli fresci, come si fossero all'hora stati cavati dalla terra, perche non si sarebbono mantenuti nel tempo del caldo se si fossero politi, sì dalla terra, come dalle sue scorze, & facilm[en]te si sarebbono incalcinati.

[IV.3] Si deve scieghiere il seme da quelle, che havranno bellissimo fondo, come Il bianco lattato, che habbi il fondo negro, che questo si giudica per il meglio.

[IV.4] Avvertinento, che quando si haverà un Tulipane bello pennacchiato, che la persona desideri conservarlo, non li facci far' seme, mà coglia il fiore, perche facendo il seme si smonge di maniera tale, che alle volte non solo si riduce in picciolissima forma, mà il più volte si perde.

[IV.5] Le semi delli Tulipani si raccogliono quando si vede cominciar' à crepare la bocciola, quale si ripone, & alle prime acque di Settembre si semina in Vaso, con mettervi terra d'horto vigorosa mezzo dito sotto, coltivandoli come li altri semi. Non si devono cavare se non il 2.o anno, sciegliendo li grossi dalli piccioli, & li grossi si possono piantare, ò in terra, ò in vaso, come più parerà, mà meglio staria in vaso sin'à tanto, che possino pro-(fol. 19r)durre fiori, che sarà il 4.o et quinto anno.

[IV.6] Avvertimento, che si vedrà à canto la corona del Tulipane alcun figlioletto picciolo, non si deve scoprire di quella scorza secca, perche verria à esser' offeso dalla terra, mà lasciarlo stare, & questa diligenza si può usare alli Tulipani di qualche consideratione, quali si devono cavare ogni anno, benche tutti vogliono l'istesso coltura, et diligenza.

[IV.7] Sogliono alcuni Tulipani mandar' fuori per mezzo la corona una radica più grossetta dell'altre, quale andando all'ingiù per quattro ò cinque dita lontano dalla madre ingrossa la sommità di essa, & genera un'altro Tulipane co'l lasciare voto il guscio della madre, & perciò nel cavarlo si deve andar' avvertito, quando si trova il guscio voto sotto di esso, si troverà il Tulipane, quale ancora stà attaccato con un filo al guscio della madre, mà questa sorte per lo più non suole esser' nel numero de buoni, la diligenza, che molti usano pare sia troppo esatta, con fabricare sotto la cassetta mattonato, acciò non si sperdino, perche non la possono fabricare tanto sopra, che non la fabrichino almeno un buon palmo, e più basso dove si pone la cipolla, acciò vi sia tanto terra, che basti per il notrimento di essa, & la cipolla, che si distacca mai si slontana per lun-(fol. 19v)ghezza di mezzo palmo. Talche pare poco giovevole anzi contro l'opinione di molti dico, [Word?] non doversi in modo veruno usare, perche piovendo l'aperture de mattoni si riempono di terra, et à guisa d'astrico si tura. Si che l'acqua non havendo dove scolare, senza dubbio alcuno ritrovandosi la cipolla oppressa da quello marcisce, tanto più, che li Tulipani di consideratione (io sono di questa opinione) non vanno sotto terra.

[IV.8] Per le pioggie, che sogliono venir' nell' Estate non si devono lasciare in terra, perche ritrovandosi poco coperti dalla terra, facilmente con il soverchio caldo, & humido causato dalle pioggie si subolliscono, et muoiono.

be five fingers apart. This is done to prevent them suddenly taking in the less pure juices and so running a severe risk of being damaged.

[IV.2] They are planted in the month of September when it is mild, and they are dug up as soon as they have shed their leaves so that they can be better preserved during the summer. They should not be cleaned of their soil nor stripped of their husks as soon as they have been dug up, but put in an open position to dry for four days. When they are dry, they should be wrapped in paper and put in a place which is cool but not damp. When it is time to plant them, they can be cleaned of their soil, and the dry husk which is not attached to the bulb can be taken away. One will find the bulblets as fresh as if they had just been dug up out of the ground, whereas, if they had been cleaned of the soil and husks, they would not have been preserved during the hot weather and might easily have been reduced to powder.

[IV.3] One should select the seed from those which have the most attractive base color, such as the milk-white variety which has a black base, for this is judged best.

[IV.4] Note that, when one has a fine flamed tulip which one wants to preserve, one should not allow it to produce seed but pick the flower because, if it produces seed, it is drained to such an extent that not only is it often reduced to a very small size but most often it dies.

[IV.5] The seeds of Tulips are collected when one sees the bud beginning to split. They should be put aside and at the first September rains sown in a pot, covered with half a finger's depth of rich garden soil, and grown in the same way as other seeds. They should not be dug up until the second year, when the large bulbs can be separated from the small ones, and the large ones planted either in the ground or in a pot, whichever seems best; however, it is better for them to remain in pots until they have been able to produce flowers, which will be between the fourth and the fifth year.

[IV.6] Note that, if one should see a little bulblet next to the crown of the tulip bulb, one should not strip it of its dry husk because it would be damaged by the soil, but one should leave it alone. The same care should be taken with tulips that are particularly prized, which should be dug up every year, although all Tulips need to be grown and carefully tended in the same way.

[IV.7] Some tulips send out from the middle of their tufts of leaves a root somewhat thicker than the others, and this travels down to a distance of four or five fingers from the mother-bulb. Its tip swells, and it produces another tulip, leaving the shell of the mother empty. When digging it up, therefore, one should note that, if one finds the shell empty, one will find the tulip below it, still attached by a thread to the shell of the mother. This variety, however, is not generally considered among the best. Some people take particular care in a way which seems exaggerated: they construct a brick case below so the new bulb is not lost. But they cannot make the case less than a good handsbreadth in height, or deeper where the bulb is planted so that there is enough soil to nourish it, whereas the bulb which detaches itself never travels further (from the mother) than half a handsbreadth. This method seems, therefore, to be of little use, and indeed in contrast to the opinion of many, I say that it should in no way be employed, because when it rains the holes in the bricks fill with soil and become blocked up like oysters. Thus the water has nowhere to drain away and will without doubt find the bulb and settle on it, causing it to rot. Moreover, in any case tulips which are particularly prized do not move around underground (I am of this opinion).

[IV.8] Because of the rains which often fall in summer, they should not be left in the ground, for they are not very well covered with soil and so the excessive heat and the humidity caused by the rains can easily cook them, and they die.

[IV.9] In quanto alli altri Tulipani detti Coloretti si possono lasciare in terra per doi anni, & non più, con ponervi sopra quando haveranno perdute le frondi quattro dita di terra, per difenderli dalli sop[radet]ti pericoli nel tempo dell'Estate, perche nel p[rim]o anno fanni il moltiplico, il 2.o l'ingrossano, & all'hora si possono cavare, ma nel 3.o tutti li figli, che per natura sua stanno involti, et attaccati alla madre, volendo far' nuova progenie, non hà tanto vigore, & così s'impic[c]oliscono, anzi marciscono, ricevendo gran humidità dalla quantità de gusci, da' quali sono vestiti insieme, & l'esperienza di non fare i fiori ce lo dimostra.

[IV.10] (fol. 20r) Il Tulipane di Persia per esser' di natura sua più esposto à resistere desidera terra più vigoroso, piantisi sotto terra due dita, non si deve seminare, perche non varia com'anco si trattiene assai immoltiplicare p[rim]a che faccia fiori.

[V] (fol. 20v)   Delli Garofoli

[V.1] Della natura di essi ne discorrerò brevemente, per esser pianta assai conosciuta. La pianta del Garofolo, acciò che facci il fiore grande, vuol esser' piantata in Vaso; essendo, che in terra non riesce, perche per lo più ò lo fà piccolo, ò si crepa, però devemo piantarla in Vaso, usandoli questa diligenza. Alli primi freddi dell'Inverno si deve cavare la pianta dal Vaso assieme con tutto il pane della sua terra, & diligentemente con un coltello andar' tagliando d'ogn'intorno per due dita detto pane, avvertendo, che resti la terra attaccata alla pianta, dopoi haver' il vaso accommodato con cocciole, e sassetti, come s'è detto, & sopra li sassetti si metterà un suolo di terra mediocre di grossezza di un dito, con mettervi sopra quattro buone dita di sangue di Bove, & poi tre dita di terra magra, con ponervi poi sopra il pane della terra, dove stà attaccata la pianta di Garofolo, qual pianta si riempirà d'intorno di terra assai grassa, con darvi l'acqua à suoi bisogni, espondendola al sole. Quando poi arrivarà il colmo dell'Inverno, che saranno grandissimi freddi si pigliarà una Caldara, & vi si porrà dentro (fol. 21r) un scorzo di pollina ò palombina, stemperandola ben bene con un mezzo barile d'acqua, con la quale si adacquarà la pianta, che si bene il Garofolo non teme molto il freddo, con tutto ciò si rende più vigorosa la pianta, si per il calor di quest'acqua. come anco, che arrivando le radiche alla terra ingrassata dal sangue putrefatto riceve grandissimo notrimento, donde nasce, che li fiori, che produce sono molto più pieni, et copiosi di frondi, avvertendo, che quando sarà passato il rigor del freddo adacquarla con l'acqua ordinaria.

[V.2] Avvertimento, mentre da un Vaso di Garofoli uno riceve due dozzine di fiori si può contentare. Si custodischino in questo modo. Si lasciaranno 20. ò 25. fusti per Vaso, secondo si vedrà la pianta vigorosa, & quando saranno alzati detti fusti, et cominciato à far bottoni in ciaschedun fusto, lasciando solo in cimo il principale, quale quando haverà allungato il cannello tanto, che si conosca che trà doi giorni sia per cominciare ad allargarsi per mandar' fuori il fiore, all'hora si dovrà leggiermente ligare il cannello con un poco (fol. 21v) di filo et diligentemente con la punta d'un stemperino si rimanderà allargando quelle fissure, che sono in cima del detto cannello, acciò che più facilmente possa uscire la gran copia di frondi, che stanno racchiuse in sì picciolo cannello, che altrimenti sarebbe impossibile venir' fuori senza farlo crepare. Quando poi si vedrà essere uscito fuori quel globolo di frondi, all'hora si porrà levar' via il filo, non vi essendo più pericolo alcuno. Et così porgerà maravilia à riguardanti il veder uscite tante frondi da un cannello così picciolo senza romperlo, ò fenderlo. Vogliono sole assaissimo et molt'aria, mà quando poi il fiori saranno in vigore se li farà havere poco sole, acciò non li secchi così presto, mà durino qualche tempo. Quando havranno finito di far fiori, se li continuarà à dar acqua secondo si vedrà il bisogno.

[IV.9] As regards those other tulips known as 'Coloretti,' they can be left in the earth for two years and no longer; when they have shed their leaves, four fingers of soil should be laid over them to protect them from the aforesaid dangers during the summer. In the first year they produce bulblets; in the second they grow larger, and then they can be dug up; but by the third year the offsets, which are naturally wrapped round and attached to the mother, all want to produce new offspring, but they do not have enough strength and so they grow small and even rot, for they take in a lot of moisture from all the husks with which they are covered, and experience proves this, for they do not produce flowers.

[IV.10] The Persian tulip [*Tulipa clusiana* DC.] is naturally more resistant; it needs richer soil and should be planted two fingers deep; it adapts to all positions. It should be taken up every year, because it moves further underground. It should not be sown, because it does not produce variations and is, moreover, very slow to propagate before it produces flowers.

[V]   Of Dianthus. [*Dianthus* spp.]

[V.1] I will only deal briefly with their nature, as they are a well-known plant. If one wants the Dianthus to produce large flowers, it should be planted in a pot, for this does not happen if it is planted in the ground, which generally makes it grow small or split. We should therefore plant it in a pot, taking particular care of it in the following way. At the first cold winter weather, the plant should be dug up from the pot together with all its clump of earth, and one should carefully cut this clump to two fingers all around, making sure that the soil remains attached to the plant, and after having prepared the pot with sherds and pebbles, as described above. Over the pebbles should be placed a layer of moderately rich [*terra assai grossa*] soil one finger thick, and over that should be put some oxblood to a depth of a good four fingers, and then three fingers of sandy soil, on top of which should be set the clump of soil to which the plant is attached; one should fill in all around the plant with very rich compost, watering it as needed and exposing it to the sun. When it is the depth of winter and the cold is most severe, one should take a cauldron and put the skin of a chicken or pigeon into it, mixing it thoroughly with half a barrel of water. The plant should be watered with this, for although the Dianthus is not very afraid of the cold, nevertheless the plant receives extra strength both from the warmth of the water and because the roots take in plenty of nourishment when the water reaches the soil enriched with the putrefied blood. As a result, the flowers which it produces are very full, with an abundance of petals. Note that when the severe cold has passed, the plant should be watered with ordinary water.

[V.2] Note: One should be satisfied when one has obtained two dozen flowers from one pot of Dianthus. They should be cultivated in the following way. One should leave twenty or twenty-five stems per pot, according to how strong the plant seems, and when these stems have grown tall and started to produce buds the size of a small bean, all the buds on each stem should be carefully cut off except for the main one on the top, which should be left. When this has grown a stalk so long that one can see that within two days it will start to enlarge to put forth the flower, then one should tie a little piece of string lightly round the stalk and carefully push the bud back with the point of a pocket-knife, thus enlarging the openings at the top of the said stalk so that the great abundance of petals, enclosed in such a little stalk, can come out more easily, for otherwise it is impossible for them to come out without splitting it. Then, when one sees that the little globe of petals has come out, one can remove the string,

[V.3] Si moltiplicono in doi modi, cioè per Cacchi, e per seme. Per seme, quale si dovrà raccogliere ben maturo, il che si conoscerà quando il cannello sarà secco, & havrà aperto l'altro cannello, che stà di dentro, che all'hora il seme sarà divenuto negro, con sciegliere quelli granelli, li quali stando nel fondo del detto cannello; perche per esperienza si vede (fol. 22r) che ne riescono più doppi, essendo i primi, che hanno ricevuto dalla pianta maggior sostanza. Si seminaranno subito, perche così si guadagna una stagione, nel modo, che s'è detto dell'Anemoni, coprendoli con un poco più di terra quanto sarebbe un mezzo dito, con tenerli di continuo adacquati, & così trà sei, ò otto giorni nasceranno. Si dovranno porre in luogo alquanto fresco, che non habbino sole più di tre hore la mattina, sinche la pianta habbia spuntato fuori la quarta fronda, che all'hora si potranno esporre al sole per tutto il giorno; avvertendo però di tenerli sempre humidi, acciò non siano abbrugiate dal caldo. Si trapiantaranno al fine d'Ottobre, perche produranno il fiore alla prima stagione.

[V.4] Molti usano piantare i Cacchi d'Ottobre, altri vi seminano attorno orzo, ò grano, acciò faccino più le radiche, mà questo lo rimetto al gusto loro. L'esperienza insegna piantarli il mese di Febraro quando si cominciano à risentire in questo modo. Schacchiando dalla pianta il cacchio con un poco del vecchio senza altremente torcerlo, & piantarlo trà la terra, e'l Vaso, stringendoli la terra intorno quanto si può, havendoli prima tagliate (fol. 22v) le sommità delle fronde. Overo tagliando il cacchio con un coltello nel mezzo del nodo, mà però nel vecchio, & piantarlo come sopra, con metter' il Vaso all'aria, mà che non habbi sole per 20., ò 30. giorni, & mantenerli sempre la terra humida. Si pianti sotto in modo, che resti fuora l'occhio, & quando si vedrà cominciare à crescere le frondi di mezzo del cacchio, all'hora s'esponga al sole, perche è segno, che hà preso, & così più sicuramente pigliano, che quando sono piantati nel mese d'Ottobre, & si custodiscono come sopra.

for there is no further danger. In this way it will afford amazement to the beholders when they see that so many petals have come out from such a small stalk without breaking or splitting it. They need plenty of sun and a lot of air but, when the flowers are in full strength, they should be given only a little sun so that they will not wither too quickly but last for some time. When they have stopped producing flowers, one should continue to water them as one sees the need.

[V.3] They are propagated in two ways, namely, by cuttings and from seed. When from seed, it should be collected when it is fully mature, and one can tell this when the stalk has become dry and the node, which is inside it, has opened out, by which time the seed will have turned black. One should select the seeds which are at the bottom of this node, for experience has shown that more double flowers come from them, since they were formed first and received more nourishment from the plant. They should be sown immediately, for in this way one gains an extra season, and in the way described for Anemones, but covered with a little more soil, as much as half a finger, and kept constantly watered. In this way they will start growing within six or eight days. They should be put in a fairly cool place, where they will get no more than three hours of sun in the morning, until the plant has sprouted its fourth leaf, when they can be exposed to the sun for the whole day. Note, however, that they should always be kept moist lest they are burnt by the heat. They should be transplanted at the end of October so that they will produce flowers in their first season.

[V.4] Many people are accustomed to plant the cuttings in October; others sow barley or wheat round them to make them produce rootstock more readily, but I leave this to their own judgment. Experience teaches they should be planted in the month of February, when they start to revive, and in the following way. One should cut the tendril from the plant with a bit of the original plant, but without twisting it, and plant it between the soil and the pot, pressing the soil as tightly as possible round it, and after having first cut off the tips of the leaves. Or one can cut off the tendril with a knife in the middle of the node—of the original plant, however—and plant it as above, putting the pot in the fresh air but without letting it have any sun for twenty or thirty days, and always keeping the soil moist. It should be planted so that the eye remains above ground, and when one sees the leaves beginning to grow in the middle of the cutting, then it can be exposed to the sun, for this is a sign that it has taken, and in this way they are surer to take than when they are planted in the month of October; they are cared for as above.

APPENDIX III

CATALOGUE OF THE FLOWER ALBUM

BIBLIOTECA APOSTOLICA VATICANA, MS. BARB. LAT. 4326

Note: The identification of the flowers by modern botanical names was done by Carla Teune of the Botanical Garden of the University of Leiden with the assistance of M. H. Hoog. Their comments were translated into English by Vanessa Bezemer Sellars. Their identifications have been reviewed and emended by Dr. Frederick Meyer of the National Arboretum in Washington, D.C., and I have added comments of my own.

All the following illustrations are from Biblioteca Apostolica Vaticana. Each plant is first identified by its modern botanical name. This is followed, where possible, by the names given identical or similar plants in Besler's *Hortus Eystettensis* and/or in the Barberini sources. These are identified as:
Bes. = Besler
Fer. = Ferrari
Inv. = Inventory
Tr. = Treatise

Fol. I View of Pastel Gondolfo
Fol. II Dedication

Eminentissimo, & Reverendissimo Sig.re mio e Pro'ne Sign.
Gradi la Santità di N. S. PAPA URBANO VIII, La Descrittione del nobilissimo stato posseduto / dalli Duchi e Principe della Rovere parto del mio / debolissimo ingegnoso Questa S. Eminenza come p. / aborro [aborto] fattola trasportare nella sue celebre librarie si co. / piace conservare tra gl' altri molti libri di grandissima / qualità e dottrina, non per altro effetto credo io che per maggiormente delettare / le persone studiose, che ni capitano acciò conesciuta la deformità di quella app: / arisca maggiore la vaghezza di questi. Et perche Em. Sig. solani [word?] in este miseris socios habere penates, accogline un altra di fiori staccata dal ste: / rilissimo Giardino della mia propria Idea, trattegiati dal naturale, dal mio roz: / zosi ma devoto e humile pennello. Questi per la varietà e diversità di colori / serviranno per abellire la deformità della sorella e tenerli compagnia. Accettila / con benigno occhio, l'irrighi con felicissima acqua della sua buona gratia, / acciò scossi dalla polvere della detrattione porghino animo i. me di dedicar: / lene due altri volumi: uno d'uccelli e l'altro dello Stato & Dominio della feli: / cissima & nobilissima Casa Barberina sotto la cui protettione io & miei figli / vivendo, & da vivere unitamente tutti li il colmo d'ogni felicità / e longa vita. Di Roma il 21 Agosto 1639
D. V. Eminenza

Humilissime et oblig.temissimo Serv.te
Francesco Mingucci
da Pesaro

Fol. 1
Lilium chalcedonicum L.
Scarlet Turk's-cap; Bes., *L. Byzantium Serotinus*
Illustrated in Fuchs' Vienna Codex ca. 1550. Vermilion-scarlet flower.

Fol. 2
Lilium martagon L.
Martagon lily; Bes., *L. montanum flore purpurescente non punctatum*
Central Europe to Siberia. Under cultivation since 830 in Switzerland. Purplish flower.

Fol. I

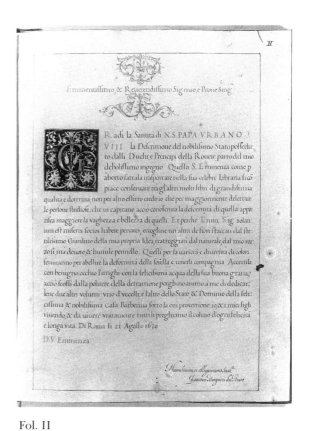

Fol. II

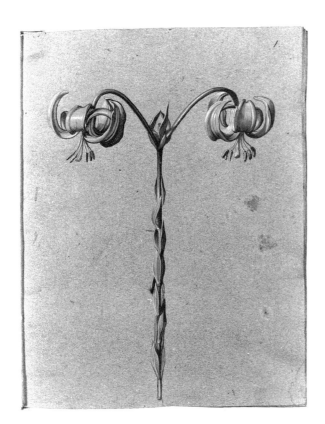

Fol. 1

Fol. 2

Fol. 3 (Pl. VI)
Narcissus tazetta L.
Tazetta narcissus; Inv., *Tazzetta della gran sorte*
Native to the Mediterranean area. In cultivation in Germany by 1557. Probably a forerunner of the modern Paper White Narcissus. This variety probably is no longer grown, although many hybrids are. Flower has white perianth, light yellow corona.

Fol. 4
Narcissus tazetta L. (Earlier *N. odoratus albus plenus* or *N. Incomparabilis Hort.*)
Poeticus narcissus; Bes., *N. orientalis maior polyanthos totus albus*; Inv., *Trombone doppio*
Probably no longer in cultivation. Flowers double, white.

Fol. 5 (Pl. V)
Narcissus tazetta L. cultivar.
Tazetta narcissus; Bes., *N orientalis major*, or *medio* or *N. polyanthus mixtus*; Inv., *N. Constantinopolitano doppio*
Double pure white form.

Fol. 6 (Pl. IV)
Narcissus poeticus L. ? or *N. pseudonarcissus* ?
Trumpet narcissus; Bes., *Pseudo N. pallidus calice amplo*; Inv., *Trombone non ha pari*
Native to Europe. Both are still in cultivation. Single flower, white perianth, corona pale yellow.

Fol. 3

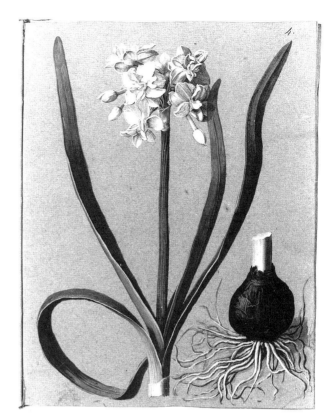

Fol. 4

Fol. 5

Fol. 6

293

Fol. 7
Narcissus tazetta L.
Tazetta narcissus; Bes., Most like *N. orientalis polyanthos mixtus*.
It is very similar to the tazetta on fol. 3. Double white perianth, shallow yellow corona.

Fol. 8
Narcissus tazetta L. 'Grand Soleil d'Or'
Tazetta narcissus; Bes., Most like *N. juncifolius praecox maior* or *N. polyanthos orientalis medio luteus odoratus maximus*
A golden yellow colored selection, not found in the wild but probably native to the Mediterranean.

Fol. 9 (Pl. III)
Narcissus jonquilla L.
Jonquil; Sweerts, *N. minor juncifolius*; Inv., *Giunchiglia*
Western Mediterranean. In cultivation in England by 1596. Flower deep yellow.

Fol. 10
Narcissus odorus L.
Jonquil; Sweerts, *N. juncifolius minor amplo calice luteus*?, *N. juncifolius latine colore*
Cross of *N. jonquilla* x *N. pseudonarcissus*. Southern Europe, in cultivation in the Netherlands by 1594. Flower yellow.

Fol. 7

Fol. 8

Fol. 9

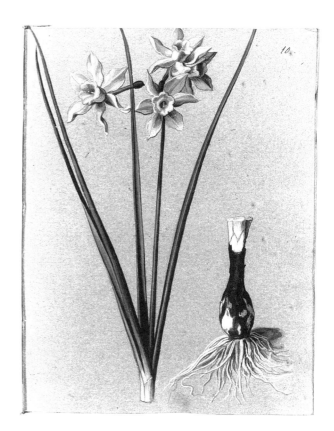

Fol. 10

Fol. 11
Narcissus jonquilla L. 'Plenus.'
Double-flowered jonquil
In cultivation by 1596 in England. Perianth golden yellow, corona double, golden yellow with white interior of petals.

Fol. 12
Dianthus plumarius L. 'Gras' (left); *D. caryophyllus* L. (right)
Carnation or dianthus; Bes., *Caryophyllus*
D. plumarius grown in Belgium by 1568. *D. caryophyllus* in cultivation since Greek antiquity, imported to Western Europe by 1270. Four individual flowers in shades of pink and salmon, petals fringed.

Fol. 13
Tulipa sylvestris L. (right). Unidentified cultivar of *T. gesneriana* (left).
Wood tulip
Central and southern Europe, North Africa, Iran. In cultivation in the Netherlands by 1594. Formerly called *T. florentina odorata* Hort. It is yellow colored and greenish on the outside, never red.

Fol. 14
Tulipa sarracenia Perrier or *Tulipa planifolia* Jord.
Tulip
This belongs to the group of the so-called "Neo-Tulips" which grow wild in the Italian region of Piedmont in the province of Aosta, and in France in Savoy. These tulips were once thought to be lost but have now been discovered growing wild and have been grouped under this name. Flower on left is dark red, the right one is ivory with rust tips.

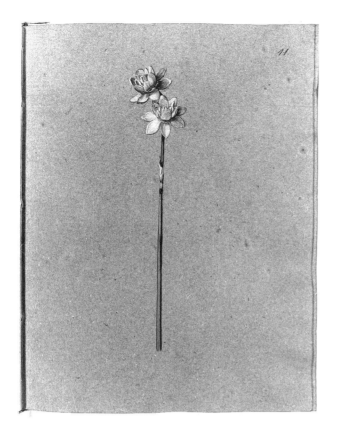

Fol. 11

Fol. 12

Fol. 13

Fol. 14

297

Fol. 15
Tulipa 'Duc van Tol' (also 'Duc van Tholl' or 'Duc van Toll')
Tulip
This is the rose colored form of the cultivar. These tulips derive from the species *T. suaveolens* Roth.

Fol. 16
Tulipa 'Duc van Tol'
Duc van Tol tulip; Bes., Most like *T. fulvo sulphurei coloris margine amplius rubinose*
Deep gold, shading to salmon. See fol. 15.

Fol. 17 (Pl. XI)
Tulipa sylvestris L.
Tulip; Bes., Most like *T. lutea lituris aureis*; Inv., *Tulipano pennacchiato di Persia*
Gold colored flower with some white on petal tips.

Fol. 18
Tulipa sp., (unknown cultivar)
Tulip; Bes., Most like *T. coccinea adhiscentibus oris*
Probably a seedling with a reddish yellow flower.

Fol. 15

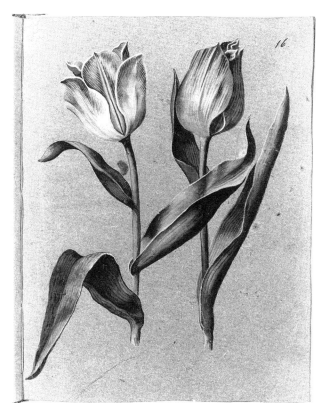

Fol. 16

Fol. 17

Fol. 18

299

Fol. 19
Tulipa sylvestris ?
Tulip; Bes., Same as fol. 17
Flower gold and red.

Fol. 20
Tulipa sp., (unknown cultivar)
Tulip
Probably seedlings. Flower on left is reddish purple, on right, brownish red with yellow edges to the petals.

Fol. 21
Tulipa sp. Could be *T. gesneriana*
Tulip; Bes., Most like *T. floribus flexis inferioribus*
An unknown variety, probably a seedling. Reddish with tones of orange.

Fol. 22
Tulipa sp.
Tulip
An unknown variety, probably a seedling. Darkish red shading to orange. Almost lily-flowered in form.

Fol. 19

Fol. 20

Fol. 21

Fol. 22

301

Fol. 23
Tulipa sarracenia Perrier or *Tulipa planifolia* Jord.
Wood tulip
See fol. 14. Flowers white at base, reddish shading to white on edges.

Fol. 24 (Pl. XIII)
Tulipa clusiana DC
Lady tulip; Bes., *T. persica*; Fer., Inv., Tr., *Tulipano di Persia*
Native to Iran and Afghanistan. The first tulips were imported to Europe from Turkey about 1554. This species was in cultivation in the Netherlands by 1606. It has naturalized in southern Europe. Flowers are red with white borders.

Fol. 25
Tulipa 'Duc van Tol'
Tulip
Rose colored. See fol. 15.

Fol. 26
Tulipa sp.
Tulip
These belong in the "Neo-Tulipa" group. See fol. 14. Flower on left is deep gold shading to red and white with dark veining. On right, the flower is a light yellow.

Fol. 23

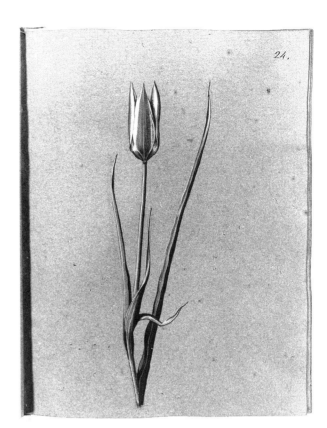

Fol. 24

Fol. 25

Fol. 26

Fol. 27
Tulipa sp.
Tulip
The flower on the right is a precursor of the so-called "Rembrandt" or broken colored tulips so highly prized in the craze for tulips in the 1630s. It is now known that the broken colors are not a natural mutation, as was believed in the seventeenth century, but are caused by a virus infection.

Fol. 28
Tulipa, probably a selection of *T. gesneriana*
Tulip
Unknown seedling with many characteristics of the lily-flowered tulip (which had been in cultivation since 1613). Flower is dark orange.

Fol. 29
Tulipa L. 'Columbus' ?
Tulip
It is highly probable that this is the late-blooming tulip "Columbus" in cultivation since ca. 1628.

Fol. 30
Tulipa L. 'Lac van Rijn'
Tulip; Bes., *T. purpurea rosea persica*
The word "lac" refers to tulips with a white edge. They were very popular in the seventeenth century. Van Rijn was a flower grower, not the artist, Rembrandt van Rijn. Flower is rose with white petal edges.

Fol. 27

Fol. 28

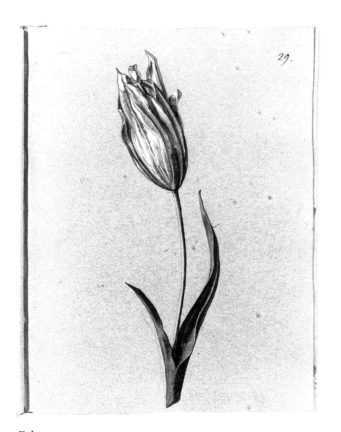

Fol. 29

Fol. 30

Fol. 31 (Pl. XII)
Tulipa gesneriana L. ?
Tulip; Bes., Most like *T. summe miniate*; Inv. *Tulipano coloretto*
Naturalized in North Italy. See fol. 14. In cultivation in the Netherlands since 1601. Dark red.

Fol. 32
Tulipa, probably a *T. gesneriana*
Tulip
There were a large number of seedling selections by the 1600s. Hybrids were probably not yet developed. Dark red.

Fol. 33
Hyacinthus orientalis L.
Roman hyacinth; Bes., *H. orientalis*; Fer., Inv., Tr. *Giacinto*
Hyacinths were imported from the Near East to Austria in the 1550s. Now only the so-called Roman hyacinths are grown. The variations in color and form, as recorded in the inventory and other sources, developed by selection, or mutation. Dark blue flowers.

Fol. 34 (Pl. VII)
Hyacinthus orientalis L.
Hyacinth; Bes., *H. orientalis violaceo colore albis linei*
See fol. 33. Pale blue flowers.

Fol. 31

Fol. 32

Fol. 33

Fol. 34

307

Fol. 35
Hyacinthus orientalis L.
Hyacinth; Bes., *H. orientalis mixtus*
See fol. 33. Dark blue flowers.

Fol. 36
Hyacinthus orientalis L.
Hyacinth; Bes., *H. orientalis flore cinereo albo* or *fl. niveo*
See fol. 33. Pinkish flowers.

Fol. 37
Hycinthus orientalis L.
Hyacinth; Bes., as for fol. 36
See fol. 33. Light blue flowers.

Fol. 38
Hyacinthus orientalis L.
Hyacinth; Bes., as for fol. 36
See fol. 33. Flowers pale blue.

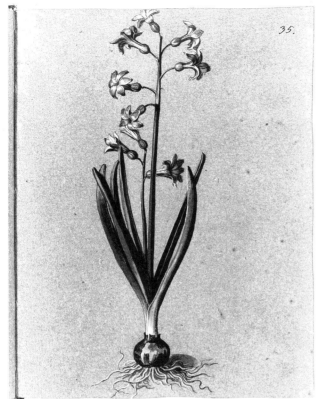

Fol. 35

Fol. 36

Fol. 37

Fol. 38

Fol. 39
Hyacinthus orientalis L.
Hyacinth
A rarity. See fol. 33. Flowers are pale blue, it is double stalked with narrow leaves.

Fol. 40
Hyacinth orientalis L.
Hyacinth; Bes., *H. orientalis variegatus*
See fol. 33. Flowers very pale lavender.

Fol. 41
Anemone coronaria L.
Anemone; Bes., *A. latifolia*
In cultivation since Roman antiquity, even the fuller forms. The indigenous plant is probably no longer in cultivation. Stalk on left has flowers pink shading to lavender, the stalk on the right has peach colored flowers.

Fol. 42
Possibly *Anemone pavonina* L.
A bizarre mutation.

Fol. 39

Fol. 40

Fol. 41

Fol. 42

Fol. 43
Anemone pavonina Lam.
Anemone; Bes., *A. latifolia*
Native to southern Europe. In cultivation in the Netherlands by 1601. Flower on left pink, on right, white.

Fol. 44 (Pl. IX)
Anemone pavonina Lam.
Anemone; Bes., *Anemone latifolia*; Inv., *Anemone*
Flowers are (from left to right) white double, pink single, pale purple.

Fol. 45
Blank page

Fol. 46 (Pl. XIV)
Punica granatum L.
Pomegranate
This is the earliest recorded representation of the double flowered pomegranate in Europe. Before, the earliest recorded date was 1827 in Germany. Native to western Asia.

Fol. 47
Ranunculus asiaticus L.
Ranunculus; Bes., *Ranunculus asiaticus grumosa radice flore pleno ruberrimo*
Belongs to the group of so-called "Turkish Ranunculus." Imported to Austria in 1580. The imported plants were cultivars which had been grown and traded in Turkey for a long time. Flowers are orange and very double or full.

Fol. 43

Fol. 44

Fol. 46

Fol. 47

Fol. 48
Anemone pavonina Lam.
Anemone; Bes., *A. latifolia flore coccinea plena*
Red double flower, but not to be confused with *A. multipetala*. Partly and fully-opened forms.

Fol. 49
Anemone coronaria L.
Anemone; Bes., *Anemone flore multiplici coccineo colore tenuifolia*
Double cultivar. Flower on left, red striated white, on right, brownish red.

Fol. 50
Anemone coronaria L.
Anemone; Bes., *A. simplex latifolia dilute purpurescens*
Single flowering form still in cultivation. Flowers reddish fading to white at tips of petals. Fully opened flower is white around center, also has bluish petals.

Fol. 51
Anemone x fulgens (DC.) RChb. Multipetela
Anemone; Bes., *A. latifolia flore coccineo plena flore pleno coccineo variegate latifolia*
Probably *A. hortensis x A. pavonina*. Only one color, scarlet red, known for this cultivar. Not hardy.

Fol. 48

Fol. 49

Fol. 50

Fol. 51

315

Fol. 52
Anemone coronaria L.
Anemone; Bes., no match but is *tenuifolia* type; Inv., *Argemone*
In the single and double flowering forms and usual colors, blue and pink.

Fol. 53
Anemone pavonina Lam.
Anemone; Bes., *A. latifolia purpuresco*
Flower on right is the *prolifera* form. The left one is double. Both are orange.

Fol. 54
Anemone coronaria L.
Anemone; Bes., *A. tenuifolia*
See fol. 50. Flowers on left are violet, on right, red.

Fol. 55 (Pl. VIII)
Anemone coronaria L.
Anemone; Bes., *A tenuifolia flore multeplici coccineo colore*
Extra double form. Flower is dark red, almost maroon. This is the type called "pluchée" (Fr.), "vellutato" (Ital.), and "velvet or plush" (Eng.) in the seventeenth century.

Fol. 52

Fol. 53

Fol. 54

Fol. 55

Fol. 56
Rosa centifolia L.
Cabbage rose; Bes., *R. centifolia rubra*
In cultivation since antiquity. A pink fully open flower and two buds.

Fol. 57
Rosa gallica L. 'Versicolor'
Rosa mundi; Bes., *R. praenestina variegata*
Imported to the Netherlands by Clusius by 1594. Shades of pink and dark red.

Fol. 58
Rosa hemisphaerica Herrm.
Rose; Bes., *R. lutea maxima flore pleno*
Formerly called *R. sulphurea Ait*, not known in the wild. This double yellow garden variety was imported from Turkey and was in cultivation in Switzerland by 1625. Golden yellow.

Fol. 59
Fritillaria meleagris
Fritillary (guinea hen flower)
Widespread in Europe. The flower is dark purple, almost black.

Fol. 56

Fol. 57

Fol. 58

Fol. 59

319

Fol. 60
Valeriana officinalis L.
Valerian, common or garden heliotrope; Bes., *V. sylvestris*
Widespread in Europe. Cultivated in western Europe by 1561. Small white flowers in dense clusters on long stalks.

Fol. 61
Possibly *Ranunculus aconitifolium* L.
Ranunculus; Bes., *R. albus flore pleno* has similar leaves but a double flower.
Native to Central and Northern Europe. It has been in cultivation in Switzerland since 830. Small pinkish flowers.

Fol. 62
Geum rivale L. Avens
Geum; Bes., *Gariophyllata montana*
In cultivation in Austria by 1584. Native to Europe, Asia, and North America. Dark purple calix, petals orange-pink.

Fol. 63
Aquilegia vulgaris L. 'Flore pleno'
Columbine; Bes., *A. flore coerulo pleno*
In cultivation in Germany by 1613 but the species was grown in the Netherlands by 1470. Blue flowers.

Fol. 60

Fol. 61

Fol. 62

Fol. 63

321

Fol. 64
Clematis viticella L. 'Flore pleno'
Clematis; Bes., *C. peregrina purpurea flore pleno*
In cultivation in England by 1597. Sepals purple, corolla pink.

Fol. 65
Aquilegia vulgaris L. 'Flore pleno'
Columbine; Bes., *A. flore pleno incarnato*
See fol. 63. Flowers pink.

Fol. 66
Aquilegia vulgaris L. 'Flore pleno'
Columbine; Bes., *A. flore pleno*
See fol. 63. Purple flowers.

Fol. 67
Ranunculus asiaticus L.
Ranunculus
See fol. 47. Flowers creamy yellow shading to pink.

Fol. 64

Fol. 65

Fol. 66

Fol. 67

323

Fol. 68
Calendula officinalis L.
Pot Marigold; Bes., *Calendula*
Origin unknown. In cultivation since Roman antiquity. Flowers orange.

Fol. 69
Convallaria majalis L. 'Rosea'
Lily of the Valley; Bes., *Lilium convallium flore incarnata*
Also *C.m. rubra* Sweet / *C.m. rosea* Reichenbach
In cultivation by 1576 in Austria. Pink flowers.

Fol. 70 (Pl. x)
Ranunculus asiaticus L. (left) and *R. acris* L. 'Plenus' (right)
Ranunculus; Bes., *R. creticus grumosa radice flore niveo* (left) *R. flore globoso* or *R. hortensis flore pleno* (right); Inv., *R. a foglia di Ruta*
For flower on left, see fol. 67. Flower on right formerly *R. var. Plenus* West / *R.a. var. multiplex* G. Don / *R. var. pleniflorus* Bergm. They were in cultivation in Germany by 1480. Flower colors: Left, white with black center; Right. pale yellow

Fol. 71
Chrysanthemum parthenium (L.) Bernh.
Feverfew; Bes., *Matricaria flore pleno*
Probably a predecessor of *C. p. fistulosum*, which has been cultivated since 1665. This is a dwarf variety. The species was in cultivation by 1561. White flowers.

Fol. 68

Fol. 69

Fol. 70

Fol. 71

325

Fol. 72
Narcissus, possibly *N. tazetta* L.
Jonquil
Flowers, golden yellow.

Fol. 73
Narcissus, not identified
Flowers pale yellow with white corolla.

Fol. 74
Santolina chamaecyparissus L. (left) and *Carthamus tinctorius* L. (right)
Left, Santolina; Bes., *Abrotanum foemina sive Chamoeay parissus*, Right, Safflower; Bes., *Coricus sativus*
Santolina is a subshrub native of the Mediterranean region. Flowers yellow.
The safflower with yellow flowers was grown in ancient Egypt where it was used as a pigment in paint. Native plant of Africa (Ethiopia and adjacent areas).

Fol. 75
Iris x germanica L.
German iris; Bes., *I. illyrica*
Origin unknown.
Lavender flowers.

Fol. 72

Fol. 73

Fol. 74

Fol. 75

Fol. 76A (Unnumbered folio)
Iris chamaeiris Bert.
Iris
Close to *I. pumila* but differs especially in the stem length and flower.
Rarely cultivated today, native to southwest Europe. Yellow flower.

Fol. 76
Iris foetidissima L.
Stinking iris; Bes., *Spatula foetida*
Native to south and west Europe. In cultivation by 1561. Purplish gray flower.

Fol. 77
Pancratium illyricum L.
NA; Bes., *Lilio narcissus hemerocallia disfacie*
Mediterranean region. In cultivation in the Netherlands by 1592. Not hardy. White flowers.

Fol. 78
Matthiola incana (L.) R. Br.
Stock, gilliflower; Bes., *Leucoium pleno flore album purpureis maculis signatum*
Native to the Mediterranean area. Has been in cultivation since antiquity. Pink double flowers.

Fol. 76A

Fol. 76

Fol. 77

Fol. 78

Fol. 79
Matthiola incana (L.) R. Br.
Stock, gilliflower; Bes., *Leucoium rubro flore pleno*
See fol. 78. Flowers double rose pink.

Fol. 80
Filipendula vulgaris Moench
Meadowsweet; Bes., *Filipendula vulgaris*
The species was grown in Germany by 1561. White flowers.

Fol. 81
Consolida regalis S. F. Gray (*Delphinium consolida* L.)
Larkspur; Bes., *Consolida regalis multiplicato incarnato flore*
Mediterranean and Near East. In cultivation since Greek antiquity. Left, double pink flowers; right, double purple flowers.

Fol. 79

Fol. 80

Fol. 81

APPENDIX IV

PLANT LISTS

1. Alphabetical list of plants in the inventory and their location in the garden
Note: Arabic numbers refer to the planting bed and row

PLANT INVENTORY LIST

Flower Names	Compartment Numbers				
	I.	II.	III.	IV.	V.
Anemone bianco fiammato d'Incarnato doppio					10
					11
					12
Anemone Carneo massimo					18
Anemone di cinque colori					4
Anemone dal fiocco verde			11.1		7
Anemone dal fiocco lionato					17
Anemone incarnato di limone bello					17
Anemone orlato					1
					2
					3
Anemone rossi col fiocco lionato		11.2		10.1	2
Anemone rossi vellutati					8
					3
Anemone Rossini					1
					6
Anemone Persichino					5
Anemone Persichino doppia			10.1		
Anemone Sanguigno doppij					4
					5
					6
Anemone scritto buono					13
					14
					15
Anemone solfarino fiammata rosso doppio					7
					8
					9
Anemoni	25.1	17A			10
	25.3	17B			20
	26.1	19.4			
	26.4				
	27.3				
	29.3				

Flower Names	I.	II.	III.	IV.	V.
Argemone carneo					14
Argemone Colombino acceso					9
Argemone cremesino					9
					13
					14
					20
Argemone il bel Tenerino					10
					12
Argemone la Guascogna					18
Argemone Madre della Celeste					12
Argemone la Massima Paonazza					12
					15
Argemone la Palidetta					18
					13
Argemone Palombino acceso					11
					14
Argemone rosino					19
Argemone rosso cremesino					11
					21
Argemone rosso oscuro					18
Argemone violaceo					9
Argemoni	25.1	17A			16
	25.2	17B			20
	25.3	19.4			22
	26.1				23
	26.4				
	27.3				
	29.3				
Garofani			9.2		
Giacinti		13.2	1.2		
		19.3	9.1		
			9.2		
Giacinti bianchi			3.1	7.6	
			4.1	8.1	
Giacinti bianchi orientali	26.3				
Giacinti buoni		1.1	5.1	1.5	
		3.1	5.2	2.5	
	5.4	3.5		5.3	
			5.5	5.5	
			7.1	6	
			8.5		
Giacinti detti del Cornaro	3.1				
	10.3				
	14.3				
	23.1				
Giacinti da Brescia					3.5

FOUNTAINS, STATUES, AND FLOWERS

Flower Names	I.	II.	III.	IV.	V.
Giacinti di Brescia	19.3	17A.3	2.4		4.2
	20.2				7.2
	20.3				8.5
Giacinti di Cornaro		2.1			
		15.1			
		16.2			
		17.2			
Giacinti odoratissimi	8.1				
	8.2				
	8.3				
	9.1				
	9.2				
	9.3				
	17.1				
	17.2				
	17.3				
	18.1				
	18.2				
	18.3				
Giacinti polianti	6.1	9.1			
	6.2	14.3			
	7.1				
	7.2				
	27.4				
	28.1				
Giacinti polianti di Brescia	13.2	4.3			
	5.3				
Giacinto doppio detto Januario					22
					23
Giacinto stradoppio					26
Giacinto verde					27
Giunchiglia dalla foglia unita	1.2	8.2	2.2	5.2	
	5.2	9.1	3.7		
		10.2	4.7		
Giunchiglia di Spagna	10.2	2.2			25
	14.4	6.3			26
	25.4	7.3			28
	26.2	17.3			
	26.4	17A.2			
	27.3	17B.4			
	28.2	18.3			
	29.2	19.2			
	29.4	19.4			

Flower Names	Compartment Numbers				
	I.	II.	III.	IV.	V.
Giunchiglia grossa di Spagna	11.2				
	12.2				
	15.2				
	16.2				
Giunchiglie					20
Giunchiglie doppie					24
Giunchiglie riflesse					19
Giungifoglie					21
Narcisi collo di camello		17.4		5.1	
				6.1	
Narcisi collo di camello doppij		6.4	7.4	3.4	
		7.4	8.2		
		8.1			
		10.1			
		11.4			
		12.4			
Narcisi Constantinopolitani	2.5		6.1	4.3	
				7.5+	
				8.2	
Narcisi Constantinopolitani doppij	1.1				
	2.5				
	2.6				
	2.7				
	2.8				
	4.4				
	4.5				
	4.6				
	21.5				
	21.6				
	21.7				
	21.8				
	22.5				
	22.6				
	22.7				
	22.8				
Narcisi Gentilini	10.5		1.1		
	14.1				
Narcisi gialli	17.2	5.1	5.3		
	17A.1	5.2	6.3		
			5.3		
			5.4		
			5.5		

Flower Names	*Compartment Numbers*				
	I.	II.	III.	IV.	V.
Narcisi gialli in oro	5.1	4.3	1.2	5.1	
	7.1	5.3	2.1	6.1	
	8.1	6.3	7.1	7.1	
	9.17	7.3	8.3	8.6	
	10.1	9.1	9.3	9.1	
	11.M	10.1			
	12.M	13.1			
	14.1	14.3			
	14.5	17B.1			
	15.M	19.1			
	16.M	19.2			
	17.1				
	18.1				
	19.1				
	20.1				
	24.1				
	25.1				
	25.3				
	26.1				
	27.3				
	28.2				
	29.1				
	29.3				
Narcisi gialli in paglia		8.1			
Narcisi in oro	1.1				
Narcisi massimi d'Olanda detto del Gaetano	6.3	2.M	2.6	1.5	
	11.M		7.5	2.5	
	12.M		8.1	3.5	
	13.M		9.2	4.2	
	15.M			4.5	
	16.M			7.2	
	19.4			8.5	
	20.M			9.1	
	2.M				
Narcisi non ha pari				1.2	
				3.2	
				4.5	
Narcisi non ha pari doppio					25
Narcisi non ha pari giallo	13.1	18.1			
Narcisi non ha pari solfarini	1.4	6.2			
		7.2			
		11.2			
		12.2			
		17.4			

Flower Names	Compartment Numbers				
	I.	II.	III.	IV.	V.
Narcisi d'Olanda minore				5.2	
				6.2	
				7.5	
				8.2	
Narcisi Solfarini	1.4				
Narcisi Tela d'Olanda			3.3		
			4.3		
Ranunculi a foglia di Ruta	18.2	11.1		10.1	24
Ranunculo scritto					28
Tazzette	28.2	1.1			
Tazzette dalla foglia unita	2.2	1.3			
	2.4	3.3			
	21.4				
	22.1				
	22.2				
	22.3				
	22.4				
Tazzette d'Olanda dalla foglia unita		21.3	6.1		
			7.1		
			11.1		
			12.1		
Tazzette d'Olanda stellate	3.3	11.1			
	10.3	12.1			
	14.3	13.3			
	23.3	19.4			
	25.3				
	29.3				
Tazzette della gran sorte	1.1	13.4	1.3	1.3	
	2.2	14.1	2.3	2.3	
	2.3	17.1	3.5	3.3	
	2.4	17A.1	4.5	4.4	
	3.1	17B.1	7.2	5.3	
	4.1	19.1	8.4	5.4	
	4.2			6.3	
	4.3			6.4	
	5.1			7.3	
	11.1			8.4	
	12.1				
	13.3				
	15.1				
	16.1				
	21.2				
	21.3				
	21.4				
	22.1				

Flower Names		*Compartment Numbers*			
	I.	II.	III.	IV.	V.
	22.2				
	22.3				
	22.4				
	23.1				
	24.1				
	25.1				
	26.1				
	27.1				
	29.1				
Tazzette della gran sorte dalla foglia unita	7.3	6.3			
	19.4				
	20.4				
Tazzette d'Olanda dico non ha pari gialli	3.2				
	19.4				
Tazzette massime		15.1			
Tromboni bianchi	1.3	1.1		2.6	
	5.3	3.1		15.3	
	8.4	8.2			
	9.4	10.2			
	13.5	15.3			
	17.4				
	18.4				
	19.1				
	20.1				
	24.3				
Tromboni della gran Tromba solfarini	10.4	18.1			
Tromboni della gran Tromba con l'ale solfarine	14.2				
	25.3				
	29.3				
Tromboni doppij		1.2	2.5	2.4	
		3.2	3.4	9.2	
		4.2	4.4		
		5.2	10.3		
			11.3		
Tromboni non ha pari				8.3	
Tromboni solfarini			3.2	3.6	
			4.2	4.1	
				7.4	
Tulipano Candido, e rosso acceso, come fiamme in tutte le foglie			10.2		
Tulipani coloretti	13.5	2.2	2.1	1.1	
	28.1	14.4	2.6	3.1	
		16.2	3.6	4.6	
		17B.3	3.8	5.6	
		17B.4	4.8	6.6	

Flower Names		*Compartment Numbers*			
	I.	II.	III.	IV.	V.
		18.1	5.6	7.1	
		18.3	5.7	8.6	
		5.8	10.1–3		
Tulipani coloretti detti Porpore		15.4			
Tulipani detti Duchi Primotici	8.5				
	9.5				
	10.1				
	14.5				
	17.5				
	18.5				
Tulipani di Persia	25.2	19.4			
	26.4				
	27.3				
	28.2				
	29.4				
Tulipani di seme	25.3				
	27.4				
	28.1				
	29.3				
Tulipani rossi e gialli		13.1			
Tulipani tela d'oro		4.5			
		5.4			
Tulipani pennacchiati	26.3	17.A3			
	27.2	19.1			
	27.4				
Tulipano Agata detta del P.re Savelli			10.2		
Tulipano pennacchiato bianco candido e rosso stamine nere fondo turchino			10.2		25
Tulipano pennacchiato bianco e rosso			11.2		
			11.3		
Tulipano pennacchiato Cera di Spagna pennacchiato di bianco					25
Tulipano pennacchiato de' SS.Lani			10.2		
Tulipano pennacchiato detto Agata di tre colori de' S.r Fabr.o			11.2		
Tulipano pennacchiato detto Bracchettone			10.2		
Tulipano pennacchiato detto il Cugino di Bosuelt			11.2		28

2. Alphabetical index to plants in the horticultural treatise

Fols.	Nos.	Italian Flower Name	Botanical Name
I,	1–30	Anemone latifolio	A. pavonina Lam.
I,	31–33	Anemone tenuifolio	A. coronaria L.
III,	33	Ciclamini autumnale	Cyclamen hederfolium Ait.
III,	33	Ciclamini primaverile	C. persicum
III,	21	Corona Imperiale	Fritillaria imperialis L.
III,	18	Fritellarie	Fritillaria sp.
V,	1	Garofoli	Dianthus sp.
II,	6	Giacinto Belgico, Hispanico, Ossoleto	Hyacinthus orientalis L.
II,	4	Giacinto bianco	H. orientalis L.
II,	7	Giacinto Cipressina	Muscari comosus (L.) Mill.
II,	1	Giacinto del collo incarnato	Not identified
II,	10	Giacinto Peruano	Scilla peruviana L.
II,	8	Giacinto "Tuberosa Radice"	Asphodelus sp.
II,	1	Giacinto turchino	Hyacinthus orientalis L.
III,	5	Giunchiglia	N. jonquilla L.
III,	7	Ginuchiglia di Spagna	N. juncifolius Lag.
III,	25	Iride Bulbose	Iris xiphium L.
III,	24	Iride "di Persia"	Iris persica L.
III,	24	Iride prima del Clusio	Iris sp.,
III,	7	Iuncifolia	Narcissus juncifolius Lag.
III,	19	Iucca	Yucca gloriosa L.
III,	15	Lilio Narciso Indico "Belladonna"	Amaryllis belladonna L.
III,	20	Martagoni	Lilium martagon L.
II,	9	Moschi Grechi	Muscari sp.
III,	7	Narcisetto giallo doppi	N. bulbocodium L.?
II,	11	Narciso collo di camello	N. pseudonarcissus L.
III,	17	Narcisi d'India	Cybistebes longifolia (L.) Milne-Redh.
III,	3	Narciso "del Cucu"	Not identified
III,	5	Narcisi dell' Arena del gran Calice	"
III,	13	Narciso "dell' Isole Virginie"	Zephyranthes Atamasco L.
II,	11	Narciso di Narbona	Not identified
II,	1	Narciso doppio	N. tazetta Flore Pleno?
III,	3	Narciso doppio "del Boncori"	Not identified
II,	11	Narciso doppio di Musarto	"
III,	7	Narciso Fraseo	"
III,	12	Narciso "Jacobeo"	Sprekelia formosissima (L.) Herb.
II,	11	Narcisi Non ha pari	N. x incomparibilis L.
III,	16	Narciso scaglioso "bifolio" o "Suersio"	Haemanthus coccineus L.
II,	1	Narciso semplice	N. pseudonarcissus L.?
III,	2	Narciso tazzetta	N. tazetta L.

III, 5	Narcisi Tromboni	N. pseudonarcissus L.
II, 11	Narciso Valdenech	Not identified
III, 10	Ornitocoli	Ornithogalum sp.
III, 22	Peonie	Paeonia sp.
III, 26	Ranuncolo bianco doppio	Ranunculus asiaticus L.
III, 32	Ranuncolos de di Sanesio	Not identified
III, 30	Ranuncolo di Tubero	"
III, 31	Ranuncolo foglia di Ruta	Callianthemum rutifolium (L.) C. A. Mey
III, 29	Ranuncolo semplice	R. asiaticus L.
III, 1–4	Tazzette	N. tazetta L.
IV, 1–8	Tulipano	Tulipa sp.
IV, 9	Tulipano "Coloretto"	T. sarracenia Perrier or T. planifolia Jord.
IV, 10	Tulipano di Persia	T. clusiana DC.

3. Modern botanical names of plants in the flower album listed alphabetically

The original identifications of the plants by Carla Teune and M. H. Hoog have been revised by Dr. Frederick Meyer. The numbers are the corresponding folios in the album.

Botanical Name	Fol. No.
Anemone coronaria L.	41, 49, 50, 52, 54
Anemone pavonina Lam.	43, 44, 48, 53, 55
Anemone pavonina Lam.?	42
Anemone x fulgens (DC.) RChb. Multipetala	51
Aquilegia vulgaris L. 'Flore pleno'	63, 65, 66
Calendula officinalis L.	68
Carthamus tinctorius L.	74
Convallaria majalis L. 'Rosea'	69
Chrysanthemum parthenium (L.) Bernh.	71
Clematis viticella L. 'Flore pleno'	64
Consolida regalis S. F. Gray., formerly *Delphinium consolida* L.	81
Dianthus caryophyllus L.	12 right
Dianthus plumarius L. 'Gras'	12 left
Filiipendula vulgaris Moench	80
Fritillaria meleagris	59
Geum rivale L. Avens	62
Hyacinthus orientalis L.	33–40
Iris chamaeriris Bert.	76A
Iris x germanica L.	75
Iris foetidissima L.	76
Lilium chalcedonicum L.	01
Lilium martagon L.	02

APPENDIX V

GLOSSARY OF TERMS IN THE INVENTORY AND TREATISE

A

acceso	flaming red
agata	color of agates = milky, pale
agrumo	name of cultivated species of *citrus*, a small evergreen vine or bush
ala/e	perianth
anemone	*anemone coronaria* L., *a. tenuifolia*
aranciato	deep orange
argemone	*anemone pavonina* L., *a. latifolia*
autunnale	autumnal
avvinato	wine red

B

bianco	white
Bosuelt	probably a botanist
botriode	grape-like clusters of flowers
bulbosa	bulbous

C

Calcedonio	Chalcedonian, i.e., near Eastern in origin can also mean bluish-white *or* translucent
calice	cup *or* corolla
candido	purest white
cannello	hollow stalk, can also refer to *Cannabis sativa*, marijuana
capigliaro	literally, capillary; rootlets
capo	head
carneo	flesh colored
cassettone	a parterre, garden area with a number of planting beds
cera di Spagna	*cera lacca*, sealing wax, usually dark red
chiaro	cloudy and smoky *or* limpid and clear
cilestro	sky blue
cinabro	blood red, brownish red, or vermilion
cinque	five
cipollo/a	bulb/s
cipressino	from Cyprus *or* cypress-shaped poplar
collo di camello	shape of a camel's neck, e.g., arched
collo intornato	a band, usually a different color than the rest of the flower, bud, leaf, or stem
colombino	dove colored = white, grayish, violet
colombino acceso	intensely dove colored
coloretto	literally, colored, a term used for single-colored flowers

colori	colors
Constantinopolitano/i	from Constantinople, i.e., of Turkish origin
corniculato	with pointed ends like a horn
corno di cervo	stag horn
corolla	part of flower, same as English
cremesino	bright red

D

di profumeria	fragrant?
dita	ca. 5 cm
doppio	double, as opposed to single blossoms

E

F

fiammato	incandescent *or* flamed
fila	row in planting beds
fila per lo lungo	row the length of the bed
fila per traverso	transverse row
fiocco	terminal of a plant, a thick bunch of greens, leaves, or flowers
foglia	leaf *or* flower petal
foglia di ruta	leaves like those of rue, *Ruta graveolens*
foglia larga	broad-leafed *or* petaled
foglia stretta	narrow-leafed *or* petaled
foglia unita	possibly an undivided corona?
Fraseo	refers to a type of narcissus; also called Roseo
fronda	most often branch but can mean large leaf
fusto	stem

G

gambo	the part of an herbaceous plant that connects the roots to the leaves and flowers, used interchangeably with *fusto*
giallo	yellow
giallo in oro	golden
giallo in paglia	straw colored
gigliato	lily shaped
giunco	rush = *juncus*
giungifolia, giuncifolia	rush-shaped leaf, i.e., very thin and long
grapoloso	shaped like a grape cluster
guida	the border of a planting bed

H

I, J

Januario	name of a garden owner
incarnato	flesh toned
incartacciato, incartocciato	wrapped in paper or with a skin-like covering

344

Isole Verginianie	mainland Virginia
iuncifolo/a	same as *giungifolia,* rush-shaped leaf

K

L
larga/he	broad
latifolia	broad-leaved *or* wide-petaled
lattato	milk colored
limone	lemon
linea retta	straight line
lionato	reddish yellow, tawny
loggetta	small loggia, balcony, or terrace
lucido	luminous, lustrous

M
macchiato	spotted
marmorino	marmoreal *or* like variegated marble
massimo	largest
mattone	brick
mazetto (mazzetto)	small bundle *or* handful
mescolato	mixed
minio	intense reddish orange color
moltiplico	propagation *or* multiplying
montagnuolo	hill *or* mount
musarte/o	a type of narcissus

N
nero	black
non ha pari	unequaled—botanical term *incomparibilis*

O
obsoleto	immature, not fully open
occhiuto	budded, with eyes like a peacock tail
odoratissimo	highly scented
Olanda	Netherlands
onione	bulb
orientale	middle eastern *or* oriental
orlato	with a different colored border
ossoleto	dark brown

P
palombino	like white bird plumage with smoky grey
paonazzo	like peacock plumage, changing purple
pedicozzo/i	tendrils or thread-like roots
pennacchiato	flamed
peonina tuberoso	tuberous peony
persichino	intensely pink, like peach flowers

pianella	tile
pilastretto	pilaster
polianto	polyanth = multi-stemmed or multi-flowered on one stem
porpore	purple
primaticcio	spring blossoming
purgato	cleansed

Q

R

racemoso	clustered, in racemes
radica, radiche	root
Raguseo	originating in Ragusa, Jugoslavia coast
ramerino	the herb rosemary
rancio	orange tree or orange colored
riccio	curly
riflesso	reflex = botanical term for blossom sharply curved in relation to stem
rigato	striped
roggio	russet, reddish
rosa secca	color of dried rose leaves
rosino	pinkish
rosso	red
rosso acceso	intense red
rosso incarnato	pinkish red
rosso oscuro	dark red

S

salsiccia	tuber or thick root
salvatico	wild flower
sanguigno	blood red
scaglioso	scaly
scarlatto, scarlattino	scarlet
schietto	smooth or unadorned
scolorito	colorless, pale
scompartimento	planting bed edged by a low hedge, bricks, or tiles
scritto	striped
semplice	single flower
si tiene nota particolare	noteworthy
spalliera	espalier
stamina	stamen
stanza/e	room/s
stellato	starred
stretto/a	straight or erect
stradoppio	extra double
Suersio	Dutch botanist, Sweerts
sulfarino	sulphur colored

T

tardivo	late blooming
tela d'oro	color of gold cloth
tenerino	diminutive of *tenero,* gentle or tender
tenuifolia	narrow-leafed *or* petaled
terra d'horto	literally, orchard/soil
tramezzato	mixed, partitioned, separated
tromba	trumpet
tuberosa	tuberous
turchino	deep *or* dark blue

U

unito	unbroken color—also used to describe leaves, meaning unknown

V

Valdenech	unidentified
vellutato	velvety, used for "plush" anemones
verde	green
verno	winter
viale di mezzo	middle path
violaceo	violet

W

X

Y

Z

zolfana	sulphur colored

Index

Part I

Index

Part II